T0351961

Shareholder Democracies?

Shareholder Democracies?

*Corporate Governance in
Britain and Ireland before 1850*

MARK FREEMAN, ROBIN PEARSON,
AND JAMES TAYLOR

THE UNIVERSITY OF CHICAGO PRESS   CHICAGO AND LONDON

MARK FREEMAN is a senior lecturer in economic and social history at the University of Glasgow, an associate member of the Centre for Business History in Scotland, and the author of several books, including *Social Investigation and Rural England, 1870–1914*. ROBIN PEARSON is professor of economic history at the University of Hull and the author of *Insuring the Industrial Revolution*. JAMES TAYLOR is a senior lecturer in the Department of History at the University of Lancaster and the author of *Creating Capitalism*.

The University of Chicago Press, Chicago 60637
The University of Chicago Press, Ltd., London
© 2012 by The University of Chicago
All rights reserved. Published 2012.
Printed in the United States of America
21 20 19 18 17 16 15 14 13 12   1 2 3 4 5

ISBN-13: 978-0-226-26187-4 (cloth)
ISBN-10: 0-226-26187-5 (cloth)

Library of Congress Cataloging-in-Publication Data

Freeman, Mark, 1974–
    Shareholder democracies? : corporate governance in Britain and Ireland before 1850 / Mark Freeman, Robin Pearson, and James Taylor.
        p. cm.
    Includes bibliographical references and index.
    ISBN-13: 978-0-226-26187-4 (alk. paper)
    ISBN-10: 0-226-26187-5 (alk. paper)
    1. Corporate governance—Great Britain—History—18th century. 2. Corporate governance—Great Britain—History—19th century. 3. Stock companies—Great Britain—History—18th century. 4. Stock companies—Great Britain—History—19th century. I. Pearson, Robin, 1955– II. Taylor, James, 1976– III. Title.
    HD2741.F8143 2012
    338.60941'09033—dc23

                                                    2011023610

Contents

Illustrations

Acknowledgments

The research for this book could not have been carried out without the assistance of a major grant from the UK Economic and Social Research Council (number RES 000 23 0096), awarded to Robin Pearson. This essential support is gratefully acknowledged. We are especially grateful to Ray Stokes, Director of the Centre for Business History, University of Glasgow, for organizing a symposium on the first draft of our manuscript, and to Naomi Lamoreaux, Bob Morris, and John Turner for agreeing to read and comment on that draft and participate in what was a day of intensive and stimulating exchange. We took away their many astute comments and suggestions and have tried earnestly to revise the book in the light of them. Our thanks also go to the anonymous reviewers of the University of Chicago Press, who provided praise and constructive criticism in equal measure; to David Pervin, senior editor at UCP, who guided the manuscript through to publication; and to Shenyun Wu, who provided technical support along the way.

Several preliminary papers dealing with aspects of our research were presented at the following conferences: the Social History Society Conference, Dublin; Economic History Society Conference, Leicester; Association of Business Historians Conference, Glasgow; European Business History Association Conference, Barcelona; International Economic History Congress, Helsinki; Economic and Social Research Council Seminar on Corporate Governance, Regulation and Development, Queen's University, Belfast; Statistics and the Public Sphere Conference, Oxford Brookes University; and senior seminars at the Universities of Athens, Seville, Exeter, Glasgow, and York and at the Business History Unit, London School of Economics. We wish to thank the participants at these meetings for their comments, as well as those with whom we have had valuable conversations about our research over the years, including Tim Alborn, Matthias Beck, Huw Bowen, Colleen Dunlavy, Roy Edwards, Chris Kobrak, Josephine Maltby, Ioanna Minoglue, John Quail, Janette Rutterford, Richard Saville, Judy Slinn, Steve Toms, Michael Turner, and Robert Wright.

Abbreviations

ACBI	Agricultural and Commercial Bank of Ireland
AGM	annual general meeting
AUL	Aberdeen University Library
AVIVA	AVIVA plc Archive, Norwich
BCA	Birmingham City Archives
BL	British Library
BPP	British Parliamentary Papers
BRO	Berwick Record Office
BSA	Bank of Scotland Archive
CCA	Canterbury Cathedral Archive
CII	Chartered Insurance Institute Library, London
CKS	Centre for Kentish Studies
CMA	Clerical & Medical Insurance Company Archive, Bristol
CRO	Cornwall Record Office
DCA	Dundee City Archives
DM	Directors' Minutes
DRO	Dorset Record Office
DUA	Dundee University Archives
EIC	East India Company
GCA	Glasgow City Archives
GL	Guildhall Library, London
GM	general meeting (of shareholders)
GRO	Gloucestershire Record Office
GULSC	Glasgow University Library, Special Collections
HLRO	House of Lords Record Office
LMA	London Metropolitan Archive
LRO	Liverpool Record Office

LTSB	Lloyd's TSB Archive
NA	National Archives, London
NAS	National Archives of Scotland
NLI	National Library of Ireland
NLS	National Library of Scotland
NMM	National Maritime Museum
NURLSC	Newcastle University Robinson Library, Special Collections
OGM	ordinary general meeting (of shareholders)
RBS	Royal Bank of Scotland Archive
RC	Royal Commission
SC	select committee
SGM	special general meeting (of shareholders)
SRO	Suffolk Record Office
TWA	Tyne and Wear Archives
ULL	University of London Library
WRO	Worcestershire Record Office

CHAPTER ONE

Introduction

The contradiction inherent in representation . . . lies in the fact that it is on the one hand necessary to the action of the masses, but on the other hand easily becomes a conservative obstacle to it. — Leon Trotsky[1]

The tension between rule and popular voice, between executive power and representation, was present at the birth of democracy. When Cleisthenes, backed by a popular uprising, drove the Spartans and their aristocratic allies out of Athens in 508 BC, he reorganized the city's constitution along lines partially recognizable to students of modern democracies. A ruling council of five hundred was established, answerable to an assembly of the people, with annual rotation of office and regular auditing of accounts. The assembly could not vote on any question not first discussed by the council, but some acts of the council were subject either to ratification by the courts or to direction by the assembly.[2] Assembly debates were genuinely popular affairs, with all adult male citizens—women and slaves were excluded—having the right to participate.[3] It is true that two key features of the Athenian constitution are alien to modern constitutions: first, most offices of state, including membership in the council, were chosen by lot rather than by election; second, the assembly held an annual ticket vote to ostracize the individual deemed most likely to threaten democratic government in the city. Modern states have opted for neither device. Both devices, however, along with other elements in the constitution of Cleisthenes, were aimed at resolving the fundamental issue in all democracies, ancient and modern, namely, control of the executive and establishment of accountability.

This issue lies at the heart of this book. Our principal finding is that there was a convergence in the forms of power and representation in

politics and business in the world's first industrializing nation. The long
search for checks and balances between the executive and legislature in
the British polity, which was already well developed by the end of the
seventeenth century, had its parallel, we argue, in corporate organizations, including the new joint-stock companies that came to dominate
important sectors of the economy during the following centuries. The
chapters that follow focus on the internal governance regimes of these
companies as the latter worked out what each perceived to be the optimal allocation of rights and obligations among shareholders, directors,
and managers. Yet much of this debate in the corporate economy mirrored, to a degree that few have hitherto remarked upon, wider constitutional debates about the relative power of the estates and classes in
eighteenth- and nineteenth-century Britain and about the role of electors and the elected and the transparency and accountability of decision
making in civil government.

In this book we define a joint-stock company as one with thirteen or
more partners and transferrable shares—this definition is explained below.[4] Our study comprises both companies incorporated by royal charter
or act of Parliament and unincorporated companies that existed under
English, Irish, and Scottish law as mere partnerships without a separate corporate legal identity. Notwithstanding their proscription under
the Bubble Act of 1720, the latter constituted more than 40 percent of
all joint-stock companies formed in Britain and Ireland during our period.[5] We explore the reasons for their proliferation in chapters 2 and
3. It is sufficient to note here that they are an important part of British corporate governance history, not just because of their numbers, but
because they experienced many of the problems of agency and representation that were faced by the corporations. It is also worth noting,
particularly for our North American readers, that the British incorporated company in our period was unlike the early US business corporation in several ways, most obviously in the degree of state regulation to
which it was subjected. While the concepts of public utility and public
welfare were applied by legislators to petitions for incorporation on both
sides of the Atlantic, they were applied with greater vigor in the young
American republic. In the United States between the 1790s and 1830s
supporters of incorporation had to work hard to counter criticisms of the
business corporation as an "aristocratic," monopolizing, and corrupting
element in the economy.[6] One consequence was a greater regulation of
corporations and their constitutions—for example in the reporting re-

quirements, in the duration of charters, and in the level of direct interference by state legislatures—than was experienced in the United Kingdom. The closer oversight of business incorporation by the New England
states soon led to its acceptance there as the predominant form for joint-
stock enterprise. Over thirty-five hundred companies were incorporated
in New England between 1800 and 1844. By the 1850s the process was
being streamlined further by the introduction of general acts of incorporation in most states.[7] By contrast, the British Parliament, backed by
a conservative judiciary, remained reluctant to make corporate privileges more freely available, even after the Bubble Act was repealed in
1825. The result was that many company promoters, particularly in England, had to organize their joint-stock ventures under a variety of legal
vehicles, including the trust, while trying at the same time to mimic the
rights enjoyed by corporations. For the most part, legislators and the judiciary left such companies to their own devices, just as they seldom in-
terfered in the operations of corporations. In the United Kingdom, unlike in the early American republic, the business corporation generally
operated no more, and no less, in the public sphere than the unincorporated company.[8] In Britain during our period, notwithstanding their different legal origins, we find that there was a convergence in the constitutions and governance of incorporated and unincorporated companies
and that this convergence manifested itself in a fundamental shift in the
power relations between shareholders and directors in both types of enterprise. The evidence for this is presented in the following chapters.

Modern Corporate Governance and Its Theories

The governance of business has been the object of considerable public and academic debate during the past two decades, prompted by instances of scandal and mismanagement, such as those at Enron and
WorldCom in the United States, Northern Rock and Royal Bank of
Scotland in the United Kingdom. Particular concerns have focused on
the quality of auditing, the role of nonexecutive directors, agency problems, and executive remuneration. It has been argued that governance
structures allowing managers to pursue their own preferences have provided a dissemblance of democracy in many firms, while sustaining elit-
ism and self-interest in the boardroom.[9] In Britain, the Cadbury Report
of 1992 recommended the adoption of independent audit and executive

remuneration committees, and from this and subsequent reports a code of best practice has been developed. In the United States, the Sarbanes-Oxley Act of 2002 required more stringent reporting of internal financial controls in corporations, brought in new rules for auditors, specified the duties of directors, and introduced a range of penalties for filing misleading financial statements, falsifying documents, and coercing independent auditors.[10]

Such governance issues are not merely pertinent to the internal affairs of large corporations but also have a resonance for the wider community of stakeholders and, more generally, for the kind of democracy we wish to see develop within modern capitalism. What has determined the type of corporate governance that we get? How can the divergent interests of stakeholders be reconciled in a viable governance system? A large body of theoretical literature has attempted to answer these questions. Agency theory in particular has focused on the misaligned incentives of two main interest groups within the firm: managers (agents), who were employed by owners (principals). While the latter sought to maximize the returns on their investments, the former sought to maximize their own utility, which might include, for example, enhanced remuneration linked to asset growth rather than profits, or power, prestige, and other forms of nonpecuniary reward. The costs of agency were threefold: the monitoring costs of the principal, the bonding costs (the guarantees) of the agent, and the residual loss to the firm caused by the divergence of interests.[11] Agency theory not only described the problem but also claimed to explain how it could be resolved. The market, it was held, conveyed the means by which managerial incentives could be aligned with those of shareholders, through devices such as stock options and the hostile takeover, disciplining managers who consistently failed to enhance shareholder value.[12]

Subsequent shareholder models of corporate governance have drawn upon this contention that there are automatic mechanisms that mitigate the agency problem between owners and managers and that these mechanisms have become refined over time. Such models hold that optimal risk allocation in an economy *depends* on the functional separation of powers between owners and managers, with the latter being responsible for decision making and the former for residual risk bearing. Shareholders are (fully) rewarded for "waiting" (deferring consumption) and bearing residual risk so that dividends equate to the payment of pure interest (waiting) plus an equity risk premium. This approach underpinned the work of Alfred Chandler on the development of the modern managerial corporation. Although Chandler himself never examined the question at any length, business historians have tended to follow him in regarding governance forms as the outcome of the internal evolution of the firm and the separation of ownership and control.[13] Agency theory, therefore, was chiefly responsible for the view—which became an orthodoxy of institutional economics by the 1980s—that shareholders, as residual risk-takers and residual claimants, merely represented one of several forms of input into the firm, with no privileged right to insist that the corporation be operated in their sole interest. This marked the final disembodiment of shareholding from control, the last stage in the long historical process, whose genesis is traced in this book, of equating the separation of ownership and control with business efficiency, and of making ownership "irrelevant."[14]

Some authors, however, have focused on the legal framework, itself contingent on historical processes, as the chief determinant of governance forms in business, thus placing the onus on the law to work out solutions to the principal-agent problem. Common-law regimes, it has been claimed, historically have provided stronger protection for minority shareholders and greater defenses for companies against arbitrary interventions by the courts and government than civil-code regimes. One consequence is that share ownership is more likely to be widely dispersed in common-law countries than under civil codes.[15] Others have regarded corporate governance as an institutional response to the company's need to reduce the uncertainty in its relationship to a changing external political environment. Roe, for instance, has argued that social democracies in post-1945 Europe weakened the ties of managers to shareholders and strengthened the power of a wider body of stakeholders, especially employees, thereby eroding the business principle of maximizing shareholder value. This, in turn, has discouraged the spread of share ownership in countries such as Germany. By contrast, in polities such as that of the United States, where the shareholder value principle has not been undermined by social democratic policies, share ownership has been more widely diffused.[16]

What relevance, if any, do the findings of this book have for the theory or practice of modern corporate governance? While this book is primarily aimed at historians rather than economists and policy makers, it is nevertheless the case that many of the issues in the present debate over corporate governance were first addressed in Britain during the period covered by our study. It is remarkable how many of those advocating remedies for corporate governance problems today appear to be entirely unaware of the fact that similar problems, with similar remedies proposed, have been recurring in business for centuries. Malcolm Salter, for example, has recently written an influential account of the Enron disaster in which he puts forward several suggestions for reform: appointing individuals to company boards who have sufficient time to devote to directing; remunerating directors more generously in order to encourage them to take their jobs seriously; obliging directors to hold a larger stake in the company; enforcing a greater division between direction and management; and boosting shareholder powers over directors.[17] These are exactly the kinds of remedies proposed in Britain during the early nineteenth century. Indeed, arguments for the importance of aligning executive incentives with the interests of the constituents they represent have been debated in Britain since the late seventeenth century, with companies frequently requiring minimum shareholding qualifications for directors.[18]

Without wishing to preempt the analysis in the following chapters, we may point to other findings from our study that speak to the models of modern corporate governance outlined above. First, this book indicates that what investors expected from corporate governance has varied greatly over time and that those expectations have been contingent on political, social, and cultural as well as economic factors. From the eighteenth to the early nineteenth century, most types of stock company in Britain anticipated that shareholders would be interested in the wider benefits that their enterprise would bring to the local or regional economy. Short-term financial rewards in the shape of dividends or gains in share values were often of secondary concern. Such shareholders expected to take an active role in the business of their firm, and the governance systems of many early companies reflected these expectations.[19] One can view the company constitution in Britain, until the 1820s at least, as a risk management asset for investors interested in the degree of "active" control that company promoters were offering them as potential voting shareholders. Investors thus bought into that asset—the governance system—at the same time as they bought shares in the enterprise. In a competitive market for capital, drawing on investors with these kinds of expectations, the degree to which a constitution was aligned with shareholder expectations of control may occasionally have been decisive for company promoters trying to get a project off the ground, although our evidence suggests that this applied in only a minority of cases.[20] The situation began to change with the rise of the "passive" or "rentier" investor during the railway age. By the 1840s, many investors in stock companies lived at a distance; relied more on intermediaries such as the financial press, solicitors, or share brokers for information about their investments; and were less interested in the management of their companies, provided their dividends kept being paid. Even at this date, however, despite the increasing disjuncture of shareholders and executives, especially in the largest firms, the belief remained widespread that the properly informed shareholder should take responsibility for actively monitoring managers and directors. Hence the call to publicize the names of company promoters and investors and the idea that personal reputations and standing rather than constitutional rules offered the best guarantee for potential investors, particularly given the continued local scope of many new share issues and the informal character of the secondary share market. Through to the end of our period, the motivation of the average shareholder was still regarded in many quarters as involving more than utility maximization. Our findings lend support to those who criticize the rationalizing assumptions of agency theory and argue that the social and political context in which a firm operates plays an important role in creating the conditions for the emergence of particular governance forms.[21] This was as true in 1800 as it is today.

Second, economic historians of Britain have argued that the change to a more flexible property-rights regime, associated with the Revolution settlement in the decades after 1688, shifted the locus of executive power from Crown to Parliament and secured the expansion of private business, including stock companies, during the long eighteenth century.[22] Parliament became a forum where land and capital resources could be reorganized, allowing groups of property owners and communities to tap opportunities for economic development. Through estate and enclosure acts and local statutory authorities, Parliament proved itself willing to alter traditional property rights in order to encourage infrastructural investment and the provision of public goods and services. Indeed, some have argued that civil liberties, and particularly the secure and enforceable rights of the individual to property, were themselves the product of the privatized, nondiscretionary access to corporate rights under common-law regimes, such as Britain and the United States.[23] The effect of the legal system and the property-rights regime on corporate governance cannot be ignored. Throughout this book, we try to assess where that effect was important and where it was not. For example, in chapter 3 we consider the system for obtaining incorporation, as well as the procedures for establishing companies without royal or parliamentary sanction, while in chapter 7 we also examine the attempts made by many such companies to use the law of contract or other devices to limit the liabilities of shareholders. Our findings suggest that the legal uncertainty surrounding the status of companies created difficulties for company promoters but did not discourage them from experimenting creatively with corporate structures. As we show in chapter 6, many of the developments in shareholder voting rights and the role of the general meeting stemmed from the problems in operating outside the legal framework of incorporation. We also show how the legal differences within Britain and Ireland ensured that specific features of corporate governance were more significant in Ireland and Scotland than in England and Wales. Provisions concerning the liabilities of shareholders particularly varied between legal jurisdictions.

Do our findings support the idea that common-law regimes provided a congenial legal environment for the growth of the joint-stock economy by protecting the interests of investors?[24] Yes, but only to a limited extent. It is true that, notwithstanding the restrictions imposed by statute law—particularly the Bubble Act of 1720—on the formation of companies without incorporation, hundreds of unincorporated companies operated successfully in Britain between 1720 and the Joint-Stock Companies Act of 1844. In part, this was possible because, for much of the period, judicial discretion was employed in a way that favored, or at least did not undermine, the security of shareholders' investments in unincorporated companies.[25] It is also true, however, that the creativity of British corporate governance structures, which we document in the following chapters, originated largely in response to the long-running legal uncertainties surrounding joint-stock companies in Scotland, Ireland, and England, rather than in response to any protection that common law offered to investors.[26]

Third, we argue that political factors were as important in shaping corporate governance systems in eighteenth- and nineteenth-century Britain and Ireland as they were in Europe and the United States in the late twentieth century, though not in the way that Roe describes. Rather than focusing on the effect of different state policies on corporate governance, we emphasize the importance of the political institutions of government in both public and private spheres—the assemblies, election procedures, franchises, ballots, and committees of local government and the rules, bylaws, and annual reports of voluntary societies. These provided cognitive models upon which joint-stock companies and the authors of their constitutions drew readily. The parallels between governance forms in the political and business environments are one of the most notable, even surprising, results of our study, and we discuss these extensively in the chapters that follow. Because of the fragmented nature of the historical evidence, it is impossible to establish with certainty a causal chain linking governance practices in the political sphere with those in the business sphere. However, the histories of the two are so strikingly similar that to ignore the parallels would be to risk jettisoning an important dimension to the story of corporate governance in Britain before 1850. We believe that the political model of government in Britain holds the key to explaining many of the developments in the governance history of joint-stock companies and that this is more than a mere speculation on our part. As we demonstrate below, contemporaries also noticed the parallels between politics and business and used metaphors from politics to analyze phenomena in company governance.

In sum, as Robert Wright has recently argued, knowledge of the repeated failure of corporate governance reforms through history will surely be useful to those engaged in the current debate over the most effective means of monitoring corporations.[27] An understanding of the complex process by which shareholders were disengaged from the companies they owned may facilitate the efforts of those today who are trying to reengage shareholders and the wider community of stakeholders in the process of governance.

Early Corporate Governance: Hypotheses and Arguments

Chapter 2 outlines the growth of the joint-stock economy in eighteenth- and nineteenth-century Britain and argues that, until recently, its size and significance have been grossly understated. Attention is increasingly being paid to some of the external issues generated by this first corporate economy. Some historians have focused on the relationship between business and the state with new research on taxation, company law, and the effectiveness of commercial lobbying.[28] Several have explored attitudes toward corporate failure and fraud and the political and social factors influencing company legislation.[29] Others have examined the gender and social composition of shareholders, their motives for investment, and the limitation of their liability.[30]

There has been less exploration of other "political" relationships that could affect the way companies did business in the past. These include some of the major issues in the current debate about corporate governance, namely the constitutional allocation of power, rights, and obligations among company directors, managers, and shareholders, and how that allocation is worked out in practice. These political relationships within the company are the principal focus of this book. Such relationships had already surfaced during the seventeenth and early eighteenth centuries in the context of wider debates about mercantilism and state policy, overseas trade, public finance, and the benefits and costs of monopoly privileges and joint-stock versus regulated companies. Indeed, many of the issues surrounding proprietorial rights and directorial powers, managerial preference, individual liability, control over share transfers, transparency, and auditing that were features of the later joint-stock economy were already present by 1700, for example in the East India Company (EIC) and the Bank of England.[31] Although there is not space to examine them here, the constitutions of the seventeenth-century chartered companies varied greatly, in their provisions for shareholder scrutiny of accounts, for instance, and gave scope for governance disputes between shareholders and executives.[32] The heterogeneity of pre-1700 governance practice and the frequent surfacing of conflict in joint-stock politics remained features of corporate governance in Britain and Ireland far into the nineteenth century.

The starting hypothesis of this book, therefore, is that in enterprises large enough for a space to develop between ownership and management, this space became a political arena in which governing executives, boards of directors, confronted their "public" legislatures, the assemblies of shareholders. The following chapters explore this hypothesis through an analysis of the institutional arrangements for, and the practice of, governance in joint-stock companies in Britain between the Bubble Act of 1720 and the Companies Act of 1844, that is, during the century or so when the legal status of the stock company in England was most uncertain and when that in Scotland and Ireland was still not entirely resolved. There are advantages to focusing on this period, for it was one in which corporate governance structures, whether in corporations or in unincorporated companies, were largely formed without state intervention or any great degree of standardization. This was the key era of experimentation in British corporate governance history, when the struggle over the powers of directors, who were also usually owners, and nondirecting shareholders was particularly acute. Before the act of 1844, there was no constitutional template for company promoters to follow, even for corporations whose charters were shaped in only the most rudimentary fashion by the standing orders of Parliament, which regulated the process by which a bill of incorporation could be applied for. By quantifying provisions in the constitutions of new joint-stock companies, we are able, first, to measure the extent and evolution of "democratic" practice in the governance of British business and, second, to explore the relationship between forms of corporate governance and the development of political institutions in Britain from the early eighteenth century through to the Victorian "age of reform." Constitutions were often changed over the course of a company's lifetime, and for some companies we have tracked such amendments. Our database, however, which is described below, is exclusively derived from the original constitutions of new companies, as these reflect the intentions of company promoters and founders and provide the best available basis upon which to make comparisons between sectors and over time.

Amid the great heterogeneity of company constitutions during this period, we discern two coexisting generic types. The first, which we call model A, was a constitution that set up the general meeting of shareholders (GM) as the source of all power within the company, having the ultimate authority over directors, managers, and employees, but also permitting power to be devolved to them. The second type of constitution, model B, represented a system of "checks and balances," in which the GM was given oversight over the directors, while the directors had a broad authority to manage the business of the firm as they saw fit and to exercise authority over company's employees. Overall, our constitutional database charts the decline in model A and the increase in popularity of model B by the 1830s and 1840s. For much of the eighteenth century, model A was favored by corporations, while model B was preferred by unincorporated companies. We endeavor to trace the complex genesis of these models and to explain these preferences in the following chapters. Our explanation refers as much to the sources of political authority within the company as it does to the changing structure of the joint-stock economy. The allocation of political authority within companies by their constitutions, we argue, was influenced in important ways by the external political environment, where the official institutions of

central and, especially, local government, as well as the forms of government adopted in the private sphere by the growing array of voluntary associations, provided cognitive models for the authors and users of business constitutions. In early corporations, authority derived from the GM,
and the small shareholder base—in many local canal, bridge, and water companies, for instance—ensured a convergence of power between
the GM and those appointed to manage the venture. The GMs of such
corporations, we argue, operated as mini-parliaments in the manner of
the EIC and older chartered monopolies, that is to say wholly sovereign
bodies, with shareholders acting as quasi-MPs, having ultimate authority over directors and employees. Unincorporated companies, because
they were constituted without the sanction of the state, were less influenced by the parliamentary ideal and always embodied a different, more
limited version of democracy, perhaps more influenced by local government and voluntary associations than by Parliament. In these companies, especially the larger ones, for example in insurance and later banking, the executive derived its political authority and decision-making
powers directly from the constitution rather than from the GM, which
assumed a more limited, monitorial role. During the early nineteenth
century, some new corporations, particularly in the railway sector, began to adopt this model-B type of constitution that divested shareholders of large amounts of authority over the governance of their companies. Certainly, part of the story that unfolds is one of businesspeople
experimenting over generations with different constitutional arrangements in order to secure the best bottom line. As our period progressed
and the competition for joint-stock capital increased, the search for economic efficiency may have been increasingly important in the shaping of
corporate governance systems.[33] However, it was not the only nor even
the major factor. The struggle for power within the joint-stock sector between shareholders and their company executives, along with the influence of institutional models drawn from the political sphere, also drove
the changes we find in British corporate governance.

The issue of democratic practice taps directly into an emerging
transatlantic debate about the historical governance of stock companies. Lamoreaux has shown that, notwithstanding the extension of general incorporation in the United States from the 1840s, for much of the
period a company's legal identity was not something that businessmen
could freely contract for but was a privilege granted by the state. Thus,
as in Britain, the choice of organizational form was restricted by con-

servative legal tradition and precedent.[34] "Public interest," rather than
the maximization of private profit, remained the key principle behind
the allocation of corporate rights in the United States.[35] Lamoreaux and
Rosenthal together, and Hilt, have each uncovered the extent to which,
contrary to the Chandlerian view, ownership and management were sep-
arated in early US corporations. Managerial voting powers were controlled by large shareholders, "oppressing" the rights of minority shareholders.[36] Some believe, however, that political models, rather than legal
constraints, were the principal influence here. Alborn has argued that
the new joint-stock banks emerging in England after 1826 were "local
republics" of shareholders, paralleling the subscriber democracies fash-
ioned by the urban middle classes through the voluntary associations of
the period.[37] Their form of "participatory" politics came under pressure
during the financial crisis of the late 1830s. Alborn contends that banks
moved quickly away from the voluntary model toward more streamlined administrations and less "democratic" constitutions under which
"virtual" rather than direct representation of shareholders by boards of
management became the norm. Such moves, he claims, had parallels in
the electoral compromise of 1832 and reflected the subsequent trajectory
of middle-class politics away from populism. Dunlavy has found a similar development in the United States after the 1830s as stock companies
moved away from a "democratic" suffrage, characterized by weighted
voting and restrictions on the concentration of shares, toward more "plutocratic" forms of governance typified by one share, one vote.[38] With
these findings in mind, this book seeks to establish and explain the existence and timing of this putative shift toward business "plutocracy"
and the "virtual" representation of shareholders by managers and directors and away from participatory democracy in which shareholders were
more fully empowered with governance rights and played an active role
in the affairs of their companies.

The Constitutional Database: Sources and Methodology

The acts that incorporated canal, bridge, dock, railway, and other companies in England and Scotland specified the capital that was authorized
to be raised by shares, bonds, or loans; set out the procedures for nego-
tiations with property owners whose land was affected by the schemes;
regulated the business operations of a company; and outlined its system

of governance, which often included the franchise, modes of election to the board, voting procedures at GMs, provision for audits, and shareholder access to company books. Companies that failed to obtain incorporation, or that did not even try, included many of the same governance regulations in their private deeds of association or articles of copartnership.

The critical questions about how power was to be divided among proprietors, directors, and managers were answered in a variety of ways by different companies. In order to investigate how such relations developed over time and by industry, region, and, in the case of Scotland and Ireland, by different legal regimes, we constructed a dataset of governance provisions from the constitutions and bylaws of 514 joint-stock companies founded in Britain and Ireland between the Bubble Act of 1720 and the Companies Act of 1844, which provided the first official registration of stock companies in England and marked the first general attempt at their regulation. Because we are interested in the internal constitutional arrangements and relations among shareholders, directors, and managers in these companies, we decided to focus on businesses with a minimum of thirteen partners holding transferable shares. This definition of a joint-stock company draws upon Charles Munn's distinction between unincorporated Scottish copartneries with thirteen or more partners and ordinary partnerships with fewer. The larger copartneries, Munn argues, were most likely to have an elected committee to run their day-to-day affairs and thus to experience a separation of powers between managers and proprietors. Incorporated and unincorporated English joint-stock companies can also be distinguished from small partnerships in this way.[39] Only a small number of firms appear to have been located right on this threshold. According to its act of incorporation, for instance, the twelve members of the New Pembrey Harbour Company (1825) were permitted to established a "board of directors," but there was some latitude in the wording of the act, suggesting that this was not required.[40] Article 46 of the act outlines the powers of the New Pembrey directors, "if any such Directors are appointed." In article 34, although the wording of the clause directs the shareholders to appoint a board, the marginal note says only that they "may" do so. This ambiguity nicely underlines Munn's organizational (rather than legal) distinction between a partnership and a joint-stock company.

With this definition in mind, a pilot survey of over sixteen thousand business records was conducted to identify companies with relevant ex-

TABLE I.I. **Companies in the database by type and subperiod**

Type	1720–89	1790–9	1800–9	1810–9	1820–4	1825–9	1830–4	1835–9	1840–4	Total
Incorporated	25	31	25	33	20	37	28	58	33	290
Unincorporated	14	3	20	8	19	33	31	72	24	224
Total	39	34	45	41	39	70	59	130	57	514

tant records, particularly constitutional documents (charters, deeds of settlement, articles of copartnery, rules, and bylaws) from the period 1720–1844. These records were located in several hundred public and private repositories throughout the United Kingdom, Ireland, and abroad.[41] From this survey and subsequent research, the constitutions of 514 stock companies were selected for inclusion in the database. Fifty-six percent of these were incorporated by acts of Parliament or royal letters patent; the rest were unincorporated companies, constituted by private articles and deeds of association or copartnery (see table 1.1). A template was constructed in order to analyze the governance provisions in the constitutions of these companies. This template was modified and revised until the final version extended to ninety closely defined variables.[42] The variables include capital structure and share denomination; size and distribution of the proprietorship; number of directors and trustees; managerial structure and organization; limited-liability clauses; procedure for calls on shares; executive control over the purchase and transfer of shares; prerequisites for share ownership; scope of proprietorial rights (including the right to appoint and dismiss directors, fix levels of remuneration, declare dividends, inspect books and accounts, comment on directorial decisions, amend the company's constitution, dissolve the company); quorums and frequency of shareholders' meetings; shareholders' voting rights; directors' duties and rights (including the right to stand for reelection); and the quality of accounting information presented to shareholders.

One problem was how to make the sample representative of the total population of stock companies in England, Wales, Ireland, and Scotland over this period, for which we have no figures. There are a few modern and contemporary estimates, however, which, supplemented by a wide range of other sources, together suggest there were at least 1,006 joint-stock companies founded between 1720 and 1844 in the five largest categories—banking, canals, railways, insurance, and gas.[43] Altogether, across all sectors of the economy we have identified some 1,400 stock companies founded before 1844. Given incomplete record survival, the actual total may be in excess of 1,500. Given time and resource constraints and the desire to ease calculation and to prevent the sample from being dominated by one or two sectors or by a particular period (joint-stock banks in England, for instance, were not permitted until 1826), we aimed to collect data on a sample of sixty companies in each of the five largest categories and on a further two hundred across all other sectors of joint-stock enterprise. Following the adjustments described below, we finished with a total of 514 companies in the database. Allowing for some undercounting, this suggests that our sample of 306 companies in the five main categories (64 banks and 62 insurance companies, rather than the target of 60, were eventually included) covers nearly 30 percent of all joint-stock banks, canal, railway, insurance, and gas companies founded between 1720 and 1844. The 514 companies in our database probably represent about one-third of all stock companies formed in Britain and Ireland in this period.

Within the five main joint-stock categories, and also the water companies, we were able to adjust the database to represent as closely as possible the actual chronological distribution of all companies (by date of foundation).[44] For example, we calculated that of the 189 insurance companies established during our period for which we knew the precise year of foundation, 3 percent were formed between 1810 and 1819; thus we endeavored to ensure that two of the sixty-two insurance companies in our sample (3 percent) dated from this period. Similarly 53 of the 189 insurance companies (28 percent) were formed in the decade 1820–29, as were 17 of our sample of 62 insurance companies (27 percent). Because of incomplete and uneven record survival, and because of the regional adjustments noted below, the fit between the chronological distributions of the sample and the total population of companies within these six industrial sectors was not exact for every subperiod, but we are confident that the sample distribution is broadly representative of the cycles of company promotion in these industries. Because of the complete absence of data elsewhere on total numbers of stock companies, no such adjustment was possible for other sectors. These unadjusted sectors—shipping, manufacturing, property, etc.—together make up 40 percent of the total database, whereas they probably accounted for about 30 percent of all stock companies in this period. Despite their overrepresentation in our database, they help demonstrate the great variety of constitutional structures and governance practices across the joint-stock economy. Table 1.2

shows the distribution of companies in the database across twelve economic sectors and by date of foundation. Figure 1.1 shows the chronological distribution of all companies in the database. The pattern generally
mirrors the familiar cycles of joint-stock promotion: the burst of canal
and dock foundations in the 1790s, the minor boom late in the first decade of the 1800s, and the major upswings in stock-company flotations in
the early 1820s and the mid-1830s, especially in gas, railways, insurance,
and banking.

We also adjusted our samples to ensure that all regions were represented. We considered using the ratios of Scottish and Irish to English
GDP as a guide, but if we had stuck rigidly to these ratios, the numbers
of Scottish and Irish companies in our sample would have been too small
for analysis. In the end, there are 120 Scottish and Irish companies in
the database, or 23 percent of the sample, distributed across all subperi-
ods (see table 1.3). This is enough, we believe, to allow us to make useful

TABLE 1.2. **Companies in the database by sector and subperiod**

Sector	1720–89	1790–9	1800–9	1810–9	1820–4	1825–9	1830–4	1835–9	1840–4	Total
Banking	3	0	2	2	2	10	15	28	2	64
Bridges	1	4	6	4	3	5	6	5	0	34
Canals	17	25	3	6	0	5	0	3	1	60
Colonial	0	1	0	0	1	4	2	4	0	12
Gas	0	0	0	5	11	8	10	17	9	60
Harbours	1	2	2	8	1	3	2	8	3	30
Insurance	5	0	15	2	11	6	3	9	11	62
Manufacturing/ trade	11	2	2	1	3	5	2	9	1	36
Property	0	0	2	1	0	1	6	15	5	30
Railways	0	0	3	6	3	7	8	19	14	60
Shipping	1	0	1	4	2	6	1	6	5	26
Water	0	0	9	2	2	10	4	7	6	40
Total	39	34	45	41	39	70	59	130	57	514

TABLE 1.3. **Companies in the database by country and subperiod**

	1720–89	1790–9	1800–9	1810–9	1820–4	1825–9	1830–4	1835–9	1840–4	Total
Colonial	0	1	0	0	1	4	2	4	0	12
England	24	30	33	34	24	43	47	91	39	365
Ireland	2	0	1	1	7	5	3	12	2	33
Scotland	13	1	10	3	7	18	5	16	14	87
Wales	0	2	1	3	0	0	2	7	2	17
Total	39	34	45	41	39	70	59	130	57	514

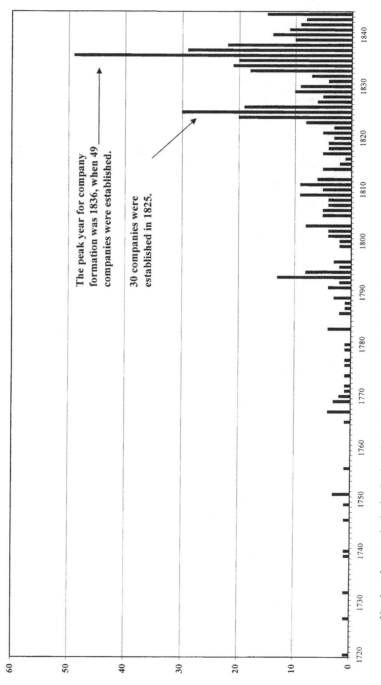

The peak year for company formation was 1836, when 49 companies were established.

30 companies were established in 1825.

FIGURE I.I. Number of companies in the database by date of establishment, 1720–1844 ($N = 514$)

comparisons between the development of corporate governance under the different legal systems in the three kingdoms by subperiod, by sector, and by size of company. Furthermore, we tried to ensure that all regions of England and Wales were covered. In sum, the database has been constructed as carefully as possible with a view to producing—as far as record survival permits—a representative account of corporate governance in British and Irish business during this period.

In addition to the 514 companies included in the database, data were also collected on over 160 other firms founded between 1720 and 1844.[45] These were excluded from the database either because a constitutional record did not survive or was incomplete or because we had already sufficient companies in a particular category.[46] As noted above, we also examined the governance provisions of nonbusiness organizations, such as municipal corporations; poor-law unions; voluntary societies; and drainage, sewer, and harbor commissions that included elective and associational elements. Thus, one area of great interest pursued in the following chapters is the convergence of governance forms across business and nonbusiness sectors. Many data on companies not included in the database derive from internal business records other than constitutional records, including minutes of company boards, committees, and GMs, as well as accounts, ledgers, bylaws, prospectuses, circulars to shareholders, and letter books. These types of records enable us to explore the extent to which the governance provisions in constitutions were put into practice in the daily operations of companies and at times of crisis caused, invariably, by poor business performance, mismanagement, or instances of fraud, when tensions rose among proprietors, directors, and officers. During such crises, boardroom attitudes toward shareholders were often exposed in the historical record and are therefore open to investigation. These internal business records have been supplemented by a great number of external sources, which give shape to the political, legal, and cultural context in which stock companies operated during this period. These include diaries, autobiographies, contemporary pamphlet literature, newspaper and periodical articles, parliamentary papers, legal treatises, and law reports. On the basis of this extensive and intensive research, we would claim that this book represents the first comprehensive examination of corporate governance in industrializing Britain and the most ambitious study of the early corporate economy yet undertaken.[47]

CHAPTER TWO

The Joint-Stock Company and Its Environment, 1720–1850

For forms of government let fools contest;
What'er is best administered is best.—Alexander Pope[1]

In many quarters, particularly among business historians with their focus on Chandlerian models of the corporation, there is little recognition that corporate governance was even an issue before 1870 or that
there was much separation between ownership and control in British
companies. This is partly due to failure to recognize the range of sectors penetrated by joint-stock companies and the growth of share ownership before the late nineteenth century. Thus "proprietorial capitalism"
is taken as an equivalence for the family firm, and the orthodox historical account remains one of a Whiggish march of progress from the one-
person firm and small partnership of the preindustrial economy to the
modern joint-stock limited-liability managerial corporation of the modern era.[2] This development, it is claimed, was determined primarily by
the increasing scale of production from the later nineteenth century and
the growing requirement for larger quantities of capital to be placed under centralized control in hierarchical organizations.[3]

In fact, the increased capital requirements associated with overseas
commerce or large-scale manufacturing or mining operations were already a common explanation for the emergence of big corporations between the late sixteenth and early eighteenth centuries, as was the desire to reduce information and transaction costs associated with market
exchange. Where risks were high and information most imperfect, in
long-distance trade or insurance, for example, regulated corporations,
joint-stock companies, and mutual associations emerged in numbers by

the early eighteenth century. After the overthrow of the Stuart mon-
archy and the Revolution Settlement of 1689, the growth of large companies was also driven by the requirement put upon groups of promoters to make loans to the state in return for corporate privileges. In itself
this was nothing new. Loans and gifts of shares had been made by several corporations to the Stuarts. The financial demands of the state during the prolonged Williamite wars against France, however, were many
times larger than they had been earlier in the seventeenth century. Cru-
cially, Parliament rather than the Crown now provided the principal
source of authority for incorporation. Investors in newly chartered companies, such as the Bank of England or the New East India Company,
were able to place their capital upon the more solid basis of parliamentary rather than royal security. New share issues expanded, and the public debt increased enormously—from £4 million to £25.5 million between
1705 and 1712 alone. A new and well-organized market for liquid securities emerged. It has been estimated that the number of investors in this
market doubled to ten thousand between 1694 and 1709.[4] The install-
ment method of paying for shares, whereby an investor's subscription to
a share was paid in small portions at fixed intervals over a period of time,
lowered barriers to the less affluent. The range of investment products
such as fixed-rate bonds, annuities, and preferential and ordinary stock,
offering different blends of risk and return, also increased. In the midst
of this financial revolution, one can also detect an increased willingness
to experiment with novel forms of business organization. As well as the
joint-stock and regulated trading corporations, there were sleeping partnerships in shipping and trade; joint-stock partnerships within craft and
merchant guilds; large mutual associations; small annuity, friendly, and
benefit societies; companies launched by municipal corporations; and,
not least, large unincorporated partnerships with transferable shares—
perhaps one hundred in England and Wales by the late 1690s, plus a
handful in Scotland.[5] By the beginning of the eighteenth century, therefore, there was a broad palette of organizational choice available to company promoters and investors.

The Bubble Act and Its Aftermath

In theory, this choice became severely restricted in England by the Bubble Act of June 1720, passed at the height of a huge speculative boom in

company promotions.[6] The legislation was the result not of a moral panic about joint-stock projects but of a cabal of South Sea Company directors pushing Parliament—where many of the company's investors sat—into protecting the price bubble that they had taken great pains to inflate.[7] The cabal aimed to deter further stock company promotion and maintain the flow of funds into South Sea shares. The act itself was a composite work. Most of its clauses dealt with the incorporation of two new marine insurance ventures, the London Assurance and the Royal Exchange Assurance. Four clauses, however, were aimed at suppressing "dangerous and mischievous Undertakings or Projects" contrived "under false pretences of publick Good." Any such undertaking established after 24 June 1718 and acting without a charter, acting under a charter granted for other purposes, acting under a charter that had fallen into abeyance by nonuse "or for want of making lawful Elections," or presuming to act as a corporate body without legal authority was declared illegal, void, and a "publick Nusance."[8] Promoters of such undertakings, and those found guilty of raising a transferable stock or making transfers or assignments of stock for such a purpose, would be liable "to such fines, penalties and punishments, whereunto persons convicted for common and publick Nusances are," including imprisonment.

The act, it has been argued, operated as a major deterrent to the formation of joint-stock companies. Its restrictive clauses, the absence of limited liability, and the long memory of the South Sea affair, purportedly diminished the market for shares and deprived industry of joint-stock capital until the act was repealed in 1825.[9] As a result, according to some, joint-stock companies were "exceedingly rare" during the Industrial Revolution.[10] This view was reinforced by historians' use of the published lists of stock prices, in which, during the eighteenth century, shares of joint-stock companies were conspicuous by their absence. The belief that the corporate sector of the economy was minimal continues to lead to the characterization of British business before the late nineteenth century as being dominated by "personal" or "family capitalism," without any division between the ownership and control of firms.[11]

This position is a caricature of the actual situation. As Dubois correctly argued some time ago, the effect of the Bubble Act was to encourage entrepreneurs seeking to raise large capitals to seek incorporation by a parliamentary act, or—where powers of eminent domain or the right to levy tolls were not required—to form voluntary unchartered shareholding partnerships of uncertain legality.[12] Recent research by Harris and others suggests that such partnerships formed under various elements of trust, partnership, equity, contract, and agency law.[13] The joint-stock organization with transferable shares, both incorporated and unincorporated, appeared in a remarkable range of British industries during the eighteenth and early nineteenth centuries and dominated some of them. Our survey of business records for this book revealed such companies for overseas trade, river navigation, canals, docks, quays, harbors, bridges, tunnels, roads, railways, sail and steam shipping, coach and ferry services, waterworks, gasworks, insurance, banking, financial investment, land improvement, colonial settlement, commercial property development, public baths, cemeteries, reservoirs, fisheries, mining, quarrying, the timber trade, brewing, distilling, flour milling, bread baking, sugar refining, and the manufacture of salt, glass, porcelain, pottery, brass, rope, boats, guns, silk, hemp, linen, and cotton and woolen cloth. Altogether we have identified over fourteen hundred joint-stock companies operating between the early seventeenth century and 1844, and this is certainly an undercount.[14] Harris has estimated that in 1740 about £18 million was tied up in the capital of English joint-stock companies and that this increased to £90 million by 1810 and to £210 million by 1840, growth that considerably outpaced the expansion of the economy as a whole.[15] The general sectors in which joint-stock companies were present—trade, transport, and manufacturing—accounted for 40 percent of British national income in 1801 and 53 percent by 1851.[16] Such companies were the dominant form of business organization in parts of these sectors, notably canals, railways, and other transport infrastructure, urban utilities, and insurance. By the early nineteenth century, therefore, far from the joint-stock enterprise having stagnated or "retreated" under the oppressive burden of legal restrictions, there were many hundreds of joint-stock companies making a significant contribution to British economic development and thousands of investors spreading the shareholding habit throughout the country.[17]

The Growth of the Joint-Stock Economy during the Eighteenth Century

It is possible to discern some periodization in the growth of this joint-stock economy, for its development was far from linear. Although the years from the Bubble Act to the 1760s were not devoid of new joint-stock companies in Britain, the number of new ventures was small relative to the periods before and after. This may have been due in part to the restrictive legislation, but it was probably also a consequence of sluggish economic growth, coupled with frequent shocks including wars, bad winters, harvest failures, credit crises and Jacobite uprisings.[18] Several joint-stock undertakings were incorporated by Parliament to improve the navigation of English rivers such as the Kennet and the Avon. In this sector, and in drainage schemes, public-private hybrid organizations also emerged in this period, in which sources of finance ranged from the private wealth of individual undertakers to compulsory district levies, fixed-interest loans and annuity loans usually secured on future toll revenue, and equity capital. The transformation of the River Don navigation between 1725 and 1733 from a nonprofit venture run by the Cutlers' Company of Sheffield and Doncaster Corporation to a for-profit venture by an incorporated joint-stock company is one example.[19] The flow of petitions for business charters, however, came to a virtual halt during the 1730s and 1740s as the attitudes of the Crown law officers, particularly under Attorneys General Yorke and Ryder, toward incorporation became tougher. In 1741 the Bubble Act was extended to America and the colonies, after it was observed by Ryder that there was no way under common law of prosecuting several Massachusetts joint-stock banks that were operating without a charter. The growth of joint-stock enterprise in Scotland and Ireland was even slower than in England, mainly owing to the relative backwardness and capital impoverishment of those economies. The linen industries received support from statutory boards in Ireland from 1711 and in Scotland from 1727, while Irish river improvements were also financed by a national Commission of Navigation (established in 1730, incorporated in 1751), but this public finance stimulated no joint-stock schemes in either the textile industries or the waterways of either country.

Between 1760 and 1800, a period topped and tailed by two booms in English canal promotions and marked by more liberal attitudes among the English judiciary toward unincorporated companies, there was a quickening in the expansion of joint-stock enterprise in transport, insurance, and Scottish banking, shipping, and fishing. Where projects had claim to a natural monopoly or a public utility, such as canals and docks, there were usually few legal obstacles to parliamentary incorporation in this period, although, as we discuss in chapter 3, the financial and political hurdles could be high. For these kinds of ventures, incorporation provided an increasingly amenable legal environment. In the canal mania of 1788–96 nearly £10 million was authorized for canal and river navigation projects. Dock capacity in England doubled during the last quarter of the eighteenth century.[20] Most of this expansion was delivered by new joint-stock corporations. Where an unincorporated stock company held out the prospect of some public benefit, company promoters were generally left alone. This was true, for instance, of insurance, where by 1800 there were some thirty companies, mostly joint-stock and unincorporated, insuring over £206 million of property and lives.[21] Such companies also received tacit recognition from the state via the licensing system introduced with the stamp duty on fire insurance policies in 1782 and the response of the attorney general to the application for a charter by the new Phoenix Fire Office in 1783. Although the application was rejected, the attorney general encouraged the promoters of the fire office to establish their enterprise on an unincorporated basis, in the full knowledge that this was a stock company with eighty-nine shareholders and transferable shares.[22]

The Scottish economy also entered a stronger phase of growth in this period. There was some agricultural improvement, and the tobacco trade and linen industry expanded rapidly. In the west of Scotland, tobacco traders invested in estates, sugar refineries, coal mining, breweries, bottle and glass manufactories, turnpikes, and a number of stock companies and larger copartneries such as the Carron Iron Company (1759), the Glasgow Ropeworks, and the Monkland Canal (1770).[23] Several fishing and shipping companies were established along the east coast. The banking system expanded, with over a dozen provincial banking companies being founded between 1747 and 1770 and a further twenty-five between 1772 and 1810, of which nine were copartnerships with thirteen or more proprietors.[24] The new banks were a response to lack of facilities provided in the regions by the three Scottish chartered banks and to the growing shortage of specie and rising demand for notes. The Bank of England's monopoly, prohibiting other banks being set up with more than six partners, worried some in Scotland.[25] The partners of the Ship Bank in Glasgow, for instance, believed that this law also applied to Scotland and confined their numbers to six. They were mistaken. Glasgow's second bank, the Arms (founded in 1750), had thirty-one partners, and its legality was never challenged in the courts, nor were the other Scottish banks that were subsequently established with more than six subscribers.[26] There was general agreement north of the border that partnerships of all types, small and large, were separate entities under Scottish law, "competent to maintain legal relations with a third party by its separate firm or name," and with the right to draw up regulations governing the conduct of their members that would stand up before the courts.[27] This was very different from the situation in England, where a partnership had no legal existence distinct from the persons composing it. The Bubble Act had little effect on this situation, whether or not it applied in Scotland—and there was much confusion about this point. Scottish law, however, did not clearly provide two critical devices for large copartneries and stock companies, namely, the right to sue and be sued in a corporate name or the right to hold heritable property in such a name. Nor did it provide limited liability for copartners and shareholders, though there was confusion about this too. The principal motive for seeking incorporation in Scotland, however, was the inadequacy of the Scottish law of partnership with regard to the ability to hold heritable property without the need to resort to the cumbersome device of a trust and the ability to undertake legal actions in the name of company officers. Separate legal personality for unincorporated stock companies and copartneries remained out of reach in Scotland before the legislation of the 1840s.[28]

In Ireland, a joint-stock economy barely emerged during the second half of the eighteenth century. Before 1767 all inland navigation projects had depended entirely upon grants from Parliament or compulsory levies imposed on local property owners. In that year, a group of twenty-five investors obtained an act incorporating the Limerick Navigation Company to make navigable a stretch of the Shannon, a project previously funded by public grants that had made little progress. The act authorized the company to raise £10,000 by subscription in £50 shares, in addition to another £6,000 granted by Parliament.[29] In 1772 the Corporation for Inland Navigation was empowered to make grants to private companies of undertakers, and this encouraged further investment. In the same year a private corporation with 177 subscribers took over the Grand Canal.[30] Other joint-stock initiatives followed, including the Lagan Navigation Company (1780) and the Royal Canal Company (1789), but, in sharp contrast to the English canal system, there was usually also an element of public funding involved. Work on other navigations, such as the Boyne, Barrow, Tyrone, and Newry, continued to be entirely financed by grants. Poor financial management, capital shortages, and faulty governance systems—most notoriously in the Grand and Royal Canal companies—were consistent features of Ireland's waterways, and this may have helped dampen investors' enthusiasm in other sectors as well. The number of Irish joint-stock companies was not large. Apart from the canal and river corporations, there were nine unincorporated insurance companies, a couple of mining companies, a glass manufacturing company in Belfast, the Corn Exchange and a fishing company in Dublin, and the Bank of Ireland, whose incorporating act of 1782 gave it a monopoly of joint-stock banking on the island.[31] Thus, against a background of increasing economic growth in Ireland, joint-stock projects remained thin on the ground.

The situation did not improve much after the Union of 1801. The Irish economy remained weak and undiversified. Services, transport (with the notable exception of coastal steam shipping), and utilities stand out as particularly underdeveloped sectors in Ireland, accounting for only 16 percent of employment, compared with 32 percent in Britain in 1841.[32] These, together with mining, were precisely the sectors in which the majority of joint-stock investment in Britain took place before 1850. Some have argued that the problem was not one of capital or investment opportunity but of a native unwillingness to invest.[33] Perhaps the reluctance of Irish investors to risk their capital outside real estate, banking, railway shares, and government securities was partly the result of the paucity of strong business networks and associational traditions in the smaller towns, in comparison with England or Scotland. The legal framework, however, was less of an obstacle. The Irish legal system, unlike the Scottish, was modeled on that of England, and much of the legislation passed at Westminster, including the Bubble Act, also applied to Ireland. The Bubble Act, however, was largely irrelevant to an economy with no history of stock speculation and a tiny corporate sector. On the contrary, there were several innovative legislative developments to promote capital pooling that remained unique to Ireland. An act of 1742, for instance, to "encourage the trade and manufactures of this Kingdom," empowered the majority in any firm with up to nine partners and up to £10,000 capital to compel any partner to meet calls on the stock and to sell "by public cant" the shares of any partner refusing to pay. This was a useful measure, though restricted to firms below our defining threshold for a stock company (thirteen partners). The removal of penal restrictions on Catholic investors was probably also important. This was begun by private joint-stock companies even before the general Catholic Relief Acts of 1778 and 1782. The act of the Limerick Navigation Company, for instance, stated that shares were "personal estate and not subject to any of the laws to prevent the growth of popery."[34] In 1772 this dispensation was extended to all inland navigation and insurance companies.[35] The Anonymous Partners Act of 1782 applied to all companies, excluding banks, discount houses, and retail shops, formed with capitals between £1,000 and £50,000 for any term not exceeding fourteen years with no upper limit to the number of partners.[36] Partners were divided into "acting partners," who were to assume the day-to-day management of the company with full liability as if they were trading on their own account, and "anonymous partners," whose liability was to be limited to the amounts they individually invested in the concern. Such firms, unlike ordinary partnerships, were to enjoy a continuous corporate existence to the extent that the death or failure of any anonymous partner did not automatically bring about the dissolution of the company. Companies could also sue and be sued in the name of the acting partners, in the form of "AB & Company," without the need to name the anonymous partners as parties to any suit. This was the first general limited-liability legislation anywhere in the British Isles and the first time that the continental type of *société en commandite*, with its division between active and sleeping partners, had been introduced in Britain or Ireland. Yet the act failed to stimulate a growth in joint-stock company promotions. The 508 partnerships registered under the act between 1782 and 1853 possessed on average a capital of just £4,134 and 3.5 partners.

Revival and Repeal of the Bubble Act

In England the period between 1800 and 1825 featured successful attacks on the East India, Bank of England, and marine insurance monopolies; further speculative booms in joint-stocks; and a revival of the Bubble Act in reaction to these booms. The tolerance shown by the judiciary and the general public that had marked the later eighteenth century, came under increasing strain with a new upswing in promotions between 1807 and 1810. During 1807 some forty-two new companies were launched, mostly in London, the largest surge of unincorporated company formations since the South Sea Bubble. Under Lord Chief Justice Mansfield (1754–88), who was generally supportive of mercantile interests, the judiciary had adopted a fairly relaxed view of such promotions, but his successors on the King's Bench, Lords Kenyon (1788–1802) and

Ellenborough (1802–18), were less pliant.[37] Criticisms in the press and satires on joint-stock enterprise mounted. The relevant clauses of the Bubble Act were reprinted as warnings to promoters and investors.[38] Promoters of multiple projects, such as William Brown and Ralph Dodd, were targeted for attack.[39]

The legal assault commenced late in 1807, when a private complaint was made by a corn-distilling firm in West Ham about Dodd's prospectus for a "London Distillery Company" with transferable shares. The attorney general swiftly moved for a rule to show why a criminal information should not be filed against Dodd. The case was argued before Ellenborough in the Court of King's Bench in May 1808, the first action brought under the Bubble Act since 1722.[40] The court refused to grant the prosecution, but Ellenborough's ruling was ominously ambiguous about the legality of such companies. There were seven further prosecutions under the Bubble Act between 1808 and 1812, and although these decisions did not interpret the act as a general prohibition of all unincorporated stock companies, the upsurge of litigation and the equivocating judgments of the courts left the legal position of unincorporated stock companies in England very uncertain.[41] Incorporation continued to be difficult. All the new insurance companies of the period that petitioned for an act were unsuccessful.[42] The early gas companies also met resistance. In industrial towns, utility companies often became embroiled in local political conflicts, with opposing parties either supporting rival companies, or with one side presenting themselves as embryonic collectivists and calling for public ownership, while others backed private enterprise.[43] Moreover, gas was a new industry, and it did not face the opposition of long-entrenched corporate monopolies. In other sectors, notably overseas trade, banking, and marine insurance, applications for incorporation challenged well-established chartered rights.

The hostile rulings of the King's Bench were widely reported in the Scottish Tory press, accompanied by fierce denunciations of such "abominable combinations," but they did not cause the same alarm among company promoters north of the border as they did in London.[44] In Scottish towns and ports the joint-stock economy boomed and diversified after 1800. New shipping, harbor, gas, water, insurance, and canal companies were formed. The year 1810 saw the first of a new breed of very large unincorporated joint-stock banks, the Commercial Banking Company of Scotland, with a nominal capital of £3 million. Others followed in the

1820s and 1830s. By 1825 the shares of more than fifty joint-stock companies, mostly unincorporated, with a combined paid-up capital of £15 million were being traded in Edinburgh.[45] In Ireland, outside canals and insurance, most growth sectors, such as cotton spinning, brewing, sugar
refining, and flour milling, continued to be organized as small partnerships.[46] The company promotion boom of the 1820s, however, witnessed
at least twenty-four new joint-stock companies, including six insurance
offices, four mining companies, three gaslight companies, three steam
shipping companies, a water company in Limerick, and a coach company in Ballymena.

In England, despite the heightened uncertainty about the legality
of unincorporated joint-stocks, the company boom of 1824–5 produced
over six hundred prospective schemes. There were features of this boom
that had not been seen before, most notably the large number of mining associations formed for Latin America.[47] The range of domestic projects launched was also wider than ever before. At Christmas 1824, well
before the peak of the boom, a firm of Edinburgh stockbrokers was advertising shares in four Scottish insurance companies, three Scottish
railroads, the Edinburgh and Leith Dock Company, the Edinburgh
Joint-Stock Water Company, the Caledonian Foundry Company, the
Edinburgh and Leith Glass Company, the Equitable Loan Company,
the Waterloo Hotel, the Theatre Royal, and the Edinburgh Subscription
Library.[48] Widespread speculation in scrip paper—advance allotments of
shares before they were issued—had not been witnessed on this scale before and drew the condemnation of Lord Chancellor Eldon in the House
of Lords.[49] The boom also elicited the now-familiar attacks on speculation and joint-stock companies.[50]

Opinions varied about how the state should respond. The ultra-Tory
Eldon argued that the Bubble Act should be applied with vigor, while a
mixed group of Whigs, liberals, and liberal-Tories wanted repeal and the
creation of new legal structures for recognizing and regulating companies.[51] Situated between the two extreme positions was the government
of Lord Liverpool, who favored noninterference in economic matters.
Laissez-faire, however, was sorely tested by the company boom and by
the pressure placed on parliamentary time by the growing number of
petitions for incorporation. At the height of the boom, the government
repealed the relevant clauses of the Bubble Act. Repeal appeared the
best way of creating greater certainty for investors, yet the government's

intention to keep a tight rein on the number of businesses receiving corporate privileges was also made clear by its failure to support calls for general incorporation and general limited liability.[52]

Several months after repeal, the bubble burst. By 1827 only 15 of the 624 companies formed in 1824–5 were trading above par, while around 500 had disappeared entirely.[53] As share prices fell, a run on banks followed. By January 1826 some eighty country banks had suspended payments or declared bankruptcy. The crisis put pressure on the government to consider the Bank of England's monopoly. With so many country banks going under, the Bank of England had patently failed in its (unwanted) role as lender of last resort, and there was also mounting criticism of its internal governance and lack of transparency toward its shareholders.[54] In contrast to England, there were only a handful of bank failures in Scotland. The strength of Scottish joint-stock banks, particularly their extensive branches, provided a model for the reform of English banking. There was also a statutory precedent in Ireland, where the Bank Act of 1821 had ended the Bank of Ireland's privileges outside a fifty (Irish)–mile radius of Dublin and permitted copartnerships of any number of persons to enter banking and issue notes.[55] The Bank Act of 1826 permitted joint-stock companies of more than six persons to do banking in England outside a sixty-five-mile radius of London, while also allowing the Bank of England to establish branches in the provinces. Such companies were given the key power to sue and be sued in the name of one or two "public officers," who were fully indemnified against losses arising out of such actions, but there was to be no limited liability for partners. All new banking companies were required to file a return with the Stamp Office containing their corporate name, the names and addresses of all the partners, the names of their "public officers," and the names of the towns where their notes were to be issued.[56] Here was the principle of registration that was to become the cornerstone of the company legislation of the mid-1840s.[57]

The bust of 1825–6, however, dented the confidence of joint-stock advocates. There was a retreat from proposals for general incorporation. Even after the repeal of the Bubble Act, great uncertainty remained about the status of unincorporated companies. It remained far more difficult to obtain an act of incorporation in the United Kingdom than in the United States. English courts were left to struggle with common-law interpretations of the problem. There followed twenty years of state ex-

perimentation with piecemeal reforms of company law, none of which
resolved the legal uncertainties under which unincorporated stock companies in England continued to labor.

From Repeal to Reform

In spite of, rather than because of, the political and legal environment,
the number of companies and the volume of share capital rocketed to
new heights, partly because of new technologies and the growing need
for large-scale capital ventures, and partly because of wealth accumulation by the expanding ranks of middle-class investors and their desire
to diversify their asset portfolios. In England in 1840 the capital of joint-
stock companies amounted to £210 million, while in Scotland there were
over one hundred stock companies with capital of £19 million.[58] In Ireland between 1825 and 1844 at least thirty-six stock companies were established, including thirteen banks, seven steam shipping companies,
and five railways. Reflecting trends in Britain, there was also a greater
diversity than before, including Irish bridge, reservoir, cemetery, land
improvement, and shipbuilding companies. Thus, between the 1820s and
the 1840s across the United Kingdom the joint-stock form of organization diffused out of the traditional sectors of transport, finance, and utilities into areas such as property development, manufacturing, and mining, which had previously been the domain of the small partnership or
the single owner.

Under the Whig governments of the 1830s, traditional attitudes toward the extension of corporate privileges largely persisted. In 1834 an
act authorized a new type of "quasi corporation," a "company, body or
association" granted letters patent by the Crown but without parliamentary incorporation, that would enjoy the privilege of being able to engage in legal actions in the name of its principal officers without having to name all its shareholders in a suit.[59] This was an attempt to shift
the growing burden of petitions for incorporation back onto the Crown,
whose officers, it was argued, would be able to process such applications
more efficiently and without the dangers of corruption to which parliamentary committees might be exposed. The problem, however, was the
narrow way that the Committee of Privy Council for Trade stipulated its
conditions for granting letters patent under the new act. The only companies that would merit approval would be those engaged in hazardous

activities, such as mining; that required large capitals, such as canals and railways; that were exposed to "extended responsibility," such as assurance companies; or that required a large number of associates to realize their objectives, such as literary or charitable societies.[60] As a result, few companies bothered to apply for the privileges afforded by the act of 1834, and even fewer received them. Of the three hundred stock companies promoted in the boom of 1834–7, just twenty-five applied under the act, and only four were successful.[61] In 1837 a new act modified this legislation.[62] It permitted the Crown to issue letters patent to limit the liability of members of unincorporated associations to the extent of their shares and required companies to register more detailed information on their shareholdings, but it still stopped well short of being a general law of incorporation.

The idea of registration, however, continued to progress in a piecemeal way. Registration addressed the demands of those calling for greater protection for the public from speculative and fraudulent promotions, while at the same time retaining the principle that individual shareholders should take responsibility for monitoring their own investments.[63] By the early 1840s there were plenty of precedents. Shipping companies had been brought under Registry Acts in 1786 and 1823.[64] Friendly societies were first registered in 1793, with subsequent legislation consolidated in 1829.[65] An act of 1817 required the certification of saving banks, with quinquennial returns to be made to Parliament.[66] Registration was extended to building societies in 1836, to joint-stock banks in 1826, and to stock companies incorporated by letters patent in 1834 and 1837.[67] Thus the idea of registration and regular returns of company information was well developed by the time the Select Committee on Joint-Stock Companies met in 1841.

The committee was a response to the company promotion boom of the mid-1830s and the failure of the acts of 1834 and 1837 to secure investors against bankruptcies and frauds. This boom was led by eighty-eight new railways, but there were also projects for shipping, mining, banking, insurance, conveyancing, investment, newspapers, gas, canals, and cemeteries. Over 2.5 million shares were issued for a total capital of £135.2 million.[68] Many of the new companies were short lived. Some were promoted with the intention of quickly finding a larger company to buy them out, and there were important merger and acquisition waves in banking and insurance in these years.[69] Other projects were outright frauds. This new boom and bust, together with the failure of the government to replace the Bubble Act with a coherent legislative framework for stock companies, revived concerns about the rights and security of shareholders. Worries about speculative or fraudulent promotions easily dovetailed into anxieties about the mismanagement of companies and the transparency and accountability of decision making by directors.

The select committee, chaired by Gladstone, published its report in March 1844.[70] It listed the deceptions that had been practiced on unsuspecting investors and recommended the compulsory publication of company accounts and a periodic audit. The report formed the basis of two acts that received royal assent in September 1844: the first, for the registration, incorporation, and regulation of joint-stock companies; the second, to facilitate the winding-up of such companies.[71] The main act put an end to the experiment to revive incorporation by the Crown. It introduced compulsory registration, undertaken in two stages, for every new partnership with transferable shares and all new companies of more than twenty-five partners, excluding banks, railways, and Scottish companies. The first stage involved provisional registration before any shares could be offered to the public by prospectus or advertisement. A company deed had to state the purpose of the enterprise, the structure of its share capital, the names of subscribers, the amount of their shares, and the names of the directors and auditors. For the first time, a standard template was provided upon which the promoters of new companies could model their constitutions. This 165-clause model constitution was consolidated for England, Ireland, and Scotland in the Companies Clauses Consolidation Acts passed in the following year.[72] The second stage involved complete registration once the shareholders had signed the deed and the first officers had been appointed. Once this was achieved, a company could enjoy many of the privileges of incorporation, including the right to sue and be sued under its corporate name, to make contracts, hold land, borrow money, assemble, make bylaws, and freely transfer shares. The liability of a shareholder for company debts was to continue for three years after the sale or transfer of his or her shares. Half-yearly returns detailing all changes of share ownership had to be submitted to the Registrar of Joint-Stock Companies. Balance sheets had to be provided to the shareholders periodically, and these were to be audited. Finally, joint-stock companies were declared illegal without registration, thus distinguishing for the first time between such companies and ordinary partnerships.

Railways and banks, the sources of some of the major frauds, were

excluded from the 1844 Companies Acts. Railway companies continued to require specific acts of incorporation, as they did before 1844.
Gladstone's Railway Act of 1844 created a railway board, fixed passen-
ger rates, required companies to present accounts, and gave the state an
option to buy new lines twenty-one years after they were authorized. A
further act passed in 1844 required each new bank of more than six partners to obtain letters patent in order to undertake banking business.[73]
The Bank Charter Act of 1844 prohibited issue of notes by new banks
and limited the note issue of existing banks, which had been widely regarded as a major factor in the banking panic of 1836–7.[74]

Gladstone hoped that the legislation would strike the right balance
between permissiveness and restriction.[75] Registration was not to be
equated with regulation, but neither was limited liability to be made
generally available. Whatever the legislators' hopes, however, there was
clearly a lowering of entry barriers to the corporate economy after 1844.
By 1854, 3,677 companies had provisionally registered under the Companies Act, and 884 of these obtained complete registration. The latter
figure represented probably more than a 50 percent increase on the total number of joint-stock companies ever established before the act was
passed.[76] It is not accurate, however, to assert, as Harris does, that entry barriers disappeared entirely and that the state's role as guardian of
incorporation became largely passive.[77] As we note below, the registration process could be used quite deliberately to prevent democratic and
working-class forms of joint-stock organization from acquiring corporate privileges.

The growing acceptance of the notion of cheap and efficient government, providing a minimal amount of oversight and protection for tax-
payers and investors, helps explain the new approach to corporate business taken by successive British administrations from the second quarter
of the nineteenth century. Joint-stock regulation made up one part of
what some historians have dubbed the "revolution in government," in
which permissive legislation was an outcome of the search for reliable
agencies to effect policies, to reduce the cost of private bill procedures,
and, in the process, to improve the self-government of the propertied
classes in their businesses and local communities. The many parallels between joint-stock politics and local government form a recurrent theme
in this book. The question, for instance, of whether the latter should be
based on a weighted franchise and select system, as many Tories argued,
or on a one-ratepayer-one-vote system, as some liberal Whigs argued,

was subject of much political debate but was also mirrored in the struggles in joint-stock companies over their franchise systems.[78] Similarly, the issue of public voting by show of hands or private voting by secret ballot was raised in both local and national politics as well as in the joint-stock sector, as were other points relating to representation, consultation, and the balance of power between executive government and its constituents.[79]

These debates centered on the problem of how best to ensure the moral self-government of companies and local communities and how to remove the old vices of corruption, apathy, lax and amateur administration, factiousness, and nepotism without applying the intrusive and costly hand of state regulation. The companies legislation of 1844–6 belonged to a new image of government, projected by both Tory and Whig administrations since the 1820s, with its roots in Pitt's premiership of the 1780s, in which efficiency and public service were held up as paramount virtues. Some historians view this as the rational outcome of a search for cheaper and less wasteful government after the high spending years of war against France. Others regard the ethos of efficiency, "civic virtue" and public service, and the gradual erosion of the worst excesses of "old corruption" as the means by which the ruling class legitimized its power when confronted by radical criticism of unreformed government.[80] The growth of the press in the early nineteenth century provided a new and powerful ally for those calling for reform in both government and joint-stock enterprise.[81] Toward the middle of the century, as ever-larger amounts of capital were at stake in the joint-stock economy, it is possible to discern the beginnings of a profound transition from an older moralizing response to business ethics, in which shareholder vigilance and the personal bonds of trust between proprietors and managers formed the principal safeguard of standards, toward a technocratic response in which professional managerial elites, regulated by their own organizations and assisted by a new framework for company law, supervised the implementation of ethical practices, though not always efficiently.[82] This transition was assisted by Victorian judicial attitudes, which increasingly tended to favor the self-regulation of entrepreneurial activities at the expense of private property rights. It was also complemented by the framework of commercial ethics worked out during this period by the nonconformist churches, which helped narrow the differences between religion and business.[83] Thus the internal changes taking place in corporate governance by the middle of the nineteenth century were accompanied by sweeping external changes in legal, political, and religious attitudes toward business.

In this, the role of the state was meant to be viewed not as a burden on the middle classes but as a guarantor of their security against speculation, monopoly, and fraud and against democratic political movements that threatened a redistribution of political power and wealth via universal suffrage, progressive taxation, and social welfare. From the 1820s, middle-class forms of association—voluntary societies and joint-stock companies included—were increasingly co-opted by working-class and petty bourgeois groups for their own ends and, in places, deployed against urban elites in the struggle over local resources, redefining the meaning of "civil society" in the process.[84] Examples include the joint-stock schemes formed by poor Scottish emigrants in 1819, the Owenite community and other cooperative projects launched on a joint-stock basis from the 1820s, the "union" mills in Yorkshire launched by collectives of small artisan manufacturers, and the chartist and communist land and newspaper companies of the 1830s and 1840s.[85] The changing legal environment, however, was not conducive to such projects. Chartists struggled between their desire to create open, democratic organizations within a joint-stock framework and their attempts to obtain legal protection by trying to make their schemes conform to the existing laws on joint-stock companies. The chartist land company, for example, was repeatedly refused permission to register under the Friendly Societies Act, and when it tried to register under the Companies Act of 1844, it fell foul of the requirement to obtain the signatures of one-quarter of its shareholders. The act was geared to ordinary companies of a few hundred shareholders, not this mass organization of forty-four thousand subscribers.[86] From the perspective of the authorities, political economists, and those traders and manufacturers whose businesses were allegedly threatened by the new schemes, there was a growing need to differentiate middle-class property rights from those of the working class as the latter began to adopt the joint-stock form for a range of projects, some with the express intent to provide an alternative to capitalist competition.

Thus there is another perspective on the company acts and other reforms of the second quarter of the nineteenth century, namely, that they aimed to legitimize middle-class forms of property (including joint-stock capital) and to offer more liberal access to it, while at same time effectively criminalizing working-class poverty (the workhouse) and refusing

legal recognition to independent working-class forms of democratic organization. This drive in the spheres of law, politics, and economics to
differentiate between the rights of different forms of property found
echoes in the internal governance of stock companies discussed in the
following chapters. From the 1830s and 1840s there were signs that the
balance of power in such companies was beginning to change. The older
proprietorial mechanisms for monitoring moral hazard, embodied in individual company constitutions and bylaws, were increasingly made redundant by general legislation that aimed to protect investors and limit
their liability, while at the same time shareholders' involvement in corporate governance was diminished by the growth of firms and internal
company reforms. As we shall see, our data reveal the beginnings of the
demise of "voluntarism" and "participatory politics" among joint-stock
companies and the expansion of executive powers and the virtual representation of the passive investor.

CHAPTER THREE

Company Formation

The practical goodness of a government depends, much more than is generally supposed, on the forms of business. — John Stuart Mill[1]

Entrepreneurs wishing to establish a company faced a number of important decisions, many of which would have a profound effect on the character and prospects of the concern. The decision whether or not to seek incorporation was perhaps the most fundamental. Incorporation offered legal security for the property invested in a company and could ensure that the liability faced by shareholders would be limited, but the process was expensive and uncertain to succeed.[2] Companies seeking to follow this route needed to obtain substantial support, both among politicians and local economic interests, most typically landowners. The surest way to do this was to win their favor by distributing shares and seats on the board to them. Beyond this, companies needed to develop strategies for winning the right kind of financial backers. Prospectuses and other literature issued by the company had to position the company in such a way as to stress both the public benefit served by the scheme and the private gain that would accrue to its investors. In addition, the size and capital structure, in particular the share denomination and the amount paid up on each share, greatly influenced the kind of proprietary the venture would attract. There were, however, many other mechanisms employed to help regulate the kind of investors a company had. These mechanisms, ranging from directorial control over share transfers to time restrictions on the payment of the first dividend, suggest that issues of class and respectability were paramount in the minds of company promoters in our period. Their popularity also hints at the importance that continued to be placed on the character of a company's proprietary and thus the influence exerted by the partnership form of organization long into the nineteenth century. All these decisions were enshrined in the company constitution—embodied in either an act of incorporation or, for unincorporated companies, a deed of settlement (articles of co-partnery in Scotland). This chapter explores the processes by which both types of founding document were drawn up. Here, as in other areas of corporate governance, companies varied enormously in their approach to the issue of shareholder participation.

Foundation and Promotion

The establishment of most joint-stock companies commenced with a se-ries of private meetings between individual projectors. This was often accompanied by a personal canvass of potential investors and patrons, including county landowners and neighboring gentry and leading mer-chants and professional men in or around the hometown of the projec-tors. The first meetings of the projectors of the Kent Fire Insurance Of-fice, for instance, were held at the Bell Inn, Maidstone, in February 1802. They divided themselves into two groups of four for the purposes of can-vassing support. The first group visited six prospective investors in Can-terbury, "all of whom were civil but not warm in the business." The sec-ond group called on Thomas Godfrey, high sheriff of Kent and MP for Ash, at a coaching inn in Rochester while he was on his way to London. Godfrey "expressed himself well satisfied with the plan," and asked to be kept informed. Further meetings of the projectors were held at inns in Sittingbourne and Tunbridge Wells, at which the "plan" of business was finalized.[3]

Following such initial meetings and private canvassing, a promotion committee was usually formed from some or all of the original projec-tors. Frequently at this point a minute book would be opened and a sec-retary or clerk appointed, whose first task would be to record the pro-ceedings of the promotion committee. The committee would decide the object of the venture, fields of business to be entered, structure of the capital stock, denomination of shares, and the procedure and terms of the issue and would instruct a legal counsel to draft a constitution, ei-ther in the form of a deed or articles or in the form of a bill of incorpo-ration. The promotion committee often provided most of a company's first board of directors. The directors were usually appointed at one of the early "public" meetings of the promoters, to which other interested parties—patrons and potential investors—were also invited.

Once the projectors of the Kent Fire Office had drafted their "plan"—a capital of £100,000 in £50 shares, with each policyholder insuring £1,000 being entitled to one share—further canvassing ensued. Early in March, two of the promoters, Thomas Lediard and William Dann, dined at Canterbury with Thomas Godfrey, who promised to "bring forward his neighbours and the Canterbury gentlemen" to meet them. Lediard and Dann also called on the Earl of Camden, Sir William Gray, Sir John Boyd, the Earl of Romney, Lords Gwydir and Whitworth, and William Pitt, while other projectors interviewed Lords Guildford and Thanet in London and the Archbishop of Canterbury and visited the Maidstone assizes to solicit the approval of the grand jury for their scheme.[4] Toward the end of the month, invitations were sent out to 179 individuals, including 32 peers, to attend the project's first "public" meeting at the Rose Inn, Sittingbourne. Forty-two turned up for the meeting chaired by Viscount Marsham, son of the Earl of Romney. They appointed Romney as governor; four trustees, namely, Marsham, Earls Camden and Darnley, and Lord Sondes; thirty-five deputy governors, including many of those who had been personally canvassed; and fifty "directors," including Godfrey, the MPs for Bromley and Chatham, and the Bishop of Rochester. Lediard was appointed "secretary, accomptant and comptroller." Three other projectors were appointed surveyor and solicitors to the new company. The Sittingbourne meeting also appointed a committee of eight, with Marsham as chair, "to propose noblemen, gentlemen and officers to patronize, support and conduct this institution." The energetic canvassing had thus been highly successful. The unwieldy first board of "directors" was largely promotional in character, designed to attract further investors from across the county. As much as £105,000 was subscribed within seventeen days. A subsequent meeting resolved to increase the capital to £200,000.[5]

As businesses that commonly found it difficult to obtain acts of incorporation, many insurance companies looked to advertise the presence of noblemen and members of Parliament on their boards or as trustees. This, it was believed, increased the prospects of a successful petition for incorporation, although its impressive array of peers did the Kent Fire Office little good when it sought incorporation in 1802 in the face of opposition from larger and more influential London insurance companies. Titled executives also lent éclat to a new venture. The first trustees of the County Fire Office in 1807 included the Duke of Rutland, the Marquis of Buckingham, and the Earls of Buckinghamshire, Upper Ossory, and Northampton, who had been assured by the company's promoter, John Barber, that the deed of settlement would "be so framed as to preclude any trouble or active duty to the noblemen who consent to become trustees."[6] Infrastructure projects, such as canals and railways, which required corporate privileges, found the support of landowners and MPs indispensable, especially as they often suffered from expensive battles between powerful interests, including rival companies, supporting and opposing their schemes. (This is discussed further below.) As a result of the extended geographies of their operations, insurance and railway companies were also great advertisers. In 1843, for instance, the directors of the Lancaster and Carlisle Railway Company ordered their prospectus to be published in fifteen newspapers between Edinburgh and London, as well as "the two Railway Papers" (the *Railway Magazine* and the *Railway Times*).[7]

This sequence—private meetings; personal canvassing of influential patrons; appointment of a promotion committee; drafting a plan, sometimes in conjunction with an engineer or surveyor as well as a lawyer depending on the type of business to be entered; advertising that plan in newspapers, by circular and by prospectus; followed by more public meetings to attract prospective investors—was common to the establishment of most joint-stock companies in the eighteenth and early nineteenth centuries. The object was always to construct a public "body corporate and politic" out of a private initiative. The line between the private sphere of projectors' discussions and the public sphere of subscribers' meetings was easily crossed. Companies had to perform a fine balancing act when advertising a scheme, stressing the benefits that would ensue to both public and private interests. Thus, a circular of the Birmingham Banking Company claimed that the bank "would tend greatly to the advantage of the mercantile and other classes of the town and neighbourhood, and afford a sufficient remuneration to the parties whose capital might be employed."[8] The prospectus of the Stirlingshire Banking Company claimed that the scheme would, "besides forming a profitable investment for capital, greatly promote the prosperity of the district by affording a judicious and uniform support to trade, agriculture, and manufactures."[9]

There were other steps that promoters could take to reinforce the public nature of their company. Insurance companies in county towns

in Shropshire, Kent, Wiltshire, and Worcestershire, as well as those in
cities such as Norwich, Newcastle, Manchester, and Leeds, enjoyed intimate links to the magistracy, officeholders, corporations, and guilds in
their areas. Company insignia were sometimes based on the town arms,
premises would be taken up in the high street, and prominent local figures would be encouraged to hold shares and sit on the board of directors. These steps amounted to "a fusion of corporate and urban identity,
of private and public interests."[10] This blending of the public and the private can be seen throughout the joint-stock economy. The initial "public" meetings of companies were often held in local hostelries such as the
Red Lion, Falkirk, and the Fountain Inn, Canterbury.[11] When more spa-
cious premises were required, other quasi-public buildings were found,
including the Newcastle Assembly Rooms and the Royal Exchange,
Leith.[12] Frequently, the connection with the public life of the community was made still more explicit. The supporters of the Blandford Gas
and Coke Company held their first meeting in Blandford Town Hall;
the shareholders of the Tunnel under the Thames Company met in Gravesend Town Hall; the first meeting of the Dartford Gas Company took
place in the local vestry room.[13] Local authorities could also be instrumental in the promotion of joint-stock services and amenities. The initial committee of the Blandford Gas and Coke Company, for instance,
consisted of the town council together with nine other directors.[14] Companies continued to embed themselves in the public sphere after they
were formed. The Ratcliff Gas Light and Coke Company, for example,
made small charitable donations to local schools and dispensaries, and
the Liverpool and Manchester Railway Company was a benefactor of
the Liverpool infirmary.[15]

At the same time, companies had to stress the private benefits that
would accrue from investment in the scheme. While the prospectus of
the Metropolitan Marine Bath Company focused on the public benefits that new bathing facilities would bring, it also suggested that the return on capital invested "cannot be less than 14 per cent."[16] The Plymouth and Devonport Banking Company pointed to "the high premiums,
borne without any known exception" by the shares of other joint-stock
banks in England and Wales.[17] General predictions of profitability, however, were not necessarily enough to get a new company off the ground.
Well after the initial phase of private canvassing by promoters, share issues were often targeted at those whose support the company wished to
attract. The Atlas Assurance Company in 1807 reserved one-quarter of

its shares "as an inducement for persons residing in the principal provincial towns."[18] Other insurance companies also reserved blocs of shares
to sell in particular localities or prioritized certain groups as investors by
carefully controlling the distribution of shares.[19] Walter Cassels, London
agent for the Northern and Central Bank of England, recounted that the
board held back a number of shares so "that the directors should have it
in their power to give shares to influential shareholders in the immediate neighbourhood."[20] Though it was a common practice, it could arouse
misgivings. Thomas Backhouse, a managing director of the York City
and County Banking Company, wrote to a business colleague that the
board had kept behind some shares "which it was originally intended to
give out to such parties as offered valuable accounts with the Bank, but
my opinion is that if we once begin to distribute them, those who don't
get them will be offended, and we shall do more harm than good."[21] Furthermore, the practice could provide an opportunity for the misappro-
priation of shares by directors for personal gain, a problem to which the
directors of the General Steam Navigation Company alluded at its first
GM. The company had made £8,309 from the sale of shares that had
been retained because they had not been taken up by subscribers at the
time of the original share issue. "Disclaiming all comment upon the conduct of other Directors in other concerns in the self-appropriation of this
incidental advantage," the directors felt that "they are the trustees of
the Shareholders, especially appointed to guard and promote their general interests." They therefore recommended that, once the expenses incurred in the formation of the company had been paid, the rest of this
money be distributed among the shareholders.[22]

Shareholders could be particularly vulnerable to dishonest share appropriations in the early stages of company formation. The East London Water Works Company ran into disaster months after its establishment in 1807. Prior to securing its act of incorporation, the directors
had sounded out the London Dock Company with regard to purchas-
ing its Shadwell and West Ham waterworks. The East London Company's engineer had valued the property at £60,000, but the directors of
the London Dock Company subsequently demanded £130,000. The directors were given only three days to reach a decision—insufficient time
to convene a GM—and were "much alarmed at the awful responsibility of their situation." The amount demanded was far in excess of what
the East London Company could afford, yet the purchase was necessary
in order to prevent competition in its own district. A director, George

Boulton Mainwaring, suggested a solution: "some most opulent and respectable persons" had agreed to take up four hundred new £100 shares toward expediting the purchase. They would be issued on the condition that they were not sold on again, to prevent any depreciation in the company's value. This option was retrospectively approved by a special general meeting (SGM) in January 1808.[23] It was hoped that the move would "secure to this undertaking the patronage and support of persons of high character and whose known honour and integrity would ensure the performance of the stipulation that such shares should not be disposed of."[24] Several directors, however, sold their shares at large premiums just a few months later. Subsequently the GM established a committee to investigate. When it reported, two directors, Mainwaring and William Hubbard, were singled out for particular censure. It transpired that the shareholders had been misled throughout the whole affair: the London Dock Company had not imposed an ultimatum of three days, and an SGM could have been convened to consider the matter at leisure. The scheme advanced by Mainwaring was in fact a plot to ensure that the extra shares were distributed among Mainwaring and his friends and not the body of the shareholders. The committee sought legal advice and was told that "the mode by which the appropriation of the 400 shares was obtained was a gross fraud on the Company." The company filed a bill in Chancery against the delinquent directors and successfully compelled them to return the money made from the transfers.[25]

Incorporation

English companies that decided to incorporate could face a long, uncertain, and expensive process to secure their objective. Before 1844, two main routes were open: applying to the Crown for a royal charter of incorporation or applying to Parliament for an act of incorporation. During the seventeenth century, under the Stuart monarchs, the former route had been particularly risky. In formal terms, a royal charter, in giving a company jurisdiction over its members and employees, delegated some of the absolute authority of the Crown over its subjects and, in doing so, asserted the royal prerogative to dispense or retract such authority at will. After the Glorious Revolution of 1688–9, however, Parliament increasingly became the source of corporate privileges and protection, and all sides quickly recognized that the Crown prerogative was now severely limited. By the reign of Anne it was widely accepted that trading companies needed to gain the "sanction of parliamentary constitutions," as one defender of the Royal African Company put it, rather than simply rely on their royal charters or letters patent.[26]

The reasons businessmen desired charters or acts of incorporation have not been much studied, but several incentives may be suggested. First, a company charter or act created a new legal personality with perpetual succession, separate from the mortality of individual company members and subject to termination only in a prescribed manner.[27] Partnership law, which held that a partnership was dissolved automatically by the death or withdrawal of one of its members, could not deliver this. Incorporation also gave a company the power to sue and be sued in its separate personality and imposed the obligation to have a common seal.[28] Furthermore, a charter or act allowed a company to own and convey assets, especially land, in its corporate name, in mortmain, and to be exempt from feudal dues for the same—an essential consideration for infrastructural projects such as canals and river navigations. Second, incorporation gave company promoters the right to make legally binding bylaws to govern their own affairs. This included the power to regulate and levy taxes on their members, to resolve their own disputes, and sometimes to adjust the liability of the company and individual members. Again, partnership law could not provide this, for it was geared to firms with only a handful of partners who usually had no need of an elaborate structure of internal regulations.[29] Third, companies might seek monopoly privileges in a trade, including exemption from customs duties and the right to defend their trade against interlopers. These powers— the possibilities of limited liability and share transferability, the trading advantages held out by the monopoly, and the tax privileges—helped attract investors to English business corporations.[30]

In Scotland, in addition to charters granted by the Crown and special parliamentary acts of incorporation, royal burghs could grant a seal of cause that was treated as a charter of incorporation. There were over eighty such burghs by 1707. Lesser burghs of barony, which numbered around 350 by this date, could grant a letter of license for incorporation in place of a seal of cause, though this letter required confirmation by the Crown.[31] Furthermore, in contrast to England, where general company legislation was entirely absent until the Victorian era, acts of the Scottish Parliament in 1641, 1661, and 1681 provided a general statutory basis for the formation of joint-stock companies, although to obtain full privileges of incorporation and monopoly trading rights it remained necessary to apply to Parliament or the Privy Council.[32] By the early eighteenth century the increasing practice of establishing stock companies under parliamentary acts undermined burghal rights of incorporation, but these did not entirely disappear. In 1747, for instance, the magistrates and town council of Glasgow incorporated the "Friendly Society of the Heretors of Glasgow and suburbs for a Mutual Insurance of Houses against Losses by Fire."[33] The exclusive trading and incorporating privileges of the Scottish burghs were not abolished until 1846, although the Royal Commission on Municipal Corporations in Scotland in 1835 found the practice had by then fallen into desuetude.[34]

During the eighteenth century, therefore, in all parts of the United Kingdom, Parliament became the chief purveyor of corporate rights. The process by which Parliament dealt with local bills was gradually standardized in an attempt to ensure that all applications were responses to genuine local needs and were dealt with consistently by the legislature.[35] In 1685, a standing order was passed to the effect that private bills had to be introduced to Parliament by means of a signed petition stating the aims of the project. An order of 1699 specified that there would be at least three clear days between each reading of a bill and a week between the second reading and the commitment so that legislation could not be sneaked through. In 1717, a further standing order made it compulsory for bills involving the levy of tolls to be referred to a select committee before they could progress.[36] The legislative loads experienced by Parliaments after 1688 were sufficiently light to ensure that these rules were subject to little change long into the eighteenth century. The volume of legislation, however, later increased dramatically: the average number of acts per session rose from 58 under George I to 254 in the reign of George III.[37] While enclosure and turnpike acts accounted for much of the increase, a rise in the number of infrastructural projects, particularly the "canal manias" of the 1760s and 1790s, also contributed. Indeed, the flurry of bills put before Parliament by the supporters of canal projects led to the imposition of new rules regulating applications for incorporation. These were designed to protect the public, and particularly landowners, from a glut of new schemes. All canal acts provided powers for the compulsory purchase of "messuages, lands, tenements and hereditaments" that were necessary for the completion of works of "public utility." By the end of the eighteenth century most acts were quite precise about the course of a canal or river navigation and how much land on either side of it could be purchased. They also specified that the schedule of lands to be purchased must be circulated to the landowners concerned, set out a valuation process, and established a jury system to arbitrate in case of disputes between landowners and the canal company. It took several decades, however, for company promoters to be forced toward a position of compliance. In the early 1770s there were complaints that landowners often "had their lands cut through by a canal, almost without any notice at all, or at least with too little to afford them an opportunity of considering the proposition maturely, and of laying their observations upon such Bills before Parliament with effect."[38] In response, the House of Commons appointed a committee in 1774 to examine ways of improving the bills procedure for drainage schemes, turnpikes, canals, and river navigations. This led to new standing orders that required that notices of all applications for bills be fixed to the door of the local quarter sessions house and be inserted in one newspaper in every county through which the canal would pass (later also in the London *Gazette*). Further safeguards included a requirement that petitioners for a bill contact all owners of land through which the canal would pass and establish whether they supported or opposed the scheme. A plan of the canal and a list of the lands it was to run through and the owners and occupiers affected, all contained in a "book of reference," together with the names of all subscribers and the amounts they had subscribed and the estimated cost of the canal also had to be included with the application. These standing orders were refined by the Commons between 1789 and 1794 and adopted by the House of Lords in the latter year.[39]

Under these rules, winning at least the consent of local landowners was essential. Directors of canal and, later, railway companies had to keep a close eye on public meetings held in towns and villages through which the line would pass, and they sometimes sent delegations of directors to talk to residents and defuse opposition.[40] Companies did their best to emphasize the public benefits of their enterprises in order to persuade landowners of their necessity, but bribes often proved more effective. At the first meeting of the Ashby-de-la-Zouch Canal Company in 1792, it was recorded that it was "the unanimous sense of this Meeting that if such Canal could be obtained it would be attended with great advantages to the Community at large. They therefore flatter themselves that the project will meet with Lord Rawdon's concurrence and patronage."[41] Rawdon was brought on board, but other landowners, notably Penn Curzon, were less amenable. Curzon attended a select committee of the company's executive to announce his opposition to the scheme and claimed that other landowners supported him. As a result of these problems, when the shares were issued, the committee of management decided to reserve 500 of the company's 1,500 shares for landowners and withheld a further 250 to be distributed during the progress of the company's bill through Parliament.[42]

Allocations of shares could win over skeptical landowners. A complementary strategy was to hand over considerable executive power to local patrons whose support was considered crucial. A committee of seven, for instance, was appointed by the Manchester, Bolton, and Bury Canal Company in 1790. Of these, four were nominated by the Earl of Derby, Lord Frey de Wilton, local landowners, and mill owners.[43] Significant incentives sometimes had to be given to interested parties in order to buy off their opposition. Attempts by the promoters of the Liverpool and Manchester Railway Company to secure an act of incorporation failed in 1825 in the face of hostility from local landowners. The route of the line was altered, but this brought the trustees of the Bridgewater Canal into opposition. As a result, the railway directors approached the chief trustee, the Marquess of Stafford. Stafford was persuaded to drop his opposition in return for the right to purchase 1,000 of the company's 5,100 shares and the permanent right to elect three of the company's fifteen directors so long as he kept his shares.[44]

Another aspect of the parliamentary process of incorporation that had a profound effect on company formation strategies was the composition of the select committees appointed by Parliament to consider bills. These committees always comprised politicians with local interests, and bills of incorporation, as in the case of the Worcester Canal in 1786, might be subject to the "strictest scrutiny."[45] As Thomas comments, "the advantage of personal, local or professional knowledge was clearly held to outweigh the danger of bias or jobbery arising from such connections."[46] This feature of the incorporation process attracted much condemnation: the radical MP Joseph Hume was "strongly impressed with the impropriety" of the system of "canvass and influence" that this rule brought about.[47] The Whig Henry Brougham thought that as well as interested voting, the system also encouraged "jobbing" in votes: that is, MPs selling their votes on the committee to the highest bidder.[48] The rule, however, also had plenty of supporters who claimed that interested voting was too complex a problem to legislate away.[49] Not until 1844 did the Commons begin to change its rules, switching to a system of impar-

tial committees in which local interests could not dominate, first for railways, and then in 1855 for all local bills.[50]

The makeup of bill committees imposed certain requirements on
companies. Rather than having to persuade an impartial jury of the
public good of a scheme, they had to ensure that they had marshaled
sufficient local political power to bludgeon their measure through Parliament. As Hume put it, "every projector of a new company" found it
"absolutely necessary to have among his subscribers a certain number of
members of parliament; without whose aid he could entertain little or no
hope of getting his bill passed."[51] Indeed, companies that were liable to
be at all controversial bulked out their boards with MPs and other prominent figures who could secure the political backing needed to ensure the
bill's success.[52] In return, MPs received shares on preferential terms "to
sell at a profit in the Bubble-market," in the words of one critic.[53] For example, the Tunnel under the Thames Company needed parliamentary
support for its ambitious scheme to dig a tunnel connecting Kent and
Essex. The first committee of management counted an earl, three MPs,
and representatives of the Royal Engineers and the Royal Navy among
its fourteen members.[54] This support, however, did not prevent the company from failing: work was abandoned in 1804 after more than half
of the capital of £30,000 had been called up. The fate of this and other
such schemes created a climate of suspicion of overly ambitious projects,
which made the process of incorporation even more perilous. The provisional committee of the St. Nicholas Bay Harbour and Canterbury Canal Company applied for an act of incorporation in 1810. The committee had to make concessions to the bill's opponents while the bill was
progressing through Parliament because of "their knowledge of the dis-
taste with which the House of Commons had received several plans of
professed improvement in different parts of the kingdom. The failure of
wild and impracticable schemes, eagerly patronized in former years, had
generated a spirit of distrust that threatened to extinguish ever so useful a project as that which the subscribers to the St Nicholas Bay Harbour and Canterbury Canal, have had in view." The bill scraped through
by 21 votes to 19. The importance of securing influence in Parliament
was highlighted when the GM went on to elect its board of directors: no
fewer than six of the twenty-one were MPs.[55] Without sufficient political
backing, companies were vulnerable to ambush by rival firms. In 1825,
Henry Whitbread presented a petition to Parliament from the directors of the London and Westminster Oil Gas Company, objecting to the

manner in which the company's bill had been "got rid of" by its parliamentary committee. "After a long and laborious inquiry in the committee," the petition asserted, "a number of persons, most of whom were interested in the Coal Gas companies, and not one of whom had attended
for a single hour during the progress of the inquiry, came down on the
last day, and voted against the bill. In this way a measure which would
have been of great advantage to the public, had been lost, and with it
no less a sum than £30,000 which had been expended in order to carry
through parliament."[56]

As Whitbread's complaint suggests, obtaining the necessary political
backing, fending off opposition, and bankrolling a bill's slow progression through its many stages in committee, could be enormously difficult
and expensive. Kostal has described how a small number of parliamentary agents and barristers were able "to create a hugely profitable car-
tel for their services" in getting railway bills through Parliament.[57] The
Great Western Railway secured its act of incorporation in August 1835.
At the GM two months later, shareholders were told that £88,710 of their
money had been spent, the bulk of it on legal costs, though construction
had not yet begun.[58] Such a heavy bill was exceptional, but it was normal for companies to be left with a substantial burden from the process
of incorporation. The shareholders of the Leeds and Bradford Railway
Company, for example, were told that the cost of their act (1844) was,
at £11,409, twice what it would been if it had not been opposed by local
landowners.[59] This expense amounted to almost 3 percent of its capital
stock (£400,000). Even once this initial cost had been borne, future payments could be necessitated by subsequent approaches to Parliament to
revise existing powers. The Dundee and Newtyle Railway Company, established in 1826 with a capital of £30,000, paid more than £299 to its solicitors between February and August 1836 to secure a bill to amend its
existing acts. When such a bill reached its final stages, the costs could
accumulate rapidly. In August, the company paid a total of £76 16s. 6d.
in the Commons and £69 5s. 6d. for committee fees, engrossing fees,
housekeeping, clerical fees, and so on. A further £23 12s. 6d. was spent
on printing the bill.[60]

These kinds of costs dissuaded many small companies from seeking incorporation. The shareholders of the Dursley Gas Light and Coke
Company—formed in 1835 with a capital of just £2,760—decided at an
early GM to erect their works without an act of Parliament. The shareholders unanimously resolved "that the Company do take upon itself all

risk and responsibility of acting without authority of Parliament—and that in case of any proceedings against the Directors or any other Person acting under their authority for any act done they be indemnified out of the funds of the Company if sufficient and if not by the Shareholders individually according to the number of their shares."[61] Even companies that were initially keen to incorporate could be persuaded otherwise when the costs and the difficulties involved became clear. In 1802, the directors of the Kent Fire Office intended to seek incorporation by act or charter once the capital was subscribed, "to Establish the Institution and especially to protect the property of the proprietors beyond the amount of their respective shares." The directors, however, reported to the shareholders that, owing to strong opposition from the London insurance offices, the application to Parliament had been withdrawn, and "from what arose during such proceedings they found it would be very difficult and perhaps impracticable to establish the institution under that mode."[62]

The growing importance of incorporation to companies can be seen in the number of unincorporated companies making explicit provision in their constitutions for a subsequent approach to the state for corporate powers. None of the unincorporated companies in our sample established before 1800 and only two of the twenty-eight unincorporated companies formed between 1800 and 1819 made this provision (see table 3.1). But the provision became common from 1824, a year when Parliament was swamped with applications from new companies. The insecurities and legal difficulties faced by unincorporated companies drove a majority to include this provision in every subsequent period up to the

TABLE 3.1. **Unincorporated companies making provision for incorporation in their constitutions**

Subperiod	Total unincorporated companies	Number making provision	Percentage
1800–9	20	1	5.0
1810–9	8	1	12.5
1820–4	19	10	52.6
1825–9	33	20	60.6
1830–4	31	22	71.0
1835–9	72	43	59.7
1840–4	24	16	66.7

Note: No unincorporated company established before 1800 made this provision.

legislation of 1844. Those that did not were mostly small companies, indicating that for them incorporation was simply too expensive an option to contemplate. Just 12.2 percent of very small and 34.8 percent of small companies made the provision, as opposed to 75.7 percent of large companies (see table 4.2 for the definition of size categories).

The Attraction of Unincorporated Companies

At least three factors induced businessmen in England after 1720 to proceed with the risk of promoting and investing in unincorporated enterprises with transferable shares. First, as noted in chapter 2, the Bubble Act remained dormant during the eighteenth century and was not revived until the company promotion boom of 1807–10, by which time there were hundreds of unincorporated companies already in operation. The hostility of the courts and the Crown's law officers to unincorporated joint-stock companies had diminished markedly during the second half of the eighteenth century. Some legislation even provided official recognition of some unincorporated companies, in insurance and shipping, for example.[63] Shipping companies in both Scotland and England fell under admiralty law, which recognized the corporate identity of a ship and facilitated the settlement of disputes between part owners. Moreover, the Registry Act of 1823 gave statutory recognition to the traditional joint-adventure system and fixed the maximum number of shares at sixty-four and the maximum number of registered owners at thirty-two.[64] Joint-stock companies were already operating coastal shipping and ferry services before 1815. After the end of the Napoleonic Wars, numerous steam packet companies were launched on east coast and Irish Sea routes, and steam ferry companies appeared on the Mersey, the Wear, the Humber, the Thames, and Strangford Lough. The great majority of these were established by private deed of settlement (in England and Ireland) or by contract of copartnery (in Scotland).[65]

Second, there was the positive effect of the law of trust, which was extensively utilized by unincorporated companies in our period. Trust law provided useful elements of perpetuity and joint holding. During the late seventeenth century, considerable progress had been made in the legal classification and definition of trusts.[66] A ruling in 1673, for instance, stipulated that assets held on trust could not be claimed by the trustees' creditors. Thus, by vesting their assets in a number of named trustees through a deed of settlement, unincorporated companies aimed to limit the liability of individual shareholders to their shares in the company.[67] It was by no means a perfect device. Trusts were not recognized at common law, and litigation in Chancery could be expensive. There was also the question of the liability and obligations of trustees to shareholders. Under equity a trust could not fail on account of the deficiency of a trustee, but any negligence or misuse of entrusted funds by trustees certainly made their personal estates liable for compensation.[68] Furthermore, trust law did not cover the question of transferable shares. Despite these handicaps, of the 224 unincorporated companies in our database, no fewer than 209 adopted the trust device. A further thirteen incorporated companies also provided for trusts in their constitutions.[69] We return to the constitutional provisions for trustees below.

Third, we must also look beyond the realm of the law, in particular to the expansion of associational culture and commercial networks, to explain the growing popularity of the unincorporated company. The voluntary association diffused rapidly throughout polite society in Britain during the eighteenth century, most notably among the urban middling classes, but also among county elites who would join urban associations for the purposes of patronage or where political or economic interests converged.[70] To come together for the benefit of an improving project became a general instinct and was seen as promoting a collective sense of civic responsibility, as well as providing a source of status, power, and social capital. For many writers, the club, society, private company, or voluntary association became a model for a moral and virtuous society at large, where individuals of politeness and property could meet on a roughly equal footing, where the exchange of ideas and information would be free, and where behavior and reputation would be monitored by mutual observation.[71] The transparency of rules and the free flow of information were essential to this vision, as was the public operation of trust and regard. As David Hume put it, among the virtuous "middle station of life" commerce between friends was tempered "by obligations given and received."[72]

Associating for a collective investment most commonly occurred among urban- or regional-based networks of capitalists. Such networks generated "institutional arrangements" that included formal rules as well as shared attitudes and value systems, the former complementing the latter. Together these could facilitate contract enforcement and reduce the risk of opportunism or malfeasance in commercial transactions.[73] "Institutional arrangements" included the regulations embodied in the constitutions of joint-stock companies. Such regulations included the check on personal liquidity provided by the paid-up subscription and the procedures for share transfer, the power afforded to proprietors to inspect company constitutions and amend them by majority vote, the power to inspect and query accounts, and the power to elect and remove directors and managers.

The civic face of social and business networks also ensured that, as noted above, many private joint-stock ventures, whether or not they were incorporated, were expressly promoted, and to an important degree legitimized, as a public good. Such ventures can be viewed as part of the great improvement movement of the eighteenth and early nineteenth centuries, which included investment in street lighting and paving, commercial exchanges, assembly rooms, coffeehouses, subscription reading rooms, and libraries.[74] Consequently, there was a convergence between the joint-stock company and other institutions of improvement. Subscription societies were noncommercial enterprises, but they aimed to give their members a moral and educational return on their money. Their forms of governance were not dissimilar to joint-stock companies, with an elected management committee and general meetings of subscribers. The unincorporated as well as incorporated joint-stock company, therefore, is properly situated in the landscape of other forms of association characterizing local and regional elites in industrializing Britain.

Unincorporated Companies: Duration and Trustees

A key characteristic of the corporation was that it was established in perpetuity and therefore outlived its founder members, unlike the private partnership, which in England had no legal existence distinct from its members. Although legally identical to ordinary partnerships, unincorporated stock companies occupied a gray area between these two. A majority of them (77.2 percent) were established for an indefinite duration, while just fifty-one (22.8 percent) imitated private partnerships in stipulating a fixed endpoint. In our sample there were also fifteen corporations that were established for a fixed duration. However, these were mostly bridge and harbor companies, which were to be converted into a trust or commission once their shareholders had received a specified return on capital invested. Most of the aforementioned fifty-one unincorporated companies specified a lifespan between seven and ninety-nine years. The modal duration was twenty-one years, adopted by thirteen companies. There were marked differences by place: twenty Scottish unincorporated companies (34.5 percent of all such companies in our sample) had a fixed term, whereas the proportion for England and Wales was 11.9 percent and for Ireland 11.1 percent. This reflected the different business cultures north and south of the border, particularly the existence in Scotland of a "half-way house," somewhere between the private partnership and the English unincorporated company. The boundary between partnership and company, as Munn suggests, was predominantly a matter of size, with the smaller joint-stocks most resembling fixed-term partnerships. Of the forty-four unincorporated companies in our sample that were established for ninety-nine years or less and specified a nominal capital, twenty-four had a capital of £50,000 or less. The fixed term could insulate unincorporated companies against claims that they were imitating corporations by establishing perpetual bodies without state sanction, but it could prove a problem after incorporation by registration was introduced from 1844. For example, the Shotts Iron Company was established for a fixed term of twenty-five years in 1824 and in 1849 was renewed for a further twenty-five years. When, in 1871, the company decided to seek incorporation, the shareholders were "advised that in consequence of the copartnership being limited [in duration] . . . they cannot obtain incorporation in perpetuity by registration" under the Companies Acts of 1862 and 1867, and instead they were required to obtain a special incorporating act of Parliament.[75]

Other important decisions facing companies were whether or not to have trustees and how to regulate their appointment and behavior. Just thirteen corporations (4.5 percent) made provision for appointment of trustees in their constitutions. Seven of these were bridge companies that placed funds in the name of trustees with instructions about how the money was to be deployed in a given eventuality.[76] Unsurprisingly, given their greater legal fragility, unincorporated companies resorted to trustees far more often: all but fifteen in our sample did so. Capital stock was held in the names of the trustees, and all actions brought by or against the company were to be performed or answered by them. In this way, as noted above, unincorporated companies hoped to obtain some of the legal security enjoyed by corporations. Small groups of trustees were the preferred option. The modal number was three. Trustees were often a small group of the wealthiest shareholders, but they could also be local notables with no direct connection to the company. Of the 222 companies making provision for trustees, 126 (56.8 percent) did not specify any share qualification for trustees, indicating that trustees did not have to be shareholders. Three specified that trustees must not be shareholders. The remaining ninety-three companies required some share qualification for trustees. In forty-seven of these, the qualification was set higher than the minimum shareholding, indicating that trustees were expected to be substantial shareholders, though in only two cases was it set higher than the directorial qualification.

Companies varied considerably in their approach to trustees. Nearly 90 percent of all companies making provision for trustees stipulated how they would be appointed. In thirty-eight companies, all but four of them Scottish or Irish, the board and/or salaried officers acted as trustees, with no process of appointment set out beyond the normal board elections and appointment of officers. In a further 106 companies (47.8 percent), the directors were explicitly given the power to appoint trustees. In only fifty-four companies (24.3 percent) were shareholders at the GM given some say over the process, and even then, the powers could be vague. The extent of shareholders' rights was determined chiefly by the size of the company. Shareholders in no less than 54.6 percent of very small companies were granted the power to appoint trustees, but this fell to 4.6 percent in very large companies. Geography was also important. Shareholders had rights of appointment in one-third of English companies but in only 11.8 percent of Irish and 7.7 percent of Scottish companies, largely because many of the latter appointed their boards as trustees. This suggests that very different cultural and legal contexts existed north and south of the border and across the Irish Sea when it came to the role and status of trustees in joint-stock companies.

Close attention was paid to the rules regulating the appointment and composition of trustees, as, in addition to their legal role, they were intended to provide an extra security to the shareholders against the actions of directors. The value of this security, however, was decidedly limited. Investments ordered by directors typically had to be authorized by the trustees, but, according to a group of actuaries giving evidence to the Select Committee on Joint-Stock Companies in 1843, trustees usually signed whatever they were ordered to by the board.[77] Trustees had no real discretion over the actions of the directors and rarely featured prominently in disputes between directors and shareholders.

Constitutions

The constitutions of both unincorporated and incorporated companies were crucial in defining the political relationships among directors, managers, and shareholders and therefore in distributing power within the company. The long-term effect of the Bubble Act on constitutions was twofold. First, there was an increase in the number and scope of restrictive clauses inserted into charters, acts, and deeds of settlement to try to preempt potential criticism or prosecution. Charters and acts, for example, commonly included clauses stating that the company would not act contrary to the Bubble Act. This was regarded as important in view of the implicit power of Parliament or the Crown to withdraw a charter if a company acted illegally or breached the conditions of its incorporation, although incorporating acts rarely referred to such power explicitly.[78] Second, the constitutions of both incorporated and unincorporated companies became more specific. More contained clauses that fixed the amount of capital that could be raised without further authority, prohibited the transfer of shares for a period after incorporation or purchase, banned interlocking directorates in other companies in the same industry, restricted the number of shares one individual could hold, and spelt out the areas of a company's activities.[79]

As the primary safeguard for shareholders in a new venture, constitutions had the power, when published in full, or in abstract, or as extracts in circulars, prospectuses, and advertisements, to attract or repel potential investors in often highly competitive capital markets. Unsurprisingly, therefore, they were often long and complicated documents, and their drafting was typically delegated to a solicitor with experience in the field. The deed of partnership of the General Steam Navigation Company was "framed by a Conveyancer of great professional experience."[80] The Equitable Gas Light Company assured its subscribers that the draft deed had been prepared by Baker and Hodgson, solicitors, "under the advice of Mr. Wilde, a gentleman of great eminence at the bar, and particularly conversant from his extensive practice with deeds of a similar nature."[81] It was common for deeds to borrow phrases and sometimes even whole clauses from earlier deeds. Interlocking networks of promoters and directors drawn from the same urban elite reinforced this tendency, as did the imitation of company deeds within individual sectors and even across different sectors. The deeds establishing the

Warwick Gas Light Company (1822) and the Warwick and Leamington Brewery Company (1833), for instance, were very similar in several respects, which is not surprising given that many of the same individuals were involved in both companies.[82]

Lawyers, however, were not usually left on their own to draw up constitutions, and this may help explain the persistent heterogeneity of the latter throughout our period. Solicitors worked in conjunction with promoters and company officers to ensure that the constitution met the company's needs. The extent to which shareholders were involved in this process, however, varied greatly between companies. An early meeting of the Lyme-Regis Gas and Coke Company appointed a committee of five shareholders "for the purpose of assisting the professional Gentlemen in drawing up rules for the future Guidance of the Company." When this was done, the draft deed "was read from the Chair and each clause separately discussed, when the same was finally settled and approved of by the shareholders."[83] An early GM of the Dursley Gas Light and Coke Company resolved "that the proposed Proprietary and other Deeds be sent to the different Professional Gentlemen who are Shareholders with a request to them to peruse same—that they be requested to confer with the Directors thereon and that a General Meeting of the Proprietors be afterwards called for the purpose of submitting the Deeds for their approval." The next GM made further revisions to the deed, regarding share qualifications for trustees and the quorum of board meetings.[84] This kind of participation could have a distinct effect on a company's constitution. Even before the Dursley Gas Company's deed was drawn up, the shareholders turned out in force at a meeting to rescind an earlier resolution in favor of a one-share-one-vote franchise and replace it with a capped voting scale.[85] There was also consultation at the Equitable Gas Light Company, whose board proposed a special committee of seven shareholders "to confer with the Directors on the provisions and clauses of the deed of settlement." The committee found the deed "to have been framed with great care and attention, and . . . well calculated to protect and secure the interests of the Proprietors; and the Committee have only found it necessary to suggest some alterations in its provisions and clauses, so as to adapt it to the present circumstances of the Company."[86] The alterations were approved by the directors.

Constitutions could be drafted very early in the promotion process, but this did not necessarily preclude shareholder input. For example, a

circular of the County of Devon Banking Company, issued before any
subscribers' meeting had taken place, contained nineteen clauses outlining the key features of the constitution from the franchise to the rotation
of directors. The circular stated that these regulations were "submitted
for the consideration of the public; but it will, of course, be competent
for any individual interested in this measure, to suggest alterations, by
which the objects of the company may be more effectually or beneficially
promoted."[87] The prospectus of the Plymouth and Devonport Banking
Company also contained a nineteen-point outline of its constitution,
though it was noted that the clauses were "subject to such modifications
as the Proprietors may hereafter determine on."[88] These clauses were not
always presented as a fait accompli. Indeed, it is noteworthy how much
space in prospectuses was taken up with constitutional information, suggesting the importance placed upon a careful analysis of the same by potential investors. There is evidence that early shareholders were able to
challenge the clauses drawn up by promoters and secure their revision.
The first meeting of subscribers of the Plymouth and Devonport Banking Company, for example, insisted on a more "democratic" franchise
and a lower share qualification for directors than had been set out in the
prospectus, revisions that were promptly incorporated in the second version of the document.[89]

This consultative approach was not the norm, however. More typically, deeds were framed entirely in private by solicitors and directors
and were then presented to the GM for approval and finally deposited
in the company office awaiting the signatures of the shareholders. Minute books rarely reveal dissent over the clauses imposed by the directors,
and active input from shareholders seems to have been nonexistent in
many cases.[90] The lack of shareholder involvement could have significant
consequences. One merchant, who had experience of companies both as
a shareholder and a director, argued that the constitutions of many companies were profoundly flawed: "the directors, when they have the deed
of settlement drawn up, take good care to give the shareholders as little power as possible." Shareholder impotence was a significant factor
behind subsequent failures, he believed.[91] Peter Laurie, a barrister who
had prepared several deeds of settlement, pointed out that "all companies are constituted for the pecuniary advantage of some of the origina-
tors, either the solicitor or the manager, or some other party . . . and the
directors are naturally anxious to avoid as much responsibility as possible, and to take as large powers as possible; of course all the responsi-

bility which they shift from themselves, and the increased powers which they obtain, are at the expense of the shareholders." Laurie claimed that the "most extraordinary clauses" could be inserted into deeds because "the parties who become shareholders in very many cases never think of reading the deed of settlement, and indeed are often not very competent to understand it."[92] Minute books indicate that shareholders sometimes asked for an abstract of the deed of settlement before signing it, but rarely did they take the time to plow through the whole thing.[93] As Laurie pointed out, relying on abstracts alone was unsatisfactory because "they depend so much upon the talent of the person who abstracts them, who may omit the most important words."[94] Even if the original shareholders did read the deed, after a few years they might make up only a small proportion of the proprietary. Those transferring into a company would never encounter its constitution unless they deliberately sought it out, for the transfer deed did not contain the provisions of the deed, though it did bind the shareholders to observe its regulations.[95]

The increasing complexities of the constitutions and affairs of unincorporated joint-stock companies and the legal uncertainties to which they were often subject encouraged those who wrote the constitutions to provide for means of settling disputes that avoided recourse to the law courts. As figure 3.1 shows, provision for arbitration between shareholders, which was comparatively rare among unincorporated companies in the eighteenth century, became the norm by the 1810s and appeared in more than 80 percent of constitutions after 1825. At the Manchester and Salford Bank (1836), for example, disputes were to be "referred to three indifferent persons," one chosen by each party to the dispute and a third chosen by these two arbiters. These three men—we have no evidence of women being chosen as arbiters by any company—were to determine the rights and wrongs of the dispute within three months.[96] These long and convoluted clauses often referred disputes to named arbiters. For example, differences between shareholders of the Glasgow and Liverpool Royal Steam Packet Company (1844) were referred by the contract of copartnery to "the amicable decision, final sentence, and decree arbitral" of Archibald Alison, sheriff-depute of Lanarkshire, or, failing him, one of a number of named individuals, mostly prominent Glasgow merchants.[97] In most sectors, provision for arbitration was the norm, although it was especially predominant in banking (92.1 percent of unincorporated banks had arbitration clauses), insurance (80.3 percent), gas (78.1 percent) and shipping (76.2 percent), whereas a minority

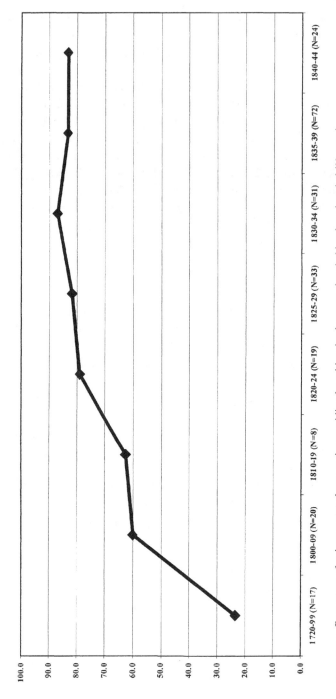

FIGURE 3.1. Percentage of unincorporated companies providing for arbitration between shareholders by subperiod ($N = 224$)

of manufacturing and property companies made the provision. By contrast, provision for arbitration was almost unknown among corporations, which was probably the result of their clearer legal status.[98]

The acts of incorporated companies, which contained their constitution, were drawn up by specialist solicitors or parliamentary agents: as the standing orders with which applicants for incorporation had to comply became increasingly complicated and demanding, it was essential that the drafting was done by experts.[99] One parliamentary draftsman, John Halcomb, stressed the effort that went into framing the bills, "great care and judgment being . . . requisite in the framing of the Preamble and clauses . . . to answer the Ends of the Parties . . . and . . . obviate such objections as are likely to arise."[100] These requirements left little room for shareholder involvement.[101] Sometimes subscribers to companies seeking incorporation would in effect renounce all rights to shape the constitution of the company. A subscription contract between the Dundee and Perth Railway Company and its subscribers to form a new company, the Kinross Junction Railway Company, authorized the directors "to do all things which may be necessary in relation to the said Undertaking or the intended application to Parliament in respect thereof as to them shall seem expedient."[102] The Brandling Junction Railway Company worked out many of the fundamental aspects of its constitution, including the number of directors, their share qualification, the appointment of auditors, and officers' pay at a subcommittee meeting of the main board, and there is no record that these decisions were put before a GM for approval.[103] Opportunities for shareholder involvement increased in 1846 when the House of Lords standing orders were amended, leading to the requirement that so-called Wharncliffe meetings be held.[104] No second reading would be given in the Lords to a company's bill unless the directors provided evidence that a meeting of shareholders had approved the bill. This was, according to Clifford, "to prevent directors of companies from promoting Bills without the knowledge or sanction of shareholders." In 1858, the same requirement was introduced to the House of Commons.[105] Subsequently, the standing orders were revised in an attempt to facilitate shareholder participation in the incorporation process. The meeting of shareholders had to be advertised in two consecutive weeks in a newspaper published in London, Edinburgh, or Dublin and in local newspapers and by circular to all shareholders at least ten days in advance of the meeting. A proxy form had to be enclosed with the circular. The bill must be submitted to the meeting and approved by the holders of at least three-quarters of the capital, in person or by proxy.[106] Even where Wharncliffe meetings were held, their form and procedures were sometimes challenged by shareholders who felt their concerns had not been fully considered.[107]

If shareholder oversight of the process of incorporation was largely absent in our period, the state's scrutiny could compensate for it. In the pre-1844 climate, when incorporation was seen as a privilege rather than a right, would-be corporations faced the possibility that the state would modify or limit the powers they sought. Admittedly, rather than shaping the internal relations between shareholders and management, the state's primary concerns were to protect the public from overpowerful companies by stipulating maximum rates of tolls or to protect landowners by trying to ensure they were adequately compensated for land lost to canal and railway companies. Care was also taken to protect existing firms whose livelihood might be jeopardized by the entry of another company into the market: whether new entrants would promote healthy competition or harmful monopoly was a debate endlessly rehearsed in our period.[108] Nevertheless, the state's concern to protect the public could also influence its response to a company's constitutional provisions. This was evident both in private bill committees and in sessions of Parliament. Railway bill committees were obliged by standing orders of 1837 to record the proposed capital of the company, the power to raise loans, the amount of shares subscribed for, the deposits paid on these, the names and addresses of the proposed directors, the shares taken by each, and details of shareholders subscribing over £2,000. It was also stipulated that no railway company be permitted to raise a sum greater than one-third of its capital by loan and that half the capital had to be paid up before the loan could be raised.[109] It is possible that a still greater influence took place behind the scenes. Before bills reached the committee, they were "narrowly sifted" by the office of the chairman of committees, and any clauses to which the chairman objected had to be removed if the bill was to have any chance of success.[110]

Incorporating bills could also be discussed in open sessions of Parliament, and heated debates frequently took place on various aspects of company constitutions. This was most obvious when companies applied to limit the liability of their shareholders: members of both houses were quick to oppose companies that sought "exclusive privileges" to compete unfairly with those whose liability was unlimited.[111] Politicians could also try to control the capital, and thereby the scale and power, of companies in order to protect the public from monopolistic corporations. In 1833, opponents of the St. George Steam Packet Company portrayed it as an "unnatural coalition" of shipowners whose huge capital would drive competitors out of business. They also objected to the powers the company's bill would give them to subsequently increase its capital by £30,000 and to form a sinking fund of £80,000, seeing this effectively as a means of bypassing the standing orders of Parliament, which required a proportion of the capital to be subscribed.[112] Against a background of increasing competition in steam shipping on the Irish Sea, the application of the Dublin Steam Navigation Company to permit its directors to raise a contingency fund of £50,000 was also opposed: "What was the object of this enormous contingency fund? It was plainly this, that if any minor speculator or shipowner presumed to place a vessel on a line already occupied by the Dublin Steam Navigation Company, this fund was to be available for his destruction. . . . It was in reality a fund for crushing marine enterprise, and deterring other merchants from honourable competition."[113] MPs could even object to the voting scale proposed by a company, as did Mr. Stanley in a debate on the Manchester Gas-Light Bill in 1824. He mocked the petitioners' stated aim of breaking up the existing "monopoly" of gas supply in the town, pointing out that the "monopolists" (the current municipal gas committee) were elected by up to twenty thousand residents in Manchester—all those possessing or occupying property to the value of £30 a year: "Of these every one had an equal vote, while, under the bill, the petitioners proposed to give votes to the proprietors of shares, whether resident or not in Manchester, according to the amount of shares, with liberty to vote by proxy."[114] This voting system would serve to create monopolies, not break them down. Thus, while MPs sometimes complained, especially during speculative "manias," of objectionable bills being "smuggled" through Parliament, the close scrutiny that was an integral part of the process of incorporation tended to encourage higher levels of transparency in incorporated company constitutions than were found in unincorporated companies.[115] This was one factor behind the development of the two generic models of company constitution that ran through our period.[116] As quasi-public bodies deriving their authority from the state, business corporations constructed their constitutions, for all their individual variety, from a democratic model in which the GM was the principal source of governance power. Transparency was a fundamental building block in this. Unincorporated companies, far less open to official scrutiny, had the option of

drawing upon a more republican "checks and balances" model of constitution, in which greater power was accorded to the executive, with the
GM acting as a passive, sometimes nearly invisible, monitor of managerial actions.

Shares: Capital Stock and Denomination

Of all the decisions that had to be made at the birth of a company, the
most important included the amount of share capital to be issued and the
denomination of the shares. Large nominal capitals increasingly came to
be viewed as an indicator of solidity and respectability. In promotional
literature, companies paraded their capitals as prominently as possible.
An early circular of the Birmingham Banking Company displayed the
subheading "CAPITAL £500,000, IN 10,000 SHARES OF £50 EACH"
on the second line. The prospectus of the Stirlingshire Banking Company proclaimed "CAPITAL, £400,000" in type nearly as large as the
name of the company itself.[117]

A tendency to hyperbole in this regard, however, bred a degree of
cynicism among the public. Nineteenth-century fiction abounded with
commentaries on the gulf between appearance and reality in the joint-
stock economy. Credit was easy to acquire through the illusion of solidity generated by a large capital. In Dickens's 1844 novel *Martin Chuzzlewit*, the secretary of the Anglo-Bengalee Disinterested Loan and Life
Assurance Company asks Tigg Montague, the chairman, what nominal
capital is to be advertised in the prospectus. Montague tells him: "A figure of two, and as many oughts after it as the printer can get into the
same line." Montague is one of Victorian fiction's great fraudsters, and
his company was based entirely on bluff: "provided we did it on a sufficiently large scale, we could furnish an office and make a show, without
any money at all."[118] The tendency, however, even among honest firms,
to inflate nominal capitals continued. It contributed, for example, to the
loss of confidence following the commercial crisis of 1866. As the finan-
cier and banker William Newmarch explained, "a company which really
required only 1,000,000l., formed itself, with a great flourish of trumpets,
two years ago, with a capital of 2,000,000l., and now it finds its shares entirely unsaleable in the market" because no one was willing to take on
the amount of overhanging liability.[119]

Setting the value of the share denomination was also recognized to be of prime importance in the process of company formation. "Probably no point ought to be more anxiously weighed," wrote one director, "than the nominal amount of the shares into which the capital of the company is to be divided."[120] The value of shares adopted had direct implications for the class of investors attracted. All but 4 of our 514 companies specified a share denomination in their constitutions. In total, twenty-eight different share denominations were adopted, though 92.6 percent of companies opted for one of seven values: £5, £10, £20, £25, £50, £100, or £500, with £100 shares being the mode (161 companies) and £93 the mean.

Shannon and Jefferys have both traced the decline in share denominations after the 1850s and the eventual adoption of the £1 share as standard from the 1880s.[121] As Cottrell has argued, however, it can be misleading to plot simple trends over time for share denominations, as they varied according to the trade cycle, tending to rise with trade booms and to fall during slumps, when investment capital was scarcer and needed to be coaxed.[122] The argument appears to hold up in our period, though we do not have enough data for each individual year to be certain. During the trade boom of 1807–10, the average share denomination of companies in our sample rose incrementally from £55 to £160, then fell away to £53 by 1814. In the early 1840s, when the railway mania triggered a wider enthusiasm for joint-stock shares, denominations rose rapidly from £18 in 1842 to £101 in 1844. In the booms of the mid-1790s, mid-1820s, and mid-1830s, however, the average denomination of new issues did not behave in so clear-cut a fashion.

More recently, Alborn has argued that we need to take into account society's changing attitudes to notions of participatory democracy to fully understand the factors behind the adoption of particular share denominations. He notes that the joint-stock banks formed after 1825 were launched on a tide of democratic rhetoric that stressed participation and inclusion. A key feature of this was a desire to reduce share denominations to make investment possible for wider groups of society. A conflict developed, however, between democratic ideals and administrative practice. In particular, the mania for investment in banks in the mid-1830s led to fears among bankers and legislators alike that the participatory politics of joint-stock banks had got out of hand because of the number of lower-income investors speculating in shares. These fears led to new policies of exclusion centered on raising the share denomination.[123]

Alborn's arguments are only partially supported by our data. The denomination of bank shares clearly fell after 1825. The average for the dozen banks in our database formed before 1826 was £297. The average for eleven banks formed in the seven years following the liberalization of the law in 1825 was £186. Once the enthusiasm for bank promotion grew, the share denomination dropped decisively, falling to £74 for the thirty-two banks formed between 1833 and 1836. According to Alborn, this experiment in participatory democracy did not last long. Citing evidence given before the secret committees on joint-stock banks in 1836–7, he concludes that there was a fundamental rejection of the principles of inclusion at this time. Certainly, some witnesses presented low share denominations as undermining the solidity of company constituencies. If the shares were set as low as £5, "butlers, ladies' maids, and all sorts of persons, will get in; it will be composed of the lowest classes," opined one banker.[124] As well as leading to "a very inferior constituency," in the view of another, small shares also led to "gambling to a certain degree in the community."[125] Shares of at least £100 were required for the purposes of "preserving a respectable proprietary."[126] Some of the older insurance offices at this time were also rather sniffy about the type of investors attracted to new competitor companies offering low-value shares.[127] These views, however, did not seem to influence practice, at least in the 1837–40 period. Nine banks in our database were formed in these years, with an average share denomination of just £25, considerably lower than the average share value of the banks in the 1833–6 period. It seems that, as in Cottrell's thesis, new banks were inclined to reduce their share denomination as far as possible in order to attract new investors in an increasingly competitive market for shares and that this aim overrode the fears, highlighted by Alborn, that this would undermine the quality of the shareholder base. It was the legislature, not the banks themselves, that eventually initiated a break in this policy. Peel's Joint-Stock Banks Act of 1844 stipulated that all new bank promotions adopt a share denomination of at least £100, which was certainly not confirming current practice in the banking sector.[128]

Trends in banking and insurance were not entirely representative of behavior in other sectors. As table 3.2 shows, denominations varied greatly across the joint-stock economy. While unincorporated companies set their share denominations nearly twice as high as their incorporated counterparts (£127 as opposed to £67), this was probably determined primarily by significant sectoral differences. Insurance and banking companies opted for the largest denominations, in part because their shares

TABLE 3.2. **Average share denomination by sector**

Sector	Average share denomination (to nearest £)
Insurance	244
Banking	128
Shipping	94
Canals	91
Manufacturing/trade	83
Harbors	74
Railways	65
Colonial	59
Bridges	58
Water	53
Property	30
Gas	28

were never intended to be fully paid up; the uncalled portion acted as security for creditors and depositors in the event of losses. Five of the six companies with share denominations of £1,000 or more were insurance companies or banks. At the other end of the scale, denominations were much lower, though only gas and property companies averaged less than £50 per share. Significantly, the only two companies in our sample established before the 1840s that issued £1 shares, the Birmingham Flour and Bread Company (1796) and the Bristol Flour and Bread Concern (1800), were small companies established to provide cheap and unadulterated provisions to the people in their communities and were intended to be as inclusive as possible, with their subscribers also being the principal customers. Conversely, shipping companies often aimed to secure wealthy merchants as shareholders who would transport their goods with the company, a trend that continued into the limited-liability age.[129] Few companies in this sector offered shares below £50, and some issued very large shares, such as the Glasgow and Liverpool Royal Steam Packet Company (1844), whose sixty-four shares were valued at £1,000 each.

These distinctions between sectors shaped practice more than geography or size of company. Geographically, there was little difference between English (average share £95) and Scottish (average £102) companies, though Irish and Welsh companies set their share denominations lower, at £80 and £49, respectively, taking into account the relative paucity of affluent investors in these poorer countries. Interestingly, overall share capital is not a reliable guide to share denomination. While medium-sized companies had much higher average denominations than small companies (£160 versus £76), large and very large companies in fact opted for smaller denominations—£79 and £138 on average, respectively. (For the definition of these size categories, see table 4.2.) This suggests that larger companies needed to attract capital from a wide variety of sources and were therefore more likely than medium-sized companies to reduce denominations in order to secure a broader investment base.

In the joint-stock economy as a whole there was undeniably a tendency, as figure 3.2 shows, for share denominations to decline over time, indicating that fears to be found in some quarters of banking and insurance were not generally held. While the average denomination for all sectors in the 1720–1825 period was £142, by the late 1830s it had fallen to just £47. Table 3.3 groups denominations in ranges of values. While fewer than 3 percent of companies established between 1720 and 1789 issued shares of £10 or under, 31.6 percent were doing so by 1840–4. Shares of £60 or more made up over three-quarters of all share denominations in the earlier period but just 7 percent by the 1840s. More important than the trend toward small shares, perhaps, was the establishment of the medium-sized share between £15 and £50 as the norm. Shares in this range made up just 18.4 percent of the total in 1720–89 but were adopted by over half of all new companies from the late 1820s, rising to 61.4 percent of all companies established in 1840–4. For Jefferys, the key factor in the trend toward smaller shares in the late nineteenth century was "the entry of the middle classes into the market for shares."[130] Although narratives stressing the "rise" of the middle classes are currently

TABLE 3.3. **Share denominations, 1720–1844**

Period	0–£1		>£1–£5		>£5–£10		>£10–£25		>£25–£50		>£50–£100		>£100	
	no.	%	no.	%	no.	%	no.	%	no.	%	no.	%	no.	%
1720–89	0	0.0	1	2.6	0	0.0	1	2.6	6	15.8	21	55.3	9	23.7
1790–9	1	3.0	0	0.0	0	0.0	0	0.0	4	12.1	27	81.8	1	3.0
1800–9	1	2.2	0	0.0	0	0.0	4	8.9	11	24.4	21	46.7	8	17.8
1810–9	0	0.0	0	0.0	2	5.0	3	7.5	16	40.0	18	45.0	1	2.5
1820–4	0	0.0	0	0.0	2	5.3	5	13.2	11	29.0	15	39.5	5	13.2
1825–9	0	0.0	1	1.4	5	7.1	11	15.7	25	35.7	24	34.3	4	5.7
1830–4	0	0.0	2	3.4	5	8.5	16	27.1	16	27.1	17	28.8	3	5.1
1835–9	0	0.0	11	8.5	23	17.7	47	36.2	28	21.5	19	14.6	2	1.5
1840–4	2	3.5	5	8.8	11	19.3	16	28.1	19	33.3	2	3.5	2	3.5

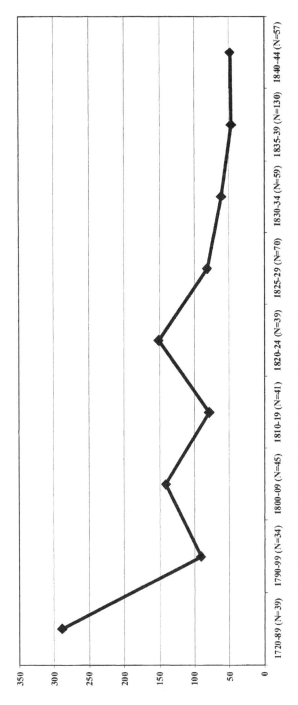

FIGURE 3.2. Average share denomination in £ by subperiod, all companies ($N = 514$)

unfashionable, our data seem to provide evidence that this process began much earlier than Jefferys contemplated. Companies were increasingly catering to pockets of middle-class investors. They were no longer
relying on the large surplus capital of the very wealthy but were not yet
soliciting the meager resources of the masses.

Shares: Restrictions and Controls

Fixing the share denomination was not the only means by which the
makeup of a joint-stock company could be influenced. A more direct
method was directorial control over the purchase of company shares.
Indeed, some believed this to be a far more potent tool than adjusting share denominations. Walter Cassels, London agent for the Northern and Central Bank of England, which issued £10 shares, was one: "I
never cared much about the nominal amount of the shares; I think it was
much the same to have a nominal share of 100 l. or 10 l. . . . it might be
said that it was liable to the objection that persons with a trifling sum of
money might become the proprietors . . . but the invariable view of the
directors was to avoid taking those very weak persons, and their applications were scarcely ever listened to."[131] Of the constitutions in our sample, 181 (35.2 percent) explicitly reserved to their directors the right to
control access to the company. Nearly all of these were unincorporated
companies. As table 3.4 shows, nearly all banking and insurance companies made this provision, as did most shipping companies. The practice was also relatively common among manufacturing, gas, and colonial
companies. Much rarer was the requirement for proprietors to approve

TABLE 3.4. **Percentage of companies in each sector
permitting directors to control access to shares**

Sector	Percentage
Banking	92.2
Insurance	91.9
Shipping	73.1
Manufacturing/trade	36.1
Gas	35.0
Colonial	25.0
Property	13.3
Water	7.5
Harbors	3.3
Canals	1.7

purchasers of shares, featuring in just nine company constitutions, four of them Scottish. This tended to occur in concerns in which the boundary between the partnership and the joint-stock company was blurred, such as the Clay Company (1795), which operated a blackball system, whereby unanimity was required among all existing members before a new partner could be admitted.[132] Directorial control over share transfers is discussed further in chapter 5.

Other steps that companies could take to attract the right kind of investor included imposing a geographical restriction on subscribers.[133] While only thirteen companies enshrined this in their constitutions, many more imposed the requirement on their initial subscribers. When the Ashby-de-la-Zouch Canal Company opened its share subscription, for example, its committee of management decided that subscribers must reside within five miles of some part of the intended canal and resolved "that speculation shall be as much discouraged as possible and to that end strict attention shall be paid to the responsibility of the proposed subscribers." No share was to be transferred until £15 was paid up. Their physical presence was also required: all subscribers had to attend a GM soon after subscription to sign the parliamentary petition and subscription paper and pay the deposit on their shares.[134]

As this example suggests, some companies were keen to dissuade "speculators" from buying their shares, particularly in boom times. Many strategies were open to them to accomplish this. For example, 125 constitutions, 24.3 percent of the total, stipulated a delay between the establishment of the company and the first dividend payment, thus discouraging those who were primarily seeking a swift return on capital. This delay could last a fixed number of years or until a certain event, such as the completion of the project or the accumulation of a certain amount of paid-up capital. Such a step, of course, would not prevent speculators from "bulling" shares: buying them cheaply and selling them quickly at a premium. But there were other means of dealing with this. One was to impose a restriction on when shares could be transferred, which sixty-seven companies (13.0 percent of the total) did. This restriction fell into two principal types. The first specified a length of time before shares could be transferred. For the Northumberland Fishery Society (1789) it was three years from the date of its act of incorporation; the American and Colonial Steam Navigation Company (1825) specified a period of just two months.[135] The second stipulated that a certain amount had to be paid up on a share before it could change hands. For the Portland

Railway Company (1825) this was fixed at just £5 per £50 share; the General Cemetery Company (1832) stipulated £15 on its £25 shares.[136] Some constitutions left scope for directorial discretion but clearly anticipated that shares would be mostly paid up before transfers could take place. The deed of the Rochester and Chatham Gas Light Company (1819) stated that no shareholder could transfer out until "the whole of his or her subscription or such part thereof as may be deemed by the said company to be necessary for carrying the said concern or undertaking into execution shall be fully paid and satisfied."[137]

Another, simpler, method was to require the payment of large initial deposits on shares. The directors of the Clerical, Medical, and General Life Assurance Society, for example, noted in December 1825, the end of a year notable for widespread speculation in joint-stock companies, that

> Some persons, who put down their names for shares at the commencement of the Institution (probably with a view of speculating) declined taking them when called upon to pay the advance of £2 10 0 per share. Others, who wished to forward the views of the Society as an useful and permanent establishment, were desirous to take a greater number of shares than the Capital enabled the Directors to grant. Accordingly, the Board was careful to distribute them in limited allotments, and this measure had the effect of spreading the Interests of the society over a wider extent, by thus attaching to it, a more numerous list of permanent Friends.

The result of this policy, the directors reported with much satisfaction, was that "the shares of the Society appear to be in the hands of permanent holders . . . no share has hitherto been sold, or even exposed for sale in the market." Even five years later, the directors told the shareholders that "most of the shares remain permanently in the possession of the original subscribers and friends of the Society."[138]

Such a step would not put off speculators at times when the potential short-term gains were far greater than the deposit. In December 1843, when interest in railways as lucrative investments was rapidly growing, the directors of the Leeds and Bradford Railway Company had more applicants than they needed for their preliminary share issue. In such cases, some of the applicants might be "speculators," but directors were able to filter through applications and select the most promising investors: the directors of the Leeds and Bradford were in the luxurious position of ordering their secretary to write to unsuccessful applicants.[139] In the railway booms of the 1830s and 1840s, railway companies were often hugely oversubscribed. In 1837 the New Gravesend Railway received 80,000 applications for its 30,000 shares; the Direct Western Railway had 1,400,000 applications for 120,000 shares in 1846.[140] Companies were not always so well positioned, however, and while keen to discourage speculation, they often had to weigh this against the necessity of securing sufficient subscribers. This was particularly important for companies seeking privileges from Parliament. Standing orders of the House of Lords in 1813 first imposed rules regarding the capital required to be subscribed before a company's bill could be read for a second time, and these were extended in 1824 "to provide against the mischief which was now going on with respect to Joint-Stock Companies."[141] The new orders stipulated that three-quarters of a company's capital should be paid up and deposited in the Bank of England or invested in Exchequer bills before a bill could be introduced into the Lords, though subsequent debates revealed that the rule was not always applied.[142] The House of Commons imposed less punitive rules six years later, insisting that a bill could not pass its second reading until half of the capital had been subscribed. This was extended in 1837 under the pressure of railway business so that one-tenth of the capital had to be paid up and deposited in the Bank of England or invested in government securities, a rule that applied to all acts of incorporation.[143] In light of these rules, insufficient evidence of investor support could undermine a company's application to Parliament. The directors of the Great Western Railway Company doubted in October 1833 that it could raise a sufficient subscription for the whole line, so they decided to apply to Parliament for permission to construct the line at its two extremities only (the London and Bristol ends) in the first instance. But even with these reduced ambitions, the company struggled to fill the share list, and the bill was defeated in the Lords.[144] When the directors regrouped after this reverse, they resolved to halve the deposit required on their shares to just £2 10s. There were subsequently fewer problems in attracting investors on these terms, and the bill passed through Parliament the following year.[145]

Conclusions

The problems initially faced by companies that, like the Great Western Railway, had to incorporate, were largely "political" in nature—having to win sufficient backing from investors and local powers to overcome local opposition and ensure that the bill of incorporation would pass through Parliament. Indeed, in many senses the problems facing all companies, whether incorporated or not, were political. All had to secure the support of local investors, and all had to don the clothing of "public" interest, for, throughout this period, the public good was the justification for most kinds of joint-stock endeavor. All faced critical decisions about the type of investor they wished to attract. The share denomination was usually seen as the most effective tool in shaping the proprietary. If it were too low, a new concern would be overwhelmed with irresponsible and unrespectable speculators; if too high, the concern risked being starved of capital. This issue was seen as so significant that it attracted the attention of legislators by 1844. The process of company formation also sheds light on the political relationships within a company. The extent to which shareholders were invited to participate in the process by which the founding constitution was drawn up varied considerably from firm to firm, and where shareholder interventions are noted in company records, they usually had the effect of increasing shareholder rights and participation. The distribution of power between shareholders and directors forms the focus of the following chapters.

CHAPTER FOUR

Constitutional Rights and Governance Practice

The Executive

The Tempter saw his time; the work he ply'd;
Stocks and Subscriptions pour on ev'ry side,
'Till all the Daemon makes his full descent
In one abundant show'r of Cent per Cent,
Sinks deep within him, and possesses whole,
Then dubs Director, and secures his soul.—Alexander Pope[1]

One powerful strand of classical economic thought held that companies could never be conducted as efficiently as private partnerships. In the absence of the exogenous controls promised by an extensive formal secondary market in shares, contemporaries continually worried about the available constraints on managerial preference and moral hazard. The debates in the 1690s about the rotation of directorships in the Bank of England and the East India Company, for example, centered on precisely this question. During the first half of the eighteenth century there were numerous accusations that the East India Company directors pursued their self-interest at the expense of shareholders, and the South Sea affair exposed rampant opportunism in that company.[2] The Scottish economist Adam Anderson reiterated a long-standing view that the joint-stock company was "never so frugally managed as private adventurers do their own money."[3] Adam Smith similarly reasoned that as directors were in control of other people's money, they would be less careful with it than with their own: "Negligence and profusion, therefore, must always prevail, more or less, in the management of the affairs of such a company."[4] Still more skeptical was the radical William

Godwin, who characterized directors as "men fattened on the vitals of their fellow citizens."[5]

It was widely recognized that constitutional restraints on directors and managers, together with organizational structures, could influence expectations of business efficiency and the attractiveness of joint-stock investment. From the early nineteenth century, entrepreneurs and others interested in the promotion of joint-stock companies went into print to defend their management systems, denying that boards of directors were inherently inefficient or corrupt.[6] Traditional attitudes, however, continued to be pervasive, and glimpses of them can be caught from various sources, from editorials of the *Times*—"what board of a company would ever have invented a spinning jenny!"—to the condemnation of railway capitalism published by Herbert Spencer in the *Edinburgh Review* in 1854.[7] Even supporters of general limited liability in the debates of the mid-1850s proceeded on the assumption, still widely held, that "joint-stock companies never will successfully compete with private enterprise and management in any well-known business, and within the range of ordinary capital."[8]

In this chapter we examine the structures of company executives, particularly boards of directors. We argue that the increasing size of joint-stock companies provoked a variety of constitutional responses and resulted in considerable variations between sectors. On the whole, however, there was a movement toward longer terms of office for directors, more onerous qualifications for service on boards, and more frequent board meetings, as well as an increasing likelihood that management would be devolved to subcommittees of the board or to a range of salaried officers. Company directors were increasingly regulated, exclusive, and professionalized. In larger companies with a more diversified shareholder base, executives increasingly supplanted many of the traditional functions of shareholders, although the latter were not entirely marginalized, as we show in chapter 5. The structures and roles of boards of directors developed in tandem with local and national government, and although it is difficult to establish causality with any certainty, we do highlight striking parallels between the "economic" and the "political" spheres.

Structure of the Board of Directors

All companies in our sample established a basic division between ownership (shareholders) and control (directors) in their constitutions. A small number of joint-stock companies did not, and these have been excluded from our sample. Some very small companies established by act of Parliament did not require a division of ownership and control because of the tiny number of subscribers involved. For example, the act incorporating the Weymouth Waterworks Company (1797) listed just six subscribers, and no board of directors was established.[9] A few larger companies also eschewed the creation of an executive. The act establishing the Company of Proprietors of the Burnley Waterworks (1819) listed forty-nine subscribers yet only made provision for GMs, which would meet "from time to time" to transact the business of the company.[10] Such companies, however, were rare. Most constitutions specified the number of directors, the quorum for board meetings and their frequency, the directors' terms of office, and in many cases also provided for the establishment of board subcommittees and the remuneration of directors and employees. It should be noted that management practice had yet to solidify into modern classifications, and this was reflected in the terminology found in company constitutions.[11] During the seventeenth and early eighteenth centuries the executive councils of the major chartered corporations had evolved from "courts of committees," or, more usually, "courts of assistants" (the latter term was also used in many unreformed municipal corporations), to "courts of directors." The majority of joint-stock companies established in the eighteenth century rejected the word "directors," and instead called their executive a "committee of management" (69.9 percent). This changed in the early nineteenth century, so that by 1840–4 over 90 percent of the companies in our sample called their executives "directors." Throughout this book we use the term "board of directors" for reasons of simplicity and consistency.

In our sample of 514 companies, thirty-three different sizes of board were adopted, ranging from one director to seventy. Only four constitutions did not specify a board size. The modal and mean number of directors was twelve; the median was nine. Companies rarely opted for very small or very large boards. Only ten companies had fewer than five directors, and only 10.8 percent had more than twenty. Board size was partly a function of company size. Boards of very large companies were nearly twice as large as those in very small companies. Large companies tended to have more shareholders and therefore a greater range of interests that desired representation on the board. Sectoral variations were also significant, as indicated by figure 4.1. Small boards were usual in companies with localized operations, such as in gas, water, and manufacturing.

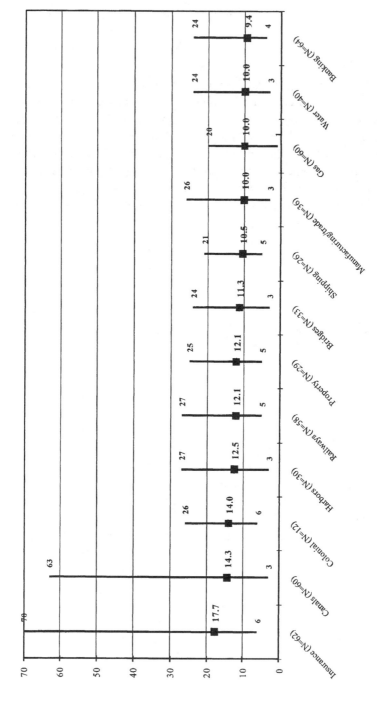

FIGURE 4.1. Board size by sector, showing mean board size and largest and smallest boards in each sector where board size is known (N = 510)

When companies were doing business in geographically broad or dispersed areas, which was often the case for canals, insurance, and railways, large boards were more common. The Oxford Canal Navigation (1769), for instance, had sixty-three directors, forming three committees of twenty-one, which supervised the construction and management of the canal in Coventry, Banbury, and Oxford, respectively.[12] Some companies had to accommodate significant outside interests. The board of the Bristol Dock Company (1803) had twenty-seven members, but only nine were shareholders elected by the GM; the rest were elected by the Common Council of Bristol and the Society of Merchant Venturers of Bristol.[13]

Companies that opted for large boards, however, did not always persevere with them. In 1792, for example, an early meeting of the Ashby-de-la-Zouch Canal appointed a general committee of sixty-three, which in turn appointed a select committee of thirty for the transaction of business. For the first few months, both committees met independently, but by 1793 the select committee became the sole instrument of decision making. This committee was in turn replaced by an even smaller committee of fifteen, with a quorum of seven.[14] In 1794 the company's incorporating act provided for a committee of management of thirteen, with a quorum of five.[15] This company's disenchantment with the very large board as a means of efficient governance seems to have been shared more widely: after 1809, huge boards became rarities. By 1840–4, more than 80 percent of companies had boards numbering twelve or fewer, while 60 percent had nine or fewer. Companies that remained attached to oversized boards were vulnerable to censure. A critic of the London and North Western Railway argued, with reference to the nation's model of political government, that companies should not use their scale of operations to justify large boards and Byzantine structures: "The affairs of England, in all their multiplicities and complexities, are managed by a Cabinet of seventeen members, each responsible for some one department: the London and North Western Railway Company is controlled by forty-five Directors, not one of whom is individually responsible before the face of the Proprietors for any department."[16] Quorums for board meetings remained fairly stable over time—the mean was 39.1 percent of the total number of directors. There was a negative relationship between the number of directors and the quorum as a percentage of the number of directors ($r = -0.64$). In practice, this meant that, although large boards nominally represented a greater variety of interests than small boards, it was still possible for small cliques of directors to dominate the politics of the bigger companies. Frequency of board meetings was less often specified in constitutions: it was often determined in bylaws and could be altered to suit changing circumstances. Larger companies were much more likely to specify the number of board meetings, and these meetings were much more likely to be frequent—often weekly rather than monthly or quarterly—indicating the perceived importance in these companies of providing for the effective transaction of business.

Larger companies also pioneered more complicated management structures, with business delegated to subcommittees of directors or to paid managers. This had been a widespread practice among the trading companies of the seventeenth century but was slower to catch on among regular joint-stock companies.[17] Of the companies in our sample, 213 (41.4 percent) made constitutional provisions for subcommittees. The most common provision (28.0 percent of all companies) was a simple ad hoc power of the board to appoint a subcommittee at any time for a specified purpose.[18] Less common, but representing a greater step toward more sophisticated management structures, was provision for some form of permanent subcommittee, stipulated by 13.4 percent.[19] The proportion of companies opting for subcommittees of either type increased from 12.8 percent in 1720–89 to 63.2 percent by 1840–4. Leading the way were the very large companies—nearly three-quarters (74.3 percent) of companies with a capital of over £1 million specified subcommittees, compared with just 17.5 percent of the smallest ones. It seems that larger companies were increasingly influencing how smaller companies approached this issue. While none of the small or very small companies established in the eighteenth century made provision for subcommittees, 52.2 percent of them did by 1840–4. The spread of subcommittee provision in joint-stock companies mirrored the tendencies in local government for functions of elected authorities to be delegated to committees. In some places, as in Westminster from 1774, statute law provided for vestry powers to be delegated to committees, and the practice became increasingly widespread under the common-law powers of vestries during the first half of the nineteenth century. An act of 1830, for example, allowed vestries to appoint lighting and watch committees, although unlike subcommittees in companies, these were elected by all those qualified to vote in the vestry.[20]

In the corporate economy as in local government, one view of sub-

committees was that they were simply the most efficient means of transacting business. One defender of joint-stock banks claimed that "by a
subdivision of labour, much useful work is accomplished, and a final determination on all subjects arrived at, in a comparatively short space of
time."[21] Such claims, however, were countered by accusations that subcommittees undermined transparency and accountability. Alongside
their regular boards, some companies even conducted "private" directors' meetings for more confidential matters, whose minutes were kept
under lock and key.[22] The committee to investigate the York, Newcastle and Berwick Railway Company, appointed after the fall of its cre-
ator, George Hudson, recommended a series of radical constitutional
changes. It deprecated the board's establishment of a committee of management, which had "virtually superseded" the board, a system that was
"pernicious in practice." Committees were justified for special purposes,
the shareholders believed, but they should be dissolved when the reason
for their formation had passed.[23]

Managers and Management Structure

Delegating most of the day-to-day work of an enterprise to paid managers was also a common strategy but one that could have drawbacks. It
was particularly common in sectors where business became more rou-
tine after an initial construction phase. Such delegation could leave companies vulnerable to the individual failings or dishonesty of managers.
Because of this, 82.9 percent of all companies specified that security was
to be taken from employees as a guarantee of honest service.[24] The sums
required varied considerably but tended to be quite substantial. In 1801,
the clerk of the Aberdare Canal had to give security for £100; in 1818,
the superintendent of the Cheltenham Gas Light Company gave security for £500.[25] In 1783, the Thames and Severn Canal required its first
clerk of the works to give security for £2,000. The York City and County
Banking Company required the same sum from its clerks in the 1830s
and no less than £7,000 from its manager.[26] Such precautions were not
always effective. When it was discovered that the principal clerk of the
works of the Equitable Gas Light Company had stolen close to £1,000,
criminal proceedings were instituted against him, but his bond proved
to be worthless.[27]

When employees were given a significant degree of autonomy, serious

abuses could ensue. Several early nineteenth-century companies encountered problems with overbearing, recalcitrant, slippery, or negligent
managers. The Norwich Union and the Kent Fire offices, for example,
were obliged to dismiss their secretaries in 1814 and 1818, respectively.[28]
When employees had commercial ties to other firms, fatal clashes of interest could develop. John Bryan, the engineer of the Maidstone Gas
Company (1823), was in partnership with the suppliers of the company's
retorts and castings and with another firm that supplied the brass work
and other fittings. By 1839, the company's costs had become suspiciously
high, and one of the directors initiated an inquiry. He found that the
prices paid by the company were up to 70 percent higher than the rates
paid by Bryan. The engineer was immediately sacked.[29]

Many factors could influence the management structure adopted by a
company. Provincial companies sometimes believed metropolitan companies to possess superior knowledge about management and went to
them for guidance. In 1819 the new Cheltenham Gas Light Company
ordered the superintendent, Benjamin Newmarch, to "go to London
to obtain every information possible for the better management of this
undertaking."[30] Some sought expertise elsewhere. George Fox, a founder
of the Plymouth and Devonport Banking Company, wrote to Hugh Watt,
manager of the Huddersfield Banking Company, one of the first to form
after the liberalization of the law in 1826, seeking advice on key constitutional issues.[31] Fox subsequently compiled extensive information on
joint-stock banks from all over the country before establishing his own
bank. Directors also looked to existing companies when making other
kinds of decisions. Early in the life of the Manchester, Bolton, and Bury
Canal Company, the GM ordered that the committee of management
"inquire what Law Clerks on other Navigations are allowed and paid for
their services" before determining the salary of their own clerk.[32]

Even after this kind of research, companies often experimented with
several different management approaches, particularly companies that
were struggling to make a profit. The history of the Canterbury and
Whitstable Railway, the first in the country to operate a regular steam
train service on its line, is instructive in this respect. The company's incorporating act of 1825 authorized a board of "at least" ten directors, to
be annually appointed. Soon the directors ran into trouble. With construction costs escalating rapidly in the aftermath of the commercial
crisis of 1825–6, they approached the largest shareholder, Lester Ellis,
for a loan, but he preferred to rent the line, and a fourteen-year lease

was agreed to in 1828.[33] By 1830, when the railway opened, the deal appears to have fallen through. However, rather than revert to a system of control by the whole board, which now numbered thirteen, the directors resolved in 1831 to appoint a committee of nine, to meet weekly.[34] This arrangement did not last long, and at the annual general meeting (AGM) that year the twelve shareholders present decided to appoint a general manager at £200 per annum, with a brief to increase the company's business. Joshua Richardson, a former resident engineer of the line, was appointed, with "full authority to act for the company without any controul except such as from time to time be imposed by Boards of Directors."[35]

The policy seemed to bear fruit quickly. Richardson discovered that a clerk had been pocketing passengers' fares without recording them in the ledger, and he was immediately dismissed. But there appears to have been a falling out between Richardson and the directors, leading to disenchantment with the system of a general manager.[36] In 1832 the board reported that "this mode of managing the Company's affairs has not answered those expectations which were at that time entertained, of its being the most efficacious in encreasing the Business and of lessening the expences attendant thereon."[37] The company's three auditors (who were also directors) were asked to inquire into the best mode of conducting the business. Their report sheds much light on the perceived merits of various systems of managing a joint-stock company. It began with more than a tinge of desperation: "Referring to the several periods of management of the Railway Company—By a Board of Directors only—By a lessee—By a committee of management—a committee of auditors—and a managing agent—it appears that the only system yet untried is that of an acting partner." Yet it saw distinct benefits attaching to this last system and, by adopting it, indicated that influences could cut across joint-stock sectors: "Adverting to other public undertakings we shall generally find those to be most prosperous where the actual Director is an Individual possessed of sufficient interest to secure his attention to its affairs [a reference to Richardson, who had not been a shareholder], and of such integrity and ability as to insure confidence. The County Fire—Equitable Life and St. Catherine's Dock Companies are well known examples."[38] The committee therefore recommended the appointment of a "Resident Director and General Comptroller of the Company's affairs." He was to have "ample powers to act on every occasion" and would thus "carry into effect necessary proceedings for the Benefit of other Proprietors.

Such an individual should have the full confidence and co-operation of all parties without which he must be frequently thwarted in his exertions for the welfare of the concern." He was to be supported by "an assistant Director at each end of the line." The meeting approved, and the directors appointed a committee of three: the resident director, William Southcott Truman, was paid £200 per annum and his two assistants each £50 per annum.[39]

By 1834 another falling-out resulted in a coup that ousted Truman, who left predicting disaster for the company. The board then abandoned the resident director system and reverted to the nine-man committee of management. The company now employed a blend of two systems: the managing committee shrank from nine to six, while two of its members were given £50 per annum for their daily attention to the business—one supervising at Canterbury, one at Whitstable. The company, however, still could not turn a profit and continued to be burdened with heavy debts. The shareholders came full circle in 1838 and voted to lease the railway.[40] In 1839, the directors reported that since leasing the line, their functions had been "reduced to a few particulars," with the lessees taking on the management of the concern.[41] This arrangement, like the others, did not work for long. The lessees fell behind on their rent and in 1841 were declared bankrupt. The directors had to take control once again. They still clung to the idea, however, that leasing the railway was the best means of securing shareholders' investments, and in 1844 they leased it to the new South Eastern Railway Company. The two lines were amalgamated in 1853.[42]

The prolonged experimentation of the Canterbury and Whitstable Railway suggests the limitations of attempting to associate particular management forms with specific sectors. Companies, particularly struggling ones, were very willing to test different systems, and they looked beyond their own sector for examples that were thought to be successful. Systems that concentrated power in the hands of few people, in the shape of managers or managing directors, though assumed to be the most efficient, were often unsuccessful. They increased the chances of arguments and acrimony between shareholders and management and within boards and, in a culture where businessmen typically held active interests in multiple companies, increased the likelihood of negligence or corruption.[43] There was thus no simple evolution toward a preference for delegation to professional managers.

Elections to the Board

Annual elections were seen as a basic marker of democracy and accountability from the late eighteenth century long into the nineteenth century,
as shown by their inclusion in Major Cartwright's *Take Your Choice*
(1776) and the People's Charter of 1838.[44] In English local government,
elections of parish officers and poor-law guardians took place every year,
but this norm was challenged during the nineteenth century. In municipal corporations after 1835, councillors were elected by rotation, giving
them a three-year term and a degree of insulation from the electorate.[45]
A similar trajectory occurred in corporate governance. The norm in the
eighteenth century was for the entire board of directors to be elected annually: of the sixty-one companies established before 1800 that specified
a term of office, only four permitted their directors more than a year in
office. Annual elections became much less common over time, a difference prefigured in Lord North's reform of the East India Company in
1773, which scrapped annual elections of the whole board in favor of annual rotations of just one quarter of the board.[46] Other companies followed this example: the proportion of companies with full annual rotation fell to under 50 percent in 1800–9, to under 30 percent in 1830–4,
and by the 1840s, nearly 80 percent of companies allowed their directors
to sit for three or more years consecutively.

Associated with this change was the increase in company size, as figure 4.2 indicates. Whereas 54.4 percent of very small companies allowed
their directors just one-year terms, this fell to 8.6 percent for very large
ones. Directors enjoyed the longest terms of office (five or more years) in
just 2.9 percent of very small companies, but in 37.1 percent of very large
companies.[47] Longer periods in office undoubtedly rendered directors
less immediately accountable to their constituents, and some companies
pushed this to extreme lengths, such as the ten-year terms of the directors of the English and Scottish Law Fire and Life Assurance and Loan
Association (1841) and the twelve-year stints at the Farmers' and General
Fire and Life Insurance and Loan and Annuity Company (1840). The
legislative reforms of the mid-1840s approved the shift away from annual terms but also tried to rein in the tendency toward very long terms.
Schedule A of the 1844 Joint-Stock Companies Act stipulated that "at
least one third of . . . directors, or the nearest number to one third, shall
retire annually, subject to re-election, if thought fit."[48] The Joint-Stock

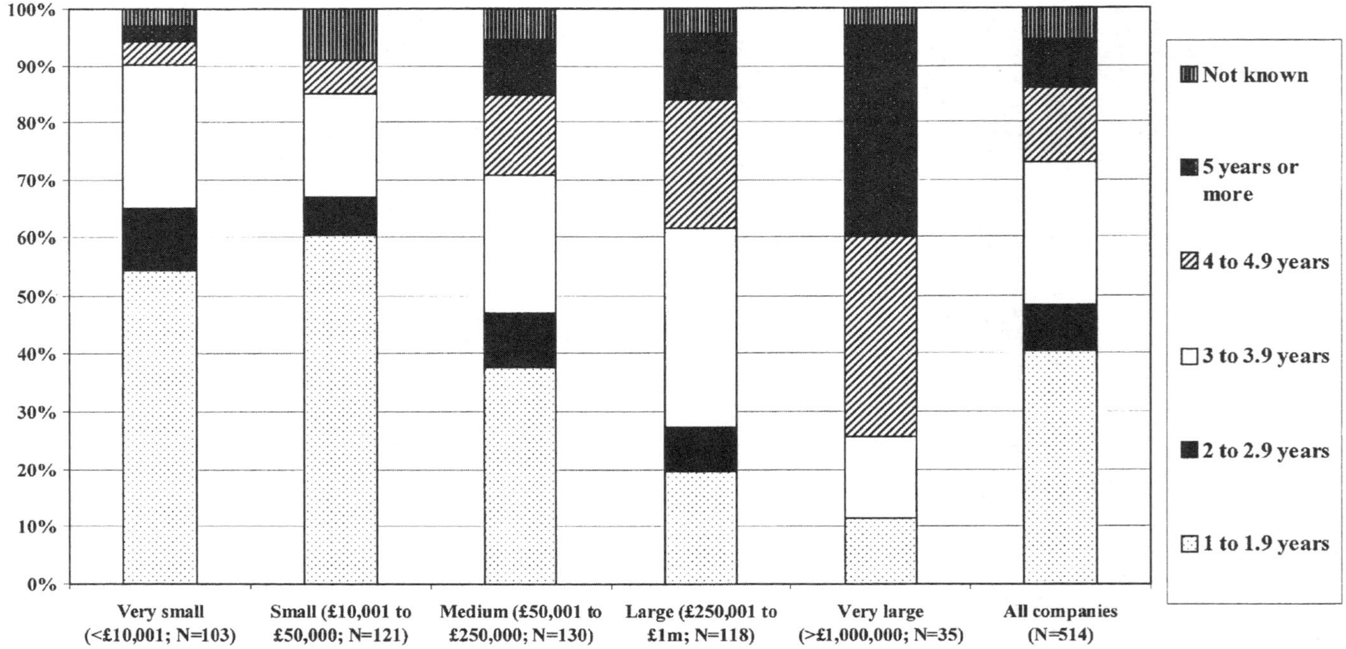
100%
90%
80%
70%
60%
50%
40%
30%
20%
10%
0%
Very small (<£10,001; N=103)
Small (£10,001 to £50,000; N=121)
Medium (£50,001 to £250,000; N=130)
Large (£250,001 to £1m; N=118)
Very large (>£1,000,000; N=35)
All companies (N=514)
Not known
5 years or more
4 to 4.9 years
3 to 3.9 years
2 to 2.9 years
1 to 1.9 years

FIGURE 4.2. Directors' term of office by size of company where size is known (N = 507)

Banks Act of the same year obliged banks to rotate at least one-fourth of the board yearly, and prevented the reelection of the retiring directors for twelve months.[49] The Companies Clauses Consolidation Act of 1845 was less prescriptive, allowing rotated directors to be immediately re-elected, but still set a default term of office (that companies were permitted to adjust) of three years.[50] But whether regular rotation was enough to render boards accountable to shareholders was another matter.

In both national and local politics, it was typical for those in power to stay in power—great electoral battles were rare. After the efflorescence of political activity in the early eighteenth century, parliamentary elections in Britain were uncompetitive affairs. In the ten general elections in England and Wales held between 1701 and 1734, 40 percent of seats were contested, but this figure fell to 29.4 percent in the twenty elections held between 1734 and 1832.[51] Figures for local government elections are harder to come by, but before the municipal reforms of 1835, in "most" corporate boroughs the municipal authority was "self-electing."[52] Although the reform of 1835 "injected party politics into municipal elections" by the 1840s, according to Doyle, "municipal politics in most places had settled into inactive one-party rule." After a flurry of contests in the 1830s, many municipal elections were uncontested thereafter.[53] Towns such as Nottingham, Leicester, Leeds, and Bradford became safe liberal havens for decades while, with the emasculation of minor township and parish institutions, such as vestries, highways surveyors, and churchwardens, several channels for popular participation in municipal politics were gradually closed down.[54]

A similar picture emerges in joint-stock companies, which is perhaps not surprising, as so many company promoters and directors were also active in local government.[55] Supporters of the joint-stock system believed that regular elections were crucial in ensuring that directors were held accountable: "the periodical retirement of a proportion of their number exposes them to the criticism and remarks of their successors."[56] Many others, however, thought that provisions for regular elections existed on paper only. Demonstrating a widespread awareness of the political dimensions of corporate governance, commentators repeatedly drew parallels between joint-stock companies and "close boroughs." In 1827, the city reporter of the *Times* noted that at the approaching GM of the Bank of England there would be three vacancies on the board to fill as a result of retirements and resignations. The election, however, "creates little interest in the city, it being well known that a seat in the

Bank direction resembles a close borough, and that the Directors in office have for many years past invariably nominated the new members."
Indeed, the reporter went on to list the three names widely expected to
fill the seats.[57] Later, the same newspaper commented that "the election
of all new directors is notoriously that of the board, and not that of the
proprietors . . . such a thing as a contested election for a seat at the board
having rarely, if ever, been heard of."[58]

This situation was frequently complained of in other companies. One
shareholder of the troubled Royal Canal Company of Ireland was highly
critical of the elections to the board, writing to the press that the lists
of qualified candidates should be circulated "at least one month" prior
to the election. At the time, the lists were withheld "until two or three
days" before the election, which seemed like a *"ruse de guerre"* to ensure the election of the board's nominees. No candidate "save those
that are in the immediate direction of the Canal have the smallest prospect of success although he possessed the most desirable qualifications
for the office of Director." The shareholder urged that "every one concerned in the Royal Canal should set his face against their Board being made a close borough which is the straight road to jobbing and all its
consequences."[59] In the 1840s two members of the Liverpool Stock Exchange wrote to the press complaining that "there is too much close borough work in the forming of the boards at all railway meetings; the places
of the outgoing directors are, in fact, filled up by the remaining members
of the board."[60] Herbert Spencer echoed these sentiments, claiming that
proprietors in railway companies had allowed their franchise to become
"a dead letter: retiring directors are so habitually re-elected without opposition, and have so great a power of insuring their own election when
opposed, that the board becomes practically a close body."[61]

Although some minute books were kept so tersely that it is not always
possible to establish whether there was a directorial contest, an extensive
examination of company records suggests that regardless of the nominal term of office, in practice there was much continuity in board membership, and it was rare for shareholders to launch challenges to sitting
directors. Even when companies had a checkered or controversial governance history, contested directorial elections were not commonplace.
The Ashby-de-la-Zouch Canal Company, incorporated in 1794, offers a
good example of continuities in management. This was an outstandingly
unprofitable concern, accumulating extensive debts during construction that were not fully paid off until 1828, when the company finally

paid its first dividend. Yet despite the fact that the entire committee of management was rotated annually, there was never a challenge posed by shareholders to its membership. Only those directors who ceased attending meetings or resigned were ever replaced. Continuities on some boards were particularly striking. In 1845, nineteen years after the formation of the Dartford Gas Company (whose directors had three-year terms), four of the nine directors elected had been on the board since its inception.[62]

Mechanisms could be introduced to combat this. Chief among these was a clause, inserted into 11.3 percent of constitutions in our sample, stipulating that some or all of the outgoing directors were not eligible for immediate reelection. This was far more common in unincorporated companies than corporations (19.6 percent versus 4.9 percent), and in banking (26.6 percent), insurance (25.8 percent) and Scottish companies (24.1 percent).[63] The provision was designed as a safety measure in companies whose directors enjoyed unusually long terms of office. Companies that blocked consecutive terms for all their directors had the longest directorial spans—4 years on average, compared with 2.4 years in companies that allowed immediate reelection or that were silent on the issue. The constitutional ineligibility of retiring directors for reelection, however, was in practice insufficient to vest effective control in shareholders, for directors had other means by which they could close down the politics of companies. In many cases, they proposed favored candidates before elections, making it clear for whom the shareholders were expected to vote. This was a practice already established in the East India Company during the early eighteenth century, when "house lists" of incumbent directors had been approved by acquiescent GMs. A company bylaw of 1734 required directors to stand down after four consecutive years in office, but the rotation principle, together with the fact that former directors were eligible for reelection after twelve months out of office, ensured longevity and continuity in the court of directors.[64] The "house list" was still operating in the early nineteenth century. In 1827, for example, the directors of the Provincial Bank of Ireland reported "that in future elections, it will greatly conduce to the harmony and cordiality which it is so desirable should prevail amongst the directors themselves, as well as to the good management of the bank's affairs, if a recommendation shall be made by them to the proprietors in favour of those candidates, whom, after due inquiry, they shall find to be the best qualified, to fill the situation." The shareholders accepted this arrangement "uniformly," according to the company's secretary: "Two or three candidates had upon more than one occasion started, but when the matter was explained to them, they have uniformly acquiesced in it."[65]

In this way, what the Webbs referred to as the "oligarchical principle" of co-option rather than election, which informed much of local government in the eighteenth and early nineteenth centuries, also had a de facto existence in joint-stock politics and continues to survive today in modern boardroom appointments.[66] Furthermore, other barriers to election could easily be erected. In several companies, if shareholders wished to mount a challenge to their board at the GM, it had to be organized beforehand, which could be a difficult task for shareholders who were geographically dispersed. The deed of settlement of the Bradford Commercial Joint-Stock Banking Company (1833) was far from unique in stipulating that candidates for the board had to give notice to the company at least seven days before the AGM.[67] These procedural features of company governance also prompted political comparisons. Writing in 1841, Thomas Corbet denounced the oligarchic tendencies inherent in joint-stock politics, which, if not constitutionally enshrined, were nevertheless widespread in practice:

> There is an incurable vice which belongs to nearly all great joint-stock companies at least; which is, that, although their constitution is almost uniformly founded or formed upon the proper principle, or *theory* of representation and responsibility, the *practice* it may be said is, nearly without exception, nomination—for the directors to name their successors, who in turn name those who named then, so that of the same set one half is alternately out and in. Lists are presented, (that is by the directors,) as we read in Sismondi's History of the Italian Democracies was the case in some of these in the election of their magistrates, not for discussion but for approbation.[68]

As Corbet implied, it would be wrong to imagine that shareholders typically clamored to sit on boards. As was sometimes the case in local government—for instance, the way the onerous and unpaid office of overseer was sometimes forced on unwilling parishioners by local justices—the lack of pay and potential workload that went with a seat on the board meant that directors sometimes struggled to fill vacancies.[69] Shareholders accustomed to the self-selecting traditions of local government service often seemed content for them to be replicated in joint-stock companies. Close social and business ties between directors and their fellow shareholders meant that the former were usually trusted to behave as they wished. According to Lewis Wolfe, a share broker working on behalf of railway companies, "a large portion" of shareholders were "friends of the Directors, particularly in some Companies—very often nine parts out of ten—and they carry what they please; they vote their own salaries, and do what else they please."[70]

Qualifications of Directors

The British state used property qualifications as a potent tool to impose limits on who could enjoy political power. The abolition of the property qualification for MPs was one of the main demands of contemporary radicals, but it was not achieved until 1858.[71] It had been introduced in 1710, standing at £300 per annum to sit for a borough and double that sum to sit for a county, although there is evidence that "the letter of the law was flouted and fictitious and temporary qualifications seem to have been common."[72] Property qualifications also formed an important part of local government rules. As the Webbs explained: "Running like a red thread through all the local institutions of the eighteenth century was the assumption that the ownership of property, more particularly landed property, carried with it, not only a necessary qualification for, but even a positive right to carry on, the work of government."[73] Reforms in local government in the early nineteenth century amended these rules, though not to democratize access to power but to incorporate new economic interests and thus consolidate the power of the propertied class. The reformed poor law in England and Wales (1834) required guardians to meet a property qualification set by the poor-law commissioners. The new municipal corporations of 1835 required councillors to hold real or personal property to the value of £1,000 or to occupy land assessed at £30.[74] Local acts governing other bodies also stipulated a range of property qualifications, such as the £20 annual ratable value for Little Bolton Trustees (1830) or £35 for the Rochdale Improvement Commissioners (1844), values that were highly exclusionary.[75]

The received wisdom was that large qualifications secured men of substantial capitals and good character and guaranteed better governance standards. General John Austin, a director of the North of England Joint-Stock Banking Company, articulated a common view when he argued that companies with low share qualifications would not be as well managed as those with higher barriers to entry. He contrasted a company where directors needed £5,000 to sit on the board and one where just £250 was required: "it is very plain they will form very different classes, and that when the directors come to be elected men more reckless and of less weight will be chosen, and of less property."[76] Despite this view, there was enormous variety in qualifications between sectors. Directors of bridge and water companies, on average, were required to hold less than £200 in shares, whereas those in colonial, insurance, and banking companies had to possess over £1,500 in shares. Exact comparisons are perhaps misleading, because shares in some sectors—especially banking and insurance—were often not paid up in full, whereas shares in infrastructural enterprises were all fully paid up within a few years of the establishment of the company. Nevertheless, in companies where the capital was not fully paid up, shareholders were still required to have the resources available in order to cover potential future calls, and if it was suspected that purchasers of shares did not have these means, then the sitting directors could block the transfer of shares to them. This being the case, the differences in share qualification suggest that directors of bridge, water, and gas companies were not required to be as affluent as their counterparts in colonial, insurance, and banking companies.

The property qualification also applied, at least technically, to women. While we have found no examples of a woman serving as an officer of a joint-stock company, there were few gender-discriminatory regulations passed by British and Irish companies during our period. Indeed, if she qualified through holding the requisite number of shares, a woman was eligible to stand as a candidate for the boards of most companies, and women do appear in the printed electoral lists of corporations such as the Bank of England and the South Sea Company.[77] If women were not elected as directors in this period, in general it was not because they were constitutionally excluded from the boardroom but because they were perceived as not having the right kind of business connections and influence. We discuss the position of female shareholders at greater length in the following chapter.[78]

Directorial qualifications were often debated within companies, especially after governance crises, with some arguing that a high share requirement artificially restricted the choice of directors, which was a greater danger than underqualified directors. The shareholders of the Equitable Gas Light Company, concerned by its poor performance, instigated a committee of inquiry into the management in 1839. When the

TABLE 4.1. **Investment required to sit on board of directors by subperiod, where investment required could be calculated**

Subperiod	Mean share qualification for directors (no. of shares)	Investment required to be a director	
		Mean (nearest £)	Std. dev. (nearest £)
1720–89 (N = 38)	2.9	482	802
1790–9 (N = 33)	3.5	330	354
1800–9 (N = 45)	5.6	534	624
1810–9 (N = 40)	6.9	566	909
1820–4 (N = 38)	11.3	918	1,111
1825–9 (N = 70)	13.0	1,001	1,637
1830–4 (N = 59)	16.0	1,101	1,555
1835–9 (N = 130)	28.0	792	1,210
1840–4 (N = 57)	26.8	841	1,279
All companies (N = 510)	16.0	778	1,217

committee discovered appalling instances of mismanagement and nepotism, one of its recommendations was to reduce the directorial share qualification from thirty shares to twenty. This would "extend the choice of Gentlemen from whom the selection may be made," which the committee considered important in securing a board less prone to corruption. The shareholders adopted the recommendation.[79] By the 1840s, instances of mismanagement and fraud by undeniably affluent directors had led to much skepticism about the automatic right of the wealthy to rule and to the floating of meritocratic ideas. As the *Leeds Mercury* opined in 1849, "Heretofore the qualification of a director or an auditor has, in most cases, been the supposed long purse, instead of the long head, of the candidate for office. Unfortunately for shareholders, they have had to pay very dearly for their experience."[80]

Nevertheless, there was a trend toward *higher* requirements over time, as is shown in table 4.1. The necessary investment increased from an average of £330 in 1790–9 to £1,101 in 1830–4, falling back a little thereafter but remaining much higher than in the eighteenth century. Large companies drove these changes, as is suggested by table 4.2. Directors in the smallest companies needed, on average, shares to the value of just £62; the largest companies insisted on investments averaging £2,673. There was a positive correlation between capital and the investment required to sit on the board ($r = 0.64$).[81] In part, of course, this may have been merely a function of company size: where share denominations varied so widely, a more revealing measure may be whether the smallest

TABLE 4.2. **Investment required to sit on board of directors by size of company, where size of company is known and investment required could be calculated (N = 506)**

Size of company	Mean share qualification for directors (no. of shares)	Investment required to be a director	
		Mean (nearest £)	Std. dev. (nearest £)
Very small (<£10,001; N = 103)	3.4	62	48
Small (£10,001 to £50,000; N = 120)	4.8	212	189
Medium (£50,001 to £250,000; N = 130)	13.1	649	628
Large (£250,001 to £1,000,000; N = 118)	38.3	1,572	1,482
Very large (>£1,000,000; N = 35)	30.7	2,673	2,075

shareholders were able to sit on the board. One hundred and six companies in our sample, 20.6 percent of the total, permitted this. Such openness came under attack in the nineteenth century: whereas 53.9 percent of companies established in 1720–89 permitted it, the proportion fell to 13.9 percent by 1835–9 (see figure 4.3). Again, the larger companies led the way: 44.7 percent of the smallest companies throughout the period permitted their smallest shareholders to be directors, compared with 4.2 percent of large companies. None of the very largest companies (with capitals over £1 million) allowed their smallest shareholders to sit on the board.[82]

This evidence supports the impression derived from politics that the importance of property ownership was entrenched rather than challenged by constitutional reforms in the early nineteenth century. However, there was another reason for inflating property qualifications, specific to joint-stock companies. Just as modern agency theory argues that share options provide incentives for directors to strive to add value for their shareholders, so it was widely argued in the nineteenth century that large qualifications helped align the interests of directors and shareholders by obliging directors to hold a significant stake in the firm. Companies paraded the large investments held by their directors in order to stress their legitimacy. The prospectus of the Monmouthshire Iron and

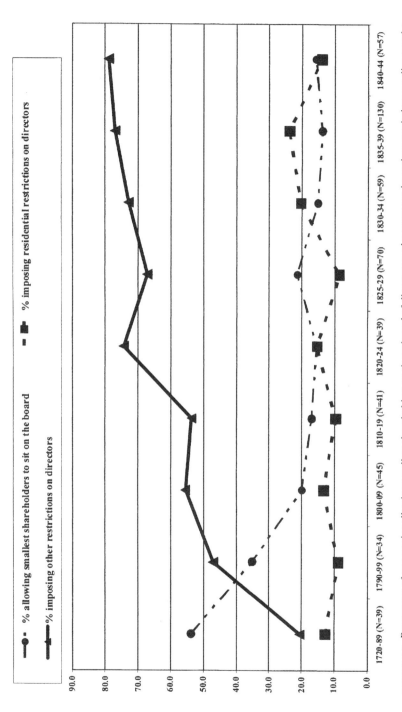

FIGURE 4.3. Percentage of companies allowing smallest shareholders to sit on board of directors and percentage imposing restrictions on directors by subperiod (N = 514)

Coal Company, for example, carried a list of the fifteen directors with the heading "holding at least twenty shares each, and several of them one hundred shares each."[83] Such was the faith in the sense of responsibility that substantial shareholdings would engender that shareholders were sometimes more enthusiastic than boards about driving the directorial qualification upward. During the 1848 GM of the Union Bank of London, one shareholder objected to the directorial qualification—twenty shares, on which £200 had been paid up—which he felt was far too low. He wanted it increased to one hundred shares and a declaration from all candidates that they were worth £10,000. This proposal drew cheers from his fellow shareholders and was not opposed by the directors.[84] The same year, the directors of the London and County Joint-Stock Bank concluded that "it would tend to the improvement of the bank, increase the public confidence, and furnish a more substantial guarantee for the attention of the directors if the qualification for a seat in the directory were increased (hear, hear)." The directors proposed an increase from twenty to fifty shares, and such was the enthusiasm for the move that they had to fend off a motion from the floor to increase it further still, to one hundred shares.[85]

While the minimum aggregate number of shares held by boards increased with the size of company, the requirements did not keep pace with the total number of shares issued by larger companies, so directors in the latter were required to hold a much lower percentage of total shares than their analogues in smaller companies: 9.8 percent of shares in very small companies, compared with 1.9 percent in very large companies.[86] In practice, directors may have held many more shares than the minimum requirement. Nevertheless, the figures suggest that shareholders were right to worry about aligning the interests of directors with their companies. They also indicate that the acute division between ownership and control, assumed to be inherent in the joint-stock company by Adam Smith and others, particularly applied to larger companies. The fact that boards in small concerns usually held a much higher proportion of the shares than in larger companies suggests a rather different relationship between directors and other shareholders, particularly where those boards were able to form a quorum at GMs on account of their shares. This is not to say, however, that there was always a complete coincidence of interests between directors and shareholders in the smaller joint-stocks.[87]

A minimum share requirement was only one of several conditions

that companies could impose on their executives. A residential qualification was another. Here too, there were parallels in local government—
though not in Parliament—for this kind of restriction. Select vestrymen
were required to reside in the parish, while under the terms of the Highway Act (1835) the parish surveyor was required to live in the parish or
in an adjoining one.[88] In Scotland, acts of 1487 and 1609 restricted the
magistracy and provostship of burghs to residents.[89] Again it is difficult
to prove with certainty that such regulations provided a model for joint-
stock companies, but the coincidences are notable. Some companies imposed residential requirements on shareholders—these are discussed in
chapter 5—but rather more imposed such requirements on directors. In
our sample, 15.8 percent of companies had a residential qualification for
some or all of their directors, although in some companies—as was the
case in Scottish burgh law—having a business in the place concerned was
taken to be the equivalent of residence. The use of residential requirements became slightly more common over our period, as figure 4.3 shows:
11.8 percent of companies established between 1720 and 1825 used them,
compared with 18.9 percent between 1826 and 1844. Company size was
again a factor: just 11.3 percent of small to medium firms imposed residential requirements, but 26.1 percent of large or very large companies
did so. Smaller firms were more likely to have a concentrated sphere of
operations and consequently a less dispersed shareholder base; in many
cases, residential restrictions would be superfluous. Residential requirements thus appear to have been primarily a means for larger companies
to try to foster a local identity, to ensure equal representation of several distinct geographical groups, or simply to ensure good attendance
and familiarity at board meetings. Geographical representation was the
priority of the Salamander Fire Office (1823), where, of the sixteen directors, four were required to live in each of the four towns where the
company transacted its business.[90] Similar requirements were in place
at the Great Western Railway Company, promoted by London and Bristol businessmen in 1835. The company's act of incorporation stipulated
that at least eight of the twenty-four directors live within twenty miles of
Bristol and at least eight within twenty miles of London.

No less than 65.2 percent of companies in our sample chose to apply
at least one additional restriction on board membership. As figure 4.3
shows, these became more widespread over time. By far the most common was a stipulation, imposed by 46.7 percent of companies, that no
acting director was to have a personal interest with the company, such as

holding an office of profit or having a contract to supply materials. The first would ensure a clean dividing line between the executive and the officers of the company, guaranteeing that there was not an unhealthy concentration of power in the hands of a single person. The second would ensure that the outside interests of directors did not compromise the interests of the company.[91] There are also political parallels with this feature of company governance. An MP still vacates his or her seat on acceptance of an office of profit under the Crown, and by-elections have been triggered by MPs accepting contracts with the Admiralty.[92] The restriction on MPs holding offices of profit dates to the constitutional compromise of 1707, which allowed a member of the House of Commons to accept an office from the Crown, provided he vacate his seat and stand for reelection.[93] From the late eighteenth century to the chartist era, attacks on government placemen in Parliament again became a stock call of reformers, which attracted legislative responses.[94] An act of 1782 renewed the prohibition on "any person concerned in any contract, commission, or agreement made for the publick service, from being elected, or sitting and voting as a member of the House of Commons," on pain of a fine of £500 per day.[95] Similarly, following the Anglo-Irish union of 1801, legislation confirmed that no person who held any office or place of profit "by any appointment subject to the approbation of the Lord Lieutenant, Lord Deputy, Lord Justices, or other chief governor or governors of . . . Ireland" could be elected as an MP, on pain of the same penalty.[96] The Municipal Corporations Act (1835) prevented councillors from serving in municipal offices, a practice widely tolerated before this. The same legislation excluded councillors who were interested, directly or indirectly, in any contract with the council.[97]

The prevalence of these restrictions in national and local government is reflected in the much higher proportion of corporations (69.7 percent) than unincorporated companies (17.0 percent) that imposed this qualification on their directors. Corporations followed the same trajectory as national and local government: while only 16.0 percent of corporations in the period 1720–89 imposed a restriction on directors holding offices or contracts, from 1835 the practice was almost universal. A related provision, found in 21.8 percent of companies, was for constitutions to prohibit interested voting by board members. In banks this usually took the form of a clause preventing directors from voting on whether to give credit to themselves, their business partners, or their relatives. In other companies, there was a prohibition on voting when the director was involved in contracts for supplying goods for the company.[98] Bowen argues that, at the East India Company in the 1820s and 1830s, "reform gradually reduced the scope for illicit activities" by directors and suggests that this reflects a period when "attitudes to public service and officeholding underwent something of a sea change."[99] Similar changes can be seen in the constitutions of other companies, whose promoters, like the members of the EIC, also had an eye on wider political developments.

Another requirement (in 18.7 percent of companies) was that directors were not to be officers or directors of, or have any other interest in, other companies, usually in the same sector. Although it was the subject of a standing order in the South Sea Company, this stipulation was rare in other eighteenth-century companies (less than 3 percent).[100] It became more widespread in the nineteenth century, mainly, it would seem, as a result of the rapid increase in numbers of companies and the temptations held out to directors to sit on the boards of several companies at once. Multiple directorships attracted much criticism. In February 1825, at the height of a company "mania," the conservative weekly *John Bull* published a list of 129 men who were on the boards of more than three companies, in order to underline "the impossibility of their doing justice either to the schemes or themselves."[101] Thirty percent of companies established in 1824–5 tried to combat this problem by imposing the restriction, and it remained a popular device thereafter. When George Hudson's railway empire collapsed in 1849, many companies acted to secure themselves against directors holding too many outside interests. A shareholder committee of the York and North Midland Railway Company secured the passage of a bylaw that no director who was a director in any other company could hold the chair or vice-chair. The spokesman for the committee argued that men occupying those positions "ought, like Caesar's wife, to be above suspicion, and entirely independent of any other company. . . . The fact of gentlemen acting on different boards of direction had been tried, and found to work disadvantageously."[102]

Various other qualifications were occasionally stipulated: 9.1 percent of constitutions stipulated that directors could not be relatives or business partners of other members of the board.[103] Four companies in our sample laid down a religious qualification. Another 3.9 percent imposed other miscellaneous qualifications. For example, eight of the seventeen directors of the Clerical, Medical, and General Life Assurance

Society had to be members of the medical profession, while the entire board of the American and Colonial Steam Navigation Company had to be natural-born subjects of Great Britain.[104]

Thus, the rapid expansion of the joint-stock sector, especially from the 1820s, increased the potential dangers faced by shareholders at the hands of their executives. Their directors might have too many outside interests to devote sufficient attention to their company, might sacrifice the company's interests in favor of other interests when it came to negotiating business deals, or might live too far from the company to be able to do their jobs properly. A company might be taken over by a particular business or family grouping, or one man might effectively take control by dominating the board and being selected as the chief salaried officer. Companies increasingly responded to these dangers by introducing safeguards into their constitutions. We see a striking decline in the number of companies willing to leave their directors free from these kinds of qualifying restrictions over time: from nearly 80 percent in the eighteenth century to barely 20 percent by the 1840s (see figure 4.3). As with residential requirements, larger companies were far more likely than smaller ones to impose these additional qualifications on directors: only 48.5 percent of the smallest companies did so, compared with 82.9 percent of very large ones, reinforcing the point that the formalized, regulated board of directors tended to replace the informal, unregulated committee of management in the larger companies.

Remuneration

Gratuitous service stemming from notions of an "obligation to serve" was one of the defining elements of central and local government in the eighteenth and nineteenth centuries.[105] Though it came under attack as a friend of corruption from the late eighteenth century, the principle of service exerted a powerful influence in the joint-stock economy. It is probably fair to state that most men did not become directors of companies in this period in order to become rich.[106] That said, only six constitutions in our sample explicitly designated the directorship an honorary office. Most companies permitted their directors to receive payment, though many constitutions were silent on the issue or made vague provision that "the company" would fix directors' pay. In the 49.4 percent that made clear arrangements for remuneration, control of directors' pay commonly rested with the shareholders. The usual stipulation (seen in 61.9 percent of companies that mentioned pay) was for the GM to fix the payment. An alternative arrangement was for the constitution to set out a rate or scale of pay for directors. In twenty companies the shareholders were explicitly given the right to alter these rates; in thirty-seven this right was not specified. In only thirty companies (11.5 percent of those that mentioned pay) were directors given the power to fix their own pay. In most of these, the scope given to directors was intended to be narrow. The River Trent Navigation (1783), for example, permitted its directors to pay themselves "a reasonable Sum of Money" to cover their expenses of attending board meetings.[107] In a few cases, provision was more open ended: the Leeds and West-Riding Banking Company (1836) permitted its board to fix remuneration for any one or more of the directors, which had to be confirmed by the written consent of three-quarters of the board.[108] But such instances were rare. Even in the many cases where pay was not mentioned, procedural records show that it was considered within the remit of the GM to decide whether, and what amount, the directors would be paid.

It was common for directors to receive no payment, except perhaps for a small fee paid for each board attendance, until the company had become profitable. Once regular dividends were being paid, shareholders could be persuaded to vote an annual salary for the board. The South Metropolitan Gas Light and Coke Company provides an example. After an early scandal in which three directors were found to be forging bills of exchange, a new deed of settlement was drawn up, and the new board of five managed to win back shareholder confidence, partly by acting without remuneration.[109] The company paid a dividend for the first time in 1836, and at the next AGM the directors argued that, as the services they had rendered to the company over the past three and a half years "must be considered a charge incurred in maturing the Establishment of the Company," they should receive a retrospective payment. This was accepted, and the shareholders voted £1,000 out of the company's capital for the directors for this period.[110] Thereafter, the directors were voted £280 per annum to divide between them.

In a climate of low or nonexistent pay, poorly attended boards were a frequent problem. At the Bridport Gas and Coke Company (1832), for example, several months could pass without any recorded board meeting because of lack of attendance.[111] In such cases, the attending directors sometimes imposed fines for nonattendance in order to motivate their colleagues; such fines were sometimes even written into the company constitution. The directors of the Cheltenham Gas Light Company (1819), for example, imposed a 2s.6d. fine on nonattenders in 1820, which was increased to 5s. in the following year.[112] Other mechanisms existed to incentivize the executive. Sometimes companies tied directors' (and employees') pay to performance. The bylaws of the Bridgewater Gas Light Company established a sliding scale, rising from 2s. 6d. per board attendance to 5s. when the dividend reached 10 percent. The clerk's annual salary was to be £25, rising to £50 when the dividend reached this level.[113]

Where directors were paid relatively highly, accusations of corruption could follow. One disgruntled shareholder of the North Midland Railway wrote to the press: "Is the fitness of the director for the post, or the fitness of the hundred a year for the director the matter of consideration?"[114] Overall, however, we detect an upward pressure on pay, especially from the 1830s.[115] The managing director of the South Metropolitan Gas Light and Coke Company, for instance, was initially paid £300 in 1835, rising to £400 in 1837 and £500 in 1839.[116] This trend can be attributed to a growing dissatisfaction with part-time directors. In the late 1840s, one large shareholder of the troubled Eastern Counties Railway believed "the time has arrived in railway affairs when those gentlemen who would best serve us as directors must be sought after . . . depend on it, when you find gentlemen offering their services to you, that very offer should induce you to look upon them with suspicion." He thought that the only men who could be effective directors were specialists who knew the work involved in managing a railway and could devote all their attentions to the concern: he thought it "impossible for a man who is engaged in active business pursuits of his own to spare the time necessary for the efficient performance of the duties of that office."[117] Such thoughts were echoed by Walter Bagehot after the banking scandals of the mid-1850s. Bagehot became convinced of the need to increase directorial pay. Many directors had low or even no remuneration, and in few companies was the pay sufficient "to induce very able practical men to devote much time to the duty. The tendency is like that of the government of a new colony—the worst qualified will be apt to take that which the best qualified are too busy to desire."[118]

Shareholders had less control over the pay of company employees than of the board. Just over one-quarter of companies (25.5 percent) clearly allowed the GM to fix the pay of some of the salaried officers of the company; 44.6 percent of companies explicitly reserved the power to the board, while the remaining constitutions either did not mention the matter or contained ambiguous provisions. Incorporated companies (37.6 percent) were far more likely to give shareholders this right than unincorporated ones (9.8 percent). This reflects the general preference of corporations, discussed further in chapter 5, for a constitutional system in which the GM exercised ultimate authority over the executive and employees, while unincorporated companies tended toward a "checks and balances" system, in which the GM monitored the executive, while the executive had final authority over the employees, including setting their remuneration.[119]

Whether directors or shareholders were in control of pay, levels of remuneration were typically low, with many employees engaged on a part-time basis. There were exceptions, with some companies happy to pay to secure the exclusive services of some employees. The superintendent of the Cheltenham Gas Light Company was required "to be in the actual employ of the Partnership from Nine in the morning until Eight in the Evening throughout the year and to devote his services exclusively to the Duties of his Employ"; accordingly, he was paid £150.[120] But not all companies were willing to pay for such close attention to their affairs. There are many instances, particularly among smaller provincial companies, of boards paying employees at such low rates that they would have no option but to work for several firms at once. When the Rochester and Chatham Gas Light Company had trouble securing a suitable superintendent, two directors were sent to London to explore options for a replacement. The superintendent of the Ratcliff Gas Light and Coke Company recommended a man who would need a salary of around £150, but Thomas Livesey, who had been involved in gas companies for twenty years, suggested that someone could be found for much less. He had secured the services of a superintendent for a small local company for just £60 per annum who could be paid so little because he supplemented his income by working as a gas fitter. The company subsequently employed a gas fitter from Chatham at just £60.[121] In some companies, pay for clerks could be as low as £10 per annum.[122]

As with directors, pay for employees increased as companies became more profitable. This was within a context of generally rising white-collar and clerical earnings, particularly after 1780.[123] Salaries were personalized in that long faithful service was rewarded by pay increases, but when an employee left, his replacement tended to be paid at a lower level.[124] Sometimes companies could not decide how much to pay their employees: shareholders at the Aberdare Canal Navigation in 1793 appointed a clerk at a salary of £20 per annum, which was reduced three years later to £10 and increased to a guinea a week in 1801.[125] Payment in the financial sector was often more generous than elsewhere, but even there, salaries were squeezed by economy-minded boards. Hugh Watt, manager of the Huddersfield Banking Company, advised George Fox of the Plymouth and Devonport Banking Company, "You should have a respectable Manager and he ought to have a sufficient income to support himself in a respectable manner; I think not less than £500 a year." Fox's brother Thomas, however, disagreed, imagining that "£250 to £300 per annum for the first year or two besides occupying the Bank house rent free would be thought liberal."[126]

Conclusions

The trends discussed in this chapter can only fully be understood by considering them alongside the changes in the rights of shareholders and the role of the GM. These are explored in chapters 5 and 6. The separation of ownership and control in early joint-stock companies, especially corporations, was often incomplete, not simply because, as Wilson argues, these companies were usually controlled and managed by those responsible for initiating the schemes, but, more important, because power was located not in the board of directors but in the GM itself.[127] When the appointment, dismissal, and remuneration of directors and employees, the audit of accounts, decisions over borrowing, and key operational issues were all decided by the GM, the executive's role was less important to the overall running of the company. It was therefore common for the executive to meet comparatively infrequently, for the rules regulating the behavior of its members to be minimal, and for it to be directly accountable to the GM, with the annual rotation of all its members as the norm.

This model of corporate governance was increasingly undermined during the nineteenth century. Particular sectors of the joint-stock economy, especially the railways, are sometimes credited with pioneering "modern" management practices.[128] It was in fact large companies generally, across the joint-stock sector—corporations and unincorporated companies alike—that drove changes in the nature of the company executive. These were the companies that were most likely to grant their directors long terms of office, thus rendering them less directly accountable to their constituents. They often developed more complicated management structures, and their directors were also more likely to meet frequently—usually weekly—to transact business as it arose. Membership of their executives was more restricted in terms of both shareholdings and other regulations. At the same time, the board of the large company as a whole owned a much lower percentage of the company's shares, therefore finally making a reality the long-held assumption that joint-stock companies represented a divorce of ownership from control. This divorce became more explicit when powers were hived off from the GM and vested in the executive. Large companies in particular were instrumental in raising the executive to a more powerful, more closed, and in some senses more mysterious position in joint-stock politics—and they were also important in downgrading the powers of shareholders and the GM in the company, as we will now explore.

Constitutional Rights and Governance Practice

The Proprietorship

The principles of a free constitution are irrecoverably lost, when the legislative power is nominated by the executive. — Edward Gibbon[1]

Shareholders, as Dunlavy has observed, are largely absent from Chandlerian representations of business history.[2] It can be argued that this absence reflects the legal distinction between the corporation and its members. In Ireland's words, the principle of the separate legal personality of the corporation "is based on a conception of the company as not merely an entity with an independent legal existence from its shareholders but an *object* which has been effectively cleansed of them."[3] For a long time, and with some notable exceptions, the legal marginalization of the shareholder was mirrored in the historiography.[4] However, as historians have begun to disentangle the complex economic, legal, and political relationships that characterized the joint-stock economy of the eighteenth and nineteenth centuries, the shareholder has reappeared as a significant figure. The motivations for investment, the mechanisms for protecting shareholders' interests, and the levels of shareholder participation in the governance of companies have all been discussed.[5] In this chapter we place shareholders center stage, examining the roles that shareholders could be called upon to perform, from the active promotion of companies to the election and appointment of directors and salaried officers, the setting of remuneration, the oversight of major strategic decisions, and the amendment of the company constitution itself. In chapter 6 we examine the various forms of franchise by which shareholders were accorded a say in company affairs and the role of the GM in corporate governance. In chapter 7, we discuss the ways in which constitutions attempted to safeguard the interests of shareholders, in particular by limiting their liability, but also by providing for company dissolution, together with other forms of protection. The picture that emerges is of the transfer of power in joint-stock company politics from the GM to the executive, with the result that shareholder participation gave way to more "autocratic" forms of government by directors and managers.

This relocation of power happened alongside—and, it can be argued, as a result of—changing motivations for investment in joint-stock companies. Debates about "prudent" versus "speculative" motives had already reached a climax in the years leading up to the South Sea crisis of 1720, and they never entirely disappeared thereafter.[6] In his study of eighteenth-century canals, Ward made a distinction between investors motivated by "economic" and "financial" considerations. The former had a direct interest in the scheme being promoted and were usually local merchants or manufacturers; the latter were rentiers, interested solely or mainly in dividends.[7] Early "economic" investment in canals gave way to "financial" investment as they began to offer returns on capital. In the same vein, Wilson applied the terms "strategic" and "speculative" to gas shareholders in the northwest of England. Early investment in gas supply was predominantly "strategic," dominated by those likely to consume the gas in their own businesses, whereas "speculative" investment grew in importance over time, with a wider geographical spread of shareholding and the rise of a rentier class, drawing the high dividends that many gas companies offered.[8] Hudson adopted a similar distinction between "economic" and "financial" investment in her study of West Midland canal and railway investors.[9] This has also been observed in shipping, where many shareholders had a personal involvement in shipping goods, but where the growth of rentier investment has also been identified.[10]

By the 1840s, if not earlier, the need to source capital from wider geographical areas, particularly in the railway and banking sectors where large firms increasingly predominated, resulted in a growing secondary market for shares and a broader investment base. By 1851, according to one estimate, there were 268,191 share owners in England alone.[11] Preda relates the growth in shareholding to the availability of financial information in the form of market periodicals and stock lists, while others have emphasized the size of returns available in the form of dividends, compared with the yield from government bonds and other alternative investments.[12] Rutterford cites an article in the *Statist* published in 1888 that distinguished between four kinds of investors: those expecting a steady return, who might otherwise invest in government bonds; those seeking high dividends and willing to take risks with their money; those who speculated with small sums; and the "premium hunter," for whom the "vitriol" of the *Statist* was reserved. Rutterford identifies two further types: the "greedy shareholder," probably a retired person or widow, and the "informed business man, happy to receive a reasonable dividend from his investment in a company with which he was probably involved, as a director or customer."[13] Only the latter corresponded in any way to the "economic" investor in the early canals, and even for him the dividend was a significant consideration. This illustrates the extent to which the predominant motivations of shareholders had shifted by the later nineteenth century.

Of course, the distinction between the two kinds of investment is somewhat artificial: it is clear that both motivations could, and did, operate simultaneously. The distinction, however, is useful for our purposes because of its implications for joint-stock politics. By the 1840s, the state recognized the changing roles of investment and began to intervene more systematically in the relationships between companies and the wider public, especially in the "network industries."[14] These attempts reflected a realization that "strategic" investment in public utilities was giving way to speculative shareholding with the maximization of returns and the search for capital gains rather than the provision of a particular service as the main objective. For most of our period, the extent of speculative investment as a gamble on the rise of share values was largely limited to the major company promotion booms such as in 1824–5. As we note below, this began to change in the railway era when company directors first tried to make a distinction between those investing for "financial" motives, with a primary interest in dividend yields, and those who speculated in "scrip"—advance allocations of railway shares before they were issued—in anticipation of selling these quickly for a profit.[15] For the purposes of the present discussion, however, we lump both types of "speculative" investor together in order to make the distinction between these types and the "economic" investor clearer. "Economic" or "strategic" investors, *ceteris paribus*, were more likely to take an active role in the government of their company. By contrast, "financial" or "speculative" investors were likely to intervene only when their returns were threatened or, less commonly, when share values suffered. The growth of a rentier class of shareholders, content to receive high dividends but capable of being moved to action when returns on capital fell, was a widely observed feature of the first half of the nineteenth century and aroused renewed concern about the evils of "speculation." It has also begun to be examined by historians. Alborn regards the shift away from shareholder participation, especially in banking, to be the result of a "political" desire among company promoters to secure a more compliant proprietary. He links this to notions of "respectability" inherent in the wider debates on the political franchise in the nineteenth century.[16] Similarly, Dunlavy links the emergence of the "plutocratic" shareholder franchise in US corporations to the transformation of the small shareholder from an active participant in corporate governance to a mere "passive investor."[17]

This chapter advances our understanding of this aspect of corporate governance by tracing more systematically the shifting constitutional balance between shareholder obligations and benefits. It shows that the right of shareholders to intervene in company affairs was traditionally bound up with various obligations and restrictions placed on shareholders, ranging from the requirement to extend the business to limitations on their freedom to contract with other companies. At the same time as they were divested of their powers over strategy and management, however, they were also shorn of their economic obligations, turning instead to ways of protecting their financial stake in the company. Thus, in an important sense, they were complicit in the reconfiguration of power within the company. Though they did this in the name of protecting their investments, the irony is that this trade-off left their investments vulnerable to depredations by unchecked directors and managers, as we demonstrate in chapters 7 and 8.

Shareholder Obligations and Benefits

It might seem obvious that the primary obligation of shareholders was to pay the calls on their shares, yet this was one of the most contested areas of joint-stock politics in our period. Calls became politicized in the late eighteenth century when responsibility for them shifted from the GM to the board of directors: while 33.3 percent of companies established between 1720 and 1789 gave the GM sole authority over all calls, this fell to just 3.6 percent of companies established after 1789.[18] Defaulting shareholders were the most common topic of discussion at the GMs of many companies.[19] Chronic nonpayment could seriously hamper a company's prospects. Failure to pay often stemmed from the straitened circumstances of individual shareholders, but it could also be caused by a loss of confidence in the viability of a scheme or the way it was being managed: companies that were plagued by defaulters also usually suffered from low attendances at GMs. Directors, therefore, had to be careful to stress that calls were made only when strictly necessary. The directors of the South Metropolitan Gas Light and Coke Company, for example, told their shareholders in 1836 that they anticipated only having to make one call that year but hoped that shareholders would cheerfully pay a second if required, as the directors "have been, and still continue most anxious to avoid all expenditure which may not tend to the interest and prosperity of the Company," and "will not unnecessarily call upon the Proprietors."[20] To try to render the call-making process more transparent and less controversial, some company constitutions, particularly in the unincorporated sector, contained a fixed schedule of calls. The Rochester and Chatham Gas Light Company (1818) issued shares of £50, and the schedule for paying up the first £35 was specified in the "deed of copartnership."[21] Even explicit provisions such as these, however, did not prevent considerable numbers of share forfeitures in the early phase of a company's life as shareholders defaulted.[22] Constitutions typically granted directors the power to enforce payment of calls through the courts and to divest defaulters of their shares in the event of continued refusal to pay. Directors, however, often proved reluctant to use these powers, preferring instead to rely on exhortation and persuasion at GMs.[23]

The extent to which the issue of calls could come to dominate a company's affairs is illustrated by the case of the Ashby-de-la-Zouch Canal Company (1794). The company's act had clear rules on payment of calls: those who failed to pay a call within thirty days could be fined up to £5 per share. The company could sue shareholders for nonpayment, and shares were forfeited if calls were not paid within six months.[24] The inadequacy of these rules soon became clear. By April 1795, £30 had been called up on each £100 share, which should have generated £45,000. The sum actually raised, however, was barely £29,000, leaving a shortfall of nearly £16,000. Letters were sent to each shareholder in arrears, and notices were placed in the press warning that if payments were not made before the next board, steps would be taken to enforce payment.[25] By the following April, after £25 more of calls, the deficit had grown to nearly £28,000. The GM unanimously voted to initiate legal proceedings against one shareholder, Bullivant, who had not paid calls on nineteen shares. Bullivant agreed to terms with the directors, but the larger problem did not recede.[26] In April 1796 the biggest defaulters received another letter threatening legal proceedings but to little avail. In the following month, the directors appointed two shareholders to "wait in person upon the Subscribers in arrear in order to receive their several arrears or to take their reasons for their withholding the payment thereof."[27] By October the deficit had swollen to over £33,000, and the directors referred the problem to the GM, which unanimously gave them authority to launch legal actions against any defaulter.[28] After three further rounds of threatening letters, the directors finally launched actions against fifty-four shareholders in November 1797 and January 1798. In April the GM voted that a list of defaulters was to be hung up in the meeting room, in an attempt to shame them publicly.[29] All of this had some effect. By October 1798, the amount owing had fallen to £22,500, but as the final calls were made over the following months, the deficit shot up again, to more than £34,000. The GM resolved that no interest be paid on calls except to proprietors who had already paid their full subscriptions.[30] Flurries of legal actions gradually had an effect, wearing down the size of the deficit to just over £14,000 by 1803.[31] The company's debts were not paid off until 1828, at which point it paid a dividend for the first time.

English court judgments had an increasing influence on the problem of making calls. Indeed, calls on shareholders, and their resistance to this liability, were the dominant issues in English legal cases involving joint-stock companies between the 1790s and the 1840s and touched upon several other aspects of the legal framework within which English stock companies operated in this period.[32] Four points emerge from a reading of these cases. First, the law courts were increasingly concerned to regulate the process of making calls, including the schedule of calls and term of notice given and the authority employed for calls and forfeitures of shares upon default of payment. This usually involved making detailed reference to a company's act of incorporation and, less frequently (because unincorporated companies appeared in the courts more rarely than corporations such as canals and railways), to deeds of settlement as the key constitutional document whose authority the judiciary sought to uphold.[33] Second, proof of share ownership became the key point upon which many of the cases turned. This issue, in turn, was central to other cases involving different categories of shareholder liabil-

ity, especially liability for company debts.[34] Third, as the number of such
cases increased, the courts became concerned to tighten the definition
of who could be sued for default. In a judgment involving the Huddersfield Canal Company in 1796, for instance, it was ruled that subscribers
were not liable for calls after they had assigned their shares.[35] Two judgments in 1840 held that directors holding shares "in trust" for a dock
company were liable for outstanding calls.[36] Fourth, following the share
boom and bust of 1835–6, there were signs of declining judicial tolerance for defaulting shareholders as numerous investors, with the help of
their lawyers, tried to wriggle out of their financial commitments using
increasingly desperate arguments.[37] Particularly with regard to railway
share issues, enormous legal problems were caused by quick transfers
of scrip and the uncertain liability of vendors for subsequent calls. As
noted above, the courts tried to follow the protocol for share transfers as
set out in company constitutions, but they also gave increasing leeway to
companies pursuing recalcitrant defaulters, for example, with regard to
irregular or incomplete entries in share transfer books.[38]

Legal proceedings against defaulters on calls did not always succeed.
In *Ward v. Matheson* (1829), the defendant refused to pay the second
call of £1 on his shares in the Edinburgh Portable Gas Company until the contract of copartnery was prepared. When the latter was finally
completed, it contained several elements that differed from those in the
original prospectus. The Lord Ordinary, and subsequently the Court of
Session, ruled that Matheson did not have to pay the call because the
changes had not been ratified by a GM. A similar decision was reached
in *Learmonth v. Adams* (1831), which related to a call made on shares in
the Commercial Marine Insurance Company of Scotland.[39] In England,
company prospectuses, when tested, were also held to be legally binding
on their promoters. The directors of the newly minted Alliance British
and Foreign Life and Fire Assurance Company were successfully taken
to court by a shareholder in 1824 because they had attempted to extend
the business to marine insurance following the repeal of the monopoly
of the two London marine insurance corporations. The plaintiff sued for
a return of his subscription on the grounds that there was no mention of
marine insurance in the company's original prospectus, which had been
issued before the repeal bill was passed.[40]

What about obligations beyond paying calls? Williston argued that
in corporations, the duties of the shareholder "were fewer and simpler
than his rights," and consisted mainly of the requirement to pay calls.[41]

Constitutionally speaking, this was true: only two corporations in our sample imposed any other constitutional requirements on their shareholders. However, where shareholders were seen as active investors promoting the broader economic interests of their company, they were expected to do more than simply hold shares. This applied to shareholders in unincorporated and incorporated companies alike. At the first ordinary general meeting (OGM) of the Insurance Company of Scotland (1821), the directors asked for "a steady and continued exertion on the part of the Partners, by bringing all the Insurances they can obtain to the Company, and by strongly recommending to their friends to become shareholders."[42] In 1838, the directors of the Ashton, Stalybridge, Hyde and Glossop Bank called on proprietors to "exert their individual and collective influence" in promoting the local circulation of the company's banknotes.[43] When a company was in dire financial straits, shareholders were expected to help by making sacrifices or by drumming up business. Several shareholders in the struggling Thames and Severn Canal Company helped in the 1790s by building boats at their own expense and letting them to the company.[44] A GM of the Medway Bathing Establishment in 1836 appointed a committee of twelve shareholders "to go round the towns to obtain subscriptions" to finance a new floating machine. When the response to a new share issue proved disappointing, the GM appointed another committee "to go round to the shareholders to get the shares taken."[45]

Obligations, often vaguely expressed, were sometimes written into the constitutions of unincorporated companies. In the contract of co-partnery of the Insurance Company of Scotland, for example, the parties "faithfully promise[d] and oblige[d] themselves severally to promote and advance the interest of this Company to the utmost of their power and ability."[46] Unincorporated companies, however, often set out additional requirements of their shareholders that went well beyond promoting the company, and this set them apart from corporations. Table 5.1 shows that in the period 1720–1809 a majority of unincorporated companies in our sample set some kind of prerequisite for share ownership. The table also breaks these requirements down by type. Arguably the key characteristic of an ideal "economic" shareholder was the transaction of business with his or her company. This was imposed as a prerequisite of share ownership in 17.6 percent of unincorporated companies established in the eighteenth century, one in four established in the 1800s, and nearly one in three of those launched in the early 1820s. In

TABLE 5.1. **Percentage of unincorporated companies imposing prerequisites for share ownership by time of prerequisite and subperiod**

Subperiod	1	2	3	4	5	6	Any prerequisite
1720–99 ($N = 17$)	23.5	17.6	5.9	23.5	11.8	5.9	52.9
1800–9 ($N = 20$)	5.0	25.0	5.0	20.0	5.0	10.0	55.0
1810–9 ($N = 8$)	0.0	12.5	0.0	0.0	0.0	12.5	25.0
1820–4 ($N = 19$)	0.0	31.6	5.3	5.3	0.0	0.0	42.1
1825–9 ($N = 33$)	0.0	3.0	3.0	9.1	6.1	6.1	24.2
1830–4 ($N = 31$)	0.0	6.5	12.9	16.1	0.0	0.0	29.0
1835–9 ($N = 72$)	1.4	8.3	5.6	4.2	2.8	1.4	22.2
1840–4 ($N = 24$)	0.0	0.0	4.2	0.0	4.2	8.3	12.5
All unincorporated companies ($N = 224$)	2.7	10.7	5.8	8.9	3.6	4.0	29.5

Key
1 = Must be approved by existing shareholders
2 = Must have some other connection with the company (e.g., transact business with it)
3 = Residential requirement
4 = Must not be involved with another company in the same sector (sometimes exempted those whose only connection was holding shares in another joint-stock company)
5 = No corporations or partnerships could hold shares
6 = Any other prerequisite

this way, joint-stock companies acquired some of the features of mutuals, where the owners were also the customers, although in most cases the customer base was larger than the proprietorship. In the eighteenth century, 23.5 percent of unincorporated companies restricted their shareholders' involvement (holding shares or office or transacting business) in competing companies. Shareholder exclusivity was most commonly insisted upon in banking (19.0 percent of all unincorporated banks), while additional connections were most commonly required in insurance (21.3 percent) and shipping (19.0 percent).

Shipping companies—the great majority of which were unincorporated—often required their shareholders to have some involvement with the trades in which their ships were engaged.[47] All the proprietors of the Stockton and London Shipping Company (1839), for instance, had to be "shippers," while in the London and Edinburgh Shipping Company (1809) each proprietor had to be "connected with some profession which leads him to ship goods" between the ports of Leith and London, although the directors could waive this requirement at their discretion.[48] The intense competition in local trading routes and the complex business connections of some investors were recognized at the Berwick Shipping Company (1820), where (among other requirements) shareholders were not permitted to ship goods, except for corn and grain, in another company's vessels on any route served by the company.[49] Manufacturing and trading companies had similar rules, sometimes reflecting the particular circumstances of their establishment. The Duns Linen Company (1765) comprised weavers and "Gentlemen" who subscribed for the purpose of organizing local linen manufacture. The "Gentlemen" were constitutionally barred from engaging in any other linen manufacture in Duns for a period of seven years.[50] At the Birmingham Flour and Bread Company (1796) and the Bristol Flour and Bread Concern (1800), shareholders were required to buy bread from their companies in proportion to the number of shares held.[51] Similarly, in insurance shareholders were often required to insure their property with their company.[52] Twenty-one percent of insurance companies in our sample imposed some such requirement. The involvement of shareholders was also actively promoted in gas companies, which were usually small in scale and territorial ambition and tended to have a local body of shareholders. Twelve of the thirty-two unincorporated gas companies in our sample had some prerequisite for share ownership: seven imposed a residential requirement.

In banking and insurance, however, directors were more concerned about the character and substance of shareholders than their place of residence or business.[53] This would ensure the availability of capital and minimize share forfeitures, while also reassuring third parties— policyholders, depositors, note holders—of the security of the concern. The promoters of the North British Insurance Company (1809), for example, were concerned "to prevent in so far as is practicable the admission of doubtful or improper names among the subscribers."[54] As discussed in chapter 3, companies often adopted large share denominations to attract the "right" kind of investor, and directors in unincorporated companies reserved the right to control access to shares. An extra layer of control was sometimes added in the eighteenth century, which shareholders themselves were called upon to exercise. At the Aberdeen Banking Company (1767), for example, the rules stipulated that GMs could expel any "improper Partner or Partners" from the company.[55]

Another way in which speculative investment could be minimized was by imposing a cap on dividends. This would encourage "responsible" investment and discourage shareholders for whom the "financial" returns on offer were the primary motivation. Forty companies, 7.8 percent of our sample, imposed a dividend cap. The lowest cap was 4 percent, and seven were at 5 percent (the traditional usury limit), but the modal figure (nineteen companies) was 10 percent. The lowest dividend caps were mostly found among unincorporated insurance companies, while the 10 percent cap was more common among corporations, especially canal, harbor, water, gas, and bridge companies. Seven of these corporations— six bridge companies, one harbor—were established with a view to their eventual conversion into trusts. Although private companies, they had a definite public purpose and would eventually be transformed into public institutions, so, to that extent, the limitations on profit making were understandable.

The flipside of the obligations and restrictions imposed on "economic" investors was the availability of benefits from the company business: for example, free or subsidized use of the canal or railway that the concern was established to build. The Midland Railway and the Manchester, Sheffield and Lincoln Railway, as well as several Scottish railway companies, allowed shareholders free passage on their trains to attend GMs.[56] The unincorporated Scarborough Cliff Bridge Company (1828) allowed holders of five or more shares to cross the bridge for free, using a ticket that could itself be sold.[57] Among our corporations, only two water companies—Liverpool (1822) and Deal (1826)—and the West India Company (1826) offered their shareholders benefits from the company's core activity as a constitutional right. In the latter case, the highly regulated benefit was the right of shareholders, with the concurrence of three-quarters of the directors, to borrow money from the company against the security of land in the West Indies.[58] This resembled the benefit available in a number of banks, particularly in Scotland, where loans could be advanced against the security of paid-up capital, although, again, this was usually subject to the discretion of the directors. Nineteen banks in our sample (29.7 percent) offered such benefits. Twelve of these were in Scotland. The earliest was the Commercial Bank of Scotland (1810), where shareholders, at the directors' discretion, could borrow up to one-half of the amount paid up on their shares.[59] The first English banks in our sample to offer this kind of benefit were formed in 1829, and others followed in the 1830s. The advisability of such loans was widely debated at the time. In 1836, Peter Watt, former manager of the Nottingham and Nottinghamshire Joint-Stock Banking Company, defended the practice, pointing out that shareholder debts to a bank were "a real and preferable *lien* over the paid-up capital and marketable value of their shares."[60] Some historians have been more critical. Checkland, for example, argued that the Western Bank of Scotland's lending to many of its 1,280 share-holders was a "dangerous policy" and a reason for its failure. By contrast, Lamoreaux, referring to New England, regards "insider lending" as more benign: banks rarely failed because of it, thanks to rigorous internal vigilance and public monitoring of bank affairs.[61]

Where shareholders were conceived of as "economic" or "strategic" investors, it was not surprising that they often attempted to enforce their will on the board of directors to advance what they saw as the economic interests of their company. Although directors and managers were eager for an active proprietary, the line between activity and interference could be a narrow one, and a sensitive board could easily take umbrage when they felt the line had been crossed. At the Edinburgh Sugar House Company (1752), many of the issues that dogged the internal politics of companies later in our period were rehearsed in a bitter dispute between the "Managers" (i.e., the directors) and their "Constituents" (the shareholders). As in other companies, the proprietors were encouraged to support the sugar house's business. In 1755 the managers "recommend[ed] to the General Meeting that in order to promote the sale of our sugar the partners will take the trouble to direct that no other be used in their Familly but what is the Manufactory of the Company and that they will recommend the Same to their Friends."[62] The managers had the power to veto share transactions and thereby to influence the composition of the proprietary. Some shareholders objected to this power, especially insofar as it applied to the disposal of shares at death. In the early 1760s growing complaints about the way the company was managed were partly assuaged by a continuation of the usual dividend, even though the profits did not warrant the payment of 4 percent. By 1762, however, the shareholders were in open revolt. The managers expressed concern "to find themselves the Objects of the Suspicion of [the GM], as Persons, who in the Purchases of the Materials of their Manufacture, have not acted agreeable to the trust hitherto reposed in them by the Company." The GM had apparently removed some of the managers' powers to import raw sugar and had insisted that a standing committee oversee their actions.[63] In response, the managers emphasized their superior knowledge of the trade, and this seems to have won the day, as the affair eventually blew over. The incident, however, shows how the encouragement of shareholder engagement could backfire on business leaders in this period.

The Accommodation of "Financial" Investment

There was a reconfiguration of the relationship between shareholders and directors during the first half of the nineteenth century. Although "financial" investment had traditionally been associated with "speculation," directors increasingly came to see the benefits of attracting investors who looked for nothing more than a reliable return on capital. Such investors were easily managed and unlikely to express an interest in strategic issues. The "financial" category of shareholders could include both speculative and steady investors. While the former could be kept out by a variety of measures from high share denominations to directorial oversight of share transfers, the latter could be let in by a relaxation of the traditional obligations imposed on shareholders. Thus, the obligations and duties that had been an important feature of company constitutions were gradually abandoned. Table 5.1 shows that the proportion of companies imposing prerequisites on share ownership declined from over 50 percent to less than 15 percent between the eighteenth century and the 1840s.

The increasing emphasis on the financial motivations of shareholders is also marked by the decline of the dividend cap. Among all companies in our sample, capping dividends became less common during the first half of the nineteenth century: 12.3 percent of companies capped dividends in the eighteenth century, rising to 20.6 percent in the 1810s, but the proportion fell to 6.1 percent in the period 1825–9 and to zero in 1830–4 before rising again to 9.6 percent in 1840–4. Companies that began life with a dividend cap sometimes regretted it as time went on. In 1828, the directors of the Liverpool and Manchester Railway, incorporated two years earlier with a sliding-scale dividend limitation, concluded that the repeal of the clause would be "highly desireable." In this instance, however, they were advised by William Huskisson, former president of the Board of Trade, that they should not attempt a repeal.[64] Indeed, from the late 1830s the revival of the dividend cap was imposed from without, by the state, which was beginning to insist on greater regulation of the "network industries."[65] The Gasworks Clauses Act and the Waterworks Clauses Act, both passed in 1847, capped the dividends of incorporated gas and water companies at 10 percent and made provision for rates to be reduced if company profits exceeded the prescribed limit.[66] Statutory dividend caps thus reflected in part the growing profitability of these companies following technological improvements. However, they also underlined the growing belief that motivations for investment were increasingly "financial" in character and that shareholders' desire for profit needed to be curbed in the public interest.[67]

As the obligations and restrictions enshrined in constitutions fell away, new clauses designed to protect the financial interests of shareholders were inserted. In this context, shareholders were not necessarily innocent victims of the reconfiguration of the balance of rights and responsibilities within the joint-stock company. Rather, they conspired in this process, enjoying their newfound freedom from responsibility and doing their best to defend the financial benefits they derived from holding shares. Some of these protections were even offered in corporations, where the supreme protection of limited liability was already available. Although in most corporations the payment of dividends from the capital stock was expressly prohibited and widely condemned by commentators as fraudulent, forty-five corporations (15.5 percent) and twenty-four unincorporated companies (10.7 percent) either gave interest on paid-up capital (i.e., had a minimum dividend) or explicitly permitted a reserve fund to be used to support the dividend. Interest on paid-up capital was most common in the eighteenth century, but it came back into favor in the 1840s. A related benefit offered by some companies—again, mainly incorporated companies—was interest on payments made in advance of calls on shares. This was less desirable from a "financial" point of view than interest on paid-up capital, but as the latter practice declined in the early nineteenth century, an increasing proportion of companies were paying interest on advance deposits. The practice was most common in railway companies (43.3 percent of companies in the sector), harbor companies (29.6 percent), and bridge and property companies (both 27.3 percent). Although not a single corporation in the eighteenth century offered this benefit, by the 1840s 72.7 percent of corporations did so: mostly railways, but also canal, property, gas, and water companies. Sometimes, as in the North British Railway Company (1844), it was available in conjunction with interest on paid-up capital.

The dividend, of course, was the most important consideration for the financial investor. During the eighteenth century both incorporated and unincorporated companies tended to permit GMs to declare dividends. The constitutions of the earlier corporations were often silent or ambiguous on this issue, but they never prevented GMs from declaring dividends, and minute-book evidence suggests that, in practice, their GMs usually declared or approved the dividends.[68] Although our database shows a dramatic increase in the proportion of new incorporated companies allowing their GMs rights over the dividend, rising from 28.0 percent in the period 1720–1825 to 79.3 percent after 1825, what was happening in these companies in the later years was almost certainly a formalization of what was a de facto situation. Conditions in the early unincorporated companies were similar to those in the corporations, the only difference being that the right to declare a dividend, either by the board or by the GM, was more often spelled out in the more detailed constitutions typical of these companies. From the 1820s, however, there was an increase—accelerating in the 1830s—in the number of unincorporated companies that explicitly denied these rights to GMs, and this was when the two types of company diverged significantly. While 79.3 percent of corporations after 1825 gave their GMs this right, only 42.5 percent of unincorporated companies did so. Insurance pioneered this constitutional feature: the earliest twelve companies in our database explicitly to deny these dividend declaration rights were all insurance firms (1780–1821). Twenty-six unincorporated companies were established in other sectors before 1821, but none of them explicitly denied shareholders this right. Thereafter, other types of unincorporated companies began to imitate insurance companies: banks (beginning in 1824) to the same extent as insurance companies (50 percent), other sectors to a lesser extent: manufacturing and trade (from 1824), shipping (1826), gas (1829), colonial (1829), and property companies (1832). The practice filtered only slowly into the incorporated sector. Just five corporations in our database explicitly denied shareholders the right to declare dividends—the first in 1834. Three were railway companies, underlining the point made elsewhere that railways in the 1830s were pioneers in the incorporated sector in circumscribing shareholder rights, albeit on a small scale in this instance.[69]

The explanation for the divergence over time between incorporated and unincorporated companies in the power over the dividend accorded to their shareholders is thus clearly associated with sectoral differences. Banks and insurance companies, almost all unincorporated, were far more likely to reserve the declaration of dividends to boards of directors (33 out of 64 banks in our database, and 33 out of 60 insurance offices) than, for example, canal corporations. This probably reflected the widespread argument that the sophisticated nature of these financial services meant that shareholders could not be trusted to have an informed input on dividend decisions, as they could not be expected to understand the financial situation of their companies. Indeed, it is notable that, among all unincorporated companies, those permitting their shareholders good access to company accounts were more likely to allow their GMs to declare dividends. Sixty percent (18 out of 30) of companies that allowed individual shareholders to inspect books, also allowed the GM to declare the dividend, compared with 38.8 percent (31 of 80) of companies that explicitly prevented individuals inspecting the books.

Some companies, both incorporated and unincorporated, guaranteed a certain level of dividend prior to reserve-fund appropriations. Although this did not amount to a minimum dividend, as it was dependent on company performance, it too went some way toward protecting the "financial" or "speculative" interests of proprietors. Thirty-seven companies (7.2 percent of the total) offered this kind of protection, all but two established in the period 1827–42, and six of them corporations. At the Exeter Water Company, shareholders could decide whether or not to establish a "sinking fund" up to £3,000, but not before a dividend of 5 percent had been paid. At the Victoria Park Company (1837), no money could be transferred to the reserve fund that would impinge on a dividend of 4 percent.[70] Of the thirty-one unincorporated companies that protected shareholders' returns in this way, twenty-six were banks, only one of which was Scottish.[71] The near absence of this provision in Scottish contracts of copartnery may reflect the other benefits widely available to bank shareholders in Scotland, particularly loans against paid-up capital, discussed above. Protections of this kind often reflected a complex balance between safeguarding the dividend and augmenting the reserve. A fairly typical example was the Saddleworth Banking Company, where up to one-quarter of the annual profits could be placed in the reserve fund, but not so as to impinge on a 4 percent dividend. One declared object of this fund was to smooth out dividend fluctuations, although this was at the "absolute discretion" of the directors. It was also explicit that any profits above £15,000 *must* be divided among the shareholders.[72] The use of reserve funds to smooth out dividend fluctuations in gas and water companies was given statutory sanction by the Gasworks Clauses and Waterworks Clauses acts of 1847, which, along with fixing the dividend cap at 10 percent, allowed the reserve fund to be used to bring the dividend up to this figure.[73]

Thus, by the end of our period, the dividend was enshrined as the most important and best-protected benefit enjoyed by shareholders, the result of a major shift in the outlook of directors and shareholders alike.

Company proprietors were well aware that regular and large dividends were very effective in securing their compliance. The Equitable Gas Light Company began paying dividends in 1833, the year its deed of settlement was signed, but it was not until 1840 that the shareholders discovered that these had been paid, without exception, from capital, and that because of incompetent and corrupt management the company had not made a profit in any year. The committee of shareholders that exposed the fraud wrote bitterly that the directors "by throwing gold dust in our eyes at every Meeting in the form of spurious and fallacious dividends . . . put the Proprietary to sleep and disarmed their vigilance."[74] Company minute books reveal that once a firm established regular dividends, shareholder interest in governance often tapered off quite dramatically. At the Uttoxeter Gas Light and Coke Company, the first dividend was declared at the OGM of 1844.[75] At earlier meetings, significant decisions had been taken regarding the leasing of the gasworks, raising money on mortgage and the issue of new shares, but subsequent minutes rarely recorded any business other than the unanimous election of the board and the declaration of the dividend.[76] In 1849 the directors openly acknowledged that shareholders' "financial" motivations were their primary concern: "The Directors beg to assure the Proprietors that the strictest economy has been studied throughout in the application of the Company's funds; at the same time keeping in view the paramount importance of preserving that efficiency, which is the true interest of the Shareholders."[77]

While directors were now encouraging "financial" investors, a line was clearly drawn to exclude "speculative" shareholders, a line that became more pronounced during the second quarter of the nineteenth century. Unrestricted trading in railway scrip during the promotion manias of 1836 and 1845 went a long way toward negating any controls that railway companies might wish to exercise over the composition of their proprietaries.[78] In the unincorporated sector, however, it was common for this right to be abridged by directorial control over share transfers. Although almost unknown in corporations (only 7 out of 290 allowed any directorial control over transferees), the right of directors to veto transfers existed in 77.7 percent of unincorporated companies. The proportion steadily increased during the nineteenth century until in the early 1840s only one unincorporated company in our sample (the Tunbridge Wells Gas Company, 1843) allowed unrestricted share transfers. Of course, even where there was no veto, shareholders still needed to find someone to buy their shares, which might not be easy in a company that was experiencing difficulties or did not pay dividends and where "economic" motivations had guided the early investors. As we show in chapter 6, legal rulings undermined directorial oversight of share transfers in some respects in the later nineteenth century, but in our period control by directors was clearly exercised, and not just at the start of a company's life.[79] Other companies set a time restriction on share transfers: some allowed transfers only at certain times of the year, others prevented the sale of shares before a certain proportion had been paid up, and others disallowed sales in the first phase of a company's existence. Such prohibitions were increasingly common over time, especially in the unincorporated sector. In total, 19.6 percent of unincorporated companies and 7.9 percent of corporations restricted share transfers in this way. They were particularly widespread in banking but could also be found elsewhere. For example, at the North of Scotland Fire and Life Assurance Company (1836) no transfer of stock was allowed within a year of the first GM, while at the Usk Tram Road Company (1814) a quarter of the £50 shares had to be paid up before they could be sold.[80] By such measures, directors could attract passive investors while keeping those with purely speculative objectives at bay.

Female Shareholders

We have written extensively before about women shareholders in joint-stock companies, so this section summarizes the findings of our earlier work, to which we refer the reader for a more detailed discussion.[81] Based on datasets showing women as a proportion of total shareholders in 191 joint-stock companies and women's shares as a proportion of share capital in 80 companies, we were able to draw several conclusions about the trends in female investment.[82] First, the presence of women shareholders in the joint-stock economy before 1850, even if minimal in places, was widespread. Fewer than one in five companies in the first dataset above had no female shareholders. Second, the proportion of women shareholders declined during the last decades of the eighteenth and the first quarter of the nineteenth century to an average of around 7 percent. The levels were higher during the first half of the eighteenth century, reaching between 10 and 20 percent of shareholders in many companies. Indeed, in the 1750s one in four owners of Bank of England stock and one in three owners of East India stock were women.[83] The decline reversed around 1830, and by 1850 the mean percentage of women among shareholders was over 20 percent. This upward trend appears to have continued throughout the rest of the century, so that in some cases, the Ulster Bank, for example, women made up as much as half of all shareholders in the decades before the First World War.[84]

Third, our data revealed that the mean percentage of share capital held by women (6.6 percent) was little more than half the percentage of women among shareholders (12.5 percent), demonstrating that on average women were twice as important to their companies in terms of numbers than they were in terms of their shareholdings. Behind this general result lay trends over time. A rise in the percentage of share capital owned by women in the 1790s and 1800s suggests that wealthier women, or at least women who were able to make larger investments, were subscribing to the joint-stock companies of this period and reducing the gap between the average shareholdings of men and women. After 1830 that gap widened again as growing numbers of female small investors entered the market for company shares, attracted by the lower share denominations of many new companies, and aided by the burgeoning financial press advertising and offering advice on railway and other share issues. Indeed, as the joint-stock economy became more diverse in this period, the increasing dispersion of female shareholding levels across the sector (measured by coefficients of variation) suggests that some types of company were more attractive to women than others. High percentages of female shareholders were to be found most often in banking, canal, and gas companies, indicating some clustering in favored investments, similar to the clustering observed by economic historians in certain "women's" trades (food, retail, textiles).[85] However, the highest standard deviations of the female proportion of shareholders occurred among insurance and railway companies, so that in these sectors the propensity for women to invest was least predictable.

Our data also confirmed that the great majority of women who owned shares were widows and spinsters holding shares in their own name and that many women's shares were held in family clusters, with their shares listed alongside those of their parents, siblings, husbands, sons, and daughters. One possible reason for the assignation of shares by men to other family members, including women, was the desire to maximize voting power by splitting shareholdings—we discuss "stock-splitting" in chapter 6.[86] Together, these factors suggest that most women bought shares, or had shares transferred to them, as "financial" rather than "economic" investors, with their interest primarily being in the dividend payment. Very few female shareholders had occupations recorded in shareholder lists, and very few reveal direct business interests in the companies they invested in. Before the Married Women's Property Act of 1870, under the English law of coverture married women were denied the right to hold shares in their own name, and a few companies did explicitly bar married women from owning shares. More frequently, however, companies required female shareholders to inform them of any change in marital status, and women were expected, upon marriage, to have their shares reregistered in their husbands' names.

The founders of some new companies also actively discouraged the purchase of their shares by women on the grounds that men were better placed to promote the business of the company, but this was relatively unusual. The great majority of companies accepted the presence of female shareholders. A few denied them the right to vote in board elections, a few restricted women to voting only by proxy, and a handful of Scottish companies barred women from acting as proxy voters for others. As we show in chapter 6, however, it was far more common for companies to enable women, together with any shareholder—male or female— living at a distance from the location of the GM, to vote by proxy without requiring them to do so.[87] Most joint-stock companies assumed that women might wish to be active shareholders, attend GMs, and vote on company affairs, and restricting women's rights as proprietors was not widespread in company constitutions. In practice, however, these rights were seldom exercised. Women were never entirely absent from governance in most companies in our period, but they participated in GMs infrequently and in small numbers.

Shareholder Powers and the Authority of the General Meeting

We now turn to more general areas of shareholders' involvement with the operations of their companies. The role of proprietors in corporate governance varied considerably, both constitutionally and in practice. Through the mechanism of the GM, shareholders had a theoretical power of oversight, and as we have seen, there were many examples of shareholders trying to use the GM to shape company policy. It was common practice in the eighteenth century for incorporating acts to include a general clause giving the GM wide-ranging powers of control over directors, even if it was not expected that these powers would be exercised in normal circumstances. A typical example occurs in the Leeds-Liverpool Canal Act (1770), which gave the board of directors the power to run the affairs of the company as it saw fit, "Provided always, That such Committee [of Management] shall from Time to Time be subject to the Examination and Controul of the said General Assembly, or other Meetings of the said Proprietors as aforesaid, and shall pay due Obedience to all such Orders and Directions in and about the Premises, as they shall from Time to Time receive from the said Proprietors at any such General or Special Assembly or Meeting, such Orders and Directions not being contrary to any express Directions or Provisions in this Act contained."[88] Thus, in theory at least, whatever rights were reserved in the act to the committee of management, in this "model-A" type of constitution the GM could overrule the committee and enforce its own will.[89] Many incorporating acts, however, were vague about the extent of shareholder involvement even in core operational decisions. In many companies, for example, borrowing could be undertaken by "the said Company": it was thus not clear whether the committee of management could borrow money without GM authority.[90] Although later acts tended to delineate the respective roles of the executive and GM more carefully, contradictory clauses could still appear. In 1844, the act incorporating the North British Railway Company explicitly set out the rights of directors and shareholders, yet even here there were ambiguities. For example, two articles vested the dismissal of salaried officers of the company in the hands of the directors, but another clause gave the GM powers of suspension and dismissal.[91] All this cautions against reading too much into many of the provisions of these incorporating acts. In practice, as our examples will show, the affairs of companies could be conducted in ways very different from those envisaged in their constitutions.

The most obvious role of shareholders in internal decision making was in the election of directors. In every company in our sample, shareholders had some constitutional involvement in the choice of directors. In 463 companies, 90.1 percent of the total, they elected all the directors, either annually or on some kind of rotation. We have identified four other ways in which directors were chosen. In six companies directors served for life or until they were removed or became disqualified. In each of these a successor was chosen by the shareholders. Second, in seventeen companies, of which sixteen were unincorporated, some directors were permanent and some temporary, although all were chosen by the shareholders: the permanent directors upon death, disqualification, or removal and the temporary directors annually or according to a stipulated rotation. There are examples of this kind of directorate in banking, insurance, shipping, and manufacturing/trade, but it was most common in the gas sector, where six companies chose their directors in this way. A third group, comprising eight companies, all unincorporated, elected some of their directors, while other members of the board were appointed by the directors themselves. Five of these were insurance companies. The final group of companies were those in which the shareholders appointed some, usually a majority, of the directors, but outside bodies either elected one or more members of the board or had ex officio representation. Twenty companies fell into this category, sixteen of them corporations. Examples occur in the bridge, canal, colonial, gas, harbor, insurance, railway, and water sectors. There was a modest increase in the popularity of nonstandard election procedures over time, peaking at 14.0 percent in 1840–4, but even in this subperiod, most companies placed the full constitutional responsibility for choosing directors with their shareholders. Those that did dilute shareholder rights in this respect were also more likely to set out longer terms for their directors. In companies that permitted shareholders to elect all the directors, the mean term of office was 2.4 years, whereas the figure for elected members of nonstandard boards was 3.3 years.

Trends in the right of shareholders to dismiss directors point clearly in the direction of a move away from shareholder participation over time. This right was widespread in the eighteenth and early nineteenth centuries: shareholders in 69.9 percent of companies established in the period 1720–99 enjoyed the right, as did 65.9 percent of those established in the 1810s. By 1835–9 the percentage had fallen to 37.7 percent, though it jumped to 63.2 percent in the following quinquennium. Variations by sector were clear: the right of dismissal existed in 79.4 percent of bridge companies and 78.3 percent of canals but in only just over one-third of gas and shipping companies. The mean nominal capital of companies where rights of dismissal existed was £277,867, compared with £414,304 where no such rights were given, indicating that larger companies were less likely than smaller ones to concede this right. The average term of office of directors was lower where the right of dismissal existed (2.4 years, against 2.6 years where no such right existed), so here too there were longer terms for directors coupled with fewer shareholder rights of dismissal.

Arguably no less important than the right to elect and dismiss directors were the procedures for filling casual vacancies on boards. Here there are revealing political parallels. In acts of incorporation, the wording used in the clauses dealing with casual vacancies often echoed contemporaneous acts for local government, where procedures varied considerably. In select vestries, under the legislation of 1819, vacancies were filled by popular election, whereas in the poor-law unions created in 1834 there were no by-elections, and interim vacancies on boards of guardians were left unfilled.[92] Select vestrymen and poor-law guardians were all elected annually, and so the procedure was less important than in the case of councillors chosen to serve in municipal corporations, who were elected for a three-year term. Under the Municipal Corporations Act of 1835, casual vacancies were filled by election within ten days of the death, resignation, disqualification, or refusal to serve of the councillor.[93] In parliamentary seats, casual vacancies were filled by means of the by-election. In our period, however, uncontested by-elections were becoming more common: the proportion increased from just under 40 percent in the Parliament of 1832–5 to almost three-quarters in that of 1841–7.[94]

Joint-stock companies initially resembled vestries and municipal corporations in relying upon popular election to fill vacancies, but over time, the choice lay increasingly with the directors themselves rather than the GM. Figure 5.1 shows the procedures for filling casual vacancies in all companies where the directors' term of office was longer than one year. In the early decades of the nineteenth century, a clear majority of companies vested in the GM the task of replacing directors who died or became ineligible for service. During the 1820s and 1830s, however, there was a definite move away from this procedure, so that by 1840–4 directors filled casual vacancies in 68.6 percent of new companies, and in a further 11.8 percent they did so subject to subsequent GM approval.[95] Even in these cases, some commentators thought that GM approval was nothing more than a formality. One author, for example, referring to the London and North Western Railway Company in 1853, pointed out that through the manipulation of proxies, directors were always able to secure the confirmation of their own nominees to vacant seats.[96] A similar trend away from shareholder participation is seen in those companies

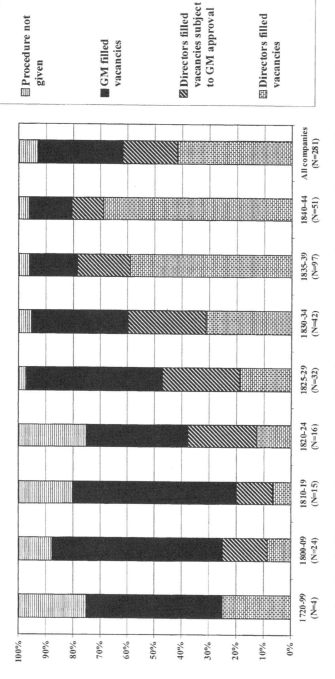

FIGURE 5.1. Procedure for filling casual vacancies on committees/boards in all companies where directors' term of office was more than one year by subperiod

where all directors were elected annually. In these companies, directors were responsible for filling casual vacancies in 11.1 percent of companies established in the period 1720–1824 but 46.1 percent in the period 1825–44.[97]

Another indication of the extent of shareholder participation was the involvement of the GM in appointing and dismissing salaried officers. Most constitutions made some provision for the appointment of managers, although such provision could be couched in fairly vague terms. A number of incorporating acts vested in the GM the right of appointing and dismissing the directors "and any Officer or Officers under them"; such "Officers," presumably, included employees. In many cases where more detail was given, the only rights of appointment conceded to shareholders were of the most senior salaried employees. In a large company, it was clearly impossible for the GM to exercise control over the appointment of numerous subordinate officials. That being said, changes over time and differences between sectors may also have reflected changing conceptions of the role of shareholders. The proportion of companies allowing shareholders some rights over the appointment of employees ranged from 90.0 percent of canals to just 10.9 percent of banks. There was a general trend for this right to decline over time. In the eighteenth century, such rights were conceded to shareholders in 79.5 percent of companies, but this fell to below 50 percent after 1820. As with many of the developments discussed in chapter 4, the larger companies led this shift away from shareholder participation. The mean capital of companies where shareholders were allowed to appoint salaried officers was £95,564, compared with £602,074 where they were not.

As with appointments, the proportion of companies established after 1800 that gave shareholders some rights over the dismissal of employees was considerably lower (between 40 and 60 percent) than it had been in the eighteenth century (over 70 percent). Even where the right was conceded, it was sometimes qualified by the requirement that directors also support the dismissal. At the Royal Bank of Liverpool (1836), for example, shareholders could only confirm (or reject) a board decision to dismiss the manager, and a two-thirds majority was required.[98] Variations by sector resembled those in the appointment of employees: 90.0 percent of canals allowed shareholders rights of dismissal, compared with just 12.5 percent of banks. Here as elsewhere in their constitutions, banks offered less participation than most other joint-stock companies. Their denial to shareholders of the right to appoint or dismiss managers was in accord with their denial of access to financial data and their exclusion of small shareholders from voting, which is discussed in chapter 6.[99]

Sectoral variations were thus an important factor behind the trends in shareholders' rights over time. In general, the procedures for the appointment and dismissal of managers and employees reflected a move away from participatory politics in the joint-stock economy. We can also see, however, the influence of the two generic constitutional models identified above, namely, those that set up the GM as the source of all power in the governance of a company and those that gave the GM authority over the directors and gave the directors the power over most of a company's affairs.[100] As noted already, corporations tended to adopt a variant of the first model, while unincorporated companies, especially the larger businesses appearing in the 1820s to 1840s, led the move toward the second. Thus, shareholders appointed the managers in 66.9 percent of incorporated companies, whereas in unincorporated companies the proportion was 28.1 percent, and the decline in these rights over time was particularly marked among the latter. As figure 5.2 shows, by the early 1840s fewer than 10 percent of new unincorporated companies granted this right to their shareholders.[101] This dichotomy between constitutional types and between corporations and unincorporated stock companies tended to reinforce itself in other areas of shareholder rights. Of those unincorporated companies that exclusively vested in the board the right of appointing trustees, only 5.9 percent (6 out of 102) permitted shareholders to appoint managers, while 92.2 percent (94 of 102) explicitly denied shareholders this right. Of those that conceded to the GM some rights of appointing trustees, 50 percent (27 of 54) also permitted the GM to appoint managers.[102]

With the data in this chapter and in chapter 6, it is possible to construct a broad profile of the type of company and constitution that offered relatively high levels of participation and accountability compared with those that did not. Companies that allowed shareholders to appoint managers also tended to give them rights over dismissal (88.7 percent of such companies), while companies that explicitly denied shareholders the right to appoint also denied them the right to dismiss (85.7 percent). Companies that allowed shareholders to appoint managers also generally held more OGMs than those that did not (1.5 per annum versus 1.3 per annum) and had directors who served shorter terms of office than those that did not (1.9 years versus 3.1 years), suggesting that such directors were more answerable to their GMs. Companies that permitted

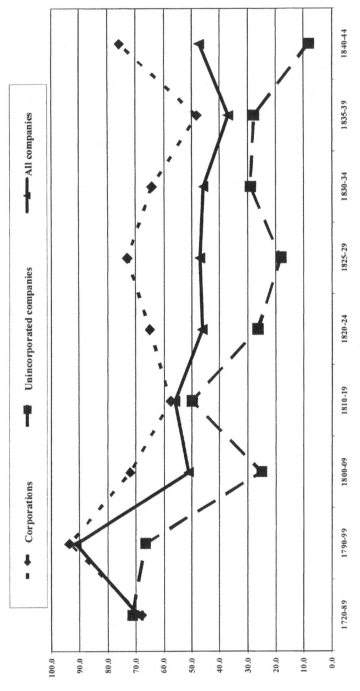

FIGURE 5.2. Percentage of companies allowing shareholder rights over appointment of managers, by type of company and subperiod

small shareholders to vote were much more likely to permit their GMs to appoint managers than those that prevented small shareholders from voting (62.5 percent versus 25.9 percent).[103] Companies that explicitly allowed the GM to declare dividends were more likely to allow the GM to appoint managers than those that explicitly denied the GM the right to declare the dividend (53.7 percent versus 11.7 percent).

In practice, especially in smaller companies, it was possible for shareholders to be actively involved in the appointment and dismissal of officers, regardless of the terms of the constitution. The Rutherglen Gas Light Company (1841) illustrates this well. Its contract of copartnery explicitly reserved to the directors the right to appoint and decide the remuneration of the salaried officers.[104] There was no explicit reference to the procedure for dismissing salaried officers. However, when the company's "gas maker," Alexander Adamson, was dismissed by the directors in 1842 without the reasons being made public, a large group of shareholders succeeded at an SGM in forcing a statement from the board regarding the dismissal. These shareholders were able to force a rather farcical compromise, whereby Adamson and his replacement, James Dowie, would each be employed for a trial period. Meanwhile, another group of shareholders began to complain about other aspects of the company's operations, and the directors themselves became divided over the Adamson-Dowie controversy. Eventually, fed up with the situation, Adamson resigned in June 1843.[105] This episode demonstrates the potential for shareholders to overturn the verdicts of a board, even where the constitution was silent on the matter and, as in this case, gave the directors control over the appointment of employees. Although the board was eventually able to make matters so uncomfortable for their engineer that he left the company voluntarily, the GM had demonstrated its potency in this trial of strength with the directors. It is significant, however, that this occurred in a small company where the shareholders were the main customers and thus could exercise additional leverage over its affairs. In larger companies, there is less evidence of shareholder intervention in appointments and dismissals, even where constitutions gave them this right. At the Insurance Company of Scotland (1821), which had some seven hundred shareholders, the contract of copartnery gave the GM ultimate, if indirect, control over the fate of the manager, although his dismissal needed first to be proposed by the board. When such a proposal was made, a GM would appoint a committee to decide whether the manager should indeed be removed.[106] When the first manager, Robert

Alexander, resigned in 1834, the directors remarked in their annual report that the aforementioned clause of the contract "placed the Manager in a great degree beyond the control of the Board" and that "it was of the utmost importance that such a state of things should not continue." As a result, they wrote a new bylaw that forced the manager to resign if five directors (of a board of eight) signed a minute requesting it. Under this bylaw, the directors themselves would be "the sole judges of the sufficiency" of the cause of dismissal. Retrospectively, this bylaw was unanimously approved at an OGM attended by seventy shareholders.[107]

Elsewhere, directors were less concerned to revise constitutional rights, seemingly secure in the knowledge that shareholders would never use them. The West Middlesex Waterworks Company's act (1806) gave the GM the right to appoint, dismiss, and set the salaries of all company officers.[108] Yet within six months, the GM had delegated the appointment of the secretary and the engineer and the fixing of all the salaries to the directors.[109] The company went on to have chronic problems with its officers. Its first engineer, the notorious Ralph Dodd, was sacked in 1806 after a disagreement with the board over the best location for the company's reservoirs.[110] His replacement, William Nicholson, had to be let go after a few months, as his "pecuniary difficulties" prevented him from doing his job properly. Nicholson was succeeded briefly by John Millington, previously clerk of the works, but he in turn was replaced by Ralph Walker in 1808. Walker resigned in 1810, his inattention to the works in favor of pursuing his own interests having been condemned by the directors. Millington once more took over but was removed months later for being "grossly and generally negligent." Only when he was replaced by William Clark in 1811 did the company find an engineer with whom they were happy. Throughout this catalog of errors, the shareholders confined themselves to occasionally confirming the actions of the board at a GM. The shareholders could hardly be described as passive during this time: there were heated disputes over a deal made by the board with one of their number to purchase land in Kensington for the erection of a steam engine and over the fact that a majority of the directors also sat on the board of the York Buildings Waterworks, a rival company.[111] Directorial elections were also regularly contested. Yet despite the liveliness of the company's politics, issues concerning employees were increasingly seen as the natural province of the board.[112]

In banking, where shareholders enjoyed explicit rights over the dismissal of salaried officers in only 12.5 percent of companies, some felt that the directors' oversight of managers was sufficient for the protection of shareholders. Writing in 1836, Peter Watt argued:

> The danger arising to the proprietary, through the necessity of intrusting their interests to a set of office-bearers, is, humanly speaking, amply checked by the constitution of joint-stock banking companies. The office-bearers enjoy official existence only so long as they act prudently and honestly. They are removable at the pleasure of the directors, on good grounds arising for their dismissal. Hence, the managers, and other office-bearers, have not only the usual motives of unblemished reputation, rank in society, and preservation of a good conscience, to induce them to act justly and honourably towards the partners of the bank, but they have the fear of instant dismissal before their eyes.[113]

The decline of shareholder rights over company employees was a significant element in the reconfiguration of the power relations within companies that took place in these years. The GM shifted from being the source of all power in the company to performing a more closely specified and restricted role within a broader system of checks and balances, characterized by directorial oversight of management and GM oversight of the board. In this reconceptualization of joint-stock politics, the directors possessed all the powers not specifically reserved to the GM. It is revealing to contrast the Leeds-Liverpool constitution of 1770 cited above with that of the Manchester and Leeds Railway Company of 1836, which stated, "Directors shall have full Power and Authority to do all Acts whatever for the Management, Regulation, and Direction of the said Company in relation thereto which the said Company are by this Act authorized to do, except such as are required and directed to be done at a General or Special General Meeting of the said Company."[114] Similar redefinitions of power relations can be found in unincorporated companies, such as the Hampshire Banking Company, whose deed of 1834 stated that "in all cases not provided for by the deed of settlement, the Directors may act in such manner as may appear to them best calculated to promote the interest and welfare of the Company."[115] In this version of joint-stock politics, shareholders were expected to be much less active in company affairs and to look mainly to the protection of their "financial" interests, which they could do through the evolving system of auditing, which we examine in chapter 8.

Constitutional Amendments

Finally, we turn to the ways in which the constitutional settlement could be changed during the life of a company. In 245 companies, 47.7 percent of the total, the GM was empowered to amend the constitution, although in 17 of these the approval of the directors was also required. In incorporating acts, the right to amend the company constitution was usually given in a longer clause outlining the rights of the GM. A typical example was the Macclesfield Canal act (1826), which, with certain restrictions, permitted the shareholders at a GM to "revoke, alter, amend, or change any of the Rules or Directions herein prescribed and laid down with regard to their Proceedings among themselves, as to them shall seem meet."[116] In all incorporating acts that permitted constitutional amendments, a simple majority at a single GM was required.[117] In unincorporated companies, by contrast, the original constitution was defended more carefully. Seventy-nine companies, 35.3 percent of all unincorporated companies, set the threshold for amendments at above 50 percent of the votes. These barriers rose over time, so that by the 1840s a majority were fixed at two-thirds or higher. Furthermore, while 97 of the 175 unincorporated companies that allowed amendments required a simple majority (or did not stipulate a threshold), many required this majority to be obtained at two successive GMs, and many also stipulated a higher quorum than normal.[118] It was particularly difficult to amend the constitution of the English and Scottish Law Fire and Life Assurance and Loan Association (1841), where 80 percent of the votes were required at two successive GMs, at both of which the quorum was twice as large as was required for normal GM decisions.[119]

There were significant differences between corporations, where amendments were permitted in just 23.8 percent of cases, and unincorporated companies, where 78.1 percent allowed amendments. Even where shareholders in corporations were allowed to amend the constitution, there were usually clearly stipulated exceptions. Of the sixty-nine corporations that allowed amendments, sixty-seven had some exceptions. All but one of these restricted changes to the procedures laid down in the act for calling GMs, the "time and place of meeting and voting," and electing directors. Eighteenth-century incorporating acts were much more likely to allow constitutional amendments than those in the nineteenth. In our sample, 73.2 percent of eighteenth-century constitutions permitted amendments, falling to 21.7 percent in the period

1800–29 and just 2.5 percent in 1830–44. In the Companies Clauses Consolidation Acts of 1845, there was no provision for constitutional amendments, demonstrating that by the time of the railway boom, the procedure was almost unknown. This sharp decline may partly be explained by the increasingly detailed constitutional provisions that were appearing in acts of incorporation. Whereas many eighteenth-century canal company acts had a single clause that contained most of the "proceedings among themselves," constitutions had become considerably more thorough by the mid-nineteenth century, and thus there may have been less need to revise them subsequently. But the decline also highlights the significance of the GM as a forum for shareholder participation in the eighteenth-century corporation and the shift toward more passive proprietaries in the nineteenth century, a passivity all the more dangerous because, as chapter 3 suggests, shareholders in corporations played little part in framing their constitutions.

Unincorporated companies were moving in the opposite direction, increasingly allowing GMs to amend constitutions, although, as noted above, procedures for doing so were often stricter than in those corporations where amendments were allowed. In the eighteenth century, 70.6 percent allowed amendments, and although this figure fell to 50.0 percent for companies formed in the first decade of the nineteenth century, the proportion steadily increased thereafter, rising to 91.7 percent in the years 1840–4. Table 5.2 shows that banks—in many respects the least "democratic" of all joint-stock companies—were the most likely to concede the right to amend. It may be that banks felt that they needed these provisions so that they would not miss the opportunity to engage in new areas of business or in branching where these were not already permitted by their deeds of settlement. Certainly several insurance companies found themselves encumbered by their original deeds restricting them to one line of underwriting or to particular forms of investment.[120] Consequently, relatively few banks or insurance companies required very high majorities at GMs to effect changes to their constitutions (table 5.2). The power to amend constitutions appears to have been less important for gas, shipping, and property companies, perhaps because their founders envisaged fewer opportunities for diversification outside their core activities, or perhaps because their deeds were less specific in the first place. After all, unlike banking or insurance companies, they were not in the business of selling trust in an invisible service or an invisible product with uncertain returns.

TABLE 5.2. **Percentage of unincorporated companies allowing constitutional amendments in main sectors**

Sector	(a) Number of companies	(b) Percentage allowing constitutional amendments	(c) Number allowing constitutional amendments	(d) Percentage of companies in column (c) requiring majority of over 50%
Banking	63	95.2	60	28.3
Gas	32	81.3	26	69.2
Insurance	61	80.3	49	51.0
Manufacturing/ trade	30	50.0	15	33.3
Property	8	75.0	6	66.7
Shipping	21	71.4	15	53.3

Notes: Companies allowing constitutional amendments include those where the directors' approval as well as GM approval was required. Column (d) expresses the number of companies requiring a greater than 50% majority as a percentage of *all* companies in column (c), including a handful where the threshold was not given and could not be assumed to be 50%.

Whereas corporations usually prohibited constitutional amendments to the procedures for electing directors and calling GMs, this kind of restriction was less common among unincorporated companies. Seventy-six companies, or 43.4 percent of all those that permitted amendments, disallowed any changes to the liability of shareholders, while 26.9 percent of such companies placed restrictions on changes to the procedure for company dissolution.[121] These types of restrictions continued to be part of the wider balance of rights and responsibilities between shareholders and company directors and managers. Nevertheless, there was a basic inequality in the power possessed by shareholders and directors over constitutions. While it was difficult for ordinary shareholders to implement constitutional changes in corporations and unincorporated companies alike, it was easier for directors to achieve the same end through means of the bylaw, as the above example of the Insurance Company of Scotland demonstrates. In corporations, too, the bylaw was a powerful instrument. Directors were usually prohibited from passing any that were contrary to the intentions of the incorporating act, but as early as 1723, in the case of *Child v. Hudson's Bay Company*, the courts upheld a bylaw that made debts of shareholders to the company a lien on their shares.[122] In unincorporated companies, especially banks that lent money to their shareholders, this provision was usually a constitutional arrangement, but the example of the Hudson's Bay Company shows that this kind of rule could be forced upon a body of shareholders without their consent. The inequality in power between directors and shareholders can also be observed in how the decision to seek incorporation—one of the most important steps an unincorporated company could take—was made. As noted in chapter 3, the constitutions of unincorporated companies increasingly made provision for a future application for corporate privileges, but in 63.7 percent of such companies the board could make the decision without reference to the GM. In general, if investors wished to shape the constitution and policy of their company, they were in a better position to do so in the early stages of its life or at crisis points and if the company was small. Once a company's affairs had settled down, it was difficult for shareholders to overcome the concerted policy of directors and managers, and, even if their rights were enshrined in the company's constitution, it was often difficult to ensure that these rights were respected.

Conclusions

The rights of shareholders examined in this chapter illustrate the great range of constitutional arrangements that were in place in joint-stock companies in our period. Sectoral differences were clearly important. This is not surprising. As Williston pointed out, "the law regulating the relations of the members [of a corporation] to each other and to the united body must differ according to the nature and objects of the corporation."[123] Small, early incorporated canal, river, bridge, gas, and water companies, for instance, mostly with a localized sphere of operations, gave greater rights to their shareholders than, for instance, the larger unincorporated joint-stock banks and insurance companies of the nineteenth century, not least because many of the former assumed a desire to participate on the part of their "economic" investors and also accepted that their businesses, sanctioned by Parliament, had a "public" purpose and accountability. It is also unsurprising that larger companies generally allowed less active shareholder participation than smaller ones. But across the joint-stock economy as a whole, and in particular among unincorporated companies, there was a reconfiguration of the power relations between shareholders and directors in the nineteenth century as companies moved from one generic type of constitution, which accorded extensive authority to the GM, to another that did not. A dual process, commencing in the early nineteenth century, divested shareholders of many of their powers and obligations. This had the effect of relocating the basis of power within companies from the GM to the board of directors and management. The trajectory was uneven and moved at different rates in different sectors. Some companies fought against the trend, and we can detect in the late 1830s and early 1840s a modest reversal of the tendency toward the removal of shareholder obligations and powers. Further systematic studies of company constitutions and governance practices will be needed to confirm trends after 1850. It is clear, however, that by the middle of the nineteenth century shareholders generally enjoyed less influence over the affairs of their companies than they had in the eighteenth century. As the number and size of joint-stock companies grew, many observers concluded that shareholders had little real power, even in areas such as the appointment of directors, where constitutional rights were almost universally vested in them. Moreover, when it came to key strategic decisions, a large body of evidence from the procedural records of companies demonstrates the relative impotence of shareholders when faced with concerted opposition from a united board of directors. As one barrister told a parliamentary committee in 1850, in joint-stock companies, "the shareholders are delivered over, bound hand and foot, to the mercy of the directors."[124] Shareholders were progressively more likely to acquiesce in this deliverance as their priorities shifted. Increasingly "financial" in outlook, they happily renounced powers that were no longer relevant to them and the obligations that had traditionally gone with them, in return for regular dividends and constitutional provisions that protected their "financial" interests. One aspect of this protection was the limitation of shareholder liability, which we discuss in chapter 7. First, however, we turn to the shareholder franchise and the company GM, where the political dimensions of business were most evident.

CHAPTER SIX

The Franchise and the General Meeting

When the people control the ballot box, they are likewise masters of the constitution.
—Aristotle[1]

This chapter examines two key features of corporate governance: the shareholder franchise, used to elect directors and for other important decisions, and the GM. Both highlight the extent to which companies were seen as political as well as economic entities. Political metaphors were widely used in the discussion of business in our period. The GM was sometimes portrayed as a company's "parliament," in which the actions of the executive could be brought to account by the legislature of shareholders. The lively proceedings at some GMs encouraged this analogy. The general court of the East India Company was described by one observer in 1807 as a "popular senate," which, unlike Parliament, carried "no impediment as to sex." It embodied an "uneasy constitutional relationship" between shareholders—including women—and directors: its proceedings were denounced by Macaulay as "riotous" and "virulent."[2] Nineteenth-century observers stretched the parliamentary analogy to other joint-stock companies. Robert Lowe called them "little republics."[3] Some boards of directors repeatedly referred to shareholders as their "constituents," as did Herbert Spencer.[4] The term was also employed by shareholders to remind directors of their responsibilities. William Davidson, a shareholder protesting against the actions of the directors of the Ballochney Railway Company in 1837, urged them to recall "their true duty to their constituents."[5] The use of political terminology by participants and observers of the joint-stock economy has been remarked upon by scholars of the period. Dunlavy, for example, has identified a move from "democracy" to "plutocracy" in shareholder franchises.[6] In this chapter, we argue that a move away from shareholder participation in the governance of companies came about not only through the evolution of less democratic franchises but also through a series of procedural changes, such as the increasing use of formal ballots, the use of proxy voting, and the increasing difficulty of summoning GMs. Many of these changes, like those discussed in chapters 4 and 5, were driven by the increasing size of companies and the growing geographical dispersal of shareholders.

We also argue that these developments are best understood in the context of simultaneous changes in national and, particularly, local government. Vernon's work, highlighting a shift from the active political participation in public arenas to a more privatized, passive form of politics, provides a useful framework for the study of joint-stock politics in this period. Vernon argues that mid-nineteenth-century England witnessed the "closure of the public political sphere": the replacement of the "direct democracy" of an earlier period with a more regulated, privatized system that effectively excluded the unenfranchised from involvement.[7] Of particular importance in this process was the demise of public institutions such as the county and town meeting. County meetings—which all ratepayers could attend—were an important feature of the eighteenth- and early nineteenth-century political landscape and could attract attendances in the thousands.[8] As Vernon observes, "The county meeting was then an indispensable occasion for the upwards and downwards communication of information and sentiment. It provided the only effective official arena in which those who were not propertied 40s. freeholders could question the use and abuse of the offices of county government."[9] Town meetings served a similar purpose and, by virtue of their inclusiveness and long history, were widely considered to command more authority than the improvement commissions that had emerged in the eighteenth century, often to oversee specific infrastructural developments.[10] From the 1830s, however, town and county meetings were in decline as instruments of government. Although in some places town meetings remained lively into the 1850s, real power in English towns was increasingly concentrated in the hands of municipal corporations, and local politics became a less public activity, more often conducted behind closed doors.[11] A similar thing was happening elsewhere in local government. The Sturges Bourne Acts of 1818 and 1819 established select vestries to administer poor relief, "emasculating" the more open vestries of the eighteenth century and their "beer hall" atmospheres.[12]

Changes to the electoral franchise played an important part in these developments. Franchises moved away from the principle of one man, one vote and began conspicuously to represent property. From 1818 the poor-law franchise was increasingly "wedded to property rights."[13] The election of select vestrymen was carried out according to a weighted franchise, in which inhabitants assessed for the poor rate at up to £50 were granted one vote each plus a further vote for every additional £25 of assessed property up to a maximum of six votes for property over £150. The same franchise was prescribed in the Lighting and Watching Act (1830) and the Highway Act (1835) and was used to elect poor-law guardians under the terms of the Poor Law Amendment Act (1834).[14] The Scottish poor-relief reforms of 1845 established elections on the basis of one vote for property valued at less than £20 with a graduated scale up to a maximum of six votes for property assessed at £500 or more.[15] Even areas of local government that did not adopt the weighted franchise—such as municipal corporations—reflected the entrenchment of property qualifications for political participation, as votes were restricted to male burgesses or ratepaying householders.[16]

Shareholder Franchises

The trend of assigning voting strength according to the amount of property was prefigured in joint-stock companies, which had long experimented with a variety of weighted franchises giving more power to larger shareholders. An early version of the graduated franchise can be found in the Greenland Company (1693), where £500 conferred one vote and £1,000 two votes, but no shareholder could cast more than this. The Harvard jurist Samuel Williston argued in 1888 that there was "gradual progress" from this low-ceiling vote capping to the situation by the second half of the nineteenth century, when capping had ceased to be the norm.[17] There has been, however, no comprehensive study of shareholder voting rights and procedures in eighteenth- and nineteenth-century Britain. Williston's account was based on case and statute law, not company constitutions, and barely considered unincorporated companies at all. In joint-stock banking, Alborn suggests that franchises became less "democratic" from the second half of the 1830s, but he bases this assertion mainly on the higher qualifications required to vote and does not attempt an analysis of company constitutions, giving an incomplete picture of trends.[18] Dunlavy has gone further, developing a tripartite typology of shareholder franchises: "democratic," consisting of one vote per shareholder; "plutocratic," consisting of one vote per share with no limit; and "prudent-mean," a term used by Alexander Hamilton referring to any franchise falling between these two extremes. Dunlavy argues that the balance of democratic, plutocratic, and prudent-mean franchises remained at around a third each for American companies chartered between the 1820s and 1850s but that during the later nineteenth century plutocratic franchises became the norm.[19] These categories, however, constitute a blunt instrument with which to analyze British and Irish franchises, because the vast majority, 84.8 percent, fall into the prudent-mean category. Only 4.3 percent of all companies in our sample adopted a "democratic" franchise, and only 9.5 percent a "plutocratic" one.[20] Clearly, the large prudent-mean category needs to be broken down if we are to uncover the changing patterns of shareholder franchises over time and between sectors.

To achieve this, the first step is to recognize the sheer variety of franchises that were in use in this period. Among the 507 companies in our database that specified a shareholder franchise, there were 233 different voting systems, of which 180 occurred only once and only 7 appeared ten times or more. We have divided these franchises into five categories, four of which are further broken down into two types, giving a total of nine franchise types. These types are fully described in the appendix to this chapter. Table 6.1 gives examples of each of the franchise types, which are arranged, crudely, in descending order of "plutocracy." The franchise had a fundamental impact on the distribution of power between different groups and individuals within a company. In the Corn Exchange Buildings Company of Dublin (1815), for example, the holder of one hundred shares had exactly the same voting strength as the holder of a single share. By contrast, at the Plymouth Union Bath Company (1828) the holder of one hundred shares was one hundred times more powerful. At the South Western Steam Packet Company (1843), where every five shares conferred one vote, the holder of one hundred shares had twenty votes. The holder of a single share had no vote at all. In between these two extremes were a range of different franchises. The right-hand column of table 6.1 illustrates the difference between the voting strength of

TABLE 6.1. **Relative voting strength of holders of 1, 2, 5, 10, 50, and 100 shares in selected companies**

Franchise type (see appendix)	Company	Franchise	Number of votes cast by holders of						Votes for 5 shares as % of votes for 100 shares
			1 share	2 shares	5 shares	10 shares	50 shares	100 shares	
1A	South Western Steam Packet Company (1843)	1 vote for every 5 shares	0	0	1	2	10	20	5.0%
1B	Plymouth Union Bath Company (1828)	1 vote per share	1	2	5	10	50	100	5.0%
2A	Liverpool and Manchester Railway Company (1826)	1 vote per share up to 20 shares; 1 vote for every 4 shares above 20	1	2	5	10	27	40	12.5%
2B	Wakefield Waterworks Company (1837)	1 vote for 1 share; 2 votes for 4 shares; 3 votes for 10 shares; 4 votes for 20 shares; plus 1 vote for every 10 shares above 20	1	1	2	3	7	12	16.7%
3A	Garnkirk and Glasgow Railway Company (1826)	1 vote for every 2 shares; maximum 10 votes	0	1	2	5	10	10	20.0%
3B	Warwick Gas Light Company (1822)	1 vote per share, maximum 20 votes	1	2	5	10	20	20	25.0%
4A	Poole Bridge Company (1834)	1 vote per share up to 10; 1 vote per 5 shares above 10; maximum 18 votes	1	2	5	10	18	18	27.8%
4B	Deptford Creek Bridge Company (1803)	1 vote for 2 shares; 2 votes for 5 shares; 3 votes for 10 shares; 4 votes for 15 shares; 5 votes for 20 shares or more	0	1	2	3	5	5	40.0%
5	Corn Exchange Buildings Company of Dublin (1815)	1 vote per shareholder	1	1	1	1	1	1	100.0%

TABLE 6.2. **Percentage of known franchise in each category by subperiod ($N = 507$)**

Franchise category (see appendix)	1720–89 ($N = 37$)	1790–9 ($N = 34$)	1800–9 ($N = 45$)	1810–9 ($N = 40$)	1820–4 ($N = 38$)	1825–9 (N = 69)	1830–4 ($N = 58$)	1835–9 ($N = 130$)	1840–4 ($N = 56$)
1. Uncapped linear	8.1	17.6	4.4	17.5	10.5	17.4	6.9	6.9	19.6
2. Uncapped graduated	0.0	0.0	0.0	0.0	0.0	8.7	17.2	19.2	26.8
3. Capped linear	56.8	73.5	53.3	42.5	42.1	29.0	20.7	21.5	10.7
4. Capped graduated	18.9	5.9	31.1	35.0	36.8	43.5	55.2	50.0	42.9
5. One-member-one-vote	16.2	2.9	11.1	5.0	10.5	1.4	0.0	2.3	0.0

five and one hundred shares in each of these companies, expressed as a percentage, as a rough guide to the impact of each franchise type on the balance of power within the company.[21]

Table 6.2 shows the five franchise categories by subperiod. Three points emerge. First, the one-member-one-vote franchise was never the norm: even in the subperiod 1720–89, it was used in only 16.2 percent of the companies for which we have data. It had largely disappeared by the late 1820s. Second, capped graduated-scale franchises were increasingly adopted, mainly at the expense of capped linear-scale franchises. Third, and most striking, an increasing proportion of companies did not cap the voting strength of large shareholders. This was perhaps the most important aspect of the shareholder franchise: where there was no cap, larger shareholders could wield considerable power.

A cap on votes could be imposed in two ways: by restricting the voting rights of large shareholders through the franchise or by limiting the number of shares that any shareholder could own. Figure 6.1 illustrates the decline in capping over our period. Before 1825, the proportion of uncapped franchises never rose above 20 percent, but they increased to 26.1 percent of the total in the later 1820s and reached 46.4 percent of all franchises by 1840–4. This chart shows that the popularity of the capped graduated scale in the unincorporated sector declined only slowly: 98.3 percent and 93.8 percent of insurance and banking companies, respectively, imposed a cap. Furthermore, caps in these sectors were usually quite low, commonly under ten votes in banks and between two and six votes in insurance. This was not necessarily the result

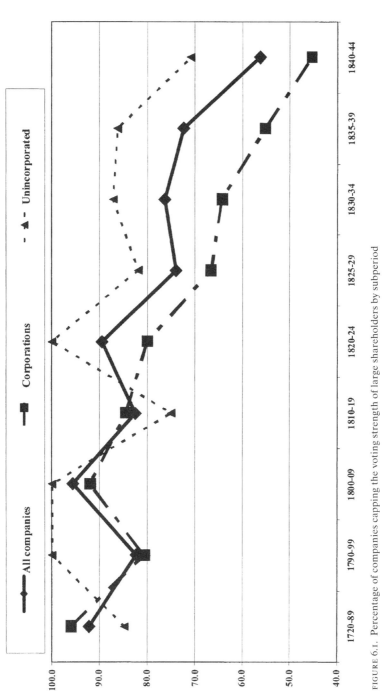

FIGURE 6.1. Percentage of companies capping the voting strength of large shareholders by subperiod

of a commitment to "democracy" or participation. The adoption of voting caps was often in fact part of a package of measures devised by company promoters to limit the potential for outsiders to take control, especially as many financial companies issued very large numbers of shares that were rarely paid up in full. These companies were more likely than others to specify a minimum period for shares to be held in order to confer a vote. In addition, over three-quarters of unincorporated companies made some provision for directorial veto over share transfers. Although such vetoes could be, and were, successfully challenged in the courts with the specific intention of strengthening shareholders' voting powers, they were part of a series of measures taken to protect companies from outside influence.

The decline in capping was much more pronounced in corporations, driven in part by the growth of the railways, where only 41.7 percent of companies imposed a cap. Indeed, railway companies tended to see the greatest displays of strength by large shareholders. Railway directors often expressed contempt for their smallest investors. In 1851, for instance, a director of the Northern and Eastern Railway thought it "too bad" that small shareholders were allowed "to take a prominent part in the proceedings of the Eastern Counties Company, and sway the decisions of a proprietary possessed of property to the amount of so many millions."[22] Other corporations were beginning to follow the example of railways in abandoning voting caps. The proportion of nonrailway corporations imposing caps stood at 82.9 percent for the period 1720–1834 and fell to 63.7 percent in 1835–44. While a small majority of companies in our sample still imposed some kind of cap by 1844, leaving voting power uncapped was sanctioned by the legislation of 1845 and 1862. Here, although the voting power of larger shareholdings was somewhat constrained by a default voting scale that allowed fewer votes per share above a set figure, the scale did not provide for a maximum number of votes.[23]

Another significant feature of shareholder participation was the role of the small proprietor. Many companies prohibited their smallest shareholders from voting at all, including, most famously, the East India Company, where in the eighteenth century a minimum of £500 of stock was required for a vote. In some companies in our sample, two shares were required to cast a vote and, in many cases, five or more. Alborn highlights concerns in the 1830s that an inclusive franchise would weaken the state "by empowering irresponsible voters." The banking crisis of 1836–7, Al-

born argues, seemed to confirm similar fears within joint-stock companies, prompting an increase in share denominations and greater efforts
to scale back shareholder participation in management.[24] As a result,
an increasing number of banking companies prohibited their smallest
shareholders from voting. Our data do not support Alborn's chronology.
Between 1720 and 1829, only six out of the nineteen banks in our sample (31.6 percent) excluded their smallest shareholders from a say in the
governance of the company, but this rose sharply to nine out of fifteen
(60.0 percent) in 1830–4. The trend continued into the second half of the
1830s, with sixteen out of twenty-eight new banks (57.1 percent) following suit. Thus, the move to exclude small shareholders from politics was
not a response to the crisis of 1836–7 but was a policy to which the majority of new banks were committed from the start of the decade.

Elsewhere, the shift toward exclusion began earlier still. Figure 6.2
shows by subperiod the percentage of companies excluding small shareholders from voting. Even in 1720–89, 16.2 percent of all companies restricted their smallest proprietors in this way, but after 1800 a rapid increase occurred, led by the unincorporated sector, peaking at 47.6 percent
of all companies in the early 1820s before stabilizing at around 40 percent for the rest of our period. The increase occurred at the same time as
the entrenchment of property qualifications in local government and can
therefore be seen as part of a consistent drive to close off popular participation in many areas of public life during the first third of the century.

Across the joint-stock economy, the exclusion of small shareholders
was driven by larger companies, especially those with low share denominations. In terms of nominal capital, companies where small shareholders could not vote were more than three times larger, on average, than
those where they could.[25] Table 6.3 shows the number and capital of companies in each sector imposing this restriction. In every sector except
railways, larger companies were more likely to exclude their smallest
shareholders from voting. They found the participation of small shareholders less appealing than smaller companies that tended to embody a
more inclusive political culture. Share denominations tended to be lower
in companies where small shareholders were excluded. In banking, the
mean share denomination was £62 where small shareholders could not
vote and £194 where they could. In insurance, the figures were £60 and
£518, respectively. These figures suggest that promoters of large companies were eager to attract the capital of small investors but not to permit them to vote. At a time of falling share denominations, companies

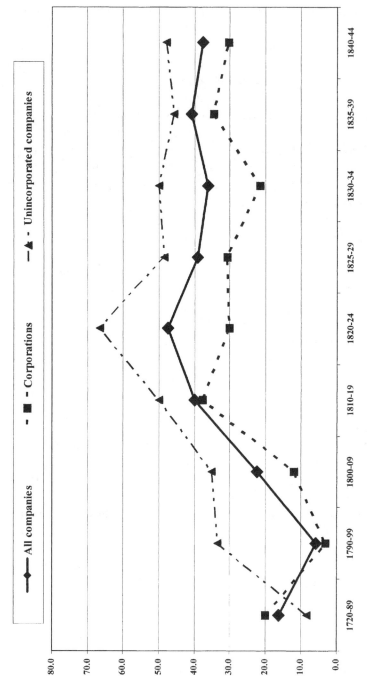

FIGURE 6.2. Percentage of companies prohibiting smallest shareholders from voting by subperiod and type of company ($N = 507$: 288 corporations, 219 unincorporated companies)

TABLE 6.3. **Exclusion of small shareholders from voting by sector and size**

Sector	Where smallest shareholders could vote		Where smallest shareholders could not vote	
	Number	Mean nominal capital (£)	Number	Mean nominal capital (£)
Banking	32	671,191	32	1,288,710
Bridges	24	38,465	9	106,820
Canals	53	123,849	7	195,357
Colonial	2	270,000	10	752,500
Gas	46	16,830	14	86,779
Harbors	17	41,229	12	324,896
Insurance	24	408,010	35	962,571
Manufacturing/trade	19	27,731	15	365,667
Property	16	12,434	14	141,643
Railways	48	472,420	12	382,577
Shipping	19	24,792	7	771,429
Water	33	31,159	7	58,930
ALL COMPANIES	333	199,750	174	615,485

reframed their constitutions accordingly.[26] Thus, the investment pool on which companies could draw was expanded, without exposing these companies to more volatile political pressures in the form of less wealthy and therefore potentially "irresponsible" voters.

Controversies over the Franchise and the Ballot

According to Dunlavy, in British corporations there was a "common-law practice of requiring that all votes at shareholder meetings be taken by a show of hands unless at least five shareholders (later reduced to three) demanded a 'poll.'"[27] Voting by show of hands rendered even the most complex franchise redundant by transforming it into a de facto one-man-one-vote system, at least until a ballot was called for. Nevertheless, there is plenty of evidence that great attention was paid to franchise design, not least by ordinary shareholders. Only seven constitutions in our sample of 514 failed to specify a franchise. At the establishment of companies, small proprietors were often eager to restrict the voting strength of large shareholders. When the Lyme-Regis Gas and Coke Company was formed in 1835, eighteen shareholders had a total of sixty-five shares. Of these, one individual, Major Henry Bayly, held fifteen. The second GM appointed a committee of five, including Bayly, to draw up "rules for the future Guidance of the Company." The GM was happy to delegate most issues to this committee, but, significantly, it reserved the decision on the franchise to itself, imposing a graduated scale. This gave Bayly four votes rather than the fifteen he would have had under a one-vote-per-share regime.[28] At another small gas company in Dursley, Gloucestershire, an early GM resolved that the franchise should be one vote per share. Soon, however, the shareholders rescinded this resolution, and decided on a more democratic franchise, whereby holders of one to five shares had one vote and holders of six shares or more had two. It is not clear whether shareholders forced this franchise onto a reluctant board, but a relatively high attendance at the meeting concerned suggests that this was a proprietorial rather than a directorial decision.[29] Elsewhere, company promoters and directors were able to thwart attempts by shareholders to impose a particular franchise. At the Dundee, Perth, and London Shipping Company (1826), some shareholders attempted to restrict the number of shares an individual could hold to sixteen, but this effort was defeated. The meeting did, however, manage to restrict to four the number of proxy votes that any shareholder could wield.[30]

In the case of decisions of particular importance, many constitutions specified a different voting scale: sometimes this was more democratic than the standard one, in other cases less democratic. For example, the decision to dissolve the company often required the consent of the majority (or a two-thirds majority) of shareholders *and* the holders of the majority of shares. In effect, this meant that the decision had to be ratified on *both* a one-member-one-vote *and* a one-vote-per-share basis.[31] This double franchise could also apply to other key votes, such as the dismissal of a director. The incorporated Swansea Gas Light Company (1830) required a three-quarters majority under its normal one-vote-per-share franchise *and* a three-quarters majority in the number of shareholders to remove a director.[32] Conversely, companies with relatively democratic franchises for normal decisions sometimes permitted larger shareholders a greater say over specific issues. In three Scottish fishing companies, the franchise was one vote per share up to a maximum of four votes, but the cap did not apply when considering the dissolution of the company or the enlargement of the capital stock.[33] In the Kennet and Avon Canal Company (1794), a cap of ten votes applied for all issues except the election of directors, where it was raised to fifty votes.[34]

Sometimes, controversy over the voting scale resulted in legal investigations. The Aberdeen, Leith, and Clyde Shipping Company was established by contract of copartnery, one section of which ruled that the directors would be annually elected by "a Majority of Stock Holders." Another section, referring to GMs, elaborated further: "it is understood that at all these meetings each partner shall be entitled to give as many Votes as he holds shares in the Company." The same article further stipulated "that the Resolutions of the Partners or a Majority of them at the General Meetings shall be binding on the Company, such resolution not being inconsistent with this contract."[35] In February 1820 an SGM resolved unanimously that, in future, the franchise for electing the directors should be one member, one vote.[36] This resolution must have occasioned disquiet somewhere in the company, because the opinion of the company's law agent was sought. As a result of this opinion, the next OGM rescinded the constitutional change. The law agent was asked to decide, first, "whether the mode of calculating Votes in Electing the Annual Committee is by the number of shares or by the number of voters" and, second, whether the resolution passed at the SGM was "inconsistent" with the contract of copartnery. His decision rested on the interpretation of the phrase "a Majority of Stock Holders," which he decided referred to those holding a majority of stock rather than a majority of individuals. He therefore ruled that the contract provided for the election of directors on a one-vote-per-share basis (the same franchise used for other decisions at GMs) and that the previous resolution was unconstitutional.[37] This is a good example of a legal rebuff to shareholders who were seeking to assert their electoral rights as they perceived them.

Voting by ballot had a long history in joint-stock politics: Charles I had tried to foist a ballot onto the East India Company as early as the 1620s. Among the companies in our sample, however, explicit constitutional reference to ballots was rare in the eighteenth century, when less than 20 percent mentioned them. They became much more common in the early 1800s, with a majority making provision for them. Although the proportion fell away a little in the early 1840s, balloting provisions remained common. The dip might have occurred because ballots were increasingly being taken for granted: that they had become the norm is suggested by their inclusion in the Consolidation Acts of 1845.[38]

While the number of shareholders required to demand a ballot was usually specified—five was a common figure and the common-law default for corporations—other aspects of ballot procedure varied enormously, creating potential for confusion. Some constitutions required ballots to be taken immediately, others that the ballot be kept open for a period

of hours, while some insisted that the ballot take place on a day subsequent to a GM and be advertised in advance among shareholders. Ballots could lead to scenes of chaos. In 1818, the shareholders of the Drury
Lane Theatre met to elect an auditor. The chairman asked the meeting
for a show of hands, but on checking the company's act, doubts arose
whether the election could be held in this way. Lord Yarmouth proposed
"that every gentleman should write his name down upon a piece of paper, with the number of shares he possessed, and that the election might
so be conducted," and much debate ensued. One proprietor suggested
that the vote be left until the next meeting, which was met with cries of
"No, no, certainly not." The issue was put to a vote, and it was decided
to proceed with the ballot. After some further discussion, a shareholder
moved that the ballot be closed, which was opposed by others, including the chairman, who argued that more time was needed to ensure they
abided by "the spirit of the act." Lengthy squabbles broke out about various aspects of the company's affairs, and when the shareholders tired of
these, cries of "ballot, ballot . . . resounded through the saloon," and the
chairman finally counted the votes.[39]

How ballots affected power relations within companies is debatable.
Where ballots were held subsequent to a GM, there was greater potential for shareholder involvement—those who were not at the meeting
could take part in the ballot—but also greater opportunity for the board
to muster its voting strength in advance of the poll and crush dissent. In
some cases, however, shareholders supported ballots as a fairer system
of voting because directors could attempt to "manage" a controversial
vote by means of the show of hands. For example, at a stormy SGM of
the Arigna Iron and Coal Company in 1825, a motion by shareholders to
appoint a committee of investigation into the profits made by the directors from the company's purchase of the land on which the mines were
situated was put to a show of hands, and only 22 out of the 157 present
voted for it.[40] These shareholders objected to the vote being decided by a
show of hands "because it was contrary to the Act of Parliament, which
expressly declares, that all questions at a General or Special General
Meeting, shall be decided by the Proprietors there present, according
to the number of votes which they are entitled to give. . . . It is therefore
evident that no shew of hands could decide as to the number of votes, as
one man might in his own right have four votes, and likewise hold four
proxies."[41] The shareholders submitted to the chairman a requisition for
a ballot, but he declared that the requisition came too late—the meeting

had just been dissolved. The shareholders then sought legal advice, and at the next OGM successfully argued that "the sense of the proprietors ought to be taken in a legal and decisive manner," and a ballot was set for the following month.[42] The board then attempted to subvert the ballot by restricting participation in it to those who had attended the OGM but in the end managed to win the vote comfortably even without the use of this "trick."[43]

By the 1830s the ballot was closely associated with the joint-stock economy, and its prevalence was used to justify calls for parliamentary reform. At a well-attended meeting of freeholders in a Hackney tavern in 1830, Sir J. S. Lilly argued in favor of parliamentary ballots as the best check upon bribery and corruption: "It had been said that vote by ballot was an un-English custom—he [Lilly] asked was the East India Company, the directors of which were elected by ballot, un-English? Were the insurance companies un-English?"[44] Recent work on the ballot, however, has suggested that, while it was a cornerstone of radical demands through the nineteenth century, it also had other, less democratic ramifications. Vernon argues that, as a result of the introduction of the secret ballot at parliamentary and municipal elections in 1872,

> many of the electoral events which had previously afforded the disenfranchised their most powerful role were eroded or abolished. No longer could the disenfranchised vote at the nomination or hold a vigil beside the hustings to intimidate the voters, nor could they deploy exclusive dealing, for how were they to tell how the shopkeepers and tradesmen had voted[?] . . . [A]fter 1872 the individual voter was less troubled by the moral, physical, and economic influence of either the disenfranchised or the employer, he and his conscience were left alone in the polling booth, it was an entirely private affair. . . . In this reading the Ballot Act . . . [was] part of the closing down of the public political sphere.[45]

Crook and Crook agree. During the nineteenth century, they assert, "Britain moved decisively from a public system to a secret system," in which voting procedures were becoming privatized and domesticated.[46] Poor-law elections for the new boards of guardians after 1834 used "private polling," involving signed voting papers delivered to ratepayers' homes, which was certainly less public than a show of hands.[47] This also became the procedure in municipal corporations from 1835 and local boards of public health from 1848.[48] In the last case, voting was by signed papers, left at the houses of voters three days in advance of the election.[49] No company in our sample entirely divorced the voting process from the GM, but some did "domesticate" certain important votes. The deed of the Hampshire Banking Company (1834), for example, stipulated that, at least twenty-one days before the OGM, the company would send out to all those eligible to vote a list of the shareholders qualified to be directors and that each shareholder would mark his or her votes against the name(s) on the list and return it by ten o'clock on the day of the GM. The votes would be counted at the GM and the result declared.[50]

If few companies went as far as some branches of local government in privatizing the voting process, their widespread use of a ballot meant that many shareholders were excluded from a full voice in the government of their company. In many cases—the 174 companies in our sample where the smallest shareholders could not participate in ballot votes—they were completely excluded. The ballot privatized the company's affairs and the role of the individual shareholder. It held out to directors the promise of an end to the potentially subversive influence of group dynamics in GMs. In this respect it is undoubtedly significant that in ten of our twelve sectors, the companies whose constitutions made provision for voting by ballot were larger than those that did not. Shipping companies that provided for ballots were nineteen times larger than those that did not; bridge companies that did were six times larger. The boards of large companies faced sizable masses of potentially unruly proprietors who, if organized, might force their will on the directors. Franchises that represented property rather than individuals and ballots that civilized and privatized the voting process offered directors invaluable methods of control, "closing down" public decision making and providing useful means of manipulating votes.

Manipulating Votes? Stock Splitting and Proxies

When the specified franchise was used, it was often susceptible to manipulation, especially by those whose shareholdings were large but whose voting strength was, in theory, comparatively small, as in the case of companies that set low maximum voting thresholds. One way in which the restrictions on the number of votes permitted to be cast by individual shareholders could be overcome was stock splitting, in other words dividing stock among individuals in order to maximize its voting strength.

Thus, for example, in a company where shareholders had a vote for every share up to a stipulated maximum, a proprietor could transfer shares beyond the maximum to a relative and thereby secure votes on the excess shares. In combination with the use of proxies, this enabled large shareholders to overcome voting caps and exercise considerable power within a company. The East India Company's franchise gave holders of £500 of stock one vote, but no further voting rights were carried by additional stock, a franchise that encouraged frenetic stock splitting during the struggle for control of the company in the mid-eighteenth century.[51] To restrict the incentives for stock splitting, a reform in 1767 aimed at the EIC but referring only to "certain" unspecified "public companies or corporations," required stock to have been held for six months before it conferred voting rights.[52] In 1773 a new sliding-scale franchise was introduced in the EIC, and the minimum period of shareholding was extended to twelve months.[53] An analogous political practice was the creation of "faggot votes," which was rife in the Scottish counties following the Reform Act (Scotland) of 1832. The adoption of a new franchise based on properties with an annual value of £10 or more meant that, in Ferguson's words, "To create votes a proprietor had only to portion up an estate into as many life-rent interests as would yield each part £10 of annual value." As a result, both Whigs and Tories inflated the size of their electorates. In Peebles-shire in the mid-1840s, for example, some three hundred votes, out of a county "electorate" of seven hundred, were "faggot votes."[54] Lord John Russell, opposing the Reform Bill of 1859, argued that the admission of forty-shilling freeholders to the borough franchise would "encourage the manufacture of faggot votes."[55] Promoters of joint-stock companies were certainly aware of the practice in the political sphere. Indeed, the same term, "faggot votes," was widely used. In 1853, for example, one reformer argued in favor of rules being introduced into railway companies to regulate voting, hoping that this would put a stop to the creation of "what are technically called 'faggot-votes.'"[56]

In our period, many constitutions made the practice of stock splitting more difficult by requiring shares to be held for a certain period of time—usually three or six months, but in some cases, as with the EIC, even twelve—before a shareholder could vote in respect of them. Fifty-one incorporated (17.6 percent) and 102 unincorporated companies (45.5 percent) in our sample had some such restriction. There were, however, comparatively few examples of explicit restrictions on stock split-

ting. Exceptions include the Royal Canal Company (1789), in which proprietors were required to take an oath before voting that they did not
hold the shares in trust for anyone else and that they had not bought
the shares with the intention to sell them straight back to the original
owner or to anyone else.[57] The Ulster Railway Company (1836) required
a forfeit of £5 per share to be paid should any shareholder "fraudulently
or collusively assign or transfer any such Shares to any other Person or
Persons, in Trust for them, him, or her, for the Purpose of obtaining a
greater Number of Votes, at any General or Special General Meeting."[58]

Such explicit rules were rare perhaps partly because directors sometimes engaged in stock splitting themselves in order to enlarge their voting power. Three days before the crucial SGM of the Arigna Iron and
Coal Company mentioned above, four directors had made a series of
transfers "evidently for the purpose of creating votes, which might be
made available at the meeting," according to the dissentient shareholders' solicitor.[59] The subsequent parliamentary inquiry established that
"from fifty to sixty new proprietors were created" in this way and that
none should have been allowed to vote in the SGM, as the company's
rules placed a block on voting for the first six months and also prohibited
share transfers when the sellers owed the company money, which three
of the directors did.[60] Although the English law courts, when confronted
with issues concerning the transfer and ownership of shares, were fairly
consistent in upholding any procedures set out in company constitutions, the silence of most constitutions on the subject placed those trying to prevent the practice on uncertain ground.[61] As a result, stock splitting continued long into the nineteenth century. In 1877, for instance,
the right of shareholders in the New British Iron Company to split stock
was upheld in the Chancery Division in the case of *Moffat v. Farquhar*,
which confirmed a similar decision made in the case of the Stranton Iron
Company in 1873.[62] As Williston explained with reference to *Moffat v.
Farquhar*, "a shareholder may distribute his stock in lots of ten among
his friends, and thereby secure, in a clumsy and troublesome way, a vote
for every share."[63]

If stock splitting and "faggot votes" caused some resentment, the use
of proxy votes to force measures onto reluctant bodies of shareholders
was perhaps the most controversial of all the procedures used to exercise power in the joint-stock company, although it has been largely overlooked, even by historians who have examined the franchise.[64] Proxy voting was outlawed in the EIC's general court—the ban aimed to restrict

the influence of Dutch shareholders—but it was allowed in another important legislative chamber, the House of Lords, until abolished in 1868.[65] Walter Bagehot was scathing about this practice, and historians have echoed his verdict.[66] Snow remarks that the practice "made the House of Lords more oligarchic and certainly less responsive to change. . . . Those who held proxies were, in fact, the select of the select."[67] Proxy votes could sometimes change the result of divisions in the House, and they attracted the wrath of reformers in the early 1830s.[68] In one division in 1833, it emerged that one peer whose vote had been cast by proxy had died on the day of the vote, probably before the division.[69] Proxy voting in local government elections worsened the abuses that arose from plural and "ticket" voting. Rent collectors and estate agents often held large numbers of proxy votes entrusted to them by local landowners. An individual at one election had as many as 833 proxies, and one critic claimed that, at Gravesend in Kent, "the proxies held by two rent-collectors alone decided the election of the majority of Poor Law Guardians."[70]

Abuses of the proxy system were also discussed by observers of joint-stock companies. Although, on the face of it, the implications of proxy voting for shareholder participation could be positive, in that it enabled shareholders to cast votes without the inconvenience of having to attend a GM, the actual effects, according to contemporaneous comment, were to strengthen the hands of directors and management. In 1853 one critic of railway companies introduced another political metaphor: "by means of the proxy system directors can always overwhelm anticipated opposition, and secure the election of their own nominee. This system has caused directorates to become close boroughs, and two or three active spirits direct the affairs of the companies."[71] Historians have concurred with his assessment. Robbins, for example, asserts that, as "railway capital became dispersed over an immense number of stockholders . . . the board could always find enough proxies to carry its resolutions and approve its selections to fill up vacancies."[72] The standard procedure for appointing a proxy, found in all acts of incorporation, for instance, allowed proxies to act on all matters, using their own "opinion and judgement" as they think proper.[73] Company records demonstrate the importance of proxies. The Great Western Railway director, George Henry Gibbs, recorded in his diary that on 16 February 1838 he was "engaged all day in writing for proxies." On 30 November in the same year, he spent another whole day "registering proxies, examining the transfers and taking measures to increase our strength," in advance of an important vote on

the Great Western's gauge. Gibbs argued that the active canvassing for
proxies by directors was necessary because of the stock-splitting activities of their opponents: "our opponents are splitting their votes, which
calls for increased exertion on our part. . . . What other course could we
possibly pursue than that of strengthening ourselves by every means in
our power?" he asked himself.[74] Gibbs's efforts paid off: the board won
the crucial ballot by 7,792 votes to 6,145. No less than 74.5 percent of
the votes supporting the board were cast by proxy.[75] The effectiveness of
this policy of "strengthening" directors' voting power can also be seen at
the Eastern Counties Railway Company, on a motion to merge with the
Norfolk Railway Company in 1849. At the GM, 138 shareholders voted
in person to approve the merger and 101 against it, a victory by 3,287
votes to 2,470. This was not a large enough majority as stipulated by the
company's act of Parliament, but 17,716 proxy votes were cast, all in favor of amalgamation, giving the pro-merger party an overwhelming victory by 21,003 votes to 2,470. Although the opponents "disputed" the
proxies, there was little that they could do.[76]

There was also conflict in other sectors over proxies. At the Dundee,
Perth, and London Shipping Company in 1832, the proposal by the directors to move into steam navigation aroused the opposition of shareholders, who resolved that "no Mandates shall be received unless they
are either holograph of the Parties or regularly held."[77] The directors just
managed to stave off a rebellion, but at future meetings they took no
chances, packing them with large numbers of proxy voters.[78] The Manchester, Bolton, and Bury Canal Company voted in July 1834 to remove
the entire board of directors; there is no record of any proxies at this
meeting. However, when in the following month a new board was elected,
more proxy votes were cast than votes in person, and seven members of
the old board were elected back onto the new board.[79] A decade later,
an SGM attended by forty-five shareholders in person and a further
twenty-nine by proxy, voted by a show of hands in favor of delaying for
six months a decision to merge with the Manchester and Leeds Railway.
A ballot was demanded, however, and a combination of the larger shareholdings of the minority and the proxy votes in their control defeated
the proposed delay by 2,518 votes to 698, a good example of how dissent
could be crushed when proxies were permitted.[80] Shareholders, though,
could also play the proxy game and ambush their board. At an OGM of
the Royal West India Mail Steam Company, the directors' report, recommending a dividend of £2 per share, was "carried by a large majority

of the proprietors present." Some shareholders then demanded a ballot and secured a bonus of £5 per share, by a majority of forty-seven—"the result of 431 votes by proxy, which one or two proprietors had obtained" prior to the issue of the directors' report. The entire board resigned in protest.[81]

Proxy voting was already common in the eighteenth century: 84.9 percent of the companies in our sample from this period allowed proxy voting for all or some shareholders, and the remaining eleven constitutions did not mention proxies. According to Williston, the absence of any mention of proxy voting in a company's charter meant that such votes were not allowed at common law; indeed, he believed, "it is very doubtful if the authority of a by-law would have been held . . . sufficient to confer the right."[82] Another authority explained that in the eighteenth century, "the prevailing view was that the shareholder must exercise his vote in person. In most cases proxies were allowed, but in the absence of such provision the shareholder had no right to appoint a proxy to vote for him."[83] As these comments suggest, the potential for controversy was always recognized, and as a result, some companies that did permit proxy voting attempted to limit its power by capping the number of proxy votes that any individual could hold. Over three-quarters of all eighteenth-century companies allowing proxies specified a cap. Proxy voting came under sustained assault in the early nineteenth century, mirroring the considerable hostility to proxies expressed in local and national government at this time. There were three strands to this trend. First, there was a decline in provision for proxy voting in company constitutions. Although the proportion of corporations allowing proxy votes always remained above 70 percent, among unincorporated companies the proportion fell from 50 percent in the eighteenth century to around 30 percent in the early nineteenth century. Second, thirty-one companies, mostly in English banking and insurance, explicitly excluded proxy voting, which had not happened in the eighteenth century. Third, sixty-five companies (12.6 percent of our sample) allowed proxy voting but confined it to certain groups of shareholders, typically women or those resident at a certain distance. The first company to do so was the East Lothian and Merse Whale Fishing Company (1751), but it was relatively unusual until the 1820s, from which point at least 11.4 percent of new companies in our sample adopted the restriction (peaking at 22.0 percent in 1830–4). Fifteen of these went further, *requiring* female shareholders to vote by proxy.

Despite the controversy surrounding it, however, proxy voting survived and became increasingly widespread from the later 1820s. By the 1840s, almost all unincorporated companies (91.7 percent) allowed some of their shareholders to vote by proxy, converging on the practice in corporations. Furthermore, capping proxy votes became increasingly rare, while legal changes normalized proxy voting. The Consolidating Acts of 1845 allowed proxy voting for all shareholders as the default position for companies thereafter incorporated by act of Parliament.[84] In a complete reversal of the eighteenth-century position, constitutional silence was now taken to prove the legality of proxy voting. A consulting actuary, in a legal handbook for insurance companies published in 1851, explained unambiguously that the right to vote by proxy "will rest upon the conditions of the Deed of Settlement; but if the Deed of Settlement is silent upon the subject, it is to be taken that he [the shareholder] has the right so to vote."[85]

Although the ballot and proxy votes stacked the odds in favor of management, votes did not always have to be won in order to achieve their objective. At a lively meeting of the West Middlesex Waterworks Company in 1810, the issue of the outside interests of the directors was discussed, particularly the fact that several also sat on the board of the York Buildings Waterworks Company. A motion calling for the dismissal of those who sat on both boards was passed on a show of hands, but then a ballot was demanded. The ballot reversed this decision, by 142 votes to 120. The close vote, however, made their position untenable, and later that month eight directors resigned.[86] In 1833, the shareholders of the Equitable Gas Light Company expressed discontent with the system of directorial remuneration written into the deed of settlement. Directors were paid on a sliding scale in proportion to revenue, but some shareholders wanted the board to be remunerated in proportion to the dividend. A proposal to change the system was twice put to a show of hands in 1834 and 1835 and was twice defeated, 20–12 and 14–11, respectively. After the latter vote the shareholders insisted on a ballot, but this went against them too, 79–37. At the next GM, however, it was reported that the directors would comply "with the wish expressed by many of the Proprietors at the late Special General Meeting" and would recommend to the shareholders a system of remuneration varying according to the dividend.[87] If shareholders displayed sufficient persistence, they could force concessions without actually mustering the numbers required to defeat the board in a vote.

Quorums and Calling General Meetings

Several other variables helped determine the level and quality of share-holder participation in joint-stock politics. Two of the most important were the size of the GM quorum and the threshold for requesting an SGM. The quorum—we use figures for OGMs because those for SGMs were often not explicitly given and were sometimes set at different thresholds depending on the issue being discussed—reflected the extent of shareholder involvement in corporate governance, with a higher quorum entailing a greater expectation of participation.[88] Indeed, in many companies, especially eighteenth-century corporations, there was a requirement to be present at OGMs either in person or by proxy, on pain of a fine. A typical example from the Warwick and Birmingham Canal Company's act of 1793 ruled that, if an inquorate meeting for the election of directors was followed by *another* inquorate meeting, shareholders who were not present, in person or by proxy, at the second meeting would forfeit five shillings, to be deducted from the next dividend payment.[89] This was common in canals, where the quorum averaged nearly a quarter of the total number of shares, and also in early railway companies.[90] The expectation of attendance, however, declined in the nineteenth century. Figure 6.3 shows that the mean quorum in eighteenth-century companies amounted to over 16 percent of total shares, whereas in the nineteenth century it never rose above 6 percent. Company size was one factor behind this decline: the correlation between the quorum as a percentage of the shares and the nominal capital of the company was $r = -0.30$.[91] As shareholder bases became increasingly dispersed, it may have been simply unrealistic to expect a large attendance at GMs. Across all sectors by the early 1840s, however, an average joint-stock company OGM could act competently if the holders of just over 4 percent of the shares were present, signaling a clear move away from direct shareholder participation in governance.

SGMs were another important mechanism of shareholder oversight. They could usually be called by directors, and most constitutions—479 of our 514—also specified a procedure for shareholders to call SGMs, usually requiring a certain number of shareholders, or the holders of a certain number of shares, to sign a requisition and send it to the directors or the secretary of the company. A higher percentage of shares needed to call an SGM suggests a lower degree of accessibility to the mechanisms of corporate governance. Conversely, a low threshold suggests that

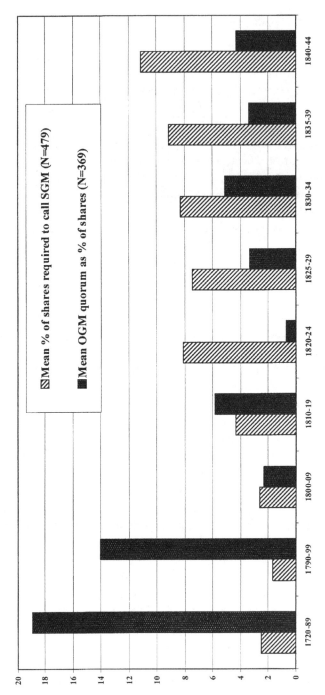

FIGURE 6.3. Mean quorum as percentage of shares and mean percentage of shares required to call SGMs by subperiod, all companies for which data are available

shareholders were able to participate more fully in the governance of the company. Figure 6.3 shows a fairly persistent upward movement in the average SGM threshold over time. By the early 1840s, the average new company required the owners of more than 10 percent of its shares to call an SGM, more than twice the percentage required on average for a GM to be quorate. This was a stiff requirement given the increasing dispersal of share ownership, especially in banking, insurance, and railways. The mean SGM threshold was comparatively high in banking (9.8 percent of the shares) and insurance (9.4 percent) and lowest among colonial (1.8 percent) and shipping companies (2.4 percent). This may reflect the large size and dispersed ownership of colonial companies and the traditional importance of shareholder participation in shipping. Gas companies had a high mean quorum for GMs (8.6 percent of the shares) *and* a high SGM threshold (10.6 percent), reflecting their local shareholder bases and small size: it would be relatively easy to get the necessary signatures on an SGM requisition, and, similarly, a high quorum was feasible. Water and harbor companies also had comparatively high thresholds. In general, although there were notable sectoral variations, the data confirm rising SGM thresholds over time in both incorporated and unincorporated companies, though the latter had higher thresholds, on average, than the former (10.4 percent against 7.5 percent).[92] This may reflect the tendency for corporations, in many sectors, to be viewed as more "public" institutions and, even in the later period, to allow their shareholders easier access to the mechanisms of governance.

Even more fundamental as an indicator of access was the number of OGMs held each year. Other things being equal, the more frequent the OGM, the more effectively shareholder oversight could be maintained. This was recognized in 1839 by John Fairfull Smith, who argued for greater publicity of the affairs of joint-stock banks, restrictions on the reelection of directors, and a semiannual OGM at which shareholders should be able to appoint auditors. In this way the prevalent "system of mystery and concealment" in banking might be undermined.[93] Thus the more frequent OGM could be viewed as part of a package of devices that promised greater transparency in corporate governance. In this light, it is significant that there was a trajectory toward fewer OGMs over time, at least until the 1830s. While the majority of companies (93.8 percent) held either one or two OGMs per annum, nineteen companies, fourteen of them dating from the eighteenth century, had more than two OGMs a year. This practice all but disappeared in the nineteenth century, and the annual OGM, used by only 38.4 percent of eighteenth-century companies, became the standard model, found in 88.1 percent of companies established in the first half of the 1830s. In the late 1830s and early 1840s, there was a revival of the semiannual OGM, perhaps indicating that Smith's arguments were resonating with some. It is significant, however, that the quarterly OGM, common in the eighteenth century, did not make a comeback, suggesting the limits to shareholder participation envisaged in these constitutions.

Another measure of shareholder access to governance, and of the extent to which a company was perceived as a "public" or "private" entity, was the way in which GMs were advertised. Here, we are focusing on the methods used to call SGMs rather than OGMs, because the latter were often held on specified dates at specified places, whereas SGMs, by their nature, always required notice to be given to shareholders in some way. Morris has described the "printed notice"—together with the GM itself, the published subscription list, the annual report, and the printed rules and regulations—as one of the core elements of the "subscriber democracies," the middle-class voluntary associations, that flourished in British towns from the 1780s.[94] This was also an issue in local government, where methods of calling vestry meetings could be contentious and perceived as partisan.[95] Almost all the constitutions in our sample specified how GMs were to be advertised to shareholders, which itself indicates the priority given to this by company promoters. The data are summarized in table 6.4. Most required either an advertisement in one or more newspapers (the newspapers were often specified) or a circular to shareholders or both of these methods. SGMs of the Irish Waste Land Improvement Society (1836), for example, had to be advertised in two London newspapers and one in Dublin.[96] In some companies—for example, the Shropshire Banking Company (1836)—the directors were required to call an SGM by circular when a group of shareholders demanded it, but if they failed to do so, then the shareholders could call the SGM by advertising in two Shrewsbury newspapers.[97] Other kinds of advertisement were sometimes specified, ranging from notices displayed on church doors and at market crosses and the Royal Exchange in London to the provision of the Rutherglen Gas Light Company (1841) that SGMs would be called "by tuck of drum, through Rutherglen, on two several days previous to the Meeting."[98] There were significant differences between corporations and unincorporated companies, and between sectors. More than three-quarters of all incorporated companies

TABLE 6.4. **Percentage of companies specifying methods of advertising SGMs by type of company and subperiod**

Subperiod	All companies				Corporations				Unincorporated companies			
	Number	Circular (%)	Newspaper (%)	Other (%)	Number	Circular (%)	Newspaper (%)	Other (%)	Number	Circular (%)	Newspaper (%)	Other (%)
1720–9	31	22.6	80.6	9.7	22	4.5	95.5	13.6	9	66.7	44.4	0.0
1790–9	33	6.1	97.0	3.0	31	3.2	100.0	0.0	2	50.0	50.0	50.0
1800–9	42	19.0	88.1	2.4	25	20.0	88.0	4.0	17	17.6	88.2	0.0
1810–9	38	31.6	84.2	2.6	31	25.8	90.3	3.2	7	57.1	57.1	0.0
1820–4	38	44.7	86.8	2.6	20	40.0	80.0	5.0	18	50.0	94.4	0.0
1825–9	67	29.9	88.1	3.0	37	18.9	91.9	5.4	30	43.3	83.3	0.0
1830–4	57	52.6	71.9	3.5	27	22.2	92.6	7.4	30	80.0	53.3	0.0
1835–9	128	50.8	70.3	3.1	58	17.2	96.6	3.4	70	78.6	48.6	2.9
1840–4	55	50.9	81.8	5.5	33	24.2	100.0	6.1	22	90.9	54.5	4.5
ALL	489	38.7	80.6	3.7	284	19.0	93.7	4.9	205	65.9	62.4	2.0

Note: Some companies specified more than one method, so percentages do not add up to 100.

used newspapers to advertise their SGMs, and this practice remained important across the whole period. Even railways, which were more likely to have bodies of distant shareholders, relied on newspapers for advertising SGMs. By contrast, after the 1820s unincorporated companies, especially in banking, gas, and shipping, tended to rely on the circular.

While there was no simple relationship between the method of advertising GMs and the transparency of governance, the method chosen reveals a great deal about a company's status as a "public" or "private" body. Contemporaries recognized that circulars were a way of avoiding the publicity that newspaper notices gave to company affairs. At the end of 1825, when the disgruntled shareholders of the Arigna Iron and Coal Company requisitioned the directors for an SGM, they also asked for a complete list of shareholders so that a circular could be sent to them outlining the reasons for the meeting. The shareholders expressed reluctance to place an advertisement in the newspapers, wishing "to avoid, if possible, the imputation of injuring the concerns of the Company, by giving unnecessary publicity to the grounds for a dissatisfaction which existed." But when the directors twice refused the requisition, the shareholders placed their notice in the press.[99] Their interest piqued, journalists tried to attend the meeting, but the directors "resolutely refused to allow admission to Reporters, and indeed, took every precaution to prevent their proceedings from finding their way to the public."[100] Nevertheless, shareholders were allowed to take notes, which "several" proceeded to do "diligently," and these notes were subsequently reported at length.[101] Over time, as table 6.4 indicates, there was a greater use of circulars to call shareholders' meetings. It could be argued that this represented an element in the privatization of the affairs of a corporation or an unincorporated company, a "closing down," in Vernon's words, of the public decision making process.[102] Public advertisement, however, remained dominant. This was reflected in the consolidating legislation of 1845, where it was provided that SGMs be announced "by advertisement" in a prescribed newspaper or, alternatively, in any local newspaper.[103] Although the shareholder in a joint-stock company was increasingly regarded as an individual owner of property rather than as a member of a collective association, the GM remained, in some senses, a "public" occasion and was still considered sacrosanct, at least in corporations. As the most important, if increasingly inadequate, mechanism for shareholder oversight of directors and managers, the GM retained an important role to the end of our period.

Conclusions

In practice, however, the effectiveness of the GM in achieving oversight was debatable. Attendances at GMs often tended to taper off after an initial burst of enthusiasm and involvement. Table 6.5 shows attendances at the first ten GMs of twelve companies from five sectors and indicates that in many cases shareholders deserted the GM within a few years of company formation. Not all companies fitted this pattern. In some, attendance rose as shareholders became increasingly concerned about the actions of their board. In others, attendance remained relatively stable. The payment of regular dividends, however, was a strong incentive for no longer attending GMs, a process we have documented elsewhere with regard to shipping companies in the nineteenth century.[104] By the mid-nineteenth century, commentators like Herbert Spencer were bemoaning the lack of shareholder participation: "Proprietors, instead of constantly exercising their franchise, allow it to become on all ordinary occasions a dead letter."[105] Few turned up to GMs, few exercised their rights, and few, it was thought, really understood what was going on in the companies that they owned. Every spring, commented the *Times*, railway companies drew up their parliamentary bills for costly line extensions and "hastily presented" them to shareholders for their approval. Only a few shareholders paid any attention, and, the *Times* reported, "many more feel that they know nothing about it, and accordingly pin their faith on the impartial judgement of some friend in the direction, who is only waiting for a good opportunity to sell, and therefore advises everybody else to hold on."[106]

Because of these well-documented complaints about the lack of shareholder participation, for many observers the comparison between GMs and Parliament seemed inappropriate. Writing in 1841, Thomas Corbet complained that

> in large public bodies which are unaccustomed to act together and which meet say only once a-year, it may be laid down almost without limitation that there can be *no discussion*. Indeed, if we refer to Parliament, it will appear it is only by the adopting of rigid rules, long training, and that experience by which a member arrives not only at a knowledge of his fellow members but of himself, that so multitudinous an assembly can be brought to act with such propriety as to admit of any business at all being done; that those who really understand the matter in hand should be allowed to take the charge, and those

who do not understand it should be induced to refrain or remain silent. Now, on the contrary, on the occasional meetings of joint-stock companies, where a knowledge in the members is wanting of themselves and of each other, it most commonly happens that fools take the lead, and wise men are reduced to the condition of, and are obliged to content themselves with being lookers-on.[107]

Corbet allowed one exception to this rule: the EIC, he thought, could be counted as a proper instance of parliamentary-style democracy in action, but, as he recognized, this was hardly typical of the joint-stock company in our period. To avoid a situation in which "fools take the lead," directors were eager to present themselves to their "constituents" as responsible wielders of authority and power, to whom the key strategic decisions within companies could and should be ceded. As chapter 5 shows, on the whole they were able to do this during our period, and as the power of the GM diminished, so did shareholder participation.

Alongside this diminution of GM power, there was a corresponding weakening of shareholder democracy. By the later nineteenth century, there was a widespread consensus that the governance of joint-stock companies had moved away from the eighteenth-century norm toward a less participatory system, just as national and local politics were turning away from the open-air, open-access public meeting in favor of the discipline of party organization and more privatized or mediated forms of political expression. This tendency was especially visible in the shareholder franchise. Dunlavy's observation that in the United States "plutocratic franchises came to seem natural, fair, and right," applies equally to the United Kingdom.[108] Stock splitting meant that curbs on the voting rights of large shareholders came to be seen as futile. Discussions on the Railway Dissolution Bill in 1846, for example, led to the replacement of the earlier graduated franchise with a simple one-vote-per-share system. The *Freeman's Journal* supported this change, arguing that the graduated scale did an "injustice" to large shareholders, and to redress this, they would have been "reduced to the clumsy but effectual contrivance of splitting up their shares for the occasion, and putting them in small parcels into numerous hands, in order to secure them their full weight on the voting list."[109] By the time of the debates on the Reform Bills of the 1860s and 1880s, it was clear that trends in joint-stock governance had overtaken those of political governance, especially at the national level. Whereas GMs had formerly been described as "parliaments," it was becoming increasingly common for the state itself to be

TABLE 6.5. **Attendance at first ten general meetings of twelve companies as percentage of best-attended meeting**

Meeting	Duns Linen Company (1765–71)	Company of Proprietors of the Chesterfield Canal (1771–8)	Manchester Bolton and Bury Canal (1791–1800)	Rochester and Chatham Gas Light Company (1819–23)	Wolverhampton Gas Light Company (1820–34)	York Gas Light and Coke Company (1823–7)	Clerical, Medical and General Life Assurance Society (1824–31)	Watford Gas and Coke Company (1835–44)	County of Gloucester Bank (1837–41)	Ashton Stalybridge Hyde and Glossop Bank (1837–50)
1st	64.1	100.0	75.4	100.0	75.0	100.0	–	100.0	70.0	100.0
2nd	100.0	64.2	59.6	81.8	93.8	–	59.3	93.8	100.0	87.5
3rd	66.7	60.4	42.1	68.2	68.8	48.8	59.3	43.8	75.0	75.0
4th	69.2	58.5	100.0	50.0	100.0	39.0	49.2	75.0	52.5	62.5
5th	64.1	64.2	75.4	77.3	68.8	31.7	42.4	75.0	62.5	68.8
6th	64.1	67.9	36.8	63.6	50.0	34.1	57.6	56.3	55.0	75.0
7th	48.7	45.3	75.4	40.9	–	24.4	100.0	50.0	57.5	37.5
8th	25.6	56.6	42.1	81.8	43.8	26.8	83.1	43.8	42.5	50.0
9th	–	71.7	35.1	54.5	56.3	31.7	42.4	43.8	45.0	15.0
10th	–	60.4	38.6	–	37.5	–	33.9	37.5	62.5	25.0

compared to a joint-stock company. Some thought that in the compari-
son, national political institutions came off worse, as "too democratic."
The future prime minister, and chairman of the Great Eastern Railway,
Robert Cecil wrote in the 1850s that

> the State is a joint-stock company to all intents and purposes. It is the combi-
> nation of a vast number of men for well-defined objects—the preservation of
> life and property. But it has this monstrous and unheard-of peculiarity, that
> it is a joint-stock company in which the shareholders vote, not by shares, but
> by heads. True, that every one has invested, so to speak, his life in the con-
> cern, and that the lives of all are equal; but, over and above this, every one
> has invested his property, and properties are not equal; and the legislation, to
> carry on which the votes are given, is almost entirely concerned with the se-
> curity and rights of property. That the shareholders should vote by numbers,
> and not by their share in the concern, is a principle which any man of business
> would at once dismiss as iniquitous and absurd.[110]

Others went further than Cecil and advocated a sliding scale of parliamentary votes based on property qualifications, not unlike those used in
some local government elections. Writing in the *Nineteenth Century* in
1883, the philosopher Norman Pearson drew inspiration from the model
company constitution outlined in table A of schedule 1 to the Companies Act of 1862 and suggested a graduated scale of parliamentary voting, whereby an annual income of £10 would confer a single vote, £40
two votes, and so on up a graduated scale to a maximum of twenty votes
given to those with an income of £35,000 and above.[111] More vehemently,
and in a private diary rather than a public forum, Thomas Sopwith, who
as a surveyor and civil engineer had worked for joint-stock companies in
the railway and mining sectors, fantasized in 1834 about his ideal election: "My plan would be to have good, strong, capacious chests placed in
the Town Hall of every county town or borough . . . and on a given day
in each year every individual in the kingdom[,] man, woman, and child,
should have full liberty to vote as often as they chose, by putting money
in the box appropriated to their respective candidates."[112]

The system in joint-stock companies of multiple votes according to the
number of shares held, and even the uncapped one-vote-per-share franchise, was widely touted by Conservatives as a natural feature of corporate governance that had always been in place. For Pearson, "In commercial matters the principle obtains a practically universal acceptance."[113]

Similarly, in 1864 Cecil, in response to a speech by Gladstone that held out the (distant) prospect of universal manhood suffrage, ridiculed the notion that "two day-labourers should outvote Baron Rothschild," and praised the plutocratic system of government in joint-stock companies:

> [Parliamentary reformers'] proposals are about as reasonable as those of a body of shareholders would be, who, having only one share a-piece, should demand that each of them should have as many votes as the holders of a thousand shares. The constitutional system under which Joint Stock Companies are managed, we believe in every country, is that which is dictated by common sense, viz., that each man should have as many votes in the government as he has shares in the concern. *It is a system whose justice has never been disputed. The question has never even been a matter of controversy.* The wildest dreamer never suggested that all the shareholders should each have a single vote, without reference to the number of shares they might hold.[114]

Cecil's endorsement of the one-vote-per-share principle went further than Pearson's and overlooked the modest curtailments of the voting rights of larger shareholders that appeared in the legislation of the 1840s and 1860s. Moreover, as we have shown in this chapter, the evidence of company records from the period before 1844 suggests that the question of the franchise had often been a "matter of controversy," despite Cecil's belief to the contrary. It is also clear that Williston's confident assertion in 1888 that the basis of shareholder voting rights had shifted decisively from one-member-one-vote to one-vote-per-share models in a relatively short space of time was misleading. We have shown that there were significant sectoral differences in shareholder voting rights in our period and that, although there was change over time, it was uneven. Like other aspects of corporate governance, this reflected the uncertainty of the legal framework of joint-stock organization and the changing size and structure of companies. Perhaps more significant than the emergence of plutocratic franchise types was the tendency toward the marginalization of smaller shareholders, who were increasingly excluded from voting at all, most systematically in the largest companies. Furthermore, developments in the range of other procedures associated with GMs in this period indicate that the principal shift was away from direct shareholder participation toward a closing down of the public sphere of joint-stock politics. This was partly embodied in constitutional provisions but was also revealed in procedural records and in pamphlet literature. The trend should not be overstated, and the evidence of this chapter suggests that it was led by unincorporated companies rather than by public corporations, but it was an important feature of the period and had significant implications for the accountability and transparency of corporate governance, to which we turn in the next chapters.

Appendix: Franchise Categories and Types

This appendix explains the five franchise categories, further divided into nine types, used in our sample of 514 companies. Examples are given in table 6.1.

Category 1: Uncapped Linear

TYPE 1A: UNCAPPED LINEAR SCALE.   This franchise type allowed one vote for a set number of shares greater than one, with no cap on the total number of votes. In table 6.1, the South Western Steam Packet Company represents this franchise type. Here shareholders had a vote for every five shares.

TYPE 1B: UNCAPPED ONE-VOTE-PER-SHARE.   These franchises allowed one vote per share, with no limit to the number of votes a shareholder could cast. We regard this as slightly more democratic than type 1A because although, as table 6.1 shows, the relative voting strength of large voters against small voters was the same as for type 1A, all shareholders, including even the smallest, were able to vote.

Category 2: Uncapped Graduated

TYPE 2A. UNCAPPED ONE-VOTE-PER-SHARE PLUS SCALE.   These allotted one vote per share up to a certain limit and then one for a set number of shares above this limit. There was an element of graduation in such franchises, in that small shareholders had a vote for every share but larger shareholders did not. At the Liverpool and Manchester Railway, as shown in table 6.1, holders of 100 shares had 40 votes, or 0.4 votes per share. Franchises of this type were particularly common in the railway sector.

TYPE 2B. UNCAPPED GRADUATED SCALE. These franchises were very similar to those in 2A, but there was no element of one-vote-per-share. In other words, there was a graduated scale right from the bottom. At the Wakefield Waterworks Company (1837), the holder of one share had one vote, four shares conferred two votes, ten shares three votes, and twenty shares four votes, and shareholders could cast an additional vote for every ten shares above twenty.

Category 3: Capped Linear

TYPE 3A. CAPPED LINEAR SCALE. This type was identical to type 1A except that there was a cap on the total number of votes a shareholder could cast. The cap varied considerably, which altered the relative voting strength of different shareholdings. At the Shotts Iron Company (1824) shareholders had one vote for every two shares, to a maximum of five votes. Holders of five shares had, therefore, 40 percent of the voting strength of those with one hundred shares. By contrast, at the Tyne Dock Company (1839) the franchise was one vote for every five shares, to a maximum of twenty votes; thus holders of five shares had 5 percent of the voting strength of those with one hundred shares, the same proportion as in those companies with franchise types 1A and 1B.

TYPE 3B. CAPPED ONE-VOTE-PER-SHARE. Here, shareholders had one vote per share up to a specified maximum number of votes. In many cases, no explicit maximum number of votes was given, but there was a maximum number of shares that an individual could hold, which acted as a de facto cap on voting strength. This franchise type embraced very wide variations. Companies adopting it included the Eastern Bank of Scotland (1838), whose shareholders had one vote per share to a maximum of four hundred votes, and the Gillingham Gas and Coke Company, where shareholders had a vote per share up to a maximum of just two votes. The example shown in table 6.1, the Warwick Gas Light Company (1822), had a cap near the average for this franchise type.

Category 4: Capped Graduated

TYPE 4A. CAPPED ONE-VOTE-PER-SHARE PLUS SCALE. These franchises were identical to type 2A except that there was a cap on the total num-

ber of votes that could be cast. Again, the level of the cap varied considerably within this category.

TYPE 4B. CAPPED GRADUATED SCALE.   This was the most common franchise type and was the most similar to the weighted franchises used in
select vestries and poor-law unions and for Scottish parochial board
elections. There was a graduated scale of voting and a cap, which varied from forty-two votes (for two thousand shares) at the Ulster Banking
Company (1836) to just two votes (for six shares) at the Leeds New Gas
Company (1835). The modal cap was four votes.

Category 5. One-Member-One-Vote

TYPE 5. ONE-MEMBER-ONE-VOTE.   This was the most democratic franchise, where each shareholder had one vote, regardless of how many
shares he or she owned.

CHAPTER SEVEN

Limited Liability
and Company Dissolution

Sound city men . . . all along have clung to the opinion, that there can be no protection to the public from mismanagement by banks, unless the responsibility of the shareholders is without limit. — *Times* (London), 22 May 1844

The preceding three chapters trace the decline of the active share-holder and the growing marginalization of investors in company decision making. This has been explained partly by the increasing size of companies and by a transition in the motivations for investment. In this chapter we consider the ways in which companies sought to safe-guard the "financial" interests of their investors, which were coming to predominate as the joint-stock economy and the secondary market for shares grew during our period. In particular, we examine the issue of shareholder liability, which exercised legislators, political commentators, company promoters, and individual shareholders during this period. The introduction of general limited liability in the 1850s is well documented, but the legal framework regulating the liabilities of shareholders before this time remains imperfectly understood.[1] Moreover, the issue has usually been viewed from the point of view of legislators and political econ-omists rather than the investors and company promoters who were sub-ject to it.[2] It was the latter who were required, where their companies remained unincorporated, to balance the need for capital with the de-sire of investors for protection from large liabilities. They also needed to protect themselves from being held personally responsible for company debts. Before the registration and limited-liability acts, however, there was widespread uncertainty about the precise liability of shareholders, which was shared by company promoters themselves.

Although shareholders in corporations generally enjoyed limited liability throughout this period, promoters of unincorporated companies sought to limit their own liability and that of their shareholders in a variety of ways through clauses inserted into company constitutions. These clauses attempted either to circumvent the unlimited liability of shareholders in law or to provide alternative restrictions on liability using a number of devices, the most important of which was provision for the dissolution of the company. Hickson and Turner have recently suggested that unlimited liability could lead to better standards of corporate governance because shareholders, especially the largest, had an obvious incentive to be vigilant and to ensure that their companies were being run efficiently and honestly. This incentive also encouraged them to participate in the governance of companies by acting as directors themselves.[3] Such arguments were commonly heard in the 1840s and were advanced again, for example, in the wake of the failure of the Western Bank of Scotland in 1857.[4] Shareholders, however, needed to be able to monitor directors and managers properly in order for unlimited liability to have a positive effect on standards of governance. This did not always happen, because in many cases the information that was available to shareholders regarding the affairs of their companies, especially in the financial sector, was imperfect. The procedures for inspecting accounts and formal auditing, which form the subject of chapter 8, therefore needed to be robust if shareholders were to protect their investments. In this chapter we conclude that fundamental governance failures in unincorporated companies undermined the potential benefits of unlimited liability and thus strengthened the arguments for general limited liability. We begin, however, by examining shareholders' and directors' liability in corporations, and then in shipping and mining, where different legal considerations applied, before moving on to the situation in unincorporated companies.

Limited Liability in Corporations

Harris has noted that even in corporations there was confusion about the extent of shareholder liability. In seventeenth-century England, when some of the major trading corporations were chartered, "there was no coherent, well-defined conception of limited liability." Moreover, "when discussing the limited liability of shareholders in a business corporation, different lawyers and historians referred to different things."[5] The two different means of securing incorporation—by act or by royal charter—added to the confusion. Harris suggests that it was *not* possible for companies in England to be *chartered* without limited liability—until the repeal of the Bubble Act in 1825 explicitly permitted the practice—whereas, for companies incorporated by *act*, a limited-liability clause was required.[6] According to Walker, the opposite was true in Scotland, where the "creation [of a corporation] by special Act included, unless it were expressly excluded, the limited liability of members for debts of the corporation."[7] In Scotland, it was also possible for a company to be *chartered* with *unlimited* liability. The charter of the Carron Company (1773), for example, stipulated that shareholders would be liable for the debts of the corporation "as fully and effectually . . . to all intents and purposes as if the said [shareholders], their successors and assigns had not been incorporated into a Body Politic and Corporate and as if this present charter had never been granted any Thing in the same or in the Usage and Practice with respect to Bodies Politic and Corporate in similar or other circumstances to the Contrary Notwithstanding."[8] Dubois argued, from the wording of this clause, that "this charter provision was thus clearly considered an exception to the usual corporation practice."[9] It was, however, an exception rather than an impossibility. The inconsistency of the legal regimes north and south of the border was highlighted by subsequent legislation. The Trading Companies Act of 1834, for example, which permitted partial incorporation by letters patent on condition that shareholders' liability was extended for three years after they had disposed of their shares, was "wholly ineffective" in Scotland.[10]

The inclusion of a limited-liability clause in incorporating acts was rare in the eighteenth century, although, contrary to Harris, this did not necessarily mean that shareholders lacked the privilege. The absence may have been because incorporation was assumed to provide limited liability, given the corporation's separate legal existence, distinct from its shareholders. Equally, it could be because in this period, as Campbell argues, limited liability was not the most important motive for seeking incorporation: the "great prize" was the legal personality that incorporation afforded a company.[11] Among twenty-five corporations in our sample established between 1720 and 1789, the constitutions of twenty-two did not mention shareholder liability at all. Of the other three, one was the chartered London Assurance in 1720, where liability was pro rata rather than strictly limited. Another was the British Fisheries Society

(1786), whose act was vague on the point, although it was clear from the preamble that one of the motivations for seeking incorporation was to limit shareholder liability. This was rather apologetically inserted into a more general plea for statutory recognition of the legal personality of the company.[12] Limited liability can be identified as a motivation for incorporation in some other late eighteenth-century cases: Dubois noted that, although the petitions of the Warmley Company in 1768 and the Albion Flour Mill in 1784 did not mention shareholder liability, it is clear from related correspondence that it was important to the petitioners. This was also true of the Sierra Leone Company (1791), whose act declared that shareholders would be responsible "to the full amount of their several and respective shares . . . but shall not be any further or otherwise liable."[13]

These petitions might seem to support Harris's suggestion that, by the end of the eighteenth century, limited liability was "an integral part of incorporation and a major motive for it."[14] It is notable, however, that none of the canal companies in our sample established during the 1790s included a full limited liability clause. A more normal provision in these years was the prohibition on calls being made beyond the value of the share, which was not the same as limiting liability, as it would not in itself protect the individual shareholder from actions by third parties. An example occurs in the act incorporating the Kilmarnock and Troon Railway (1808), whereby "it shall not be lawful to make any further Call upon any Proprietor or Proprietors who shall have paid to the Company, in Obedience to the said Calls or otherwise, the full Amount of the Sum which by his, her, or their, Subscription, he, she or they had undertaken to pay for his, her, or their said Share or Shares."[15] The general absence of full limited-liability clauses suggests that the issue may not have been in the minds of many company promoters at the time. Indeed, not until the 1840s did a majority of corporations stipulate a limitation of liability in their constitutions, as figure 7.1 shows. As late as the 1830s, of eighty-six corporations in our sample, only twenty-four (27.9 percent) employed a limited-liability clause. For English and Welsh corporations, the legislation of 1825 had little effect on the explicit liability provisions in their acts. Even in the period 1830–4 just 37.5 percent of new corporations in England and Wales specified limited liability. Only in Scotland was there a noticeable shift in practice after 1825. All of the thirteen Scottish corporations established after this date in our sample had limited-liability clauses, compared with just half of those established earlier

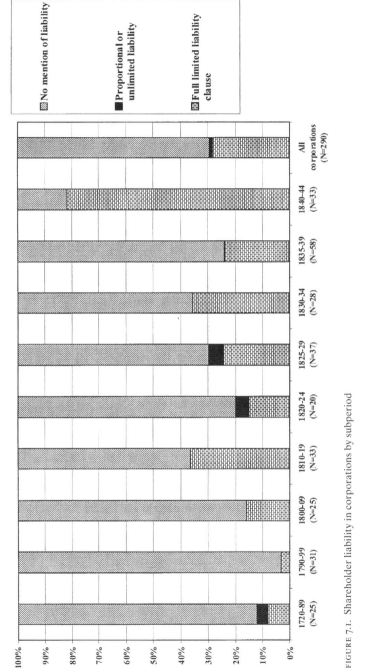

FIGURE 7.1. Shareholder liability in corporations by subperiod

(eight of sixteen). This change might be explained by the desire for explicit shareholder protection in a confusing legal climate, as discussed above. The importance of 1825 as a watershed is illustrated by the acts of the Monkland and Kirkintilloch Railway (1824) and the Ballochney Railway (1826). The latter is an almost exact copy of the former, except for a limited-liability clause having been added.[16] There were also significant variations by sector: 53.6 percent of incorporated gas companies established over the whole period had limited-liability provisions, but only 31.8 percent of corporations in the property sector. Of the thirty-three incorporated bridges, shareholders in just one company—the Gosport and Haslar Bridge (1834)—enjoyed the protection of a limited-liability clause.[17]

As the nineteenth century progressed, company promoters increasingly emphasized to their shareholders the protection that came with incorporation, even if confusion remained about the exact meaning of limited liability.[18] In 1802, for example, the promoters of the Kent Insurance Company ordered that "application should be made for an Act of Parliament or Charter or both if necessary to establish the Institution and especially to protect the property of the proprietors beyond the amount of their respective shares."[19] By the 1820s, entrepreneurs were seeking limited liability with unprecedented regularity. The directors of the General Steam Navigation Company (1825) reported in 1827 that they had been investigating the possibility of getting an incorporating act "by which responsibility is limited to the actual Partners and to the extent of their Interests."[20] Not only would this directly benefit the shareholders, they claimed, but it would also enable the business to grow in the future. When the act was passed in 1831, the directors congratulated themselves on this "concession . . . so valuable," referring to the "notorious fact that the Public have been apprehensive of embarking in a Concern where serious losses might be sustained and where each individual might be called upon in the first instance to make good such losses."[21]

It was probably not until the 1840s that limited liability could be identified as the chief distinguishing feature of the incorporated company. By that time, the limited-liability clause was a nearly universal feature of acts of incorporation. A typical clause enacted "that no Shareholder of the Company shall be liable for or charged with the Payment of any Debt or Demand due from the Company beyond the Extent of his Share in the Capital of the Company not then paid up."[22] Even with this protection, however, shareholders could still find themselves liable for heavy costs, and it was possible for creditors to sue individual shareholders for the debts of a company. For example, in *Malcolm v. West Lothian Railway Company* (1835), the Scottish Court of Session held that each shareholder "was liable *in solidum* to the extent of his subscribed stock" with regard to third parties. Although this company's act of Parliament directed that calls be made in proportion to the amount of stock subscribed, this did not prevent remedies against individuals.[23] A judgment in England in 1843 held that the remedy of plaintiffs for expenses incurred in securing an act of incorporation was not only against the funds of the company but also against the individual shareholders.[24] Other similar rulings, however, as with cases involving liability for calls on shares, hung on the disputed question of how to define share ownership. In 1829, for instance, in *Bourne v. Freeth* a person who had put his name to a prospectus for a whiskey distillery company but never paid his subscription was held not to be a shareholder and therefore not chargeable as a partner for goods supplied to the company.[25]

Although it was often advocated, the *en commandite* partnership, whereby managing partners were fully liable but ordinary shareholders' responsibility was limited to the amount of their shares, was not introduced in Britain in our period. The Anonymous Partners Act (1782) permitted the establishment of such companies in Ireland, but most of the companies established under it were very small.[26] In corporations established by act of Parliament, directors were liable, in the same way as other shareholders, to the extent of their stock and no further. Indeed, some incorporating acts moved even further away from the *en commandite* principle by giving additional protection to the directors of the company.[27] This took the form of an indemnity clause preventing a creditor from suing the directors individually. A typical example appeared in the Cheltenham Water Works Company's act (1824), which ruled that "no Member of the Committee for the Time being shall become personally answerable for the Performance of any Agreement into which he shall or may have entered, as one of such Committee, on behalf of the said Company."[28] Similar protection was given in 32.1 percent of corporations: the earliest example was in 1802, but the practice did not become general until the late 1830s. In the period 1720–1834, 9.0 percent of corporations provided for directors' indemnity. In 1835–44 the proportion was 82.4 percent. A majority of railway, water, and property companies had indemnity clauses, as did a significant minority of harbors, but it was rare in other sectors. Irish companies also protected their directors: again, this was rare before the mid-1830s and general thereafter. In Scotland, a different clause was used, which protected directors from the failings and malpractices of company employees and their fellow board members: "the said Committee of Management shall not be answerable for Mistakes or Omissions, nor for the Sufficiency or Responsibility of any Security or Securities to be taken under the Authority of this Act; nor for Receipts, Acts, or Commissions of the Treasurer, or any Clerk, Agent, or Servant of the said Company; nor any One of the said Committee for the others, but each of them for his own Receipts and Intromissions only."[29] Provisions such as these made it clear that directors' legal liabilities were restricted, in contrast with Irish companies established under the legislation of 1782. Many unincorporated companies tried to imitate the protections afforded to directors and shareholders. We discuss these below, but first we turn to the particular circumstances in shipping and mining.

Limited Liability in Shipping and Mining

Among unincorporated companies, in two sectors—shipping and metalliferous mining—specific regulations applied that had implications for proprietors' liability. In shipping, the traditional joint-adventure or part-ownership system—whereby one ship was owned by a number of proprietors—offered a measure of protection for shareholders. In the nineteenth century, joint-stock companies were beginning to take the place of the part-ownership system, but the latter remained in use well into the twentieth century at many ports. In this system a ship was divided into a number of transferable shares, commonly sixteen, thirty-two, or sixty-four, and owned jointly by a number of investors as "tenants-in-common." Investors were liable for the costs of the ship (as distinct from trading losses) only in proportion to their individual stake in the vessel.[30] As one Scottish legal ruling declared in the 1750s, "joint proprietors of ships are never subjected beyond the value of the ship."[31] This form of ownership was given statutory force by the Registry Act of 1823, which fixed the maximum number of owners at thirty-two and the maximum number of shares at sixty-four.[32] Moreover, shipping in both England and Scotland fell under the jurisdiction of the Admiralty courts, which recognized the ship as a separate corporate entity and offered a facility for part owners to settle disputes.[33] With the rise of joint-stock companies,

however, each owning several ships, the opportunities to limit one's liability in shipping diminished. At the same time, shareholders had fewer
opportunities for monitoring the activities of those who had direct responsibility for ships.[34] As early as the 1820s, the investor in the joint-
stock shipping company was in much the same position as his counter-
part in other sectors, although shipping companies with mail contracts
were more likely to be awarded charters and thereby have limited liability, as happened to thirteen new companies between 1837 and 1854.[35]

Mining was the other sector in which companies operated in a distinct legal environment. Until the late nineteenth century, metalliferous
mining in Cornwall and Devon was carried out mainly under the cost-
book system, regulated by the local stannary courts. Under this system,
a group of working tin miners—"adventurers"—could come together
in a type of extended partnership to obtain the rights to a mineral lode
and start operations with little or no pooled capital.[36] They would divide
the business traditionally into eight transferrable shares, or multiples of
eight, and employ a "purser" to keep their accounts. The purser, or, in
bigger companies, a committee of management comprising the larger
shareholders, would enter all revenue and expenditure in a "cost book,"
which also contained the names and shares of the adventurers and the
rules under which the business operated. The purser or managerial committee would call periodic meetings of the adventurers at which profits
would be distributed or calls made on shares to pay for losses. Unlike ordinary partnerships, the cost-book companies enjoyed a separate legal
identity under stannary law and could sue and be sued in the name of
the purser or other officers. By the nineteenth century the cost-book system had extended out of Cornish tin mining into copper and lead mining
and into other mining areas in Wales and Ireland. The Companies Act
of 1856 finally removed the legal recognition of cost-book companies operating outside the jurisdiction of the stannary courts.[37]

Historians have disagreed about the relative economic benefits of
the cost-book system and the joint-stock company form in mining. They
have agreed, however, about the advantages of the cost-book system to
local shareholders.[38] In particular, Burt and Kudo argue that, "in principle, the cost book adventurer's liability was unlimited and very similar to that of a member of an ordinary partnership" but that in practice
there were many curbs on liability. For example, the rules of cost-book
companies often limited the amount that could be called against each
share. While this did not restrict shareholders' liabilities to third parties,

it did restrict them *inter se*. There were limitations on the borrowing that could be contracted by pursers and managers, major contracts required the approval of a GM, bank loans were "almost entirely prohibited," and shares could be relinquished at any time. Moreover, short accounting periods of three to six months enabled cost-book adventurers to keep a close eye on their investments. The growth in size of cost-book companies, together with the widening geographical spread of the investment base, placed these mechanisms under strain, but they did exist.[39]

Thus, it is clear that various protections were available to shareholders in cost-book companies but that full limited liability was not enjoyed. Nevertheless, this did not prevent mining companies' exploiting the legal uncertainties in the sector to promote themselves to potential investors as quasi-limited-liability institutions. One example was the Marke Valley Consolidated Mines, a London-based company established in 1839 to mine copper, tin, and lead near Liskeard in Cornwall. According to its "rules and regulations," which doubled as a prospectus, the responsibility of the shareholders *inter se* was "limited to the amount of their respective shares."[40] In the same document, an unnamed "professional adviser" suggested that, in effect, a form of *en commandite* partnership operated in mining:

> The holder of a share in this undertaking . . . will not be liable, as a partner, to any of the engagements of the mine, unless he shall elect to be registered as a shareholder in the share register of the undertaking, and shall otherwise interfere in the management thereof. . . . In trading companies, which a mining concern is not, every partner is liable, and the directors, or managing partners, are treated, at law and in equity, as the agents of the whole or congregated co-partnership, and, as such, can involve their partners in the trading liabilities. In a Mining Company, unless the shareholder shall have been placed on the cost book, with his own direct authority, or shall have interfered in the mining transactions, and sanctioned the debts incurred, he is not liable, and cannot be compelled to pay the debts or liabilities of the mine.[41]

The promoters of the Marke Valley Consolidated Mines tried to take advantage of the confused boundary between the joint-stock and cost-book company forms, and of uncertainties about the liability regime under stannary law, to portray their company as a particularly safe investment. Such claims received short shrift in the courts, however, as demonstrated in 1832, when Lord Brougham ruled that the limited-liability clause in the constitution of a joint-stock mining company did not have any standing in law.[42]

Some of the controlling mechanisms discussed by Burt and Kudo, which protected shareholders without limiting their liability, were also adopted by unincorporated companies in other sectors. The usefulness of these mechanisms was questionable, particularly where directors and managers were able to act without effective shareholder oversight. They helped promoters, however, to present their ventures as safe havens for investment. In an environment where shareholders were increasingly concerned for their "financial" interests, it was important to argue that investment was not significantly riskier in banking, insurance, and manufacturing than in incorporated canals, railways, and other infrastructural projects. We now turn to the main ways in which this was done.

Limited Liability in Other Unincorporated Companies

Promoters of unincorporated companies were unable to offer their subscribers the protections available in corporations and could also find themselves liable for considerable debts, in their capacities both as shareholders and as directors or trustees. It was important, therefore, that they protect themselves from being held liable and also reassure shareholders about the safety of their investments. Most unincorporated companies—84.4 percent of the total in our sample—indemnified directors from personal responsibility for actions undertaken on behalf of the company and bound the shareholders to relieve them in the event of losses. In Scotland, there was often a clause almost identical to the standard indemnity clause in acts of Parliament, as given above.[43] In English and Welsh deeds of settlement, a long standard clause stipulated:

> That the directors, trustees, and other officers, for the time being, of the said company, and each and every of them . . . shall be indemnified and saved harmless out of the funds or property of the company; from and against all costs, charges, losses, damages, and expences, which they, or any of them . . . shall or may bear . . . form or on account, or in consequence of any contract or engagement, which shall or may be entered into for or on behalf of the company . . . and that any one or more of them shall not be answerable or accountable for the other or others of them; but each of them for his own acts, receipts, neglects, and defaults, only.[44]

As Harris has explained, the attractions of trusteeship in a company established by deed of settlement were paltry. Trustees could incur liabilities to third parties for contracts made on behalf of the company and also to the shareholders themselves if they could be shown to have been negligent in their duties.[45] Consequently, among unincorporated companies established in England and Wales, only 14.0 percent failed to indemnify their trustees in this or some similar way, and a third of these had no provision for trustees at all. Eight out of eighteen unincorporated Irish companies in our sample used a very similar indemnity clause.[46] In Scotland, it was common for the board of directors to act as the trustees, and as such they enjoyed the benefits of the standard indemnity clause. Moreover, in the clause vesting trusteeship in the board, shareholders were also usually "bound and obliged to relieve" those who acted as trustees "of every obligation come under by them in virtue of the powers hereby granted."[47]

Unincorporated companies, therefore, attempted to follow corporations in restricting the liabilities of the executive. To attract capital, however, it was important also to convince potential subscribers that they could safely invest. A number of strategies could be adopted. First, it was possible to mimic corporations and write a limited-liability clause into a constitution. This could take a relatively simple form, as was the case at the Kirkintilloch Gas Light Company (1838), whose contract of co-partnery stated that "the said Partners shall be liable only each for the amount of the share, or shares, held by him, or her, respectively."[48] Alternatively, a long and complex clause could be inserted, as was often the case with insurance companies.[49] Our sample of unincorporated companies indicates that the inclusion of limited-liability clauses was relatively common, though with no clear trend over time; 29.5 percent of all unincorporated companies attempted to limit the liability of shareholders in this way, and we have examples from almost every sector in which there were unincorporated companies and from almost every year from 1825 to 1844.[50] The practice varied considerably by sector, as demonstrated by figure 7.2. Of course, limited liability was much more important in the financial sector than elsewhere: losses at a gas company were less likely to be catastrophic than at a bank or insurance company. This factor, however, does not entirely explain the sectoral trends. While only four of our thirty-two unincorporated gas companies (12.5 percent) had limited-liability clauses, the practice was even rarer in banking, which we discuss below. It was most widespread in insurance, where forty-two

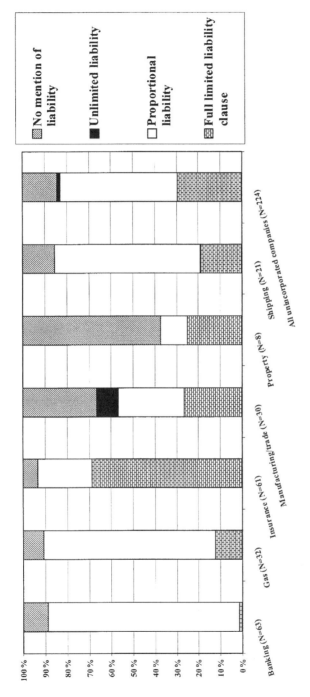

FIGURE 7.2. Shareholder liability in unincorporated companies by sector (main sectors only)

out of sixty-one unincorporated companies (68.9 percent) tried to limit shareholder liability to the extent of the unpaid portion of their shares. All seventeen English insurance companies in our sample established between 1805 and 1824 had a limited-liability clause in their deeds of settlement. Insurance company promoters, like those in the mining sector, emphasized the limitation of liability in their communications with shareholders. In the abstract of the deed of the Farmers' and General Fire and Life Insurance and Loan and Annuity Company, for example, the long and complex clause limiting the liability of shareholders was given in full, "in respect of its importance to the shareholders," thereby promoting the company as a safe haven for investors' money.[51] Unsurprisingly, this attempt to restrict liability was not publicized when the company advertised for customers.[52]

Some contemporaries cast doubt on the legality of limited-liability clauses. Such a clause, declared Lord Chancellor Brougham in 1833, was "wholly nugatory . . . as between the company and strangers and can serve no purpose whatever."[53] Limited companies were widely criticized throughout the period as reckless, speculative, un-English bubble schemes, undermining ethical standards by disavowing the duty of businessmen to pay their debts, and the law served to enforce prevailing moral values.[54] The Joint-Stock Companies Act of 1844 defended creditors' rights. Section 68 permitted them to proceed against individual shareholders if they had failed to secure a remedy against the company, having done due diligence according to earlier sections of the act.[55] Before and after the passage of this act, however, companies, particularly in insurance, often attempted to circumvent such proceedings by the use of contracts. In most cases, insurance companies that limited the liability of their shareholders stipulated that this limitation should be written into all contracts entered into by the company.[56] For example, one policy of insurance issued in the 1840s by the Merchant Traders Ship Loan and Insurance Association contained the proviso "that the said policy, or anything therein contained, shall in no case extend, or be deemed or construed to extend, to charge or render liable the respective proprietors of the said company, or any of them . . . to any claim or demand whatsoever in respect of the said policy . . . beyond the amount of their, his or her individual shares or share in the capital stock of the said company."[57] Harris has cast doubt on the effectiveness of such clauses, arguing that, "even in the insurance sector, the limitation of liability was only partial, and in other sectors, in which there was no practice of drafting standard written agreements, almost no limitation was in fact achieved."[58] He argues that policyholders could use these provisos in policies to negotiate lower premiums, although in Pearson's large study of insurance companies in the period 1700–1850, no evidence has been found to substantiate this assertion.[59]

The evidence of case law suggests that limitation of liability—both for executive officers and shareholders—by contract was increasingly tolerated, especially in England, during the first half of the nineteenth century. The protection of shareholders, however, depended on the wording of the policy. In the case of *Alchorne v. Saville*, decided in 1820, Alchorne sued three directors and trustees of the Hand-in-Hand Fire Insurance Office, which had not paid the sum due on his policy within the agreed time. The policy, which the three defendants had signed, stipulated that "we the trustees and directors of the said society, whose names are hereunto subscribed, do order, direct, and appoint the directors for the time being of the said society to raise and pay, by and out of the monies, securities and effects of the said contributionship, pursuant and according to certain deeds and settlements" the sum insured. The King's Bench agreed that those who signed the policy were not "personally liable," and the plaintiff's remedy could not be against them.[60] This judgment protected individual directors and trustees and was reinforced in the following year in *Andrews v. Ellison*, where the plaintiff's policy with the National Union Fire Association made clear that "neither of them the said directors who [signed the policy] . . . should as members of the said society, be subject or liable to any demand for loss or losses, except under the articles establishing the said society, and as was provided by the same." Although the judgment held that the funds of the company were sufficient in this case, it was clear that the defendants were liable only in the terms set out in the deed of settlement, which was explicitly referred to in the policy.[61]

Further protection was extended in several decisions in 1849. *Dawson v. Wrench*, decided in January of that year, reiterated the principle, set out in *Andrews v. Ellison*, that those who signed a policy were not personally liable.[62] In *Hassell v. Merchant Traders Ship Loan and Insurance Association*, the Exchequer court held that, because Hassell had signed a policy containing a proviso limiting the liability of the association's shareholders, he was not entitled to proceed against an individual shareholder under section 68 of the Joint-Stock Companies Act.[63] Simultaneously, the court of Queen's Bench ruled, in a case brought by Halket against the same company, that the relevant sections of the act did not apply, "for that Act was not intended to do away with the effect of any special contract entered into with companies."[64] Citing this case in a manual for insurance company promoters published in 1851, the actuary James Henry James asserted that it was probably not worth applying for incorporation, because limited liability was in any case "virtually given to assurance societies with respect to policy-holders by their own instruments; which, viewed as contracts between party and party, can be at all times pleaded, in preference to those provisions of the [1844 act] which negative the principle of a limited liability."[65] Thus, although it would not be legally acceptable to bind third parties by a limited-liability clause in a deed of settlement (this was clearly prohibited by the 1844 act), the use of contracts could afford the necessary protection to shareholders.[66]

Two factors, however, militated against the limited liability of shareholders in unincorporated companies. First, the common practice in the financial sector of requiring only a proportion of shares to be paid up meant that shareholders could be liable to the extent of the unpaid amount of their shares. This could be sufficient to drive shareholders to bankruptcy. In the case of *Reid v. Allan*, decided in 1849, the defendant had paid only £5 on his £100 shares and was found liable to meet the plaintiff's demands in full, as his unpaid shares were sufficient to do so.[67] Second was the legal difficulty associated with transferring liability when transferring shares. One solicitor explained the problem: those interested in unincorporated joint-stock companies assumed that by the sale of shares, "the purchaser immediately stands in law in the place of the vendor, to all intents and purposes. But the sale cannot by law have this effect in perhaps one case in a thousand. It cannot have this effect where contracts have been entered into and are not yet completely executed and at an end, or where there is any debt owing either by or to the partnership."[68] Shareholders selling their shares would continue to be legally liable for all company debts contracted during the period of their share ownership, and this liability would continue indefinitely; transfer only ended liability for the *future* acts of the company.

Legislation from the 1820s endorsed the principle of extended liability after transfer but placed limits on it, in an attempt to give clarity to the law and thus improve the attractiveness of unincorporated company shares. Shareholders in banking companies were made subject to a three-year extended liability regime by the act of 1826 permitting joint-stock banking in England: creditors could proceed against any shareholders who were shareholders at the time their contract was entered into, with a three-year limit on such actions.[69] Extended liability also featured in the Trading Companies Act of 1834, which permitted partial incorporation by letters patent, and it was extended to all companies registered under the legislation of 1844.[70] It was subsequently enshrined in the Joint Stock Companies Act of 1856: three years for unlimited companies, and one year for limited companies.[71] However, the extent to which extended liability was enforceable was being doubted in the 1830s by Charles Poulett Thomson, president of the Board of Trade. In a letter to the attorney general, he highlighted the problems associated with extended liability. How were liabilities to be divided between past and present shareholders? Did the length of time spent holding a share affect liability?[72] These doubts proved to be well founded after high-profile failures such as the Royal British Bank, none of whose former shareholders contributed to the settlement with creditors.[73] By the 1860s, the opinion was frequently expressed that residual liability offered no real protection to creditors. Edmund Church, a chief clerk in the Rolls' Court, argued that it was impossible to make past shareholders liable in the courts: "no call has ever been, so far as I know, made upon the past shareholders."[74]

In Scotland, some legal judgments caused confusion as to the extent of shareholder liability. It has been argued that elements of a limited-liability regime—akin to *en commandite* partnerships—were present in the eighteenth century and that, "perhaps for a time at any rate," non-managing shareholders had limited liability under Scottish common law.[75] This argument rests on a single decision of the Court of Session, in the case of *Stevenson v. Macnair* (1757), in which the court ruled that Macnair and the other nonmanaging partners of the Arran Fishing Company were not liable beyond the extent of their stock for the company's debts; the idea of the *société en commandite* was explicitly mentioned in the pleadings of the company.[76] Walker has suggested, however, that the 1757 judgment was probably a "judicial aberration" and is unlikely to have reflected the general direction of Scottish common law.[77] Campbell argued that the ruling was "forgotten" under the growing influence of English law north of the border. Indeed, in 1772, shareholders of Douglas Heron and Company, also known as the Ayr Bank, were held liable for the debts of the failed company. The nineteenth-century legal authority George Joseph Bell suggested that the unlimited liability of the Ayr Bank shareholders resulted from the fact that it traded under a "personal firm," Douglas Heron and Company, rather than a descriptive name (Ayr Bank or Arran Fishing Company), but this is unconvincing.[78] Indeed, the position of shareholders in Scotland was probably not very different from that of their English counterparts. According to McLaren's notes to Bell's commentaries, "The true principle is, that a trader cannot limit his responsibility for debts, except by a special stipulation with his creditor in each case," as was provided for by most insurance companies.[79]

There is even a case for arguing that there was a stronger culture against limited liability north of the border. Adam Smith's condemnation of exempting "a particular set of dealers from some of the general laws which take place with regard to all their neighbours" influenced subsequent Scottish authorities, notably J. R. McCulloch, who was an outspoken critic of limited liability.[80] By the time of the 1854 royal commission on the law of partnership, of fifteen Scottish witnesses, only five advocated the concession of general limited liability.[81] This antipathy was reflected in the behavior of Scottish companies, which were less likely to provide explicitly for the limited liability of shareholders: 20.7 percent of our Scottish sample did so, compared with 32.9 percent of unincorporated companies in England and Wales. Before 1826, the differences were particularly striking: 28.6 percent of Scottish and 63.9 percent of English unincorporated companies (we have no Welsh companies from this period) limited the liability of their shareholders. This can be partly explained by sectoral differences in the samples: banks account for 30.8 percent of the Scottish unincorporated companies before 1826, whereas insurance companies represent a larger proportion (60.5 percent) of English unincorporated companies in the same period. However, there were also striking differences among insurance companies north and south of the border, suggesting national as well as sectoral factors mattered. Whereas 79.5 percent of English insurance companies provided for limited liability, only 33.3 percent of their Scottish counterparts did so. Two out of three Irish insurance companies had a limited-liability clause.

Banking was the only sector in which the limited-liability clause was almost unknown. Although the extent of possible losses in banking would have made protection particularly attractive to potential investors, both the government and the banks themselves were reluctant to undermine the principle of unlimited responsibility, long perceived to be reliable proof of the creditworthiness of a bank. Consequently, the take-up of limited liability was slow even after the reform of 1858 that allowed banks to exercise the option.[82] In law, the protection conceded to shareholders in other sectors often did not apply to banks. Joint-stock banks were explicitly prohibited in England and Wales by an act of 1708, while in Ireland, the Anonymous Partners Act excluded banking companies.[83] The same was true of the acts of 1855 and 1856 allowing for general limited liability by registration. Only one unchartered bank in our sample, the short-lived Royal Bank of Australia (1840), made any attempt to provide for limited liability, and this was a rather clumsy imitation of the practices of insurance companies. Such attempts were highly unusual: banks were far more likely, as Munn points out, to parade their unlimited liability in order to boost confidence in their operations.[84]

An almost universal practice among banking companies, and more common than full limited liability in most other sectors, was for constitutions to make shareholders, among themselves, liable only in proportion to the shares they held. Under this regime, although an individual shareholder might be held liable *in solidum* for a company's debts in an action by a third party, he could then take legal action to ensure that the other shareholders paid their share of the debts. The County of Gloucester Bank (1836) was typical, stipulating that "each of the Proprietors shall as between themselves be entitled to and interested in the profits, and liable to the losses of the Company, in proportion only to his share or shares in the capital or joint stock thereof."[85] Over half (53.6 percent) of our 224 unincorporated companies operated a proportional or pro rata liability regime. After banking, the regime was most common in gas and shipping. Proportional-liability clauses were especially prevalent in Scotland. Whereas Scottish companies were less likely to provide for the full limited liability of shareholders, no less than 75.9 percent of all Scottish unincorporated companies provided for the proportional liability of shareholders. In contrast, only 48.3 percent of English and Welsh companies did so. The limits of its usefulness were demonstrated in 1772 by the fate of the shareholders of the failed Ayr Bank. Though liable for the debts of the company in proportion to their shares, many were ruined by the collapse.[86] Nevertheless, legislation in 1826 endorsed the principle of pro rata liability for banks, while the act of 1844 stipulated that any shareholder who was adjudged liable for the commitments of a company could recover these sums on a proportional basis from the other shareholders.[87]

The importance of the liability regime—whether fully limited or proportional—to shareholders is demonstrated by the obstacles that were placed in the way of altering it. This is demonstrated by the restrictions that were placed on constitutional amendments. As we saw in the previous chapter, most unincorporated companies—175 of the 224 in our sample (78.1 percent)—allowed the constitution to be amended by the shareholders. In all sectors, however, many companies disallowed certain kinds of constitutional amendments. Of the 175 unincorporated companies that allowed amendments, 76 (43.4 percent) disallowed amendments to the liability of shareholders. The figure rises to 60.0 percent for companies with a limited-liability clause. Such restrictions protected shareholders from an unwanted change in the liabilities to which they were exposed.

Alternative Forms of Shareholder Protection

Limited-liability clauses were only one way in which unincorporated companies could seek to make investment safer. A range of other mechanisms designed to protect shareholders were also inserted into constitutions. Some of these related to the procedures regulating calls on shares. Nearly half of the unincorporated companies (46.9 percent) capped the amount that could be called at any one time, and others stipulated a maximum that could be called in any one year. More than half (57.1 percent) stipulated a minimum notice that had to be given when making a call, ranging from four to ninety days (one month was the mode). A further quarter insisted upon a minimum length of time between calls, most commonly three months. All these provisions were far more common in the constitutions of corporations. However, twenty-seven unincorporated companies (12.1 percent), compared with just eighteen corporations (6.2 percent), gave GMs authority over all or some calls that could be made on shares. Although this would not affect shareholders' or the company's relationships with third parties, it represented another means of proprietorial oversight and, as we have seen, received some support from the courts.[88]

Borrowing was another important area affecting shareholder liability. In cost-book mining companies, borrowing was highly regulated and effectively impossible without shareholder approval or the explicit authority of the company's constitution.[89] In our sample of joint-stock companies, a majority (51.0 percent) of corporations specified that borrowing had to be approved by GMs. By contrast, the constitutions of unincorporated companies were generally silent on the matter. This silence can be interpreted as permissive or restrictive. Borrowing was explicitly permitted in just twenty-nine cases, and of these shareholder approval was required in only ten. Sixteen of these twenty-nine companies, however, imposed a cap on the amount that could be borrowed. Despite the lack of constitutional provision, in practice, major borrowing decisions seem to have been normally reserved to GMs. When borrowing was undertaken without shareholder approval, considerable disquiet could be raised about the extent of their liability for this debt. At the Ayr Bank, for example, following the failure of 1772, a committee of investigation protested strongly that all the shareholders were being held proportionally liable for debts arising from an issue of annuities approved by a GM, the attendance at which had consisted mainly of shareholders already in debt to the company.[90] Disquiet usually arose, however, after the event, for shareholders were generally happy to consent to whatever loans the board chose to contract, especially when these spared them from calls on their shares. For example, once half of the capital of the Great Western Railway had been called up, the board, with the unanimous support of the GM, opted to borrow the equivalent of the remaining half of the capital (£1.25 million) as well as the £833,333 additional borrowing authorized by the act of incorporation, "with a view to limit or defer the future Calls on the Proprietors."[91] Borrowing in excess of the sum authorized by act of Parliament was very common among railway companies.[92]

Some constitutions tried to protect shareholders from unauthorized or reckless borrowing. The directors of the Falkirk Gas Work Company (1829), for example, who enjoyed in most respects the protection of a standard Scottish indemnity clause limiting their responsibility for acts legally undertaken in their capacity as directors, were, notwithstanding this, forbidden either to borrow money on the company's behalf or to contract any debts greater than the capital stock. If they did, then they would be "jointly and severally liable to relieve the Company of such debts or money borrowed; and the Partners of the Company shall not collectively or individually, be liable in payment of any part thereof."[93] Shareholders in other Scottish gas companies enjoyed similar protection.[94] In England and Ireland, the same kind of protection was sometimes available. At the Preston Gas Light Company (1815), it was provided that "the Trustees shall not contract any debt to a greater amount than the funds in their hands will be sufficient to satisfy, and if they contract any such debts, they shall be themselves alone personally liable for the debt."[95] When this company was incorporated in 1839, the act explicitly provided limited liability for the shareholders.[96] Similarly, at the unincorporated Ballymena Gas Light Company (1842), although there was no attempt to limit the liability of shareholders to the amount of their subscriptions, and although there was a general indemnity clause for directors and trustees, the directors were personally liable for any debts they contracted beyond what was in the hands of the trustees or treasurer.[97] This company—echoing a common practice in the cost book system—also allowed shareholders the option of withdrawing from the company without further liability, provided their shares were fully paid up.[98] A slightly different division of liabilities occurred in the Union Lime Company of Aberdeen, where shareholders stood "bound for the debts and deeds, to the extent of their respective shares" only but agreed to relieve members of the Committee of Management of all liability for a cash account amounting to £500.[99] Other kinds of limitation reflected the specific circumstances of a company's foundation. The contract of copartnery of the London, Leith, Edinburgh and Glasgow Shipping Company (1820), for example, which was an amalgamation of two earlier companies, limited the responsibility of shareholders of each of the previous companies for the debts of the other.[100]

Another basic but essential way for shareholders to control their liability was to enable them to transfer their shares. Shares in unincorporated companies were not as easily transferable as those in corporations. Most unincorporated company constitutions (77.7 percent) gave directors the power to veto transfers and thereby control access to their company's shares. Specific provision for the relinquishing of shares to the board upon the demand of a shareholder, common in the cost-book system, was hardly ever made in joint-stock companies.[101] Most unincorporated constitutions, however, permitted but did not oblige directors to purchase shares on behalf of the company, enabling investors more easily to leave a company to which they no longer wished to belong, though such transfers would be subject to the extended liability described above.

The ability of shareholders to dissolve companies was probably the most important mechanism for controlling liability. This has rarely been acknowledged by historians.[102] Charles Coquelin, however, writing in 1845, noted that, "by such a clause, frequently resorted to in England, the principle of unlimited responsibility was in some degree neutralized."[103] In the modern context, the notion of dissolution as a protection for investors was recognized in the Insolvency Act (1986), which made *directors* "liable for the debts a company incurred after the point when they might reasonably be expected to have closed it down."[104] Allowing for the dissolution of a company by shareholders permitted, at least in theory, a form of controlled liability for investors. The issue of permanence versus temporariness was important in the context of defining shareholder liabilities. Corporations were usually established in perpetuity. There were exceptions. Fifteen corporations in our sample were established for a fixed term.[105] Eight of these (one harbor and seven bridge companies) were designed to be converted into trusts after achieving their objects.[106] In addition, two corporations established by charter—the New Brunswick and Nova Scotia Land Company (1834) and the Peninsular and Oriental Steam Navigation Company (1841)—had procedures for dissolution. In Scotland, corporations could be dissolved by forfeiture if they "abused the powers intrusted with them."[107] The constitution of the Bank of Ireland (1783) provided for dissolution by the Irish government on twelve months' notice or on petition by the Bank itself.[108] In the great majority of acts, and even in charters, however, there was no mention of dissolution. In total, 273 of the 290 corporations in our sample (94.1 percent) were established for an infinite duration and with no provision for the shareholders to dissolve. As the shareholders in these corporations generally enjoyed limited liability, there was less need to provide them with this additional protection.

By contrast, among unincorporated companies, the right of shareholders to dissolve the company, either in the normal course of events or in particular circumstances, or both, was general. Such rights were important because, as Lord Eldon's decision in the High Court of Chancery in the case of *Van Sandau v. Moore* in 1826 made clear, "the common principles of partnership," whereby any partner could dissolve the concern on giving notice to the other partners, could not and did not apply in the case of unincorporated joint-stock companies. Van Sandau was aggrieved that the deed of settlement of the British Annuity Company, in which he had purchased shares, was inconsistent with the prospectus that had induced him to do so. He argued that the company, like any partnership, should be dissolvable on notice given by any partner; however, there was no provision for this in the deed of settlement. Moreover, as Eldon remarked, even under the "common principles of partnership," all partners would have had a right to notice of dissolution, and Van Sandau had not given notice to all the shareholders in the British Annuity Company, who numbered around 250.[109] In practice, such notice would be virtually impossible to give to such a large body of shareholders. Eldon's ruling was followed in several later judgments that upheld the authority of the GM over dissolution and declared that a company could not be dissolved by a single shareholder seeking to settle his or her accounts.[110] As the barrister and social reformer John Malcolm Ludlow observed in 1848, Eldon's refusal to sanction the dissolution of the British Annuity Company in this case "went far towards securing to joint-stock companies in general one of the most essential of corporate privileges, that of perpetuity."[111] In 1844, the schedule of provisions in the model deed of settlement attached to the Joint-Stock Companies Act did not include a dissolution clause, and there was no mention of dissolution anywhere in the text of the act.[112] However, most unincorporated joint-stock companies established before 1844 had rather more protection for shareholders in the form of provisions for dissolution. Of the 224 unincorporated companies in our sample, 182 gave the shareholders some right of dissolution, while a further 11 companies were established for a specific period of time, giving shareholders in 86.2 percent of unincorporated companies some protection of this kind.[113] In the banking sector, where shareholders had significant liabilities, every unincorporated bank in our sample except one had procedures for dissolution, while the one banking corporation—the Royal Bank of Scotland (1727)—did not. It was essential for banks, wishing to attract capital without the protections of limited liability, to be able to offer shareholders provisions by which their company might be dissolved in the event of losses.

Procedures for dissolution can be divided into two kinds: general rights, whereby shareholders could dissolve the company in normal circumstances, and special rights, which allowed for dissolution in particular circumstances, usually large losses. General rights of dissolution involved a vote at a GM. In many companies, the confirmation of a second GM was necessary, and often a large vote in favor, commonly a two-thirds or three-quarters majority, with a large quorum was required. In eight cases, the threshold was 80 percent or more of the votes, and at one company—the Agricultural and Commercial Bank of Ireland (1836)—the consent of every single shareholder was required in order to dissolve in normal circumstances. General rights of dissolution were accorded to shareholders in 161 unincorporated companies (71.9 percent), although in 50 of these (31.1 percent) the consent of the directors was also required. These rights became increasingly common. Among the 146 unincorporated companies established in 1826–44, no fewer than 117

(80.1 percent) conceded these rights. Although there is no direct link between the general procedures for dissolution and the limitation of shareholder liability, the provision for dissolution was certainly part of a wider package whereby shareholders were able, if they worked together, to protect their investments.

This protection is demonstrated more clearly by special rights of dissolution. In some cases, the constitution stipulated that the company would automatically dissolve if losses reached a certain specified amount.[114] More commonly, as in the case of the ill-fated Northern and Central Bank of England (1834), if losses reached a certain amount (in this instance the whole of the reserve fund plus a quarter of the paid-up capital), the directors were obliged to summon an SGM at which it was in the power of one shareholder, or sometimes a group of shareholders, to insist upon dissolution. At such a meeting it was also lawful, if desired by the majority of shareholders, to vote to continue the concern, provided they bought out the shares of the dissentients.[115] At the National Bank of Scotland (1825), if a quarter of the paid-up capital was lost in any year, a quarter of the partners holding at least one-quarter of the stock could dissolve the company, whereas if half the capital was lost, any one shareholder could do so.[116] A special right of dissolution could exist alongside a general right. At the Agricultural and Commercial Bank of Ireland, for example, although dissolution in normal circumstances required the consent of all the shareholders, any single shareholder could dissolve the company if a quarter of the paid-up capital had been lost.[117] Among all unincorporated companies, eighty-three (37.1 percent of our sample) allowed special rights of dissolution. It was a feature of nearly all unincorporated banking constitutions (92.1 percent) but also occurred in insurance (19.7 percent), shipping (28.6 percent), manufacturing (20.0 percent), and in one gas company (Stroud Gas Light and Coke, 1833).

These clauses were explicitly designed to act as a de facto limitation of liability. The constitution of the Glasgow and Stranraer Steam Packet Company (1843), for example, stated that the intention of the automatic dissolution clause was "to prevent the Subscribers from ever being called on for a larger sum, than their original subscriptions."[118] The prospectus of the Stirlingshire Banking Company (1831) claimed that "the risk and responsibility of the Partners, would . . . be sufficiently limited by a clause providing for the dissolution of the Company in the event of a certain proportion of its advanced capital being at any time lost, and by laying aside a considerable part of the profits to form a sinking fund."[119] Peter

Watt, an Edinburgh accountant and former manager of the Nottingham and Nottinghamshire Joint-Stock Banking Company, explained in 1836 that the new English joint-stock bank constitutions embodied one "essential improvement" on the Scottish system that had influenced them, namely, "a solemn stipulation and covenant between the members, 'That, should even a *fourth part* of the capital be ever lost, the company shall be held to be dissolved.' From the inevitable operation of this most important and salutary stipulation, no loss *beyond a proportional part of the paid-up capital can ever take place* in any joint-stock bank which admits this important clause into the conditions of the association."[120] According to Watt, "it was always a matter of the utmost difficulty in Scotland to procure a wealthy nobleman or landed proprietor to become a proprietor of bank shares, except in the chartered banks of Scotland, where the responsibility is limited to the value of the share."[121] The new Scottish banks of the 1830s adopted the English practice: no Scottish bank in our sample established after 1826 failed to provide some kind of special rights of dissolution. Watt claimed the credit for the clause in the Central Bank of Scotland, which provided for special rights of dissolution in the event of the loss of a quarter of the paid-up capital, and which, he said, was designed "to limit the responsibility of shareholders."[122] Company promoters, however, who asserted that this clause amounted to full limited liability, could leave themselves open to criticism. Daniel O'Connell condemned the "wild scheme of what is called 'the Commercial and Agricultural Bank' [which] holds out a promise of limiting the liability of shareholders. As a lawyer and an honest man I am bound to denounce that delusion: the partnership as between the partners themselves may be dissolved by losses to a particular amount, but as between the partners and the public the liability necessarily continues for all the notes and engagements."[123]

The importance of special rights of dissolution becomes particularly clear if we examine them in conjunction with liability provision. Table 7.1 cross-tabulates limited liability provision and rights of dissolution in all unincorporated companies in our sample. It shows that, among the sixty-six unincorporated companies *with* a limited liability clause, only seven (10.6 percent) had special rights of dissolution. By contrast, among the 158 unincorporated companies *without* this clause (that is, where liability was proportional, unlimited, or not mentioned at all), shareholders had special rights of dissolution in 76 (48.1 percent). The importance

TABLE 7.1. **Shareholders' rights to dissolve unincorporated companies**

	All unincorporated companies		Companies with limited liability provision		Companies without limited liability provision	
	Number	%	Number	%	Number	%
General rights	161	71.9	43	65.2	118	74.7
Special rights	83	37.1	7	10.6	76	48.1
No mention of dissolution	42	18.8	21	31.8	21	13.3
Total number of companies	224		66		158	

Note: Percentages do not add up to 100, as many companies had both general and special rights of dissolution.

of these clauses is further underlined by restrictions on constitutional amendments. Table 7.2 shows the proportions of unincorporated companies with and without special rights of dissolution that prohibited amendments to the procedure. Row (b) shows that, among the seventy-six companies *with* special rights of dissolution and *without* a limited liability clause, forty-two (55.3 percent) prohibited amendments to the procedure for dissolution. By contrast, as row (a) shows, just two of the seven companies *with* both special rights of dissolution and limited liability did the same. Overall, very few companies, as demonstrated by columns (d), (e) and (f) of table 7.2, restricted amendments where there were only general and not special rights of dissolution, regardless of whether there was a limited liability clause.

Despite their sacrosanct status in many unincorporated company constitutions, special rights of dissolution were far from an infallible means of protection for shareholders, because directors could choose not to reveal losses, and shareholders might not detect them. Referring to Irish joint-stock banks, Hickson and Turner explain that special rights of dissolution were in place but would have been difficult to exercise in practice. In the Belfast-based banks that they examine, any one shareholder could dissolve the company if one-third of the capital was lost. It required the consent of one-quarter of the shareholders in the event of the loss of 20 percent of the capital and half the shareholders when losses amounted to 10 percent. As Hickson and Turner point out, "this provision may have prevented shareholders from losing their initial investment by restraining the risk-taking behaviour of the directors. However,

TABLE 7.2. **Restrictions on constitutional amendments in unincorporated companies with special rights of dissolution (N = 83), 1720–1844**

	(a) Number *with* special rights of dissolution	(b) Number prohibiting amendments to dissolution procedure	(c) Column (b) as % of column (a)	(d) Number *without* special rights of dissolution (but with general rights)	(e) Number prohibiting amendments to dissolution procedure	(f) Column (e) as % of column (d)
(a) Companies *with* a limited liability clause	7	2	28.6	38	1	2.6
(b) Companies *without* a limited liability clause	76	42	55.3	61	2	3.3
(c) All unincorporated companies (a) + (b)	83	44	53.0	99	3	3.0

given that accounts were only published annually and may have been opaque, it might have been difficult for shareholders to ascertain how much capital a bank had at any particular moment."[124] An example of the chaos that could occur in such circumstances arose at the Agricultural and Commercial Bank of Ireland, where, as we have seen, there were special rights, and very stringent general rights, of dissolution. The bank suspended payment in November 1836 and was eventually wound up in the 1840s. The financial information available to shareholders was woefully deficient, and in any case there was no attempt by any shareholder to dissolve the bank, perhaps because the required amount of capital had not actually been lost. The shareholders, however, found an alternative means of limiting their liability. Most of them had not even signed the deed of settlement, and a judgment in 1844 ruled that these shareholders were not liable for the uncalled portion of their shares.[125] The company eventually had to obtain an act of Parliament to assist with the dissolution of the bank. The act gave powers to the courts to wind up the affairs of the bank and conceded that "the Law is defective in the Means of making the Members of Joint Stock Companies Contributories for paying their Debts in full . . . and also in the Means of adjusting the Rights of the Members of any such Company amongst themselves, and finally winding up the Affairs of such Company."[126] Making shareholders pay their debts was indeed difficult, as they could adopt a number of strategies for evading liability during the process of winding up, forming associations for defense and engaging solicitors to spot legal loopholes. Nevertheless, the shareholders of the Ayr Bank in 1772, the Northern and Central Bank of England in the late 1830s, the Royal British Bank in 1856, the Western Bank of Scotland in 1857, and the City of Glasgow Bank in 1878 all found themselves liable for considerable extra payments after the collapse of their companies. In all these cases, there were special rights of dissolution for the protection of shareholders, but they were not exercised, at least not in time to prevent shareholders' being called upon for additional liabilities.[127]

Even if shareholders were capable of interpreting financial data, what was made available to them was often inadequate. The questions of liability and dissolution were bound up with more general issues of monitoring and governance in the unincorporated joint-stock company, in the same way as monitoring mechanisms in the cost-book companies aided the process of "controlling" shareholder liability. However, whereas in the stannary jurisdiction "the average cost book adventurer had at least the opportunity of knowing the extent of his liability" and of participating in any decisions to increase that liability, this was much less true for the shareholder in an unincorporated joint-stock company.[128] In cost-book companies, shareholders could inspect the books of the company at any time. This was also broadly true in joint-stock corporations. Of the 290 in our sample, 165 allowed inspection of accounts by shareholders at any time, and only 4 explicitly disallowed it. By contrast, a culture of secrecy operated in other sectors, such as banking, which made monitoring by shareholders of the affairs of their companies, and by extension their liabilities, much more difficult. Eighty of our 224 unincorporated companies prohibited the inspection of account books by individual shareholders, and only 44 explicitly permitted it. Generally, a shift away from transparency occurred in these years. We examine this in more detail in the following chapter.

In this context, shareholders could try to use their unlimited liability as a moral argument for greater transparency from the board, though such attempts did not always succeed. At the Ashton, Stalybridge, Hyde and Glossop Bank (established in 1836), the AGM of 1840 heard that bad debts hung over the bank, and one shareholder suggested that a "public accountant" be appointed to scrutinize the affairs of the company. This shareholder, a Mr. Earnshaw, said that "the meeting might think he was taking a deal upon himself in broaching these matters, but he thought that when the whole of a person's property was at stake, and what he knew of individuals in the room who had toiled hard for forty or fifty years to acquire what property they possessed, he thought he was fully warranted in making these observations."[129] Earnshaw attempted, without success, to force the directors to produce a more detailed report of the company's assets and liabilities. Matters came to a head three years later, when another shareholder proposed the appointment of a committee of inspection to make an accurate estimate of the losses incurred by the company and to "judge of the propriety of having its affairs wound up." The GM turned to the deed of settlement and found that the shareholders had no power to dissolve the company at that time. Only when the reserve fund and one-quarter of the paid-up capital had been lost could an SGM dissolve the company without the directors' approval.[130] A group of shareholders, however, managed to force an SGM on the issue, where a vote was taken by show of hands on the question of dissolution. Twenty-six voted in favor, forty-nine voted against. Immediately, six shareholders, together holding some fifteen hundred shares, sold their shares to the directors.[131] Sometimes quitting a company that had lost a shareholder's trust was the only way for an investor to limit his or her liability. In this case, however, under the terms of the banking legislation of 1826, the shareholders remained liable for the bad debts of the company for three more years.

Conclusions

In the joint-stock economy as a whole, no trade-off existed whereby investors were assured of limited losses in return for surrendering rights of inspection of accounts and general oversight of the company. Quite the reverse: with regard to access to accounts, shareholder rights were strongest in incorporated companies, where limited liability was (in most cases) already enjoyed. Unincorporated companies, however, were keen to market themselves as safe havens for capital, and to do so, entrepreneurs devised a raft of constitutional measures designed to regulate and control shareholder liabilities. These included imitating the limited liability available to investors in corporations but also embracing such rights as proportional liability, rights over calls and borrowing, protection from the consequences of unauthorized borrowing, restrictions on constitutional amendments, and finally, the safety net of dissolution. The inclusion of some or all of these benefits in company constitutions was an important feature of promotional strategies.

For joint-stock politics to work, shareholders needed access to accurate and full information relating to company affairs. Informed shareholders were the best guard against bad government, a view endorsed by the Select Committee on Joint-Stock Companies in 1844. Full publicity of information, its report argued, "would baffle every case of fraud."[132] The problem was that corporate scandals indicated that directors could not always be trusted to ensure the smooth operation of mechanisms for controlling shareholder liability, and boards with something to hide were undoubtedly aided by the limits imposed in many unincorporated companies on shareholder access to accounts. Indeed, some shareholders probably lacked even a basic understanding of their rights and liabilities. In sixteen companies (all in banking or insurance), they were not even permitted to inspect or take extracts from the company's constitution, which they had signed, and by which they were bound to abide.[133]

By 1854, the nonparticipation of shareholders in the direct management of companies was viewed by many observers as a reason to limit their liability. Thus the *Economist* remarked, "It may be said that if men are liable to the whole extent of their property, the sense of responsibility must induce to greater prudence and caution. This is not to the point, inasmuch as the shareholders who might be so influenced have practically little or no share in the management."[134] Four years later, when limited liability was granted to banking companies in the wake of a series of failures, unlimited responsibility was portrayed in Parliament as one of the central causes of mismanagement and crisis.[135] Although limited liability would be unfair to bank depositors and its introduction would weaken incentives for shareholder oversight, the existing protections afforded to shareholders, in the form of special rights of dissolution, were "practically useless." This was the verdict of the anonymous author of the diatribe *How to Mismanage a Bank*, written in the aftermath of the failure of the Western Bank of Scotland:

> It was intended in cases where the liability was unlimited, to secure that the loss never should exceed a certain proportion of the original stock, but it has utterly failed to afford such protection. The Western Bank had such a provision in its contract, that if on balancing the books such a loss "*appeared*," the result should be immediate dissolution. But such a loss never *appeared*;

that was carefully avoided. . . . A little "jugglery of figures" was all that was required to hide the truth, and in such circumstances it is to be feared such modes of concealment will be so often practised, that shareholders must look to other quarters for some security against ruin.[136]

Legislators had become convinced of the intrinsic shortcomings of unlimited liability and of its unsuitability in an age of rapid economic growth. The evidence considered here, however, suggests that unlimited liability was chiefly undermined by the governance failures that permitted directors of unincorporated companies to conduct their business in a greater degree of secrecy than was generally possible in companies incorporated by the state. Although clumsy methods of shareholder protection could be resorted to by insurance companies, whose attempts to use contracts to restrict liability were increasingly tolerated in the legal environment, these were more suitable in some sectors than in others. Alternative protective mechanisms required transparent governance, which was often noticeably absent in banking. Greater oversight of company affairs was not only increasingly necessary but also increasingly difficult as the number and size of joint-stock companies grew. The changing dimensions and mechanisms of transparency and accountability are the subject of the next chapter.

Transparency and Accountability

Did you ever expect a corporation to have a conscience, when it has no soul to be damned, and no body to be kicked?—Edward, 1st Baron Thurlow[1]

The liberal political tradition prized publicity and detested secrecy. Jeremy Bentham believed that publicity was essential if freedoms were to be safeguarded, for secrecy bred injustice: "In the darkness of secrecy, sinister interest, and evil in every shape have full swing. . . . Where there is no publicity there is no justice. Publicity is the very soul of justice. It is the keenest spur to exertion and the surest guard against improbity."[2] The *Times* agreed: "Publicity is the first principle of our political institutions. On it we depend for liberty, order, honour, and all that makes life tolerable."[3] Secrecy was a vice: "Incompetence loves secrecy—idleness loves secrecy—corruption loves secrecy."[4] These principles were widely thought to apply to the economic sphere as well. John Stuart Mill, for example, idealized small societies in which commercial activity was regulated by an informed public opinion that had access to reliable information.[5] Long before the advent of nineteenth-century liberalism, the joint-stock company had been a site where these ideas were discussed and tested. Questions of auditing procedures and accounts, secretive loans and transfers of stock, and the transparency of financial information had been raised in the Bank of England and the East India Company in the 1690s, in the South Sea Company in 1720–1, during the crisis in the EIC from the 1760s, and at the fall of the Ayr Bank in the 1770s. For some, joint-stock companies represented models of transparency compared to secretive private firms. Proponents of joint-stock banks legitimized them by comparing their accountability with the habits of secrecy that characterized private banks. In 1833, one such commentator asked who was best able to conduct the affairs of a bank prudently, "those who are under *surveillance*, or those who are not?—those who have no power whatever individually over the funds?—who are a constant check on each other?—who every year are bound to come to their account of what shall have done or left undone?—or those who, in the face of the total ignorance of their customers . . . are certainly beset—though their probity and honour resist it—with the temptation of entering into improvident investments or advancements."[6] According to this view, transparency meant responsible management and, therefore, stability and profitability. The protective mechanisms discussed in chapter 7 were only of use to shareholders insofar as they had access to reliable information. Similarly, the democratic control of companies, discussed in chapter 6, could function meaningfully only when information about company activities was freely circulated. Corrupt or inefficient management could be concealed if a company's transactions were cloaked in secrecy. In this chapter we examine the mechanisms for shareholder oversight of accounts. Constitutional provisions ranged from a general right to inspect all documents relating to the company to a complete bar on any access and from vague provisions for GMs to "audit" annual accounts to formal independent auditing procedures.

Traditionally, the process of auditing, both in companies and in poor-law administration, involved an oral examination, in the dictionary sense of *audit* as "a hearing, an audience . . . a judicial examination." In addition to the oral inquiry, there was a long history of the audit also involving a physical cross-checking of documents. The *Oxford English Dictionary* cites a fifteenth-century reference to the audit as an "official examination of accounts with verification by reference to witnesses and vouchers."[7] By the early nineteenth century this had developed into the standard "bookkeeping audit," in which the auditors, whether external or internal to the company, prepared the same accounts that they were required to check. The common procedure, if carried out in full, was to "close off" the account books, reconcile the cash books and bank statements, check the "postings" (transfers) of figures from one ledger to another, vouch the transactions with documentary evidence such as invoices, "cast" (add up) the columns of figures in the cash book and ledgers, and draw up a trial balance. In a "pure" audit, the task of the auditor would be to check whether these procedures had been carried out correctly by the company's clerks. In our period, however, the auditor would usually be undertaking some or all of these procedures for the first time. Indeed, the standard "sherry and biscuits" audit did not involve much in the way of vouching transactions or checking figures.[8]

The vitality of accounting history has ensured a large literature on accounting practices, the emergence of the accountancy profession, and the legislation regulating the publication and audit of accounts.[9] But there are sizeable gaps in the historiography. Most notably, there is an emphasis on the second half of the nineteenth century, after the acts of 1844, 1855 and 1856 first imposed, then partially removed, accounting and audit requirements on companies.[10] Moreover, existing work based on the evolution of regulatory codes tells us little about how company audits actually operated and does not explore the dynamics between shareholders and directors in relation to such audits. Business practices in this area prior to 1844 remain to some extent a mystery, about which unsupported generalizations are often made. Thus, it has been claimed that "until at least the middle of the 19th century, shareholders were considered to have an inherent right to inspect their companies' books of account."[11] In fact, as this chapter will show, while access to account books was permitted by most corporations, in the unincorporated sector a culture of secrecy restricted access not only to accounts but also to most other documents. Even in corporations, shareholder rights were being eroded, albeit not consistently, long before the mid-nineteenth century. There was no straightforward trajectory from transparency to opaqueness, and variations between sectors were considerable, though large companies proved consistently keener to limit the information available to shareholders and to impose intermediaries between the shareholders and company accounts. The chapter will show that the first half of the nineteenth century saw a gradual and uneven move across the joint-stock economy away from general rights of shareholders to inspect account books and toward a more restrictive environment in which proprietors were increasingly required to be content with summary accounts or balance sheets circulated at GMs. Direct oversight of accounts, by individual shareholders or by GMs, was replaced by more formal scrutiny of accounts by ad hoc or regular auditors. These developments reinforced the gradual exclusion of shareholders from participation in the other aspects of governance discussed above and did not necessarily provide for a more effective representation of their interests.

Shareholder Oversight

Joint-stock companies faced similar issues of transparency and accountability as other political bodies, such as municipal corporations and poor-
law boards. It is, therefore, unsurprising that there was an interchange of
ideas and practices between institutions, not least because individuals
moved freely between them as businessmen, councillors, mayors, attorneys, accountants, and MPs.[12] Although references to local government
audit in England can be traced to the fifteenth century, it was the emergence of formal poor-law institutions, financed by compulsory rates, that
spurred the development of accounting and auditing procedures. Thus,
under the terms of the Poor Relief Act (1601), the churchwardens and
parish overseers who administered the poor law were required, within
four days of relinquishing office, to deliver to two justices of the peace an
account of all monies received, or assessed and still to be received, plus
all stock they held. This account did not necessarily need to be in writing
and may have been simply a "hearing."[13] Such provisions were vague and
relatively informal and perhaps not widely enforced; they certainly did
not amount to an independent audit. Similarly, pre-1835 municipal corporations kept books of account in the hands of a steward or treasurer.
These were apparently audited annually, but it is not clear by whom, and
there was no statutory procedure.[14] The Municipal Corporations Commission, whose recommendations lay behind the reform of 1835, heard
repeated complaints "of revenue misapplied, debt contracted, and property alienated—of the absence of all accounts and the denial of all accountability by certain corporations."[15]

In the eighteenth century, more formal accounting procedures were
introduced to poor-law institutions. Under the terms of the Poor Relief
Act (1743), wardens and overseers were required to keep "a just, true,
and perfect account, in writing fairly entered in a book or books to be
kept for that purpose," which could be inspected by any ratepayer "at all
seasonable times," on payment of a fee of sixpence. The officials were
also required to present the accounts to justices of the peace and ver-
ify them under oath.[16] Dubois suggests that it was rare for a similar right
to be conceded to the shareholder in early joint-stock companies: "in
most companies he was permitted to examine only those accounts that
were submitted to the general court, and his access to other papers was
carefully restricted."[17] The 1733 act of the South Sea Company, for ex-

ample, confirmed the company's practice of making only summary accounts available to shareholders, a secrecy also applied to other papers. The South Sea directors resolved in 1735 that shareholders were not permitted to peruse "the Papers relating to the Correspondence and General Affairs of the Company."[18] This, however, was not typical. In our sample, among corporations established in the period 1720–89, 68.0 percent explicitly permitted shareholders to inspect the account books at all times, casting proprietors in a role analogous to that of ratepayers. For example, in the River Dee Navigation Company (1740) shareholders had access, "at all seasonable Times," to the "Books of Accounts, Cash and other Books" that contained "all Accounts and other Matters concerning the said Company; their Joint Stock, and their Dealings and Transactions, and the Rents, Issues, and Profits of the said Company, and the Assignments to be made of their Stock."[19] In the last decade of the eighteenth century the right to inspect the books became even more widely available, being enshrined in twenty-seven of the thirty-one corporations in our sample for those years.

The right of inspection was also fairly widespread in eighteenth-century unincorporated companies: exactly half of those established in 1720–89 permitted individual access to accounts. The two unincorporated Scottish banks in our sample for this period, however, both restricted access to account books to three proprietors "concurring together," who could then inspect the books only in the presence of two directors.[20] These clauses were precursors of the tighter restrictions on access to accounts and other documents that became more widespread among both incorporated and unincorporated companies during the nineteenth century.

One such restriction was to confine inspection of the books to a specified period, usually either side of the OGM. An early example of this arose in 1776, when the general court of the East India Company resolved that the accounts submitted to it would be made available at India House for a week before the OGM for the inspection of the proprietors.[21] The first in our sample to include a similar provision was the Caledonian Insurance Company (1805), where the account books and balance sheet were open for inspection for fourteen days either side of the annual election of directors.[22] It seems to have been particularly favored north of the border, where it became the standard practice in Scottish water and gas companies. It was also echoed in the provisions of the Royal Burghs

Act and Parliamentary Burghs Act (both 1833), which regulated burgh elections in Scotland. Here, the magistrates and council were required to make accounts available in the town clerk's or treasurer's office for inspection by electors for a fortnight before the election.[23] The practice spread and, as figure 8.1 shows, became dominant in the incorporated sector across Britain in the 1840s. It was the default position for corporations in the Companies Clauses Consolidation Acts of 1845.[24]

Some companies went further and denied individual access altogether. Denial was particularly prevalent in banking, where 73.4 percent of companies barred shareholders from any access to books of account, and the remainder were silent on the issue. This was the only sector in which not a single constitution allowed individual shareholders to inspect the books, although few (14.5 percent) insurance companies permitted the practice either. Banks and insurance companies were especially concerned not to lose a competitive edge by providing rivals with a sight of lists of their account holders and policyholders. Such restrictive provisions were rare outside banking and insurance, although we have nineteen examples from other sectors where it was either explicit or implicit that individual shareholders could *not* inspect the account books; fifteen of these were unincorporated, and all but two were established in or after 1825, suggesting the influence that banks had on other sectors in this respect. Figures 8.1 and 8.2 show that both incorporated and unincorporated companies were curbing shareholder access to accounts in the nineteenth century but that the latter were moving more quickly in this direction. Large unincorporated companies were more secretive than smaller companies. The mean nominal share capital of the thirty companies permitting access at all times was £31,967, compared with £756,725 for the eighty that explicitly denied access. The contrast is perhaps exaggerated by the large nominal capitals of the banks and insurance companies that formed the bulk of the latter group, but it is clear that it was large companies driving the change. The mean capital of the nineteen companies outside banking and insurance that denied access was £165,537, over five times that of the thirty unincorporated companies permitting access at all times.

Instead of allowing either free or restricted access to *individual* shareholders, some companies—following the model of the two eighteenth-century Scottish banks—permitted only groups of shareholders, acting together, to inspect the account books. Thirty-eight companies, 7.4 percent of the total, operated this system. Only four were corporations.

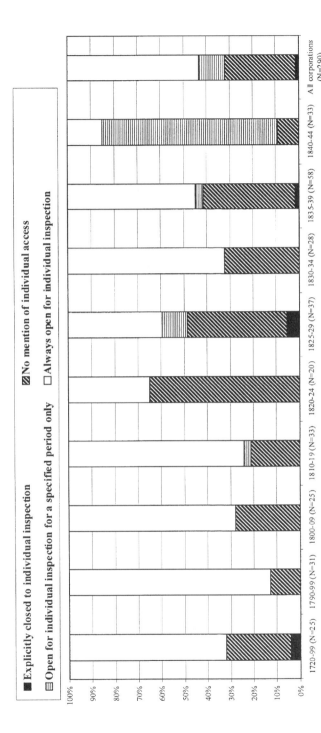

FIGURE 8.1. Individual access to account books in corporations by subperiod

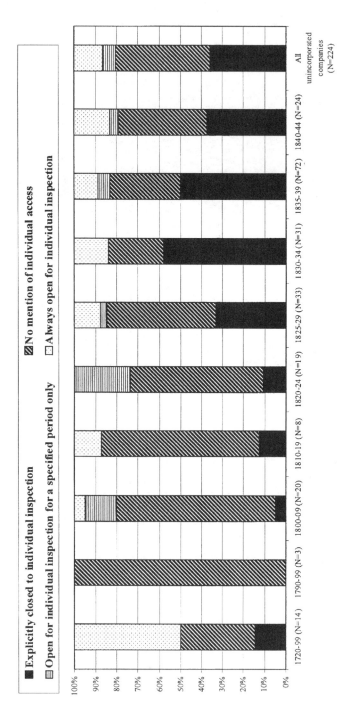

FIGURE 8.2. Individual access to account books in unincorporated companies by subperiod

Some constitutions set a threshold in terms of the number of shares or shareholders that could make such a demand. For example, at the United Kent Life Assurance and Annuity Association (1824) the books could be examined by any three proprietors of five shares each or by any person insured by the company for two years for £1,000 or more.[25] Here and elsewhere the GM could vote to give individual shareholders access to the accounts. In other cases, a single shareholder could inspect the books, but only if he or she held a specified number of shares. Such a system operated at the Royal Canal Company (1791), where the threshold was three shares.[26] Such systems diminished the rights of the smallest shareholders in particular. Some companies allowed *individual* inspection of books for a specified period and *also* permitted collective requisition at other times. The London and Edinburgh Shipping Company (1809), for example, opened its books to all shareholders either side of the OGM but stipulated that "no Partner or Partners shall be entitled, at any other time, to demand the use or inspection of the Company's books, unless specially authorized by a general meeting, or by an order from the Directors."[27] In addition, some companies allowed group requisitions *only* during a specified period. Seven of the thirty-eight companies allowing group requisitions raised this additional barrier to access; all seven were unincorporated.

There was also the issue of access to documents other than account books. Some companies, especially in the unincorporated sectors, were wary of allowing shareholders such access. It was not unknown for individual shareholders to be barred from inspecting the constitution itself. In seven companies the deed of settlement could only be consulted by a group of shareholders acting together. Shareholders, however, could challenge such restrictions in the courts. In 1840, it was ruled that the fact that a shareholder had covenanted in the deed of settlement not to call for the inspection of the company documents was not a bar to his moving for their production in an action brought by him against the company.[28] The GM was explicitly empowered to call for the deed of settlement in fifteen unincorporated companies, such as the Brandon Gun Flint Company (1838), where the GM could "call for, inspect and examine" any papers including the deed of settlement, or, alternatively, ten shareholders with twenty shares (ten percent of the total) could demand to see the documents; while they were not placed entirely out of reach in this way, they were made far less easy to consult.[29]

Two particular documents stood out, however, and were often made more widely available: the share register and the loan register. In corporations, a majority of constitutions (59.7 percent) explicitly stipulated that the share register should be open for inspection by individual shareholders, a proportion that increased at the end of our period. This practice was enshrined in the Companies Clauses Consolidation Acts, which required a "Register of Shareholders" to be made open to all shareholders at all times rather than only during the period in which the account books could be inspected.[30] In unincorporated companies, the picture was less clear. The share register was unambiguously open to inspection by individual shareholders in just thirteen unincorporated companies. However, constitutions sometimes granted right of access to "books of account and all other documents and writings," and shareholders in such companies could, of course, claim that the share register was one such document.

A standard clause in incorporating acts (though, again, rarely featuring in deeds of settlement) permitted shareholders and other interested parties to inspect the company's register of borrowing: 75.0 percent of incorporating acts had this clause.[31] It was usually part of the section that dealt with powers of borrowing and was separate from the clauses permitting inspection of other documents, where these existed. The clause was nearly universal among railways (all but one in our sample) and widespread among bridge, canal, harbor, and water companies. The register of borrowing was the most "public" of all documents relating to a company, showing some of its external relationships. Indeed, the clause ensuring its openness to interested parties became more ubiquitous over time, appearing in 93.8 percent of incorporating acts in the period 1840–4. Even though, as chapter 5 shows, many corporations were permitted to amend the parts of their incorporating acts that related to their proceedings among themselves, access to the loan register could not be amended. A loan register could be quickly checked for breaches of constitutional restrictions on investments and lending or for "loans to sundry" entries of the type misused by the South Sea Company directors. On occasion such information was used to criticize investments, for example at the County Fire Office in 1823, when shareholders disapproved of the decision to purchase risky foreign securities and low-interest Exchequer bills.[32]

In many cases, the exercise by shareholders of the right to inspect documents was, in practice, difficult, and they could be met with unhelpfulness on the part of company staff. It was revealed to the Lords Committee on railway audits, for example, that the accounts of the North Wales Railway Company had been deliberately kept "in such a manner as to be utterly unintelligible to a person who inspects them."[33] Shareholders attempting to exercise their right to access the company's loan register faced severe obstacles: "the most vexatious difficulties and excuses were interposed to prevent any effectual inspection; and when an inspection was at length permitted, it was discovered that these loans were entered in the ledger in cipher." The key to the cipher was in a private ledger, which staff kept hidden.[34] Shareholders of other concerns complained to the press that they were discouraged from visiting their company offices to examine the accounts because this was "construed into an invidious visit" and they were "received with ill-will, ill-humour, or ungraciousness of manner."[35]

Just as rights of individual inspection eroded over time, a similar process occurred with the rights of the GM to inspect and audit company accounts. The original GM "audit" was probably similar to the local government audit, which was a ritualized, public event and was often—like the GMs of eighteenth-century companies—held in a public house.[36] The right of GMs to call for and examine the books of account was a widespread feature of constitutions in the eighteenth century, more so among corporations (78.6 percent) than in unincorporated companies (47.1 percent). Five of our twenty-five corporations founded in 1720–89 *required* account books to be presented to the OGM and conceived of the audit, unambiguously, as an annual event. More common in this period (twelve of the twenty-five) was a clause such as the one included in the Leeds-Liverpool Canal act (1770), in which all GMs were given the "Power to call for, audit, and settle all Accounts of Money laid out and disbursed on account of the said Navigation."[37] By the time of the canal mania of the 1790s, this was the standard form of audit provision: twenty-seven of the thirty-one corporations established in this decade, mostly canal companies, adopted the "power to call for, audit, and settle" wording. Strictly speaking, this did not make an audit necessary, but our reading of eighteenth-century minute books suggests that where any form of audit was prescribed, books were usually presented to the OGM as a matter of course. Across the eighteenth-century joint-stock economy, the ubiquity of provision for audit by the GM demonstrates the expectation and apparent practicability of shareholder oversight and participation.

Constitutionally, at least, an unmediated relationship between directors and shareholders was reflected in the public audit of accounts at the GM, though when shareholders sought elucidation of the accounts at GMs, they sometimes encountered obstructive and unhelpful directors.[38]

There was a gradual, if uneven, decline in the proportion of companies that either required account books to be presented to the OGM or allowed GMs to demand them. Despite the uneven trajectory, the contrast between the start and the end of our period is stark. In the eighteenth century, 71.2 percent of constitutions stipulated this right. By 1840–4, this figure had fallen to just 29.8 percent. Instead of full account books, companies were increasingly likely to present *summary* accounts to the OGM. As figure 8.3 shows, unincorporated companies made this provision in large numbers even in the eighteenth century, but the practice remained uncommon in corporations until the later 1830s, when it became general.[39] This was partly driven by the railways, where the complexity of company affairs and the voluminous documentation that was produced meant the physical examination of accounts at GMs was becoming less practical.[40] Of the forty-one railway companies in the sample founded in 1830 or later, thirty-three (80.5 percent) provided for summary accounts to be presented at the OGM. Of the thirty-three, only four permitted the account books themselves to be called for and examined by the meeting. Other sectors present a similar picture. For example, among incorporated harbor companies, none of the twelve established before 1825 provided for summary accounts, and seven allowed individual inspection of the account books. Of the fifteen founded after 1825, ten required summary accounts to be presented, with just three of these continuing to allow individual access to account books at all times and three for specified periods only. The diffusion of summary accounting can be seen as primarily an effect of the increasing size of companies. The mean capital of the eighty-eight corporations that required summary accounts to be presented at the OGM was £357,267, compared with just £111,214 for those that did not. Among railway companies, the respective figures were £695,818 and £159,449.

The requirement to present only summary accounts provided scope for deception or omission, whereby directors could avert potentially uncomfortable confrontations at GMs. The diary of a director of the Great Western Railway, George Gibbs, demonstrates that boards were willing to conceal information from shareholders when this was considered in the company's best interests. The costs of this railway were increasing

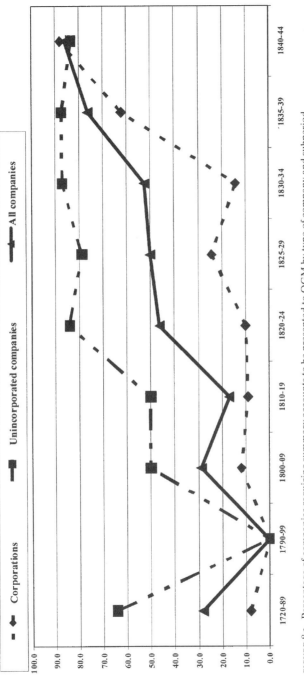

FIGURE 8.3. Percentage of companies requiring summary accounts to be presented to OGM by type of company and subperiod

faster than anticipated in the 1830s, and shortly before the OGM in 1838 the company's London secretary advised the board not to give shareholders precise figures but to "draw up such a paragraph for our report as, without in the least deceiving the public, would not give them at once the real state of the case."[41] The shareholders were successfully misled, giving thanks at the meeting to the directors for their exertions and "for the very candid and satisfactory Report."[42] Even where deliberate obfuscation did not take place, it was pointed out that the affairs of many companies were so extensive and complex "that the directors can prepare almost any statement they like for the proprietary" safe in the knowledge that most shareholders would not be able to make sense of it.[43] Even in statements affirming directors' commitment to transparency, the devil was in the detail. At one board meeting, the Great Western directors stated that "this board has always been most anxious to afford every information to their proprietors *which it may be in their opinion wise and prudent to communicate.*"[44] Moreover, boards that did respond to demands for simple and straightforward statements could use the opportunity to conceal rather than clarify important information. For example, the summary accounts presented by the directors of the West Middlesex Waterworks to the 1827 GM were much less detailed than hitherto. The directors explained that in framing the accounts, they had "endeavoured to render them so simple in their construction as to afford full and clear information on the essential points of Income and Expenditure." This also meant, however, that the accounts conveyed far less information. The sums now came under a small number of headings, and directors' pay was subsumed under "current expenses," making it impossible to identify their remuneration. It was perhaps not a coincidence that this step was introduced soon after the board adopted a policy of paying directors for attendance at subcommittees as well as at general boards.[45]

Boards used the language of openness and straightforwardness in their annual statements to shareholders, but this did not mean investors were safe. The directors of the recently formed Coventry and Warwickshire Bank assured the GM in 1839 that their object was "to put forth only a fair and moderate representation of the state of the Company, without wishing to excite undue expectations by an embellished report of its future prospects, rather being desirous of leaving the Proprietors at large, to form their judgment and to draw their own conclusions from general observations, more particularly as so great a majority of shareholders are resident in and near Coventry." But despite such commitments, and despite the local shareholder base, it proved easy to conceal troublesome reality for some time. Three years later, the shareholders were beginning to suspect something was wrong and to request returns of the number of accounts held by customers who had previously been insolvent or bankrupt and by those who lived more than twenty miles from Coventry. Soon afterward, the bank's general manager, James Beck, resigned, and at the next GM, the board told the shareholders that after Beck's departure, they had investigated the company's books and closed the accounts of the most dubious customers. The bank had made so many losses that only £15,535 of the paid-up capital of £58,850 remained.[46] No wonder that it became a commonplace by midcentury that balance sheets could be made to convey any impression desired by the board. In the view of political economist J. R. McCulloch, the annual publication of accounts gave shareholders no protection, as it was easy to "dress up a return, to make a rickety or bankrupt concern appear to be flourishing and wealthy."[47]

The ideal of transparent governance could be undermined by the behavior of shareholders as well as directors. Some sources give the impression that shareholders made little attempt to probe company accounts. Mechanisms to ensure directorial accountability were useless if shareholders were unwilling to make them work. McCulloch thought that in small partnerships, each partner exerted himself "to obviate extravagance or mismanagement in the conduct of the business," but in larger companies, "ordinary individuals [felt] that their efforts [were] apt to be of little avail," and so gave up trying to hold directors to account.[48] The accountant Robert Palmer Harding told a select committee of his experiences as an auditor for an unnamed company. Unhappy with the way in which the accounts had been prepared, he wrote a report for the GM but recalled that attendance at the GM was poor. The chairman read the directors' report "and referred to having had a report from the auditors, saying that he was satisfied that the shareholders had confidence in the directors, and did not require the auditors to tell them how to conduct their business. The shareholders were satisfied with that statement, and I ceased to be auditor at that meeting. The report that I sent in was not read, nor were the grounds of complaint that I brought before the board ever made known to the absent shareholders."[49]

When shareholders were dissatisfied with their treatment, however, they did sometimes take steps to secure better access to information. In 1840, for example, the directors of the Great Western Railway acceded to the shareholders' demand that, in future, the report and accounts be printed and distributed on the morning of the GM, to give them "the best opportunity of considering any matter to be discussed, when they assemble to express their sentiments on the general interests of the undertaking."[50] The morning of the GM, however, was too late as far as some observers were concerned. An anonymous pamphlet of 1853 urged that reports and accounts "should be in the hands of shareholders at least a week before general meetings, for it is absurd to suppose that there can be discussion and deliberation, if only the directors are in possession of facts connected with the subjects under consideration. To give proprietors reports and accounts ten minutes before the meetings take place, is to make these half-yearly gatherings mere matters of form, which most certainly the Legislature never intended."[51] There is evidence that shareholders in some companies were already insisting on this. In 1844 Mr. Coppinger, a proprietor of the Dublin and Drogheda Railway, successfully persuaded the board to print and circulate "the various reports and statements of accounts" one week before each GM, a system he claimed was already in place at the Hull and Selby Railway, in which he held shares, and at "most of the well-regulated companies throughout England."[52] The shareholders would thus be able to "make valuable suggestions, and to put questions, the replies to which might be of interest both to the public and this company." The directors consented but expressed concern that such advance publicity "might forestall the interest of the half-yearly meetings, and prevent a numerous attendance."[53] Thus, organized shareholders could combine at GMs to secure precirculation of accounts from their directors, but because this was rarely conceded in company constitutions, less organized shareholders were unlikely to enjoy this luxury. Even when accounts were precirculated, the extent to which they conveyed the real state of the company's affairs varied enormously, in many cases deliberately so.

Committees of Inspection and Standing Audits

In many companies, when shareholders were dissatisfied with the accounts presented by directors, there was provision for the appointment of a committee of inspection to investigate the affairs of the company in more depth. This provision introduced intermediaries into the relationship between the body of shareholders and directors and tended to be available most commonly when individual rights of inspection of accounts were not enshrined in the constitution. They had a long heritage. Dubois pointed out that the committee of inspection was a tool resorted to by shareholders of the York Buildings Company in 1726, the South Sea Company in 1732, the Free British Fishery in 1753, and the East India Company in 1772.[54] Our research suggests, however, that they did not become a common feature of corporate governance until well into the nineteenth century. The first such examples in our sample appear in two Scottish corporations established in 1806: the Glasgow, Paisley and Ardrossan Canal and the Glasgow Waterworks. At the latter, the GM was entitled to select three or more proprietors (who were not directors) to examine the accounts and report back to the next GM.[55] Committees of inspection could also be appointed in three other Scottish companies before 1825.[56]

The first English example of a committee of inspection in our sample was at the Huddersfield Banking Company (1827), where the GM could appoint a committee of three shareholders with the power "to call for the production of all books, vouchers, and documents" and interview "the manager, accountant, clerks, or other officers of the Company."[57] Procedures of this kind became the norm in joint-stock banks after the reforms of the mid-1820s. Of the thirty-nine banks in our sample established after 1825 in England and Wales, only seven did not provide for ad hoc committees of inspection, and five of these provided instead for a standing audit. In banking, shareholder oversight was necessarily more indirect than in sectors where the requirements of secrecy did not apply, and the committee of inspection or ad hoc audit became the standard mechanism for ensuring some kind of control over the management. Outside banking, however, ad hoc audit was also adopted in 16.6 percent of companies formed after 1825. The size of the committee envisaged varied from one to twelve members, with the mode being three.[58] Almost half of the companies permitting ad hoc inspections were railways. All of these were established between 1833 and 1843, and most did not allow individual shareholders to inspect the account books. That the committee was seen as an alternative to direct inspection of accounts is shown in table 8.1. Of companies allowing access at all times, just 6.7 percent provided for committees of inspection, whereas of companies denying individual access, exactly half allowed for ad hoc committees. There was also a clear tendency for larger companies to provide for ad hoc audit. The difference was particularly great in the case of

TABLE 8.I. **Individual access to account books and provision for ad hoc committees of inspection, all companies**

Individual access to account books	Committees of inspection permitted		No mention of committees of inspection	
	Number	%	Number	%
Access explicitly denied	42	50.0	42	50.0
No mention of access	25	13.2	164	86.8
Access within a set period	2	4.3	44	95.7
Access at all times	13	6.7	182	93.3

corporations, where the mean capital was three and a half times greater in those with ad hoc audit provision (£527,581 as opposed to £151,563).[59] Despite the ad hoc committee's status as an alternative, mediated form of access to accounts, boards seem to have been aware of the power they potentially gave shareholders. Interviewed before the select committee on joint-stock companies in the early 1840s, one anonymous merchant stated that committees of inspection could work, where shareholders had the power to appoint them, "but the directors, when they have the deed of settlement drawn up, take good care to give the shareholders as little power as possible."[60]

Wright argues that the ad hoc committees were effective tools of shareholder oversight and that "the simple threat of stockholder activism, if credible, was probably sufficient to keep most managers in line."[61] It is not clear, however, how "credible" the ad hoc audit committee actually was. Certainly, the committee did help check abuses in some cases. In 1839, some of the Bristol proprietors of the Equitable Gas Light Company (1832) received information that the company, despite paying regular dividends of between 3 and 4.5 percent, had in fact never been financially sound. A few days before the OGM they sent a delegation to confront the directors. The shareholders were permitted to see the accounts, and "upon a very cursory examination of these they were convinced that the Company were not in a state that would warrant a Dividend at all." They told the directors they would move for a committee of inspection at the GM, and the chairman, Treherne, threatened to resign if such a motion were carried. Just before the meeting, the delegation had another interview with the board, and Treherne, "finding his menaces of no avail thought proper to accede to that which he knew he could not effectually resist." At the meeting, he announced that, contrary to the circular summoning the meeting, the state of the concern did not warrant the declaration of a dividend. A committee of investigation of seven shareholders was unanimously appointed.[62]

The committee hired two "most able" accountants from Bristol to work with the company's accountant. Although the books were "fraught with contrivances to give a deceptive aspect to the Company's affairs," between them they established that the rumors were true and that all of the dividends had been paid out of capital, for in reality, the company had made losses of over £20,000, and the capital stock had been reduced by more than £50,000.[63] The committee revealed a systematic policy of wastefulness and corruption. One director was in the habit of receiving 2 guineas upon each shipload of coals received, amounting to about 140 guineas a year, while negligence in the collection of rates cost the company thousands of pounds a year. The board appointed an "extravagant number" of officers, who had received "the enormous sum" of £19,889 in salaries. A brother-in-law of a director was initially appointed as an accountant on an annual salary of £200. His complete unfitness for the situation was pressed upon the board, which eventually made him superintendent of the works, "a most important office, where he is known to be equally incapable of its duties" and where his accounts were "slovenly and unsatisfactory." Other ill-advised appointments included Treherne's young son, who, with no relevant experience, was employed at the works. During this time, the directors drew fees totaling £7,750. After hearing these revelations, the GM passed a motion of no confidence in the directors and appointed a committee to appoint a new board and introduce constitutional reforms to make future impropriety less likely. The company resumed dividends in 1843.[64]

While the committee of inspection placed the Equitable Gas Light Company on the road to recovery, it was not always an effective means of ensuring accountability, since efforts to appoint such committees were often easily resisted by boards of directors. For example, at their 1835 OGM, shareholders of the South Metropolitan Gas Light and Coke Company unsuccessfully moved for a committee to be appointed to examine the accounts. There were further angry confrontations the following year and again in 1840 when the directors twice more managed to thwart attempts to secure a committee.[65] At every step, the board frustrated attempts to subject its actions to the scrutiny of the shareholders. Even when a company was on the edge of failure, a committee of inspection could be resisted. At the Ashton, Stalybridge, Hyde and Glossop

Bank, encumbered with bad debts, a proposal was made from the floor at the OGM in 1843 to establish a shareholders' committee that would estimate the losses of the company and "judge of the propriety of having its affairs wound up." There was no explicit provision for such committees in the deed of settlement, nor, as it transpired, did the deed give shareholders the power to dissolve the company without the directors' prior recommendation. Some shareholders demanded an SGM, but the directors refused to concede one, and shortly afterward the outgoing board members were easily reelected.[66]

The appointment of committees of inspection was vigorously resisted into the second half of the nineteenth century. Robert Stewart argued in 1853 that directors and managers were in the best position to understand the affairs of a bank and protect the interests of not only its customers but also its shareholders, who undermined their own self-interest by the appointment of audit committees:

> Suppose that, at the annual general meeting of the shareholders of such a bank, after a satisfactory report has been made by the directors, some shareholder gets up and proposes that auditors be appointed to inspect the position of the bank, and to report thereon to the shareholders. Two or three suitable persons, in the opinion of the shareholders present, are appointed; but it is not unreasonable to infer that one or other of these is appointed from his noisy, bustling interference at the public meetings of the bank. Such an auditor or auditors, to support their reputation, must at least make a fuss, if they do nothing more, in executing their trust. They are "nothing if not critical"; they are appointed with the very object of tracing whether there may not be some weak or wrong points in the management of the directors; and from such elements is it not rational to expect an occasional discovery of mare's nests? Suppose these to be industriously hunted up and proclaimed aloud to the shareholders, a panic instantly ensues among them, the shares of the bank fall in value, the public takes the alarm, the depositor withdraws his money, and a greater blow is struck at the prosperity of the bank than the directors will be able to repair in seven years. Too late the shareholder finds that his interests have been destroyed by the precipitancy and self-sufficiency of one or two men [who have rushed] into a consideration of the delicate negotiations and personal interests of the customers of the bank, which could only be properly managed or appreciated by those who thoroughly understood them, viz., the directors and manager.[67]

Over time, the committee became an even harder tool for shareholders to deploy successfully. First, constitutions began setting higher majorities at GMs before a committee could be appointed. Second, shareholding thresholds for membership of ad hoc committees were imposed. In the case of the Burton, Uttoxeter and Staffordshire Union Banking Company (1839), as in many others, the shareholders appointed to the committee had to be qualified to act as directors, which required a nominal investment of £4,000, of which £1,000 was paid up.[68] Small shareholders, who were often unable even to cast votes in banking companies, as shown in chapter 6, were in these ways increasingly marginalized from the process of holding boards of directors to account.

Dissatisfaction with the weaknesses of the ad hoc audit led to calls for the appointment of standing auditors. A movement toward the latter can be detected in both the joint-stock sector and in local government during the first half of the nineteenth century. Under the terms of the Poor Rate Act of 1810, powers of audit were given to justices of the peace, and under Hobhouse's Act of 1830, parishes could adopt a new form of elective local government, with "provisions for publicity" and independent "Auditors of Accounts."[69] According to Sidney and Beatrice Webb, provisions of this kind could be related to the emergence of salaried professionals in local government: for example, the paid parish overseers of the poor, who were appearing in the eighteenth century and were given legislative sanction by the Sturges Bourne Act of 1819.[70] According to Snell, the auditing of parish accounts became "a serious occasion" in the nineteenth century. By the 1860s, overseers were required to keep seven different kinds of account book, and collectors of poor rates an additional three.[71] Further steps were taken with the poor-law and municipal corporation reforms of 1834–5. The former allowed boards of guardians to elect their own auditor and to fix his remuneration, though vesting the power of appointment in the boards undermined the effectiveness of the measure.[72] The latter stipulated that meetings of the new elected municipal councils should be open to members of the public and that municipal accounts should be annually audited and published as an "abstract."[73] The "elective audit" was carried out by three auditors, two of whom were elected by the ratepayers and subject to the same property qualifications as councillors and one of whom was appointed by the mayor.[74]

From 1844, legislation slowly began to press further still toward the idea of an *external* audit. In 1844, a reform to poor-law accounting procedures in England and Wales created a group of district auditors, although the appointment of new auditors was vested in the chairmen of boards of guardians. Thus a body of external auditors was created, but the procedure for appointment was not yet independent. Not until 1872 were district auditors appointed directly by the local government board. District auditors took responsibility for auditing sanitary districts' accounts from 1872, and county councils' and parish councils' accounts from 1888 and 1894, respectively. Municipal borough accounts, even as late as the 1930s, were not audited by district auditors, although many carried out a professional audit as well as the "elective audit," which was biannual under the terms of the Municipal Corporations Act (1882).[75]

The spread of standing audit provisions in local government was sometimes cited by those who wanted to see them extended to joint-stock companies. John Grey V. Porter wrote to the *Times* in 1847 that a large meeting at Enniskillen unanimously proposed that new legislation be enacted for Ireland requiring that each railway company be audited by two men "of high character" to be appointed by the government. The existing system, whereby shareholders audited company accounts, did not inspire public confidence: "We have also a good parallel example in support of this suggestion. There are 130 Poor Law unions in Ireland, and their accounts are audited by four auditors appointed by the Poor Law Commissioners, and with great satisfaction to the public."[76] Similar suggestions were made for banking. Following the bank failures of 1836 and 1837, Daniel Hardcastle Jr., the pseudonymous author of a tract titled *Banks and Bankers*, argued that the mismanagement of these years could have been avoided "if all joint-stock Banks had been bound by law from the period of their first establishment to the observance of a few simple rules, for the proper audit and frequent publication of their accounts."[77] According to Hardcastle, a full annual audit should be carried out "by competent persons specially appointed for the purpose, not by the directors, but by the shareholders at a public meeting."[78] Arguably, the standing audit ensured more rigorous shareholder oversight, giving a measure of ongoing supervision of the direction and management of companies.

It should be emphasized that the external audit was as yet barely used. Among the 514 company constitutions in our sample, only 8 provided unambiguously for an external audit. Seven of these were corporations. The earliest was the Calder and Hebble Navigation (1769), where the GM had the standard power to "call for, audit, and settle" the accounts, but where there was disagreement, the accounts would be "ad-justed and settled" by any three or more of the commissioners appointed by the incorporating act to deal with disputes between the company and third parties.[79] Arguably, this was not a standing audit at all, but later companies made more clear-cut provision. For example, the Leeds Waterworks Company (1837) was required to submit its annual accounts to the accountants and auditor, or treasurer, of the Leeds borough coun-cil, which was then entitled to publish as much of the accounts as it saw fit, at the company's expense.[80] An alternative provision was found at the Hythe Hard Company (1844), where an auditor was to be appointed by the chairman of the Hampshire quarter sessions and to report on the accounts twice yearly.[81] Provisions of this kind were rare, however, and their low incidence anticipated the reluctance of mid-nineteenth-century legislators to require independent external audits.

Much more common was the internal standing audit or, in some cases, a constitutional provision for an audit that could be *either* inter-nal or external.[82] Across our sample as a whole, and including all forms of standing audit, 145 companies (28.2 percent) made some such provi-sion.[83] The number of auditors stipulated varied from one to nine, but the modal number was two (fifty-three instances). As was the case with ad hoc committees, the average capital of companies that provided for standing audit (£500,741) was considerably greater than in those that did not (£280,267). Larger companies were thus driving the shift away from direct shareholder involvement in company accounts and toward the use of intermediaries. Figure 8.4 charts the progression of the standing au-dit from eighteenth-century oddity to the norm by the 1840s. Unincor-porated companies were quicker to embrace standing auditors, but by the 1840s they were overtaken by the corporations, 63.6 percent of which made provision for them. The standing audit was most common in colo-nial companies (83.3 percent) and insurance (62.9 percent), followed by shipping (46.2 percent). By contrast, it was almost unknown in the canal sector. The high proportion of audit provisions among insurance compa-nies reflected the need for some kind of formal mediation between the interests of shareholders and policyholders, particularly with the growth of "with-profits" policies after 1806 and the need for the valuation of company assets at regular intervals.[84]

Auditors could be elected by a variety of stakeholders. In life as-surance companies, shareholders sometimes appointed two auditors and policyholders another two.[85] Only seven companies—all banks or

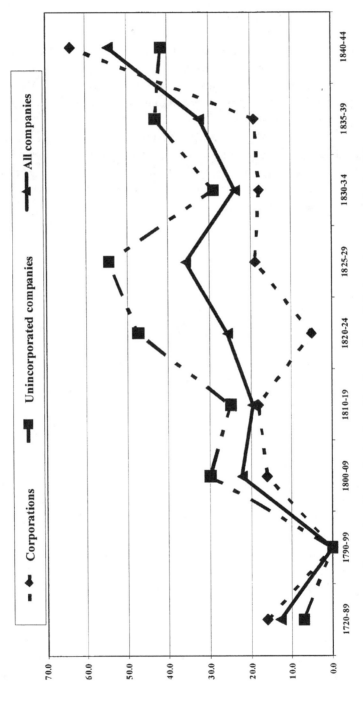

FIGURE 8.4. Percentage of companies with constitutional provision for standing audit by type of company and subperiod

insurance companies—vested the choice of auditors in the directors, a practice analogous to the appointment of poor-law union auditors by the boards of poor-law guardians. The vast majority of companies reserved the power to shareholders, a practice normalized by the legislation of 1844–5. The Companies Clauses Consolidation Acts of 1845 stipulated a default audit provision whereby the shareholders would elect two auditors from among their number, one to be rotated annually.[86] For companies regulated by the Joint-Stock Companies Act (1844), the appointment of auditors was also explicitly reserved to the shareholders.

Another important question was who would perform the audits.[87] The act of 1844 did not prohibit the appointment of directors as auditors, although, as one commentator remarked, "such an appointment would, upon general principles, be both impolitic and very unpalatable to the shareholders."[88] Nor did it stipulate that auditors had to be shareholders, and this provided the means by which audits could become the domain of full-time professional accountants rather than amateur shareholders. Matthews, Anderson, and Edwards note that "increasingly companies changed their articles to allow public accountants to be employed directly as auditors and, to facilitate this process, the initial requirement of a share qualification was gradually phased out."[89] In our period, however, there is little evidence of this taking place. Of the 145 companies making provision for standing audit, 107 (73.8 percent) imposed a share qualification for the auditors, a proportion that remained relatively constant across our period. Companies were clearly keen to keep audits "in house," not least because this kept costs down. While auditors were usually paid for their efforts, the pay granted by GMs was usually low, frequently as little as £10 or £20 a year, underlining the auditor's status as a part-time amateur.

Just as ad hoc audits were not an infallible protection for shareholders, the standing audit did not inevitably offer shareholders the security that they wanted, especially when directors and auditors colluded in hiding the true state of the company from the shareholders. A long-running dispute at the Gas Light and Coke Company (established by charter in 1812 but operating to a governance structure outlined in an act of 1810) illustrates the potential for conflict over the extent of information made available by auditors.[90] The company constitution made no provision for any kind of audit, nor were shareholders permitted to inspect the account books. Nevertheless, in 1813 a body of three auditors was created by a GM resolution, after a dispute between the GM and directors. By 1824, James Barlow, a former director, was attacking the effectiveness

of the auditing procedures. In a pamphlet addressed to the shareholders, the self-styled "Old Proprietor" recalled that an auditor at the OGM
in November 1824 "said something about a hope . . . that the meeting
would not expect him to wade through the reports of his predecessors;
that he never did understand them, and that in his opinion they were not
to be depended on."[91] Looking at the previous auditors' accounts from
June 1824, Barlow complained that the auditors had lumped items together into large categories, so that about £500,000 of expenditure was
not properly accounted for in the summary presented to the OGM. Of
this, £144,700 was *entirely* unaccounted for. Barlow requested access to
the account books so that he could investigate the matter himself. The
directors refused, and as a result Barlow went into print with his complaints. Barlow conceded that "in large public concerns, where the transactions are to be audited by a large Proprietory, the particulars are of
necessity greatly condensed, for the express purpose of expeditious and
satisfactory conclusions being formed on them."[92] In his view, however,
this necessity did not excuse the levels of inaccuracy and evasiveness that
he believed he found in the auditors' reports.

Other critics of the internal audit saw the procedure as holding inherent dangers for shareholders. In 1853, Robert Stewart distinguished between three "kinds or degrees" of audit in banking. First, there were cursory audits that merely certified "the correctness of the accounts" and
were "peculiarly the work of an ordinary accountant . . . a mere inspection of figures." Such an audit was "superficial and unsound, and but ill
calculated to answer the end it has in view." A second kind of audit was
common in railway companies, where the accounts were inspected and
the plant and property also examined and valued. According to Stewart, this kind of audit was also used by some banking companies and,
unlike the first kind of audit, "may be regarded as extending . . . to the
business of the bank, the department of the directors and manager."[93]
A third kind of audit extended to "what may be called a *moral element*
of consideration."[94] For Stewart, any bank audit necessarily fell into this
third category and therefore involved a "degrading" and unjustifiable interference with the honorable class of men who occupied seats on the
boards of joint-stock banks. Compulsory and continuous bank audits
"deterr[ed] first-class men from connecting themselves with joint-stock
companies," and the requirements of the 1844 banking legislation were
"vicious and dangerous."[95]

Conclusions

Like the ad hoc committee of inspection, the standing audit can be seen as an alternative to direct shareholder participation in company affairs. In this context, specialized auditing diminished shareholder participation by introducing intermediaries into the relationship between proprietors and managers. The development of the audit, then, was another aspect of a move away from transparency and participation and mirrored the increasingly "virtual" representation of shareholders that is documented in chapter 6. Companies' increasing reliance on audit by committee, accompanied as it often was by the withdrawal of the rights of individual shareholders or GMs to inspect accounts, represented a shift to "indirect" representation. Shareholders were increasingly obliged to rely on elected representatives to ensure the veracity of accounts, a system with many limitations, not least because auditors were widely perceived as the creatures of boards of directors, even when they were elected by the GM.[96] Shareholders found themselves having to take much more on trust, relying on the auditors to do a competent and honest job and depending on the directors not to bully and cajole the auditors. As most audits remained internal, paralleling the "elective audit" of municipal corporations, the independence and rigor of the procedure might be called into question. For their part, directors could fall back on the notion of "honourable secrecy," a central element of British political life, according to Vincent, and clearly also identifiable in Victorian boardrooms.[97] Directors interpreted any shareholder attempt to lift the veil of secrecy as an affront to their honor and, according to Herbert Spencer, regularly threatened resignation "to stave off a disagreeable inquiry" into their affairs by shareholders.[98]

Directors were so successful at keeping secrets from shareholders that it was increasingly argued that external forces should be brought to bear on companies to ensure that they were governed honestly and efficiently. We suggest in chapter 7 that existing forms of shareholder protection were inadequate in cases where transparency was lacking in company affairs. In the light of these failings of corporate governance, some observers looked to the press, others to the government, to complement or replace functions traditionally performed by shareholders. These observers were convinced that the existing tools of "stakeholder activism" offered insufficient protection. In 1845 the financial journalist David

Morier Evans hailed the "influential and impartial press" that now protected railway shareholders: "The poor shareholder, instead of remaining the passive spectator of the waste of his capital . . . has the comfort
of knowing that, by the vigilance of the press, he is afforded an opportunity of . . . inquiring into the real evils affecting the property with which
he is connected."[99]

Around the same time, there were moves to make companies more
directly accountable to the general public. Twenty-eight companies in
our sample, mostly corporations dating from the 1840s, stipulated that
there should be some kind of public access to summary accounts. For example, an abstract of the accounts of the Birkenhead and Claughton Gas
and Water Company (1841) was to be given to the clerk of the peace for
Chester and open to the inspection of members of the public on payment
of one shilling.[100] In total, over two-thirds of corporations formed in the
period 1840–4 made this kind of stipulation. These publicity clauses anticipated the Joint-Stock Companies Act of 1844, which required companies that registered under it to present a balance sheet to shareholders
at the OGM; to file it with the registrar of joint-stock companies, where
it could be accessed by the public; and to provide for it to be audited.
While these requirements were removed by the legislation of the mid-
1850s, state protection of shareholders was a frequent demand in these
years. In 1849, the Lords Committee on railway audits recommended
the appointment of one "public" (that is, state-appointed) auditor to
each company to act with the auditors appointed by the shareholders,
who would be empowered to make independent reports to the shareholders. This proposal was successfully resisted by the railway interest,
but calls for the introduction of government auditors, not merely in the
railway sector but across the joint-stock economy, did not disappear and
were given added weight by major scandals such as the Royal British
Bank failure of 1856.[101] The notion of audit by untrained shareholders
also came under pressure with the emergence of the accountancy profession. Provincial societies of accountants began to be formed in Scotland in the 1850s and from the 1870s in England.[102] Pamphlets and man-
uals for the instruction of company auditors were prepared by qualified
accountants in an attempt to raise standards.[103] The gradual and uneven
trajectory toward the professionalization and systematization of audits
was paralleled in the local government sphere.

These were all steps marking the gradual erosion of traditional conceptions of companies as "little republics" embodying a form of par-

ticipatory politics. Such steps were taken first by large companies: re-placing access to full accounts with access to summary accounts and introducing intermediaries in the relationship between shareholders and the accounts. Large companies were pioneering a new form of corpo-rate governance—more professional, more streamlined, less participa-tory, and, as argued in chapter 4, with less accountable and more exclu-sive boards of directors—which gradually filtered down to the joint-stock economy as a whole. How best to ensure transparency and account-ability continued to be debated beyond 1844, but, significantly, the pa-rameters of the argument contracted in the latter half of the nineteenth century, revolving around access to the balance sheet only, not the full account books, which it was increasingly assumed were out of bounds to shareholders.[104] Similarly, it became received wisdom that audits were best performed by small committees or, later, by professional firms of accountants, certainly not by the shareholders as a whole. The GM was gradually sidelined in the politics of the company. As investment be-came less centered on local firms, observed one director, scattered pro-prietaries became "incapable of acting in the mass."[105] Moreover, the GM was coming to be seen by many as an inappropriate forum for full and frank discussion of accounting data. Journalists attended with in-creasing regularity, proceedings were widely reported in the press, and it was recognized that whatever information was issued to the GM was in the "public" domain. This became a compelling justification for secrecy: it would, after all, be commercial suicide for companies to make sensi-tive data available to competitors. Consequently, the notion that the GM represented a "parliament" with sovereignty over a company's internal affairs faded to the extent that, late in the century, one solicitor could argue that if shareholders wanted reliable accounting information, they should not raise the issue at the GM at all but instead approach the di-rectors and obtain it privately.[106] Whether there had ever been a "golden age" of transparency in the affairs of joint-stock companies is doubtful, if only because directors were always tempted to encroach on the rights of shareholders. Yet what is clear is that, by the 1840s, growing numbers of shareholders were being stripped of their political rights, and, though not yet moribund, their participation in joint-stock politics was clearly in decline.

CHAPTER NINE

Conclusion

Conflicts between shareholders and directors over the distribution of power stretch back to the birth of the joint-stock economy in the seventeenth century. The new political economy that emerged in the mid-eighteenth century took managerial opportunism as a given among the list of features that were held to thwart "monopolistic" joint-stock companies—a belief reinforced by the behavior of company directors in the South Sea crisis of 1720 and in the struggle for control of the East India Company in the 1760s and 1770s. As a result, the company constitutions of the eighteenth century attempted to keep opportunities for corruption to a minimum. The principal safeguard was the sovereign power of the GM. The GM appointed and dismissed directors and managers, it audited accounts, and it was the public forum in which all interests in the company, large and small, came together to exercise their will. Mismanagement would be discouraged because the behavior of all agents would come under the close scrutiny of the GM, and problems would thus be resolved. These provisions may not always have worked, but they demonstrate an awareness among company promoters of the need to achieve a constitutional balance between the executive, in the form of directors and managers, and the legislature, in the form of the body of shareholders assembled at the GM. The pervasiveness of political metaphors in the pamphlet literature and procedural records of joint-stock companies is evidence that these balances were viewed in political terms, reflecting the reshaping of the governmental landscape—national and local—in the same period.

Corporate governance was always evolving, and several clear trends have emerged from our analysis. Notwithstanding the great heterogeneity of constitutions that governed joint-stock companies throughout our period, we can discern a long-run transition from one generic model, which placed supreme direct authority in the GM of shareholders, to another model, which placed considerable power in the hands of directors. This broad shift between constitutional models was accompanied by many particular trajectories of governance practice, most but not all of which moved in the same direction. Chapter 4, for instance, shows that board sizes were decreasing and terms of office increasing from the early nineteenth century and that this development was driven by the larger companies. In chapter 5, we document the decline of the active shareholder and the marginalization of GMs in key areas of decision making, including the appointment of salaried officers and the filling of casual vacancies on the board. Chapter 6 confirms a shift away from democratic governance, showing that the exclusion of small shareholders from the franchise increased over time, especially in unincorporated companies, and that voting caps were increasingly abandoned. Other features of the GM and voting procedures, such as proxy voting, were also open to abuse, and many observers complained that joint-stock democracy existed in theory but not in practice. Chapter 7 identifies some of the ways in which unincorporated companies attempted to circumvent the unlimited liability of their proprietors, but these protections did not work in practice because directors were able to conceal the true state of companies' affairs from their "constituents." In chapter 8 we chart a decline in individual and GM access to account books and, by the early 1840s, a nearly universal provision for summary accounts only to be presented to the GM, a development led by the unincorporated sector but increasingly seen in corporations from the mid-1830s. Similarly, standing audits became the norm around the same time, with unincorporated companies again leading the way.

Drawing more general conclusions from these data about the changing balance of power within companies is perhaps hazardous. Some features of company constitutions can be seen as both enhancing and restricting shareholder participation. For example, the availability of proxy voting can be seen as an enabling mechanism, giving the individual a voice in the governance of a company in a period when the increasing geographical dispersal of shareholders made the casting of a vote in person more difficult. On the other hand, it was commonly observed that boards of directors were able to manipulate proxies in order to achieve the outcomes they wanted from GMs. Similarly, provision for a standing audit might be seen as a protection for shareholders from possible mismanagement or fraud by directors and managers. It might, however, compound the exclusion of shareholders from the day-to-day oversight of their executives. Moreover, our analysis of governance focuses on the original constitutional documents and thus reflects the intentions of the founders of new companies. In many cases, subsequent constitutional documents—amending acts of Parliament, supplementary deeds of settlement, and so on—contained major revisions of the procedures set out in the founding constitution. Significantly, these often marginalized shareholders further. For example, the Manchester and Liverpool District Banking Company (1829) originally allowed local shareholders to elect local directors at each branch on an annual basis, but a supplementary deed of settlement in 1843 restricted this right and also allowed the general board of directors to appoint two or three managing directors and to vest almost all its powers in the latter.[1] More important, constitutional provisions were not necessarily followed in practice. We have provided many examples of directors riding roughshod over the supposed rights of shareholders and other examples where the latter were simply not interested in active involvement, even when their input was desired by directors. Although in some cases GMs demonstrated an awareness of their constitutional rights, in other cases these rights were probably a mystery to most of the shareholders, particularly in the twenty-three cases where individuals were not even permitted to read the constitution by which their company was governed.

Despite these provisos, we have identified nine variables that seem to reflect, fairly unambiguously, the extent of shareholder participation and have used these to calculate a general corporate governance index.[2] The higher the score on this index, the higher the level of shareholder participation envisaged in the company constitution. Figure 9.1 shows the average of this index by subperiod and type of company. A clear move away from shareholder participation is apparent, although this graph suggests that it was largely complete by the second half of the 1820s. It also shows that, from the 1720s to at least the 1820s, there was greater scope for direct shareholder involvement in corporations than in unincorporated companies but that by the late 1830s the two types of company had converged on a historically low level of shareholder participation. Table 9.1 shows the average of the corporate governance index by sector, effectively summarizing many of the sectoral differences that are explored in chapters 4 through 8.

Why did this happen? Four interlinking factors lay behind the dramatic redistribution of power within the joint-stock company during the first

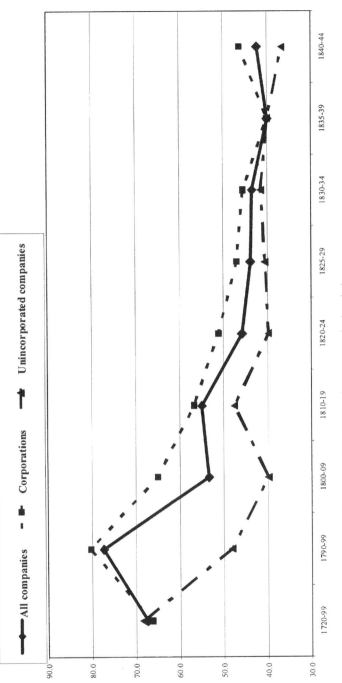

FIGURE 9.1. Corporate governance index, mean value, by type of company and subperiod

TABLE 9.1. **Mean corporate governance index by sector ($N = 486$)**

Sector	Index
Canals ($N = 48$)	75.1
Bridges ($N = 34$)	59.8
Water ($N = 40$)	51.1
Gas ($N = 60$)	48.6
Manufacturing/trade ($N = 34$)	47.2
Property ($N = 29$)	47.1
Shipping ($N = 25$)	46.0
Harbors ($N = 29$)	44.1
Railways ($N = 52$)	42.9
Insurance ($N = 59$)	40.3
Banking ($N = 64$)	37.0
Colonial ($N = 12$)	29.2

For calculations, see chapter 9, note 2.

half of the nineteenth century. First was the influence of a changing political culture. The major political issue preoccupying British elites from the 1790s to the 1840s was how to contain the power of a burgeoning, unruly populace, thrown into turmoil by industrialization and urbanization and drawn to the political radicalism finding expression in France. The response was multifaceted, but two key aspects were, first, to entrench the power of property by revising franchises to minimize the power of those with little or no property and, second, to reassert control over the process of politics by neutralizing or closing down public forums for political activity. These processes can be traced at the levels of national and, in particular, local politics. County and town meetings declined and were replaced by smaller, more intimate bodies, often with a restricted membership. The emergence of the select vestry in the 1810s was perhaps the best example of the replacement of popular decision-making arenas with more formalized, exclusive bodies of leading citizens. Although popular participation in the choice of members of municipal corporations was extended in the mid-1830s, other legislation of the 1830s and 1840s strengthened the hands of the propertied classes in local government.[3] Local government and business were dominated by the same elites, which makes it difficult to establish causal flows between, for example, developments in local government and shareholder franchises. There seems, however, to have been a feedback mechanism at work among national, local, and joint-stock politics. All three followed a similar trajectory and behaved in a mutually reinforcing way, seeking to reassert elite control and buttress the power of property against the people. Whether the aim was to contain unruly East India Company shareholders in the 1770s or stave off the threat posed by radical corresponding societies in the 1790s, the implications were the same. Politics and corporate governance, although nominally inclusive, took an increasingly plutocratic trajectory, in which "virtual" rather than "direct" representation became the norm and intermediation between governors and governed became more common.

These trends were reinforced by a second factor: the changing nature of urban business networks through the first half of the nineteenth century and the consequent reduction in the face-to-face relationships between investor groups. Face-to-face exchange and the associated high-trust relationships in small urban communities had, in theory at least, made possible the direct oversight of company executives by close-knit groups of shareholders, whose interests usually converged with those of their leaders and with the local "public interest." This public interest enabled companies to form and raise capital from members of local elites, who often had some kind of "economic" interest in the venture. This feature of the corporate landscape was in clear decline by the 1830s, and proprietaries came to be made up of geographically dispersed investors.[4] A move away from a local proprietary clearly made it more difficult to replicate the eighteenth-century model of the active shareholder. Expectations of shareholder participation were therefore reduced, while at the same time, as demonstrated in chapter 5, shareholders themselves increasingly tended to pursue their "financial" interest in companies. This diminished shareholder participation and was reflected in the declining provision for shareholder involvement in various areas of decision making, notably the appointment of salaried officers, the dismissal of directors, and the filling of casual vacancies on the board.

Fortifying these tendencies was the growing scale of joint-stock company operations. Although there were some very large companies—in terms of capital and number of shareholders—in the eighteenth century, our period saw an increase in average company size.[5] The boards of larger companies were confronted with the most diverse, anonymous, dispersed—and therefore most threatening—bodies of shareholders, and the need to control them was felt more urgently. Thus, the largest companies pioneered constitutional innovations that curbed the power of the GM and asserted the authority of the executive. Larger companies tended to allow directors to serve longer, insulating them from "public" opinion, and to require more substantial investments from their board members, making it harder for small investors to enter management. The boards of large companies also delegated responsibilities to subcommittees or managing directors, weakening chains of accountability. Generally, large companies allowed the GM a less active role in governance: their shareholders were far less likely to be able to appoint managers, for example. They also led the way in implementing the ballot—a privatized voting process—and divesting the smallest shareholders of their voting rights in an attempt to control the GM as a forum of political debate. These innovations came to be adopted by other companies, regardless of size, by the end of our period.

Large companies were also the most likely to pioneer the introduction of intermediaries in the relationship between directors and shareholders, a development that was also evident in local government. More formal mechanisms for audit and the production of summary accounts demonstrate the beginnings of a move away from a direct relationship between governors and governed and the rise of a mediated relationship, characterized by channels of information that increasingly bypassed the GM. Although this process was not complete by the end of our period, there was clearly a downgrading of the expectation that individual shareholders and the GM would ever examine company account books. Shareholders whose interest in a concern was primarily "financial" were content to become less active in company affairs and were thus prepared to relinquish many of their powers along with their former responsibilities as "partners" in return for the protection offered by intermediaries—initially the auditor but increasingly the financial press and ultimately the state. How well this alternative model of governance could really protect shareholders, however, was very much in doubt. Contemporaries pointed to the many weaknesses of early accounting and auditing processes and highlighted the powerlessness of shareholders in the face of directorial power. Even where constitutions provided for shareholder participation, the practical realities of company operations could render these constitutional rights meaningless. Many of the examples from company records that we have drawn upon in this book tell a similar story, of shareholders finding themselves unable to overcome the resistance of a determined and united board of directors.

The nature of the evidence available, however, may exaggerate the impotence of shareholders by the end of our period. Minute books do not record all aspects of the relationship between directors and shareholders. Sometimes we can detect traces of the influence that could be brought to bear informally in private meetings between directors and larger shareholders. While minute books chronicle time and time again the ability of directors to win crucial votes by marshaling proxy votes, shareholders did not always have to win a vote to influence company policy. Often a significant display of dissent was sufficient to cause the board to rethink. Angry shareholders were bad for business—they might cease paying calls on shares or offload their shares onto the market en masse and cause a collapse in the company's share value. Though usually content to trust directors, shareholders could be spurred into action by company disasters, and their efforts to secure better governance could meet with success in such conditions. The joint-stock boom of the mid- to late 1830s saw the formation of a number of fraudulent or badly mismanaged companies. The exposure of the Independent West Middlesex Fire and Life Assurance Company fraud early in 1841 led to a parliamentary investigation into that and nine other failed companies. The evidence accumulated led to a new awareness of how flaws in governance regimes could facilitate and perpetuate frauds. The committee's report gave examples of how this worked. Sometimes, as in the case of one unnamed company, shareholders were deprived of essential rights: "Owing to the want of power to inspect the books and papers of the Company, and to call a meeting, the Shareholders were unable to remove their Directors on discovering the mismanagement of the concern."[6] In other cases, problems arose when the constitution allowed a company's affairs to be dominated by a single individual. One insurance company was originally bona fide and was directed by a "respectable" board, but the original board members gradually retired, leaving the concern to the manager. The committee noted that the company's rules stated that "this officer was to hold his office for life" and that "in other cases of a fraudulent kind provisions are made of a similar nature." While such provisions could occasionally be found in honest concerns, the Select Committee on Joint-Stock Companies reported in 1844 that "it is probably a common characteristic of the worst kind of cases, and it is always liable to the disadvantage of inducing a want of care and attention on the part of the persons in whose favour it is made."[7]

It is perhaps no coincidence that in the wake of such revelations, we can identify a return, albeit only a partial and temporary one, to more transparent practices and shareholder participation in the constitutions of companies established in the early 1840s. This is highlighted in the corporate governance index (see figure 9.1), where it seems to have chiefly been a characteristic of corporations. Corporations in the 1840s gave their shareholders more rights over the appointment of managers than their 1830s counterparts and were more likely to specify shareholders' rights to access accounts (though these were more likely to be restricted to a period around the GM). While it is difficult to prove a causal link here, we can see the process happening within individual companies. As mismanagement was identified, shareholders acted to obtain better governance mechanisms to secure their property in the future. This happened in the railway companies dominated by George Hudson, whose misconduct "was discovered, investigated, and made public in the form of detailed reports entirely as a result of efforts by shareholders."[8] Hudson's accounts were questioned, committees of investigation appointed, and their twelve reports received in a flurry of activity at the York, Newcastle and Berwick; Eastern Counties; and York and North Midland companies during 1849. A range of measures was implemented. At the York, Newcastle and Berwick company these included abolishing standing subcommittees, streamlining the board, increasing the remuneration of directors, redefining the roles of employees, and improving the system of audit, all designed "to strengthen and to concentrate responsibility."[9]

The press was keen to stress that the problems encountered by the railway companies had "arisen *solely* from the infatuated blindness of shareholders to their own interests . . . and *not* from any essential defect in that principle of self-government and self-control which forms part of the constitution of all other commercial associations."[10] Despite their former negligence, the shareholders' decisive intervention showed that government interference, such as the proposals being made for audit by government appointees, was unnecessary.[11] Yet such paeans to laissez-faire ignored the point that since 1844 the state had acknowledged that it had some responsibility for ensuring good corporate governance, by imposing a variety of governance rules on companies registering under the Joint-Stock Companies, Joint-Stock Banks, and Companies Clauses Consolidation acts.[12] These rules ranged from specifying a minimum number of directors and capping the directorial term of office to guaranteeing shareholder access to accounts and making audits compulsory. They also stipulated procedures for calling GMs and SGMs and for filling casual vacancies and set a minimum share denomination.

Legislative interventions in the second half of the nineteenth century did not point in one single direction. The state oscillated between a determination to make shareholders regulate their own companies and an admission that it needed to play a larger role in mediating between shareholders and directors. The legislation of 1844–5 initially seemed likely to lock the state into a path of ever-increasing intervention. In 1850, Francis Whitmarsh, the joint-stock companies registrar, wrote to the Board of Trade with extensive suggestions for improvements to the law of 1844. Whitmarsh wanted more power to vet deeds of settlement registered with him. Currently, many "speculative promoters" inserted clauses for remunerating themselves "to a very large amount." He had objected to these clauses and had sometimes succeeded in inducing the promoters to make the clause subject to the approval of a GM. As he explained to the board, "It has sometimes been a case of sharp contest, and parties have doubted my right to require it, in which they probably were correct, but knowing how few shareholders acquaint themselves with the contents of the Deed when they sign it . . . I have persisted in my objection."[13] Whitmarsh also wanted companies to return minutes of all GMs, allowing him to check for consistency between the wishes expressed at GMs and company applications for amendments to deeds. George Taylor, Whitmarsh's assistant, complained that the balance sheets returned to the office were not audited properly, and he lobbied for the implementation of an official audit of company accounts by a Board of Trade appointee to be substituted for, or added to, the existing internal audits.[14] Such proposals would have made the registrar a powerful arbiter of company constitutions. The state, however, resisted this step in the Joint-Stock Companies Act of 1856, which repealed the act of 1844, with its insistence on the production of audited balance sheets and other regulations, replacing them with a "model" constitution that companies were free to adopt, adapt, or ignore as they saw fit. The move was a restatement of faith in the ability of shareholders to regulate their companies. While the concession of limited liability would insulate them from the worst effects of fraud, the removal of state guarantees to minimum standards of corporate governance meant that shareholders could not simply sit back and watch the dividends roll in. They would have to attend GMs to ensure good governance and to monitor their boards. The arrival of general limited liability did not mark official acceptance of the rentier shareholder.[15]

However, confidence in the ability of shareholders to keep the executive in check was undermined with the exposure of a succession of major frauds through the second half of the century. Some of the worst cases led directly to further legislative interventions: this was the case with Companies Acts of 1867 and 1890, while legislation relating to railways in 1868, life assurance companies in 1870, banks in 1858 and 1879, and building societies in 1894 all ensued from scandals in these particular sectors. Of course, there was a sense in which these could be seen as knee-jerk reactions to palliate public opinion, halfhearted measures that were not serious attempts to improve the regulatory machinery.[16] They had, however, an incremental effect on governance standards. A compulsory audit for joint-stock banks, for example, was legislated in 1879 following the City of Glasgow Bank failure and for all companies under the Companies Act of 1900.

Tracing the precise trajectory of company constitutions after 1844 would require another major study. Companies after 1844 operated in a different legal climate from that which had pertained hitherto. Most obviously, the old category of the unincorporated joint-stock company with transferrable shares, which was nothing more than a partnership at law, ceased to exist and was replaced by the legally registered joint-stock company with some of the privileges of a corporation.[17] The numbers of such registered companies soared in the decade following the 1844 act.[18] The state, made aware of the impact of constitutional arrangements on both the honesty and business performance of companies, henceforth took a much closer interest in relations between directors and shareholders. The extent to which this involvement put an end to the heterogeneity of constitutional provisions identified in this book is unclear, given the lack of systematic research on the topic. The effect on the quality of governance seems mixed, and so far, studies have considered only accounting and audit provisions. One study of thirty iron and steel companies registered under the 1862 Companies Act indicates that firms systematically watered down the model accounting provisions recommended by the statute.[19] On the other hand, another study of over a thousand companies in 1886 shows that many exceeded the legislative enactments in their provisions for audit, appointing professional accountants in their articles of association.[20]

There is sufficient evidence, however, to suggest that the trends we identify in the first half of the nineteenth century continued into the second half. Innovations in our period came to be regarded as common sense, completing the process of redefining the role of the shareholder and the status of the company itself. The political role of shareholders was further scaled back as the emphasis lay increasingly on their "financial" interests. This can be observed in an article in the *Railway Record* in 1852 bemoaning the insecurity of joint-stock company property in general and particularly railway property. This was partially a result of the inability of shareholders to hold management to account: "as the case now stands, directors have practically all the power, whether for good or evil; shareholders have none—or none that can be brought, in case of need, into serviceable action." The journal, however, went on to claim shareholders possessed nothing but a "financial" stake in their company, which, as we have already suggested, rendered their property *more* vulnerable:

> We freely concede that the rights and powers of directors and shareholders ought not to be co-ordinate. Shareholders, in relation to a railway, stand in a very inferior position to that of directors. The shareholder has only a pecuniary stake in the property; he is only interested so far as the profitable employment of his stake is concerned. The extent of protection which the law ought to be called upon to give him is, that his money should be put to the purpose for which it was subscribed or invested—that he should have as large and as regular a return for it as the profits will fairly afford, and that in no case should either principal or interest be damnified by any underhand proceedings of the Directors. . . . The shareholder should be effectually protected from such injuries, and should be armed with ample legal powers to protect himself. *But here his rights and his powers should cease.*[21]

This shrunken view of the obligations and rights of shareholders would not have been recognized fifty years earlier, and it compromised subsequent attempts to reform corporate governance, whether initiated by shareholders or the state.

We have repeatedly stressed how companies were embedded in a public, political culture; that they were "political" entities just as much as municipal corporations or voluntary societies; and that their development throughout our period followed trajectories similar to both local and national politics. There are, however, signs that by midcentury, while the state was coming under increasing democratic pressures, companies were more successful in escaping the currents of reform and fol-

lowing a different path. In the autumn of 1848, one anonymous corre-
spondent of the *Times* commented:

> We are an aristocratical nation, and this is both our strength and our weak-
> ness. . . . In every association of men in this country for any purpose whatever
> there is an attempt made by the few to usurp all rule, authority, and power. . . .
> [W]e have wisely reformed, without abolishing, our aristocratical institutions.
> We have had our Parliament reformed, our Church partially reformed, our
> municipal corporations reformed; but it is remarkable that our commercial
> associations have wonderfully escaped the liberalizing and improving ten-
> dencies of the age. This has arisen in newly-formed bodies, chiefly from the
> governing body framing its own act of Parliament or deed, as the case may be,
> and thus giving themselves just the amount of power they may think agree-
> able or convenient. . . . Where these traditionary and high Tory notions of
> government prevail, to ask for information respecting details or management,
> is resented as an imputation on the ability or integrity of the "Board."[22]

These remarks are suggestive of the way in which companies were beginning to carve out a separate sphere for their operations, which could
be termed "private." This reconceptualization had a tangible aspect:
companies literally retreated from the public sphere and became more
private institutions. The example of the London and Edinburgh Shipping Company is representative of broader trends. It was established in
1809, and the early GMs were held in public locations, alternating between Leith (the Exchange Coffee House) and Edinburgh (the Exchange Coffee House or the Waterloo Tavern), typically with high attendances. By the 1850s, the venue for GMs was the company's office,
with very few shareholders in attendance except for the members of the
board.[23] The public life of the company was in this way both privatized
and neutralized. GMs were no longer the chief source of power and the
site of decision making; their powers were largely redistributed among
the executive. When investors were motivated primarily by "financial"
considerations, it naturally followed that, within the company, it should
be property that was represented, without limit, and not people. Company franchises moved more confidently down this path just as the national polity was beginning to reconsider its stance on the issue.

In the face of the increasing exposure given to company affairs by the
developing financial journalism and investor literature of the late nineteenth century, directors began to articulate their right to conduct their

affairs in private more vociferously. In 1895, Harold Brown, a solicitor and member of the London Chamber of Commerce, argued that the increased publicity that some shareholders and certain elements in the press were calling for was "directly contrary to the principle which prudent business men and traders pursue with reference to their own businesses, viz., they keep their information jealously to themselves. Companies, to be successful, must . . . as far as possible, conduct their business on the same lines as private traders." If shareholders wanted information from the directors, "they should go to them and get it privately." Such methods of protection made a mockery of notions of constitutional safeguards and placed the onus instead upon the "inside information" and personal influence possessed by wealthy shareholders who moved in the same social circles as the directors. Brown admitted as much when he argued that "companies cannot give detailed information in general meeting, or even in private, with safety, except to large shareholders."[24]

Whereas companies had originally been "companies of proprietors," emerging out of the associational civic culture of early modern Britain, by the end of the nineteenth century they had successfully redefined themselves as private entities, cleansed of their shareholders. The irony is that two elements of this process of redefinition ultimately weakened their claims to exemption from state intervention. Originally formed by local communities to answer specific needs, they came to exist mainly to make a profit for shareholders and thus posed a potential threat to the public, necessitating regulation. Given the increased scale of operations of most companies, they were reliant on widening their shareholding base. The new proprietaries were no longer drawn exclusively from community elites but might be "as ignorant as gate-posts" and were therefore unable to regulate their companies effectively.[25] Again, the argument for greater government intervention slowly became more persuasive. These factors set the scene for the more heavily regulated but no less contested corporate environment of the twentieth century.

Notes

Chapter One

1. Trotsky, *History of the Russian Revolution*, 1:352.

2. Aristotle, *Athenian Constitution*, 251–307.

3. Ober, *Mass and Elite*; Fox, *Classical World*, 91–6; Ste. Croix, *Class Struggle*, 97.

4. See p. 14.

5. Forty-four percent (224 out of 514) of companies in our sample were unincorporated; see table 1.1.

6. Maier, "Revolutionary Origins"; Handlin and Handlin, "Origins of the American Business Corporation"; Hurst, *Legitimacy of the Business Corporation*; Novak, *People's Welfare*; "Incorporating the Republic."

7. Kessler, "Incorporation in New England," table 1.

8. The handful of great chartered corporations, such as the East India Company and the Bank of England, were exceptions that prove the rule. These do not form part of our constitutional database (described below), although we do pay attention to their governance history.

9. Maclean, Harvey, and Press, *Business Elites*, 122. The growth in executive remuneration relative to average manual salaries, by a factor of ten between 1960 and 2000, has fueled British discontent about "fat cats." Cf. Offer, *Challenge of Affluence*.

10. Mallin, *Corporate Governance*, 19–38; Kim and Nofsinger, *Corporate Governance*, 27–35.

11. Jensen and Meckling, "Theory of the Firm."

12. Cf. Kim and Nofsinger, *Corporate Governance*, 12–5, on the *misalignments* that arose out of the use of stock options for executive remuneration in the 1990s.

13. Chandler, *Visible Hand*; Herrigel, "New Wave"; Cheffins, *Corporate Ownership and Control*.

14. Fama, "Agency Problems"; Fama and Jensen, "Separation of Ownership and Control"; Shleifer and Vishny, "Survey of Corporate Governance." For a recent overview, see Clarke, "Introduction."

15. La Porta et al., "Law and Finance."

16. Roe, *Political Determinants.*

17. Salter, *Innovation Corrupted*, 245–77.

18. See, chapter 4, pp. 93–8.

19. The role of shareholders in company governance is discussed in chapters 5 and 6.

20. See chapter 3, pp. 59–60.

21. Gomez and Korine, "Democracy," 747; Johnson, *Making the Market*, 229–32.

22. Bogart and Richardson, "Property Rights"; North and Weingast, "Constitutions and Commitment."

23. Wallis, Weingast, and North, "Corporate Origins."

24. La Porta et al., "Law and Finance"; Shleifer and Vishny, "Survey of Corporate Governance."

25. As Arruñada and Andonova have pointed out, however, examples of judicial discretion to protect shareholders can also be found in civil law systems. Arruñada and Andonova, "Common Law and Civil Law."

26. In this sense, our findings support Cheffins's recent argument that common law did not matter *much* as an historical determinant of British corporate governance structures. Cheffins, *Corporate Ownership*, 51–5.

27. Robert E. Wright, "Introduction."

28. Beckett and Turner, "Taxation and Economic Growth"; O'Brien, Griffiths, and Hunt, "Political Components"; Dietz, "Politics of Whisky"; Harris, "Political Economy."

29. Alborn, "Moral of the Failed Bank"; Robb, *White-Collar Crime*; Searle, *Morality and the Market*; Garnett, "Commercial Ethics"; James Taylor, *Creating Capitalism*; James Taylor, "Commercial Fraud"; James Taylor, "Company Fraud"; Jones and Aiken, "British Companies Legislation"; Laurence, Maltby, and Rutterford, *Women and Their Money.*

30. Hickson and Turner, "Shareholder Liability Regimes"; Hickson and Turner, "Trading in the Shares"; Davies, "Joint-Stock Investment"; Reed, *Investment in Railways*; Broadbridge, "Sources of Railway Share Capital"; Sarah J. Hudson, "Attitudes to Investment Risk"; Ward, *Finance of Canal Building*; Wilson, *Lighting the Town*; Carlos, Maguire, and Neal, "Financial Acumen"; Carlos and Neal, "Women Investors"; Freeman, Pearson, and Taylor, " 'Doe in the City' "; Freeman, Pearson, and Taylor, "Between Madam Bubble and Kitty Lorimer."

31. Cf. the debate on the Privy Council's proposed reform of the EIC franchise in 1692. Nottingham, *Propositions for Regulating the East India Company*,

11 Feb. 1692; East India Company, *Humble Answer*, 28 May 1692. For similar disputes in the Bank of England, see Anon., *Observations upon the Constitution of . . . Bank of England*.

32. Cf. the highly oligarchic constitution of the Royal Fishing Company with that of the Royal African Company, which provided its shareholders with more "liberal" access to accounts. Carr, *Select Charters*, no. 22, pp. 182–5 (Royal Fishing Company); Royal African Company, *General Meeting*, 19 Dec. 1671, article VIII; Davies, *Royal African Company*, 157.

33. Anderson and Tollinson, "Myth of the Corporation."

34. Lamoreaux, "Partnerships, Corporations."

35. Wallis, "Constitutions, Corporations." See also Handlin and Handlin, "Origins of the American Business Corporation"; Maier, "Revolutionary Origins"; Novak, *People's Welfare*.

36. Hilt, "When Did Ownership Separate from Control?"; Lamoreaux and Rosenthal, "Corporate Governance."

37. Alborn, *Conceiving Companies*. On voluntary associations, see Peter Clark, *British Clubs and Societies*; Morris, *Class, Sect and Party*.

38. Dunlavy, "Corporate Democracy"; Dunlavy, "Citizens to Plutocrats."

39. Munn, "Scottish Provincial Banking Companies." Some brewery firms straddled this line. Most had fewer than ten partners, but, for instance, the Meaux Reid Griffin Brewery in 1809 had twenty. Mathias, *Brewing Industry*, 316–9.

40. 6 Geo. IV (1825) c. 115.

41. The pilot survey was carried out using the online catalogs of the UK National Register of Archives (NRA) and the National Archives (NA), supplemented by printed guides to records in individual industries, along with a range of secondary literature. The catalogs and guides did not always identify ownership, and many firms turned out to be small partnerships. Archival research, however, also revealed many stock companies not found in the original survey.

42. A booklet, *Summary of Variable Codes*, was prepared to explain the meaning of each variable and how the data were entered from the original records into the database and the codes used. This booklet has been deposited together with the database itself at the UK Data Archive, University of Essex, under the title *Constructing the Company: Governance and Procedures in British and Irish Stock Companies, 1720–1844* (AHDS SN 5622).

43. The total of 1,006 is calculated from a great variety of sources, of which the following were the most important: for all sectors, Fenn, *Compendium of Funds*; for insurance (195 companies), Robin Pearson, *Insuring the Industrial Revolution*, 16, fig. 1.1, plus additional life and marine companies found in the pilot survey referred to in the text; for railways (204), Bagwell, *Transport Revolution*, 93–4 (railway companies "sanctioned" by act of Parliament 1825–44), plus companies established before 1825 found in the pilot survey; for canal and river

navigation companies (167), Cook and Stevenson, *British Historical Facts*, 188–91 (canal acts, 1759–1827), plus additional companies found in the pilot survey; for gas (283), Falkus, "British Gas Industry"; for banks (157), Newton, "Change and Continuity," 1, and Scottish provincial banking copartneries from Langton and Morris, *Atlas of Industrializing Britain*, 148.

44. We used the count of water companies established by act of Parliament to 1840 as given in Hassan, "Growth and Impact of the British Water Industry," tables 1 and 3.

45. This figure does not include files compiled on pre-1720 stock companies.

46. Around twenty of this miscellany were mutual insurance, annuity, loan, and benefit societies; a few were partnerships of less than thirteen, and a few were *en commandite*-type companies (that limited liability for some members) formed in Ireland under 21 Geo. III (1782) c. 46 (Ir.).

47. With few exceptions, historical surveys of corporate governance continue to be focused on the twentieth century. Maclean, "Corporate Governance"; Cheffins, "History"; Herrigel, "New Wave." An exception is Robert E. Wright, "Introduction."

Chapter Two

1. Pope, "Essay on Man" (1744), epistle iii, line 303, in Pope, *Poetical Works*, 267.

2. Wilson, *British Business History*; Wilson and Thomson, *Making of Modern Management*.

3. Devine et al., *Industrial Economics*, 84–5; Boyce and Ville, *Development of Modern Business*, 38–9.

4. Michie, *Global Securities*, 29. See also Dickson, *Financial Revolution*.

5. The figure is estimated from Scott, *Joint-Stock Companies*, 1:327–36.

6. 6 Geo. I (1720) c. 18. For accounts of the bubble and subsequent crash, see Scott, *Joint-Stock Companies*, 1:388–438; Carswell, *South Sea Bubble*; Neal, *Financial Capitalism*, 62–117; Dickson, *Financial Revolution*, 90–198.

7. Scott, *Joint-Stock Companies*, 1:411; Harris, *Industrializing English Law*, 60–78.

8. The Bubble Act seems to have been drafted in haste. It offered no definition of "undertaking" by number of partners or size of capital. The raising of *any* transferrable stock was banned. Clause 20 referred to the means by which merchants and traders might have remedies against "the Persons, Societies or Partnerships . . . who contrary to this act shall be engaged in such unlawful undertaking," but clause 25 exempted from the act "any home or foreign trade in Partnership in such manner as . . . may be legally done according to the Laws of this Realm now in force." The act did not use the term "company" except with

reference to the existing chartered corporations, the South Sea and East India companies.

9. By 4 Geo. IV (1825) c. 94. For such claims, see Scott, *Joint-Stock Companies*, 1:438; Patterson and Reiffen, "Effect of the Bubble Act"; Wilson, *British Business History*, 44–5; Mirowski, *Birth of the Business Cycle*, 271–6; Crafts, "Industrial Revolution."

10. Mokyr, "Editor's Introduction," 103n.

11. Wilson and Thomson, *Making of Modern Management*, 11.

12. Dubois, *English Business Company*.

13. Harris, *Industrializing English Law*; Robin Pearson, "Shareholder Democracies?"; Anderson and Tollinson, "Myth of the Corporation."

14. The five largest groups were insurance (201 companies, excluding mutuals), gas (200), joint-stock banks (177), canals (177), and railways (167). A complete list is available from the authors. Indications that some of these numbers are too low are given by, for example, Bagwell, who counts 178 railway companies "sanctioned" by act of Parliament in the period 1825–44 alone, and Falkus, who counts 283 incorporated and unincorporated gas companies between 1816 and 1844 (although some may have been municipal enterprises). Bagwell, *Transport Revolution*, 93–4; Falkus, "British Gas Industry." These numbers do not tally with those given in chapter 1, n. 43, first, because the former also include joint-stock bank and insurance companies founded before 1720 and, second, because we have identified individually more joint-stock banks and canals but fewer gas and railway companies than the totals given in the published sources listed.

15. Harris, *Industrializing English Law*, 194–6. National income rose by an annual average (not compounded) of 6 percent between 1688 (figures for England and Wales only) and 1841 (Great Britain). Estimated stock capital rose by an average of 11 percent between 1740 and 1840. National income figures from Mitchell, *Abstract of British Historical Statistics*, 366.

16. Mathias, *First Industrial Nation*, table 26.

17. Mirowski, "Rise and (Retreat) of a Market."

18. Ashton, *Economic Fluctuations*; Fisher, *Industrial Revolution*; Mirowski, *Birth of the Business Cycle*.

19. Willan, *Don Navigation*, 24–32.

20. Deane, *First Industrial Revolution*, 77, 80; Mathias, *First Industrial Nation*, 112. On dock building in London, see Deane and Cole, *British Economic Growth*, 236; Daunton, *Progress and Poverty*, fig. 11.2.

21. Robin Pearson, *Insuring the Industrial Revolution*, appendix A, 374–5, table 1.1.

22. Trebilcock, *Phoenix Assurance*, 1:72. The Phoenix shares were fully paid up at £50 each. By 1788 the number of shareholders had risen to 188, holding 1,200 shares.

23. Devine, *Tobacco Lords*, 23, 26, 37, 75. All the Glasgow tobacco firms had fewer than nine partners, though they were generally larger than their English counterparts.

24. Munn, *Scottish Provincial Banking Companies*, 58, table 5.

25. 7 Anne (1709) c. 7, clause 61.

26. Munn, *Scottish Provincial Banking Companies*, 6. Larger unincorporated copartneries in whale fishing were also not obviously illegal in Scotland. See Jackson, "Government Bounties."

27. David M. Walker, *Legal History of Scotland*, 6:712–3.

28. Freeman, Pearson, and Taylor, " 'Different and Better?' "

29. 7 Geo. III (1767) c. 26 (Ir); Murphy, "Limerick Navigation Company."

30. 11 & 12 Geo. III (1771–2) c. 31 (Ir); NLI, P434 (9), Grand Canal Company, Proprietors of Stock, 1772.

31. Based on a dataset of ninety joint-stock companies that we have identified for Ireland between 1720 and 1850. This is unlikely to be complete, but we are confident that it captures the great majority of Irish stock companies in this period.

32. Geary, "Act of Union," table 10.

33. Lee, "Capital"; Cullen, *Economic History of Ireland*, 129.

34. 7 Geo. III (1767) c. 26 (Ir.), clause 18, cited by Wall, "Catholics in Economic Life," 46.

35. 12 Geo. III (1772) c. 25 (Ir.).

36. 21 & 22 Geo. III (1782) c. 46 (Ir.).

37. Oldham, *English Common Law*, 174; Harris, *Industrializing English Law*, 234.

38. *Morning Chronicle*, 9–20 Nov. 1807, 7 Jan. 1808; *The Satirist, or Monthly Meteor*, 4 (1809): 29–35.

39. *Morning Chronicle*, 9 Nov., 16 Nov. 1807; *The Satirist, or Monthly Meteor*, 4 (1809): 368–75.

40. This was the first case brought under the general sections of the act. There had been, however, several cases relating to marine assurance brought under the provisions in the first part of the act. Harris, *Industrializing English Law*, 236n19.

41. Harris, *Industrializing English Law*, 236–41; James Taylor, *Creating Capitalism*, 102–4.

42. The British, the Globe (both 1799), and the Kent (1802).

43. For examples from Newcastle, Leeds, Rochdale, and Sheffield, see Robin Pearson, *Insuring the Industrial Revolution*, 255–7; Fraser, "Politics of Leeds Water"; Garrard, *Leadership and Power*, 149; Dennis Smith, *Conflict and Compromise*, 84.

44. *Aberdeen Journal*, 2 Dec. 1807; *Caledonian Mercury*, 30 Nov. 1807.

45. Michie, *Money, Mania and Markets*, 39, 45, 71.

46. Cullen, *Economic History of Ireland*, 92–4; Beckett, *Making of Modern Ireland*, 241–3; Ó Gráda, *Ireland*, 276.

47. Fenn, *Compendium of Funds*, 138. See also English, *Complete View*; Jenks, *Migration of British Capital*, 110–2.

48. *Scotsman*, 25 Dec. 1824.

49. James Taylor, *Creating Capitalism*,108.

50. For critics, see Anon., *List of Joint Stock Companies*; *Scotsman*, 29 Dec. 1824, letter from "A Calm Observer." For defenders, see John Taylor, *Statements respecting the Profits of Mining*; Rawson, *Present Operations*.

51. Harris, *Industrializing English Law*, 245–8.

52. Ibid., 246–9; James Taylor, *Creating Capitalism*, 120–1.

53. Hunt, *Development of the Business Corporation*, 47n94; English, *Complete View*. On the boom and bust, see James Taylor, *Creating Capitalism*, 121–2; Kynaston, *City of London*, 1:63–72.

54. Clapham, *Bank of England*, 2:13, 41–2. Not until 1832 did the bank directors begin to submit to shareholders' meetings accounts similar to those they were compelled to present to the Secret Committee of the House of Commons. Acres, *Bank of England*, 1:319–21.

55. 1 & 2 Geo. IV (1821) c. 72.

56. 7 Geo. IV (1826) c. 46.

57. The bank's monopoly in London was ended in 1833. Clapham, *Bank of England*, 2:87–113.

58. Harris, *Industrializing English Law*, 194–6; Michie, *Money, Mania and Markets*, 39, 45, 71. James Taylor, *Creating Capitalism*, 131, table 6, counts 61 Scottish stock companies in 1837 and 111 in 1841. These may be underestimates, but they are probably reasonably good indicators of the rate of growth of the Scottish joint-stock economy in these years.

59. 4 & 5 Will. IV (1834) c. 94. The following paragraph is based on Harris, *Industrializing English Law*, 271–3; James Taylor, *Creating Capitalism*, 125–8.

60. *Copy of a Minute of the Lords of the Committee of Privy Council for Trade, dated 4th November 1834*, BPP (1837) XXXIX.

61. James Taylor, *Creating Capitalism*, 128n144, 130.

62. 1 Vict. (1837) c. 73.

63. For examples of calls for company licensing and registration, see An Old Merchant, *Remarks on Joint Stock Companies*, 97–8; Mundell, *Influence of Interest*, 150; and the evidence of Peter Laurie, Christopher Cuff, and others in *SC on Joint-Stock Companies*, BPP (1844) VII, pp. 61–2, 74, 84.

64. 26 Geo. III (1786) c. 60; 4 Geo. IV (1823) c. 41.

65. 33 Geo. III (1793) c. 54; 10 Geo. IV (1829) c. 56.

66. 57 Geo. III (1817) c. 130.

67. 6 & 7 Will. IV (1836) c. 32 (building societies); 4 & 5 Will. IV (1834) c. 94 (trading companies); 1 Vict. (1837) c. 73 (trading companies).

68. Calculated from *SC on Joint-Stock Companies*, BPP (1844) VII, appendix 4.2.

69. Robin Pearson, *Insuring the Industrial Revolution*, 199–212; Sykes, *Amalgamation Movement*, 1–4.

70. *SC on Joint-Stock Companies*, BPP (1844) VII.

71. 7 & 8 Vict. (1844) c. 110; 7 & 8 Vict. (1844) c. 111.

72. 8 Vict. (1845) c. 16 (England and Ireland); 8 Vict. (1845) c. 17 (Scotland). Shareholders of English or Irish companies residing in Scotland who defaulted on calls were to be pursued under the Scottish act.

73. 7 & 8 Vict. (1844) c. 113.

74. 7 & 8 Vict. (1844) c. 32. On the note-issue question, see "The Bank of England and the Country Banks," *Edinburgh Review*, 65 (Apr. 1837): 61–87.

75. James Taylor, *Creating Capitalism*, 142–3.

76. Registration figures from ibid., 146, table 9. For our count of over fourteen hundred companies before 1844, see pp. 15–6.

77. Harris, *Industrializing English Law*, 284–5.

78. Prest, *Liberty and Locality*, 10–1.

79. Poor-law elections for the new boards of guardians after 1834, for instance, used "private polling," with signed voting papers delivered to ratepayers' homes, which was certainly less public than a show of hands. The system also gave the most votes to the largest property owners, based on the argument that these groups would be less susceptible to bribes and corruption at elections. As we will see in chapter 6, similar arguments were put forward for the disenfranchisement of small shareholders. Vernon, *Politics and the People*, 155, 337; Rose, "Administration of the Poor Law," 133–4.

80. Stedman Jones, "Language of Chartism"; Harling, *Waning of "Old Corruption."*

81. James Taylor, *Creating Capitalism*, chapter 2.

82. Alborn, "The Moral of the Failed Bank"; Robb, *White-Collar Crime*, 169–80.

83. Garnett, "Commercial Ethics"; Hilton, *Age of Atonement*, 255–67; Simpson, *Victorian Law*.

84. Morris, "Urban Associations."

85. On emigrant companies, see *Caledonian Mercury*, 28 June 1819. For early share-issuing cooperatives, see Durr, "William King." On union mills in the West Riding, see Pat Hudson, *Genesis of Industrial Capital*. For Chartist joint-stock projects to finance newspapers and working men's halls, see Epstein, "Organisational and Cultural Aspects."

86. Yeo, "Practices and Problems."

Chapter Three

1. Quoted in Moore, "John Mill of John Company," 171–2.

2. The advantages of incorporation are discussed more fully with reference to limited liability in chapter 7.

3. CKS, U2593/B6/1, Kent Fire Office, DM, 15 Feb., 20 Feb., 23 Feb., 27 Feb. 1802.

4. All these gentlemen had Kentish estates, and some held offices in the county, such as Camden (lord lieutenant) and Whitworth (deputy lieutenant).

5. CKS, U2593/B6/1, Kent Fire Office, DM, 1 Mar., 4 Mar., 29 Mar., 5 Apr., 26 Apr. 1802.

6. GL, MS 31910/1, County Fire Office, Minutes of County Meetings (Leicestershire), 20 Nov. 1807.

7. NA, RAIL 346/1, Lancaster and Carlisle Railway Company, Minute Book, 6 Dec. 1843.

8. Birmingham Banking Company, *Circular*.

9. Stirlingshire Banking Company, *Prospectus*, 8 June 1831.

10. Robin Pearson, *Insuring the Industrial Revolution*, 237. See also Pearson and Richardson, "Business Networking."

11. Hosting the Falkirk Gas Work Company, NLS, Dep. 240/10, Falkirk Gas Work Company, GM, 18 June 1832; and the St. Nicholas Bay Harbour and Canal Company, R/U1231/O3, St. Nicholas Bay Harbour and Canal Company, Proprietors' Meeting, 18 June 1813.

12. Hosting the Brandling Junction Railway Company, NA, RAIL 64/1, Brandling Junction Railway Company, Committee and Shareholder Meeting Minutes, 27 Aug.1835; and London & Edinburgh Shipping Company, *Scotsman*, 16 Apr. 1836.

13. DRO, BZ/C/1/1, Blandford Gas and Coke Company, Minute Book, 23 Aug. 1836; BL, Add MS 27880, Tunnel under the Thames Company, Minute Book, 18 July 1798; CKS, SEG/AM9/1, Dartford Gas Company, Minute Book, 25 July 1826.

14. DRO, BZ/C/1/1, Blandford Gas and Coke Company, Minute Book, 23 Aug. 1836.

15. LMA, B/RGLC/1, Ratcliff Gas Light and Coke Company, Minute Book, 13 Oct. 1824; NA, RAIL 371/1, Liverpool and Manchester Railway Company, Minute Book, 18 Mar. 1829.

16. Metropolitan Marine Bath Company, *Prospectus*, 2.

17. Plymouth and Devonport Banking Company, *Prospectus*.

18. GL, MS 16170A/1, Atlas Assurance Company, Directors' Minutes, 6 Apr. 1808, Prospectus, Article XVI.

19. Robin Pearson, *Insuring the Industrial Revolution*, 243–4.

20. *Secret Committee on Joint-Stock Banks*, BPP (1836) IX, p. 96.

21. LTSB, A46d/3, Fox Family Papers, Thomas Backhouse to George Fox, 10 May 1831.

22. NMM, GSN/7/1, General Steam Navigation Company, Minute Book, 11 Aug. 1825.

23. LMA, ACC 2558/EL/A/1/48, East London Waterworks Company, Minute Book, 7 Jan. 1808.

24. Ibid., 6 Oct. 1808.

25. Ibid., 17 Nov. 1808, 6 Apr. 1809.

26. Davenant, *Reflections upon the Constitution*, 10–1, 28, 43.

27. A small number of acts—15 of the 290 in our sample—limited the life of a corporation, although 9 of these did not stipulate a number of years. See pp. 55–6 in this chapter and the discussion in chapter 7, pp. 200–1.

28. Holdsworth, *History of English Law*, 8:198; Blackstone, *Commentaries*, 1:463.

29. The right to make bylaws had been of particular importance before the Revolution of 1688, when such authority derived almost exclusively from rights bestowed, in theory *ex ante*, by the Crown. Royal sanction was deemed essential because subjects had no right to combine without it, and unauthorized assemblies were likely to be regarded with suspicion by the authorities. Holdsworth, *History of English Law*, 8:201.

30. Holdsworth, *History of English Law*, 8:205; Harris, *Industrializing English Law*, 18–9.

31. Mackenzie, *Scottish Burghs*, 117–9; David M. Walker, *Legal History of Scotland*, 4:316–7.

32. Campbell, "Law and the Joint-Stock Company," 136–7.

33. Glasgow City Council, *Extracts from the Records of the Burgh of Glasgow*, 6:515–7.

34. Mackenzie, *Scottish Burghs*, 1, 145.

35. Until 1797, acts of incorporation were officially designated "public acts" (that is, acts receiving the public assent, *le roi le veut*, as opposed to "private acts" receiving the private assent, *soit fait*). In 1797, the public acts were divided into two series: "public general acts" and "public local and personal acts," with acts of incorporation falling into the latter category. On the classification of these by the King's Printer, see Lambert, *Bills and Acts*, 172–86.

36. P. D. G. Thomas, *House of Commons*, 57–60.

37. Ibid., 61. See also Hoppit, "Patterns of Parliamentary Legislation."

38. Ellis, *Practical Remarks*, vii. Ellis seems to have paraphrased the remarks of Frederick Montagu, the chairman of the Commons committee on standing orders, *House of Commons Journals* 35 (15 Nov. 1775): 443–4.

39. *House of Commons Journals* 44 (15 July 1789): 537, 47 (15 May 1792): 797, 49 (16 Apr. 1794): 473–4; Ellis, *Practical Remarks*, 103–4, 108–9. This power of

compulsory purchase (or "eminent domain" in American parlance) continued into the railroad era and is still current today. The standing orders were gradually applied to other works such as docks, harbors, bridges, tramways, and railroads. The procedures were finally consolidated in the Land Clauses Consolidation Acts, 8 Vict. (1845) c.18 (for England) and 8 Vict. (1845) c.19 (for Scotland), which closely resembled the orders of 1774. See Cobb, "Sources for Economic History," 161–3; Kellett, *Railways and Victorian Cities*, appendix 3.

40. NA, RAIL 250/1, Great Western Railway Company, Minute Book, 1 Mar. 1834.

41. NA, RAIL 803/1, Ashby-de-la-Zouch Canal Company, Minute Book, 30 Aug. 1792.

42. Ibid., 18 Oct., 8 Nov., 23 Nov. 1792.

43. NA, RAIL 458/1, Manchester, Bolton, and Bury Canal Company, Minute Book, 3 Nov. 1790.

44. 7 Geo. IV (1826) c. 49; NA, RAIL 371/7, Liverpool and Manchester Railway, GM, 29 May 1826; Pollins, "Finances of the Liverpool and Manchester Railway," 92.

45. Pratt, *A Brief Reply*, 6. According to this spokesman for the company, the Worcester Canal bill "was corrected, altered, and amended, by the Committee with unusual care . . . and not approved, till every objection had been attended to." Such scrutiny in committee, however, was invariably also time constrained; see Lambert, *Bills and Acts*, 57–9.

46. P. D. G. Thomas, *House of Commons*, 58.

47. *Hansard*, 2nd series, 11:910 (27 May 1824).

48. *Hansard*, 2nd series, 12:635–6 (23 Feb. 1825).

49. For a defense of the system, see Sir Robert Peel, *Hansard*, 2nd series, 12:981 (10 Mar. 1825).

50. Williams, *Private Bill Procedure*, 1:85–91. The Lords reformed its practice before the Commons: in 1837, it adopted standing orders by which all opposed private bills were referred to a committee of five disinterested peers. Rydz, *Parliamentary Agents*, 93.

51. *Hansard*, 2nd series, 11:913 (27 May 1824).

52. Civil servants were in demand too: in the 1850s, a parliamentary return reported that at least 121 civil servants were directors, managers, secretaries, or clerks of joint-stock companies. *Statement of names of permanent public officers who hold employment out of their office, as directors of life assurance, railway, banking or commercial companies in 1852*, BPP (1854) XXXIX, 339.

53. Hudson Gurney, *Hansard*, 2nd series, 12:982 (10 Mar. 1825).

54. BL, Add MS 27880, Tunnel under the Thames Company, Minute Book, 14 Dec. 1798.

55. East Kent Archive, R/U1231/O3, St. Nicholas Bay Harbour and Canterbury Canal Company, Printed Minutes, 25 June 1811.

56. *Hansard*, 2nd series,13:1013 (2 June 1825). It was common for committee members to attend only the final day of deliberations in order to cast their votes: the bill of the Great Western Railway passed its committee stage in 1835 by 33 votes to 21. Of the thirty-three, twenty-nine had not attended on any other occasion. Lord Kenyon, *Hansard*, 3rd series, 30:1012 (27 Aug. 1835).

57. Kostal, *Law and English Railway Capitalism*, 130. On the mid-eighteenth century origins of private parliamentary agents, both Commons clerks and outsiders, see Rydz, *Parliamentary Agents*, chapter 2; and Lambert, *Bills and Acts*, 47–51.

58. NA, RAIL 250/1, Great Western Railway Company, Minute Book, 29 Oct. 1835.

59. NA, RAIL 350/1, Leeds and Bradford Railway Company, Minute Book, 28 Aug. 1844.

60. DUA, MS 105/II/6/13, Dundee and Newtyle Railway Company, Bill of Costs, 1836.

61. GRO, D2516/9/1, Dursley Gas Light and Coke Company, Minute Book, 20 July 1835.

62. CKS, U2593/B1, Kent Fire Office, Deed of Settlement, 7 Dec. 1802.

63. On insurance, see chapter 2, p. 25.

64. 4 Geo. IV (1823) c. 41. Freeman, Pearson, and Taylor, "Technological Change," 576.

65. This derives from a count of fifty-two shipping companies that we have identified, the earliest established in 1747, the latest in 1844. To our knowledge, no one has yet attempted a complete count of such companies.

66. Holdsworth, *History of English Law*, 6:641–4.

67. Daunton, *Progress and Poverty*, 239. For a more skeptical view, see Harris, *Industrializing English Law*, 152–9.

68. Sanders, *Laws of Uses and Trusts*, 152. In a much-cited case from 1765, it was ruled that the trustees of a joint-stock company, rather than the proprietors, were liable for the value of shares that had been transferred under a forged letter of attorney without the forgery being detected: "A trustee, whether a private person or body corporate, must see to the reality of the authority empowering him to dispose of the trust money." Ashby v. Blackwell and Million Bank Co. (1765) Amb 503, 2 Eden 299.

69. Two-thirds of the 222 companies named between one and five trustees, with three being the modal number.

70. On the rise of associations, see Peter Clark, *British Clubs and Societies*; Spadafora, *Idea of Progress*, 81–4.

71. "Association" never attracted the pejorative meaning among public authorities in eighteenth-century Britain that the term "combination" did. Workers' combinations were, of course, outlawed by various statutes.

72. Hume, *Selected Essays*, 7. On the economy of mutual obligations, see Offer, "Between the Gift and the Market."

73. Casson and Rose, "Institutions and the Evolution of Modern Business"; Macaulay, "Non-Contractual Relations in Business"; Pearson and Richardson, "Business Networking."

74. Grady, *Georgian Public Buildings*; Borsay, *English Urban Renaissance*.

75. 34 Vict. (1871), c. 17, preamble.

76. For example, the bridge not being completed within a specified period: 49 Geo. III (1809) c. 142 (Vauxhall Bridge Company); 51 Geo. III (1811) c.166 (Southwark Bridge Company).

77. *SC on Joint-Stock Companies*, BPP (1844) VII, p. 148.

78. Almost none of the corporations in our sample had a clause referring to dissolution by Parliament or the Crown. For further discussion, see chapter 7, pp. 200–8, where we also discuss *shareholders'* powers to dissolve *unincorporated* companies.

79. These issues are examined further in chapters 4 and 5.

80. NMM, GSN/7/1, General Steam Navigation Company, Minute Book, 11 Aug. 1825.

81. LMA, B/EGLC/12, Equitable Gas Light Company, Minute Book, 26 July 1832.

82. For further discussion of this, see chapter 4.

83. DRO, BZ/4/1, Lyme-Regis Gas and Coke Company, Minute Book, 9 Feb., 19 Feb. 1835.

84. GRO, D2516/9/1, Dursley Gas Light and Coke Company, Minute Book, 16 Oct., 20 Nov. 1835.

85. GRO, D2516/9/1, Dursley Gas Light and Coke Company, Minute Book, 15 July, 7 Sept. 1835. The attendance at the meeting was high (eighteen) in the context of other meetings of the company. For analysis of franchise types, see chapter 6.

86. LMA, B/EGLC/12, Equitable Gas Light Company, Minute Book, 26 July 1832, 6 June 1833.

87. County of Devon Banking Company, *Circular.*

88. Plymouth and Devonport Banking Company, *Prospectus*, 30 Sept. 1831.

89. Plymouth and Devonport Banking Company, *Prospectus*, n.d. The prospectus stipulated that ten shares were needed to cast one vote. This was reduced to five shares in the deed of settlement. The directorial qualification was halved from thirty shares to fifteen.

90. For example, CKS, SEG/AM9/1, Dartford Gas Company, Minute Book, 25 July, 12 Aug. 1826.

91. Evidence of "A. B.," *SC on Joint-Stock Companies*, BPP (1844) VII, p. 104.

92. Ibid., pp. 11, 67.

93. LMA, B/S.Met.G/III/1: South Metropolitan Gas Light and Coke Company, DM, 20 Feb. 1834.

94. *SC on Joint-Stock Companies*, BPP (1844) VII, p. 20.

95. Ibid., p. 68.

96. Manchester and Salford Bank, *Deed of Settlement*, art. 80.

97. Glasgow and Liverpool Royal Steam Packet Company, *Contract of Copartnery*, art. 45.

98. Only two corporations in our sample—the Corn Exchange Buildings Company of Dublin (1815) and the Peninsular and Oriental Steam Navigation Company (1841)—made this provision.

99. Rydz, *Parliamentary Agents*, chapter 2.

100. John Halcomb, *A Practical Treatise of Passing Private Bills through Both Houses of Parliament*, quoted in Rydz, *Parliamentary Agents*, 47.

101. As with unincorporated companies, however, whose original subscribers had to sign the company deed of settlement before they could receive their shares, the original subscribers to incorporated companies had to sign a subscription list, and this list of names was usually then reproduced in the preamble to the company's act of incorporation, signifying their acceptance of the company's constitution.

102. DUA, MS105/IX/1/2, Kinross Junction Railway Company, Subscription Contract, n.d. [1845?].

103. NA, RAIL 64/1, Brandling Junction Railway Company, Minute Book, 7 Sept. 1835.

104. Wharncliffe meetings were named after Lord Wharncliffe, lord president of the council in Peel's second ministry. He had chaired various railway committees in the House of Lords, for example that on the Oxford and Great Western Railway Bill in 1837, HLRO, HL/PO/PB/5/3/3. There is no mention of Wharncliffe meetings in his *Oxford Dictionary of National Biography* entry, Norgate, "Wortley, James Archibald Stuart, first Baron Wharncliffe (1776–1845)."

105. Clifford, *History of Private Bill Legislation*, 2:784.

106. Dodd and Wilberforce, *Guide to the Procedure upon Private Bills*, 111–2.

107. HLRO, HL/PO/PB/19/1, Minutes of proceedings on the petition for the London and North Western Railway (Sutton Coldfield Branch) Bill, examiners' evidence, 26 and 27 July 1859.

108. See, for example, the debates on the Marine Society Fishery Bill, *Hansard*, 1st series, 1:1048–53 (27 Mar. 1803); and the St. Catherine's Dock Bill, *Hansard*, 2nd series, 11:95–101 (2 Apr. 1824).

109. *Resolutions and Standing Orders regulating Practice of House of Commons with regard to Private Bills*, BPP (1837) LI, p. 15.

110. *SC on Private Business*, BPP (1837–38) XXIII, p. 9; Rydz, *Parliamentary Agents*, 53–4.

111. See, for example, the debate on the Marine Insurance Bill, *Hansard*, 1st series, 15:399–424 (14 Feb. 1810).

112. *Hansard*, 3rd series, 18:993–7 (19 June 1833).

113. James Emerson Tennent, *Hansard*, 3rd series, 18:1296 (28 June 1833).

114. Stanley, *Hansard*, 2nd series, 11:12 (30 Mar. 1824).

115. Evidence of this greater transparency will be explored in detail in the following chapters.

116. See our discussion of model A- and B-type constitutions in chapter 1, pp. 11–2; chapter 5, p. 128; chapter 9, p. 241.

117. Birmingham Banking Company, *Circular*; Stirlingshire Banking Company, *Prospectus*.

118. Dickens, *Martin Chuzzlewit*, 370–2.

119. *SC on the Limited Liability Acts*, BPP (1867) X, p. 64.

120. Loftus Fitz-Wygram, *Limited Liability Made Practical. Reduction of the Capital of Companies and the Sub-Division of Shares* (London, 1867), quoted in Jefferys, "Denomination and Character," 45.

121. Shannon, "First Five Thousand Limited Companies"; Shannon, "Limited Companies of 1866 and 1883"; Jefferys, "Denomination and Character."

122. Cottrell, *Industrial Finance*, 81.

123. Alborn, *Conceiving Companies*, chapter 4.

124. Evidence of John Harding, *Secret Committee on Joint-Stock Banks*, BPP (1836) IX, p. 135.

125. Evidence of Simon Martin, ibid., p. 147.

126. Evidence of General Austin, ibid., p. 130.

127. Robin Pearson, *Insuring the Industrial Revolution*, 240.

128. 7 & 8 Vict. (1844) c. 113, art. 2.

129. Jefferys, "Denomination and Character," 53.

130. Ibid., 51.

131. *Secret Committee on Joint-Stock Banks*, BPP (1836) IX, p. 96.

132. DRO, PH 526/1, Clay Company, Minute Book, 17 Nov. 1795.

133. For further discussion of shareholder qualifications, see chapter 5.

134. NA, RAIL 803/1, Ashby-de-la-Zouch Canal Company, Minutes of Subscribers' Meetings, 23 Nov., 20 Dec. 1792.

135. 29 Geo. III (1789) c. 25, art. 27; 6 Geo. IV (1825) c. 167, art. 23.

136. 6 Geo. IV. (1825) c. 121; 2 & 3 Will. IV (1832) c. 110, art. 90.

137. CKS, SEG/AM26/1, Rochester and Chatham Gas Light Company, Deed of Copartnership, 20 July 1818 (written into start of minute book), 14–5.

138. CMA, Clerical, Medical, and General Life Assurance Society, Minute Book, 1 Dec. 1825, 4 Mar. 1830.

139. NA, RAIL 350/1, Leeds and Bradford Railway Company, Minute Book, 30 Dec. 1843. This was in part because the provisional committee had allotted themselves nearly one-third of the shares issued at this stage.

140. Pollins, "Marketing of Railway Shares," 233.

141. Williams, *Private Bill Procedure*, 1:44; *Hansard*, 2nd series, 11:856 (25 May 1824).

142. *Hansard*, 2nd series, 11:1076–7 (2 June 1824), 11:1100–2 (9 June 1824).

143. Williams, *Private Bill Procedure*, 1:65–6.

144. NA, RAIL 250/1, Great Western Railway Company, Minute Book, 18 Oct. 1833, 10 Apr., 26 July 1834.

145. Ibid., 2 Sept. 1834, 28 Aug. 1835.

Chapter Four

1. Pope, "Epistle to Bathurst" (1733), in Pope, *Poetical Works*, 313.

2. See Martyn, *Considerations*, 31; Anon., *Collection of Papers*, introduction, viii.

3. Anderson, *Origin of Commerce*, 3:101.

4. Adam Smith, *Wealth of Nations*, 2:741. Cf. also Pollard, *Genesis of Modern Management*, 23–6.

5. Quoted in Porter, *Enlightenment*, 399.

6. See Eden, *Policy and Expediency*; Boult, *Law and Practice*.

7. *Times* (London), 9 Nov. 1840; Spencer, "Railway Morals."

8. William Thomson (an Edinburgh shipbroker), *RC on Amendments in the Law of Partnership*, BPP (1854) XXVII, p. 76.

9. 37 Geo. III (1797) c. 129.

10. 59 Geo. III (1819), c. 32, art. 5.

11. This point is also made in Wilson, *Lighting the Town*, 122.

12. NA, RAIL 1063/498, 9 Geo. III (1769) c. 70, 66–7.

13. 43 Geo. III (1803) c. 140, art. 11.

14. NA, RAIL 803/1, Ashby-de-la-Zouch Canal Company, Minute Book, 7 Sept., 22 Sept. 1792, 18 July 1793.

15. 34 Geo. III (1794) c. 93, art. 90.

16. Whitehead, *Railway Management: A Second Letter to George Carr Glyn*, 15.

17. The 1621 bylaws of the East India Company, for instance, provided for "selected committees" to be appointed for specific functions and listed eight of them. There were fifteen by 1626. East India Company, *Lawes or Standing Orders*; Chauduri, *English East India Company*, 31.

18. Sometimes the powers of the subcommittee were circumscribed in particular ways. Typical was the County of Gloucester Bank (1836), whose deed

forbade the subcommittee from making calls on shares. County of Gloucester Bank, *Deed of Settlement*, art. 66.

19. A handful specified a managing director or made arrangements for a standing committee or a combination of standing and ad hoc committees.

20. Keith-Lucas, *English Local Government Franchise*, 37–8, 227.

21. Anon., *Remarks on the Formation and Working of Banks*, 15.

22. Trebilcock, *Phoenix Assurance*, 1:xviii, 759–60.

23. *Daily News*, 8 Oct. 1849.

24. By a standing order of the House of Commons in 1794, new canal companies had to include in their bills of incorporation a clause that required such security—no amount was specified—from company treasurers, receivers, and collectors "for the faithful execution" of their offices. *House of Commons Journals* 49 (16 Apr. 1794): 473–4.

25. Glamorgan Record Office, D/D B Ca 1, Aberdare Canal Navigation, Minute Book, 10 July 1801; GRO, D2516/1/1, Cheltenham Gas Light Company, Minute Book, 25 Sept. 1818.

26. GRO, TS166–7, Thames and Severn Canal Company, Minute Book, 24 June 1783; LTSB, A46d/3, Fox Family Papers, Thomas Backhouse to George Fox, 10 May 1831.

27. LMA, B/EGLC/12, Equitable Gas Light Company, Minute Book, 27 May 1841.

28. Robin Pearson, *Insuring the Industrial Revolution*, 249, 251–4.

29. CKS, SEG/Aa2, Maidstone Gas Company, Coal and Coke Account.

30. GRO, D2516/1/1, Cheltenham Gas Light Company, Minute Book, 23 Apr. 1819.

31. The original letter does not survive, but see LTSB, A46d/3, Fox Family Papers, Hugh Watt to George Fox, 2 Sept. 1831.

32. NA, RAIL 458/1, Manchester, Bolton, and Bury Canal, Minute Book, 26 June 1794.

33. CCA, CC/W9/5, Canterbury and Whitstable Railway Company, Letter Book, 77–83, 93.

34. CCA, CC/W9/1, Canterbury and Whitstable Railway Company, Minute Book, 9 May 1831.

35. Ibid., 7 July, 1 Aug., 18 Aug., 10 Oct. 1831.

36. Ibid., 14 Nov., 5 Dec. 1831, 27 Aug., 24 Sept. 1832.

37. Ibid., 5 July 1832.

38. The latter referred to John Thomas Barber, later known as Barber Beaumont, founder and managing director of the County Fire Office; to William Morgan, chief actuary of the Equitable Assurance Society; and to Thomas Rhodes, site engineer of the St. Katherine Dock Company. Robin Pearson, "Beaumont, John Thomas Barber," D. L. Thomas, "Morgan, William," Crompton, "Rhodes, Thomas," all in *Oxford Dictionary of National Biography*.

39. CCA, CC/W9/1, Canterbury and Whitstable Railway Company, Minute Book, 27 Aug. 1832.

40. Ibid., 3 Feb. 1838.

41. Ibid., 1 Aug. 1839.

42. Ibid., 5 Oct. 1844, 21 June 1853.

43. The early history of the General Steam Navigation Company provides another example: NMM, GSN/7/1, General Steam Navigation Company, Minute Books, 1825–8.

44. D. G. Wright, *Popular Radicalism*, 30, 40; Thompson, *Chartists*, 57–60.

45. 5 & 6 Will. IV (1834) c. 76, art. 38. Earlier examples of rotation can be found, however: Keith-Lucas, *Unreformed Local Government*, 93–4.

46. Bowen, "'Little Parliament,'" 868.

47. There was a positive association between nominal capital and term of office ($r = 0.34$, calculated for the 487 companies where the term of office was known) and between term of office and date of establishment ($r = 0.35$, calculated for the 480 companies where the term of office and nominal capital were known).

48. 7 & 8 Vict. (1844) c. 110, Schedule A, art. 12.

49. 7 & 8 Vict. (1844) c. 113, art. 4.

50. 8 Vict. (1845) c. 16, art. 88.

51. O'Gorman, *Voters, Patrons and Parties*, 106–12, table 3.3.

52. Innes and Rogers, "Politics and Government," 565; Sweet, *English Town*, 36.

53. Doyle, "Changing Functions of Urban Government," 301.

54. Fraser, *Urban Politics*, 29–30, 133–53, 284.

55. See chapter 3, pp. 42–3.

56. Anon., *Remarks on the Formation and Working of Banks*, 14.

57. *Times* (London), 6 Apr. 1827.

58. *Times* (London), 23 Nov. 1837.

59. *Freeman's Journal and Daily Commercial Advertiser*, 15 Aug. 1820.

60. *Liverpool Mercury*, 10 Oct. 1848.

61. Spencer, "Railway Morals," 252. See also the case of the Hibernian Bank, *Freeman's Journal and Daily Commercial Advertiser*, 5 Dec. 1843.

62. Calculated from CKS, SEG/AM9/1, Dartford Gas Company, Minute Book, 1825–53.

63. The latter may have reflected the long-standing requirement, dating to the fifteenth century, that Scottish burgh officers change annually, although legal decisions had amended this somewhat, so that a change was usually held to be a requirement only every second year. Connell, *Treatise on the Election Laws in Scotland*, 312–3.

64. In 1754 over half the court had been in office for over a decade. Bowen, *Business of Empire*, 67–8. The published "house lists," however, became objects

of great public scrutiny during the hotly contested elections of the 1760s and 1770s. See *London Evening Post*, 4–6 Apr. 1765, 5–8 Apr. 1766.

65. Recounted by James Marshall, secretary to the bank, *Secret Committee on Joint-Stock Banks*, BPP (1837) XIV, p. 285.

66. Webb and Webb, *English Local Government*, 374–5; Cheffins, *Corporate Ownership and Control*, 30–2; Maclean, Harvey, and Press, *Business Elites*, 178–9.

67. Bradford Commercial Joint-Stock Banking Company, *Deed of Covenants*, art. 55.

68. Corbet, *Inquiry into the Causes*, 96–7. Original emphases.

69. Snell, *Parish and Belonging*, 363, discusses parish overseers. For the struggle to fill board vacancies, see Samuel Bignold, *Secret Committee on Joint-Stock Banks*, BPP (1836) IX, p. 171.

70. *SC on the Audit of Railway Accounts*, BPP (1849) X, pp. 227–8.

71. 21 & 22 Vict. (1858) c. 26.

72. O'Gorman, *Voters, Patrons and Parties*, 117–8.

73. Webb and Webb, *Statutory Authorities*, 386.

74. Keith-Lucas, *English Local Government Franchise*, 227–9.

75. Garrard, *Leadership and Power*, 13–4.

76. *Secret Committee on Joint-Stock Banks*, BPP (1836) IX, p. 128.

77. See, for instance, *A list of the names of all such proprietors of the Bank of England who are qualified to vote* (1803, 1812, 1819, 1836); South Sea Company, *A list of the names of all such proprietors of the capital stock of the Governor and company of merchants*.

78. See chapter 5, pp. 125–7.

79. LMA, B/EGLC/12, Equitable Gas Light Company, Minute Book, 31 Oct. 1839, 29 Jan., 4 Mar. 1840.

80. *Leeds Mercury*, 13 Oct. 1849.

81. Calculated for the 506 companies where the capital was known and the investment required to sit on the board could be ascertained. The latter figure refers to "normal" directors only: those sitting ex officio and those subject to different qualifications have been omitted.

82. The right of small shareholders to sit on the board is, admittedly, a crude measure of shareholder participation. The exclusion of small shareholders could vary considerably in its severity. For example, many companies permitted holders of two or three shares to sit on the board, whereas the Agricultural and Commercial Bank of Ireland (1836) required directors to hold three hundred shares, and two insurance companies—the Alliance Marine (1825) and the Protestant Dissenters' and General Life and Fire (1838)—required a nominal investment of £10,000 from each of their directors.

83. Taunton Record Office, Monmouthshire Iron and Coal Company, Prospectus, 11 Nov. 1836.

84. *Morning Chronicle*, 13 July 1848. It was formally adopted at the company's next meeting: *Daily News*, 12 July 1849.

85. *Morning Chronicle*, 8 Dec. 1848.

86. The correlation between nominal capital and the percentage of shares required to be held by the board was $r = -0.28$, calculated for the 502 companies where nominal capital was known and where the minimum percentage of shares held by the board could be calculated.

87. Wilson argues that a division between ownership and control rarely occurred in early provincial utilities, but we think this overstates the case. Wilson, *Lighting the Town*, 123. For further discussion of the separation of ownership and control, see chapter 5.

88. Keith-Lucas, *English Local Government Franchise*, 226–8.

89. But eighteenth-century legal judgments undermined these requirements: Connell, *Treatise on the Election Laws in Scotland*, 312–24.

90. GL, MS 11935E, Sun Fire Office, Take-Over Papers, Salamander Fire Office, Deed of Settlement, 18 Jan. 1823, 52–3.

91. Cf. the "heated debate" over this issue in the East India Company in 1726–7, Dubois, *English Business Company*, 296.

92. Craig, *Chronology of British Parliamentary By-Elections*, x.

93. 6 Anne (1707) c. 7, art. 25. Cf. Gunn, *Beyond Liberty and Property*, 9–11, 62–3.

94. Harling, *Waning of "Old Corruption."*

95. 22 Geo. III (1782) c. 45, art. 9; Keith-Lucas, *English Local Government Franchise*, 174.

96. 41 Geo. III (1801) c. 52, arts. 5–6.

97. This caused difficulty when a councillor was a shareholder in a company that had a contract with the council, a problem resolved by legislation in 1869: Keith-Lucas, *English Local Government Franchise*, 174–6.

98. See, for example, the act of incorporation of the Stockport Gas Light Company, 6 Geo. IV (1825), c. 21, art. 23.

99. Bowen, *Business of Empire*, 125.

100. Dubois, *English Business Company*, 296.

101. *John Bull*, 6 Feb. 1825.

102. *Daily News*, 30 Nov. 1849. See also the report of the committee of investigation of the York, Newcastle and Berwick Railway, *Daily News*, 8 Oct. 1849.

103. It was also a normal requirement that the clerk and treasurer of incorporated companies be different people.

104. CMA, Clerical, Medical, and General Life Assurance Society, Deed of Settlement, 14 Feb. 1827, art. 140; 6 Geo. IV (1825) c. 167, art. 26.

105. Webb and Webb, *Statutory Authorities*, 351.

106. However, a seat on the board could open up insider borrowing opportu-

nities for directors on personal and other securities, including shares. For this phenomenon in New England banks, see Lamoreaux, *Insider Lending*; and in British insurance companies, see Robin Pearson, *Insuring the Industrial Revolution*, 331–2.

107. 23 Geo. III (1783) c. 48, art. 48.

108. Leeds and West-Riding Banking Company, *Deed of Settlement*, art. 55.

109. The managing director, however, received an annual salary of £300.

110. LMA, B/S.Met.G/II/1, South Metropolitan Gas Light and Coke Company, Minute Book, 26 Jan 1837.

111. DRO, BZ/2/1/1, Bridport Gas and Coke Company, Minute Book, 1833–45.

112. GRO, D2516/1/1, Cheltenham Gas Light Company, Minute Book, 19 Aug. 1820, 14 Dec. 1821.

113. Somerset Record Office, DD/GA/2/5, Bridgewater Gas Light Company, Minute Book, 17 June 1834.

114. *Northern Star*, 11 July 1840.

115. On the "unmistakable" upward trend in managerial salaries between the 1760s and the 1830s, see Pollard, *Genesis of Modern Management*, 165–73. Salaries of engineers—"the linchpin of gas company management"—rose from the 1840s. Wilson, *Lighting the Town*, 156.

116. LMA, B/S.Met.G/II/1, South Metropolitan Gas Light and Coke Company, Minute Book, 22 Jan. 1835, 14 Dec. 1837, 24 Jan. 1839.

117. *Daily News*, 14 May 1849.

118. Bagehot, "Sound Banking," in Bagehot, *Collected Works*, 9:309.

119. See chapter 5, pp. 127–37; chapter 1, pp. 11–2; and chapter 3, pp. 65–6.

120. GRO, D2516/1/1, Cheltenham Gas Light Company, Minute Book, 25 Sept. 1818.

121. CKS, SEG/AM26/1, Rochester and Chatham Gas Light Company, Minute Book, 1 Mar., 26 Mar. 1836. Livesey was deputy governor of the Gas Light and Coke Company, chartered in 1812. See Everard, *History of the Gas Light and Coke Company*, 111–4.

122. GRO, D2516/9/1, Dursley Gas Light and Coke Company, Minute Book, 11 July, 16 July 1836.

123. Boot, "Real Incomes."

124. DRO, BZ/2/1/1, Bridport Gas and Coke Company, Minute Book, 3 June 1833, 2 Dec. 1839, 2 Aug. 1844, 13 Aug. 1845.

125. Glamorgan Record Office, D/D B Ca 1, Aberdare Canal Navigation Minute Book, Minute Book, May 1793, 14 July 1796, 10 July 1801.

126. LTSB, A46d/3, Fox Family Papers, Hugh Watt to George Fox, 2 Sept. 1831, Thomas Fox to George Fox, 11 Nov. 1831.

127. Wilson, *Lighting the Town*, 123.

128. Gourvish, "Railway Enterprise"; Chandler, *Visible Hand*.

Chapter Five

1. Gibbon, *Decline and Fall of the Roman Empire*, 1:66.

2. Dunlavy, "From Citizens to Plutocrats," 67.

3. Ireland, "Capitalism without the Capitalist," 41. Original emphasis.

4. Exceptions include Ward, *Finance of Canal Building*; Richards, "Finances of the Liverpool and Manchester Railway Again"; Vamplew, "Scottish Railway Share Capital"; Gourvish and Reed, "Financing of Scottish Railways."

5. By, for example, Alborn, *Conceiving Companies*; James Taylor, *Creating Capitalism*; Robin Pearson, "Shareholder Democracies"; Carlos and Neal, "Women Investors"; Hickson and Turner, "Trading in the Shares of Unlimited Liability Banks"; Acheson and Turner, "Investor Behaviour."

6. Anon., "Caveat against Bubbling"; Carlos, Maguire, and Neal, "Financial Acumen."

7. Ward, *Finance of Canal Building*, chapter 5.

8. Wilson, *Lighting the Town*, 82–9, 113–8.

9. Sarah J. Hudson, "Attitudes to Investment Risk."

10. Hill, "Galloway Shipping," 112. See also Freeman, Pearson, and Taylor, "Technological Change."

11. Preda, "Rise of the Popular Investor," 208.

12. Ibid.; Michie, *Money, Mania and Markets*, 27–30.

13. Rutterford, "History of UK and US Equity Valuation Techniques," 119.

14. Foreman-Peck and Millward, *Public and Private Ownership*, chapter 2.

15. See below, p. 124.

16. Alborn, *Conceiving Companies*, 85–8, 98–119.

17. Dunlavy, "From Citizens to Plutocrats," 86–7.

18. Fifteen companies, all established after 1824, delegated to the GM the authority over *some* calls, usually those above a certain specified amount.

19. See, for example, Glamorgan Record Office, D/D B Ca 1, Aberdare Canal Navigation, Minute Book; BL, Add MS 27880, Tunnel under the Thames Company, Minute Book.

20. LMA, B/S.Met.G/II/1, South Metropolitan Gas Light and Coke Company, Minute Book, 27 Jan. 1836.

21. CKS, SEG/AM26/1, Rochester and Chatham Gas Light Company, Deed of Copartnership, 20 July 1818, 5–6 (engrossed into Minute Book).

22. Wilson, *Lighting the Town*, 78.

23. There were significant doubts in the minds of some directors whether they really could take their shareholders to court over nonpayment: see, for example, BL, Add MS 27880, Tunnel under the Thames Company, Minute Book, 8 Nov., 15 Nov. 1802.

24. 34 Geo III (1794) c. 93, arts. 88, 95, 137.

25. NA, RAIL 803/1, Ashby-de-la-Zouch Canal Company, Minute Book, 6 Apr., 8 Dec. 1795.

26. Ibid., 4 Apr., 2 July 1796.

27. Ibid., 20 Apr., 31 May 1796.

28. Ibid., 3 Oct. 1796.

29. Ibid., 14 Nov. 1797, 12 Jan., 2 Apr. 1798. The list included Bullivant, who seems to have reneged on his undertakings.

30. Ibid., 1 Oct. 1798, 1 Apr. 1799, 7 Apr. 1800.

31. Ibid., 3 Apr. 1803.

32. This statement is based on a survey of 116 such cases between 1796 and 1843, the majority occurring after 1825. Thirty-three of these concerned the issue of calls, where companies were suing to recover unpaid subscriptions or shareholders were resisting calls as illegal. The cases were extracted in summary form from the LexisNexis database, http://www.lexisnexis.com/uk/legal.

33. Examples include Stratford and Moreton Railway Company v. Stratton (1831) 2 B & Ad 518; Baillie v. Edinburgh Oil Gas Light Company (1835) 3 Cl & Fin 639; Birmingham, Bristol and Thames Junction Railway Company v. Locke (1841) 1 QB 256.

34. See, for example, Cromford Railway Company v. Lacey (1829) 3 Y & J 80; London and Brighton Railway Company v. Wilson (1839) 6 Bing NC 135. Shareholder liability is discussed more fully in chapter 7.

35. Huddersfield Canal Company v. Buckley (1796) 7 Term Rep 36. On the variety of restrictions imposed by companies on when shares could be transferred or sold, see below, pp. 124–5.

36. Preston v. Grand Collier Dock Company (1840) 2 Ry & Can Cas 335; Mangles v. Grand Collier Dock Company (1840) 2 Ry & Can Cas 359.

37. On the crisis of 1836–7, see Kostal, *Law and English Railway Capitalism*, 18–21.

38. See, for example, South Eastern Railway Company v. Hebblewhite (1840) 12 Ad & El 497; London and Brighton Railway Company v. Fairclough (1841) 5 JP 513. On the difficulties caused by a high volume of scrip trading in identifying shareholders and liability for calls, see the evidence of John Duncan, *SC on Joint-Stock Companies*, BPP (1844) VII, pp. 164, 167, 170.

39. Ward v. Matheson (1829), 7 S. 409; Learmonth v. Adams (1831), 9 S. 787.

40. See John Duncan, *SC on Joint-Stock Companies*, BPP (1844) VII, p. 166; Raynes, *History of British Insurance*, 242.

41. Williston, "Law of Business Corporations," 160.

42. NAS, GD 354/1/1, Insurance Company of Scotland, Sederunt Book, 15 June 1822. On exhortations of this kind, see Robin Pearson, "Shareholder Democracies?," 852.

43. RBS, ASH/8/1, Ashton, Stalybridge, Hyde and Glossop Bank, Minute Book, 30 July 1838.

44. GRO, TS166, Thames and Severn Canal Company, Minute Book, 24 Jan. 1797.

45. Medway Archives, DE 279, Medway Bathing Establishment, Minute Book, 7 Mar., 8 Nov. 1836.

46. NAS, GD 354/1/13, Insurance Company of Scotland, Contract of Copartnery, art. 1.

47. Only five of the twenty-six companies in our shipping sample were incorporated. Three of these five were ferry companies.

48. Hackney Archives Department, D/B/NIC/2/18, Stockton and London Shipping Company, Arts. of Partnership, 2; NAS, GD301/58/3, London and Edinburgh Shipping Company, Contract of Copartnery, art. 4.

49. New shareholders were not required, however, to break any of their existing agreements. BRO, 10/1/31, Berwick Shipping Company, Arts. of Agreement, 16–7; Tony Barrow, "Corn, Carriers and Coastal Shipping."

50. NLS, MS 3707, Duns Linen Company, Rules and Regulations, engrossed in the front of the first Minute Book.

51. Bristol Record Office, 39049/1, Bristol Flour and Bread Concern, Deed of Formation, 1; BCA, MS 232/1, Birmingham Flour and Bread Company, *Printed Articles*, 7–8.

52. Robin Pearson, *Insuring the Industrial Revolution*, 246–7.

53. The main exception seems to have been where companies were actively seeking to extend their business in particular districts.

54. Quoted in Robin Pearson, "Shareholder Democracies?," 850.

55. BSA, ABC/1/1/1, Aberdeen Banking Company, Contract of Copartnery, art. 19.

56. Robbins, *Railway Age*, 75. Common though these rights were, they were rarely provided for in constitutional documents.

57. Scarborough Cliff Bridge Company, *Deed of Settlement*, 37–8.

58. NA, C66/4303, PR 7 Geo. IV (1826), part 1, no. 1, West India Company, Charter.

59. RBS, CS/362, Commercial Bank of Scotland, Contract of Copartnery, art. 15.

60. Watt, *Theory and Practice of Joint-Stock Banking*, 25–6.

61. Checkland, *Scottish Banking*, 467; Lamoreaux, *Insider Lending*, 5–6.

62. Edinburgh Central Library, qYHD.9111.8, Edinburgh Sugar House Company, Minute Book, 9 June 1755.

63. Ibid., 21 May, 14 June 1759, 11 June 1760, 28 June 1762.

64. NA, RAIL 371/1, Liverpool and Manchester Railway Company, DM, 8 Sept. 1828; 2 March 1829.

65. From the 1830s caps were increasingly inserted into acts that authorized

gas companies to enlarge their capital. Wilson, *Lighting the Town*, 110; Foreman-Peck and Millward, *Public and Private Ownership*, chapter 2.

66. Rates could be reduced proportionately by the Court of Quarter Sessions (or in Scotland by the sheriff) if in the preceding year profits had exceeded the amount required to pay a 10 percent dividend and maintain a reserve fund of 10 percent of nominal capital. 10 & 11 Vict. (1847), c.15 (Gasworks Clauses), art. 35; 10 & 11 Vict. (1847) c.17 (Waterworks Clauses), art. 80.

67. The effectiveness of dividend caps, however, was probably limited: Foreman-Peck and Millward, *Public and Private Ownership*, 45–6; Wilson, *Lighting the Town*, 52–3, 111.

68. LMA, ACC2558/WM/A/1/5, West Middlesex Water Works, Minutes of General Meetings, 27 July, 2 Nov. 1819.

69. See chapter 8, p. 222.

70. 3 Will. IV (1833) c. 32, art. 79; 7 Will. IV (1837) c. 30, art. 61.

71. This was the Clydesdale Banking Company (1838), which offered both dividend protection *and* loans against paid-up capital, as did five English banks.

72. RBS, SAD/2, Saddleworth Banking Company, Deed of Settlement, art. 38.

73. 10 Vict. (1847) c. 15 (Gasworks Clauses), arts. 30–4; 10 Vict. (1847) c. 17 (Waterworks Clauses), arts. 75–9.

74. LMA, B/EGLC/12, Equitable Gas Light Company, Minute Book, 29 Jan. 1840.

75. Staffordshire County Record Office, D800/4/1, Uttoxeter Gas Light and Coke Company, Minute Book, 18 Apr. 1844.

76. Ibid., 22 Oct. 1840, 5 Jan. 1843, 1 Feb. 1844.

77. Ibid., 19 Apr. 1849.

78. John Duncan, *SC on Joint-Stock Companies*, BPP (1844) VII, pp. 164–6.

79. See chapter 6, p. 160.

80. AVIVA, North of Scotland Fire and Life Assurance Company, Contract of Copartnery (1836), art. 18; 54 Geo. III (1814) c. 101, art. 44. Another abridgement of transfer rights came with the extension of liability after transfer, which we discuss in chapter 7, pp. 194–5.

81. Unless stated otherwise, this section draws on Freeman, Pearson, and Taylor, "'Doe in the City'"; and Freeman, Pearson, and Taylor, "Between Madam Bubble and Kitty Lorimer."

82. These datasets overlap with but do not mirror the constitutional dataset of 514 companies that underpins the present book. Shareholder data exist for some companies whose constitutions have not survived, and other companies whose constitutions are included in our present dataset have no surviving shareholder records. Nevertheless, the works referred to in n. 81 together amount to the largest study of women shareholders hitherto undertaken for Britain in this period.

83. Bowen, *Business of Empire*, 107–8.

84. Acheson and Turner, "Impact of Limited Liability." Indeed the trend continued into the 1930s, see Rutterford et al., "Gender and Investment."

85. Barker, *Business of Women.*

86. See, chapter 6, pp. 158–60.

87. See, chapter 6, p. 163.

88. 10 Geo. III (1770) c. 114, 42.

89. On model-A and model-B constitutions, see chapter 1, pp. 11–2.

90. See, for example, 4 & 5 Will. IV (1834) c. 85, art. 43.

91. 7 & 8 Vict. (1844) c. 66, arts. 83, 103, cf. art. 104.

92. 59 Geo. III (1819) c. 12, art. 1; 4 & 5 Will. IV (1834) c. 76, art. 38.

93. 5 & 6 Will. IV (1835) c. 76, art. 48.

94. Thereafter, the proportion of contests steadily increased: Craig, *Chronology of British Parliamentary By-Elections,* 313.

95. Both corporations and unincorporated companies exhibit a similar trend, although it was slightly more pronounced in the case of the former.

96. A Member of the Stock Exchange, *Shareholders' Key,* 43. For a similar view, see Corbet, *Inquiry into the Causes,* 96–7.

97. There were 117 such companies in the first period and 89 in the second. The GM was responsible for filling casual vacancies in 47.0 percent and 37.1 percent of cases, respectively, and there was a large decline in the proportion of constitutions where no procedure was set out.

98. Royal Bank of Liverpool, *Deed of Settlement,* art. 11.

99. See chapter 6, pp. 150–3; chapter 8, pp. 214–9.

100. See above, chapter 1, pp. 11–2; chapter 3, pp. 65–6.

101. The graph (a) excludes companies where rights of appointment were neither reserved to directors nor allowed to shareholders; (b) includes all companies where there were any stipulated shareholder rights over the appointment of any employees, even where the directors were responsible for the appointment of junior officers; and (c) includes all companies where all rights of appointment of salaried officials were reserved to the directors.

102. These figures exclude companies where the entire board functioned as trustees.

103. Shareholder franchises are fully discussed in chapter 6.

104. NAS, GB 1/105/1, Rutherglen Gas Light Company, Rules and Regulations, 1841, art. 11.

105. GCA, RU 4/6/128/1, Rutherglen Gas Light Company, Minute Book, 25 Aug., 26 Sept., 27 Sept., 8 Nov., 8 Dec. 1842, 5 June 1843.

106. NAS, GD 354/1/13, Insurance Company of Scotland, Contract of Co-partnery, art. 22. Shareholder numbers from NAS, GD 354/1/2, Insurance Company of Scotland, Sederunt Book, 15 June 1830.

107. NAS, GD 354/1/3, Insurance Company of Scotland, Sederunt Book, 16 June 1834.

108. 46 Geo. III (1806) c. 119, art. 21.

109. LMA, ACC2558/WM/A/1/1, West Middlesex Waterworks Company, Minute Book, 12 Aug., 8 Oct., 12 Dec. 1806.

110. For more on Dodd's involvement with other companies, see James Taylor, *Creating Capitalism*, 94–7.

111. LMA, ACC2558/WM/A/1/1, West Middlesex Waterworks Company, Minute Book, 6 Nov. 1810.

112. For another example, see LMA, B/EGLC/12, Equitable Gas Light Company, Minute Book, 4 Mar. 1840.

113. Watt, *Theory and Practice of Joint-Stock Banking*, 5–6.

114. 6 & 7 Will. IV (1836) c. 111.

115. LTSB, A/53/1/a/2.0, Hampshire Banking Company, *Deed of Settlement*, art. 83.

116. 7 Geo. IV (1826) c. 30, art. 92.

117. Only one corporation in our sample required a larger majority: the Peninsular and Oriental Steam Navigation Company. It is notable that this company was established by deed of settlement and incorporated by charter. NMM, P&O/51/17/1, Peninsular and Oriental Steam Navigation Company, Deed of Settlement, 25 Jan. 1841, art. 46. The company's royal charter of incorporation was dated 1840 (patent rolls, 4 Vict., part 16, no. 16).

118. Examples include Blaenavon Iron and Coal Company, *Deed of Settlement*, art. 58; BCA, MS 232/2, Patent Shaft and Axle Tree Company, Deed of Settlement, art. 42.

119. English and Scottish Law Fire and Life Assurance and Loan Association, *Deed of Settlement*, arts. 89, 92, 102. The usual quorum was twenty shareholders; for constitutional amendments it was forty.

120. Robin Pearson, *Insuring the Industrial Revolution*, 338.

121. We explore these issues more fully in chapter 7.

122. Child v. Hudson's Bay Co. (1723), 2 P Wms 207; Williston, "Law of Business Corporations," 122–3.

123. Williston, "Law of Business Corporations," 123.

124. John Malcolm Ludlow, *SC on Investments for Savings of Middle and Working Classes*, BPP (1850) XIX, p. 6.

Chapter Six

1. Aristotle, *Athenian Constitution*, 253.

2. Bowen, "Investment and Empire," 194; Bowen, "'Little Parliament,'" 857, 859, 863.

3. Quoted in Micklethwait and Wooldridge, *The Company*, 60.

4. See, for example, NAS, GD354/1/2, 4, Insurance Company of Scotland,

Minute Books 15 June 1826, 15 June 1829, 15 June 1836. Spencer quoted in Alborn, *Conceiving Companies*, 202.

5. GULSC, UGD8/3/13, Ballochney Railway Company, Minutes of the General Meeting, Protest by William Davidson [1 Feb. 1837?].

6. Dunlavy, "From Citizens to Plutocrats."

7. Vernon, *Politics and the People*, 337; Kirk, "Post-modernism," 73.

8. Keith-Lucas, *Unreformed Local Government*, 42–3.

9. Vernon, *Politics and the People*, 31.

10. On the role and importance of parish and township meetings, see Garrard, *Leadership and Power*, 116–8; Fraser, *Urban Politics*, 25–8.

11. On the gradual decline of vestry institutions with the increase of municipal authority from the 1840s, see Fraser, *Urban Politics*, 25–110. For municipal politics becoming "less consultative" and "more controllable," and the "disappearance" of "direct public participation," see Garrard, *Leadership and Power*, 172, 214; see also Vernon, *Politics and the People*, 65.

12. Fraser, *Urban Politics*, 29.

13. Vernon, *Politics and the People*, 46.

14. Keith-Lucas, *English Local Government Franchise*, 226–9.

15. Dunlop, *Law of Scotland*, 131–2.

16. Keith-Lucas, *English Local Government Franchise*, 228.

17. Williston, "Law of Business Corporations," 157.

18. Alborn, *Conceiving Companies*, 109–11.

19. Dunlavy, "From Citizens to Plutocrats," 76–84. See also Dunlavy, "Corporate Democracy."

20. For seven companies (1.4 percent) the franchise could not be ascertained. In the absence of a specified franchise procedure, the common law default was voting by show of hands with one vote per person. Because of uncertainty about the exact position in these seven companies, however, they are excluded from the calculations in this chapter.

21. It should be noted, however, that for many franchise types, the ratio of votes accorded to five and one hundred shares would have been very different had different companies been selected. Moreover, many companies disenfranchised their smallest shareholders, and this is not fully incorporated into this typology. We discuss this issue in more detail below.

22. This influence had led to the Eastern Counties Company rejecting amalgamation with the Northern and Eastern. *Times* (London), 20 Feb. 1851.

23. The 1845 default was one vote for every share up to ten, for every five shares between ten and one hundred, and for every ten shares beyond that. 8 Vict. (1845) c. 16, art. 75.

24. Alborn, *Conceiving Companies*, 174.

25. The means were £615,485 (standard deviation £978,354) and £199,750 (standard deviation £414,599), respectively.

26. On share denominations, see chapter 3, pp. 66–72.

27. Dunlavy, "From Citizens to Plutocrats," 85.

28. DRO, BZ/4/1, Lyme-Regis Gas and Coke Company, Minutes of General Meetings, 9 Feb. 1835.

29. GRO, D2516/9/1, Dursley Gas Light and Coke Company, Minutes of General Meetings, 15 July, 7 Sept. 1835.

30. DCA, GD/DPL/2/1, Dundee, Perth, and London Shipping Company, Minutes of General Meetings, 29 Nov. 1826.

31. Examples include the Saddleworth Banking Company (1833); the Blaenavon Iron and Coal Company (1838); and the Newcastle Commercial Insurance Company (1839).

32. 11 Geo. IV (1830) c. 17, art. 23.

33. East Lothian and Merse Whale Fishing Company; Edinburgh Whale Fishing Company; Fife and Anstruther Whale Fishing Company.

34. 34 Geo. III (1794) c. 90, arts. 82–3.

35. All quoted in the opinion of the company's law agent, engrossed at AUL, MS 3697, Aberdeen, Leith, and Clyde Shipping Company, Minute Book, OGM, 5 Dec. 1820.

36. Ibid., SGM, 1 Feb. 1820.

37. Ibid., OGM, 5 Dec. 1820.

38. 8 Vict. (1845) c. 16, art. 80; 8 Vict. (1845) c. 17, art. 83.

39. *Times* (London), 7 May 1818.

40. *Morning Chronicle*, 7 Dec. 1825; *Times* (London), 27 Feb. 1826.

41. *Morning Chronicle*, 9 Dec. 1825.

42. *Morning Chronicle*, 27 Feb. 1826.

43. *Times* (London), 16 Mar. 1826.

44. *Times* (London), 16 Dec. 1830.

45. Vernon, *Politics and the People*, 158.

46. Crook and Crook, "Secret Ballot," 469.

47. Vernon, *Politics and the People*, 155, 337; Rose, "Administration of the Poor Law," 133–4; Crook and Crook, "Secret Ballot," 456.

48. Keith-Lucas, *English Local Government Franchise*, 227–30.

49. Legislation in 1845 set Scotland on a similar course for nonburghal poor-law parochial boards. 8 & 9 Vict. (1845), c. 83, art. 24.

50. LTSB, A53/1a/2.0, Hampshire Banking Company, Deed of Settlement, 2 July 1834, art. 86.

51. Sutherland, *East India Company*, 16, 100–9.

52. 7 Geo. III (1767) c. 48.

53. Bowen, "Investment and Empire," 198; Bowen, " 'Little Parliament,' " 868.

54. Ferguson, "Reform Act (Scotland) of 1832," 109, 111.

55. May, *Constitutional History of England*, 1:455.

56. A Member of the Stock Exchange, *Shareholders' Key*, 44.

57. Royal Canal Company, *Charter*, 18–9.

58. 6 & 7 Will. IV (1836) c. 33, p. 44.

59. *Times* (London), 16 Mar. 1826.

60. *SC on Origin, Management and State of Arigna Iron and Coal Mining Company*, BPP (1826–7) III, pp. 10, 427. The directors of the Imperial Manganese Mining Company were also accused of stock splitting: *Morning Chronicle*, 5 Nov. 1825.

61. During the first half of the nineteenth century, the problem of stock splitting seems rarely to have been brought before the English courts. This conclusion is drawn from our survey of 116 cases involving stock companies between 1796 and 1843. See chapter 5, p. 113.

62. 7 Ch. D. 591; Law Rep. 16 Eq. 559.

63. Williston, "Law of Business Corporations," 158.

64. In his recent book, McQueen mentions proxy voting but argues, incorrectly, that it was a rarity outside the railway sector in our period and that its advent marked the end of limited-liability enterprises as "little republics." McQueen, *Social History of Company Law*, 114, 196–7. As we show, the majority of company constitutions permitted proxy voting, even in the eighteenth century, and, although the practice was controversial, by itself it was not fatal to the notion of shareholder democracy.

65. Bowen, "Investment and Empire," 200.

66. Bagehot, *English Constitution*, 148.

67. Snow, "Reluctant Surrender of an Absurd Privilege," 61.

68. A division was the separation of members of the legislature into two groups in order to count their votes.

69. Ibid., 69.

70. Salmon, *Electoral Reform at Work*, 197–8; Keith-Lucas, *English Local Government Franchise*, 128.

71. A Member of the Stock Exchange, *Shareholder's Key*, 43.

72. Robbins, *Railway Age*, 75.

73. See, for instance, article 44 of the Croydon, Merstham and Godstone Iron Railway Company act, 43 Geo. III (1803), c. 35. It was generally assumed, however, that the proxy holder would vote according to the wishes of the proxy giver. Although this does not seem to have been regulated by companies in any way, under common law shareholders had the right to revoke their proxies at any time, provided notice of such intention was given before or at the GM concerned. Emden, *Shareholders' Legal Guide*, 324.

74. Gibbs, *Birth of the Great Western Railway*, 32, 58–9.

75. NA, RAIL 250/1, Great Western Railway Company, DM, 10 Jan. 1839.

76. *Daily News*, 4 July 1849.

77. DCA, GD/DPL/2/1, Dundee, Perth, and London Shipping Company,

Partners' Meeting, 12 July 1832. "Holograph" here refers to a power of attorney that was wholly in the handwriting of the shareholder.

78. Freeman, Pearson, and Taylor, "Technological Change."

79. NA, RAIL 458/1, Manchester, Bolton, and Bury, Canal Company, SGM, 25 July, 1 Aug. 1834.

80. Ibid., SGM, 5 Dec. 1844.

81. *Times* (London), 14 Apr. 1856.

82. Williston, "Law of Business Corporations," 158.

83. Levy, *Private Corporations and Their Control*, 1:52. See also Emden, *Shareholders' Legal Guide*, 322.

84. 8 Vict. (1845) c. 16, arts. 76–7; 8 Vict. (1845) c. 17, arts. 79–80.

85. James, *Practical Application*, 81.

86. LMA, ACC2558/WM/A/1/2,West Middlesex Waterworks Company, Minute Book, 6 Nov., 15 Nov., 10 Dec. 1810.

87. LMA, B/EGLC/12, Equitable Gas Light Company, Minute Book, 29 Aug. 1833, 18 Apr. 1834, 26 Feb., 27 Feb., 9 Apr. 1835.

88. It is not always clear whether proxy votes could count toward the quorum, but we have assumed in all cases of doubt that they could; in many constitutions this was made explicit.

89. NA, RAIL1063/381, Warwick and Birmingham Canal Navigation, Act of Parliament, 33 Geo. III (1793) c. 38, pp. 29–30.

90. Examples include the Forth and Clyde Navigation and the Droitwich Canal (both 1767), the Leeds-Liverpool Canal (1770), the Foss Navigation and the Derby Canal (both 1793), the Kilmarnock and Troon Railway (1808, not in our sample), and the Croydon Merstham and Godstone Iron Railway (1803).

91. Calculated for the 367 companies for which there were data relating to the quorum in terms of shares (either given or calculated from the quorum in terms of numbers of shareholders) and nominal capital.

92. Unlike changes in quorum size, there was no association between SGM threshold and company size ($r = -0.04$, calculated for the 476 companies for which there were data on nominal capital and SGM thresholds).

93. John Fairfull Smith, *Proposed Alterations in the System of Joint Stock Banking*, 15–7, 24–5.

94. Morris, "A Year in the Public Life."

95. Vernon, *Politics and the People*, 197–8.

96. 6 & 7 Will. IV (1836) c. 97, arts. 36–7.

97. Shropshire Banking Company, *Deed of Settlement*, arts. 77–8.

98. Shareholders would also be notified by circular. NAS, GB1/105/1, Rutherglen Gas Light Company, Rules and Regulations, n.d. [1841], art. 10. The church door was an important place for the dissemination of local information. Overseers were required to place a range of notices on the doors of churches in their

parishes, even after the reform of the poor law in 1834. Snell, *Parish and Belonging*, 339–65.

99. *Morning Chronicle*, 9 Dec. 1825.

100. *Morning Chronicle*, 6 Dec. 1825.

101. *Morning Chronicle*, 7 Dec. 1825; *Times* (London), 7 Dec. 1825.

102. Vernon, *Politics and the People*, 158.

103. 8 Vict. (1845) c. 16, art. 71; 8 Vict. (1845) c. 17, arts. 74, 140.

104. Freeman, Pearson, and Taylor, "Technological Change."

105. Spencer, "Railway Morals," 420–1.

106. *Times* (London), 17 Aug. 1853.

107. Corbet, *Inquiry into the Causes*, 97–8.

108. Dunlavy, "From Citizens to Plutocrats," 83.

109. *Freeman's Journal and Daily Commercial Advertiser*, 13 May 1846.

110. Anon., *Oxford Essays*, 4:63.

111. Norman Pearson, "Manhood Suffrage."

112. This statement was made during Sopwith's observation of an election at Leeds in 1834: Richardson, *Thomas Sopwith*, 98.

113. Norman Pearson, "Manhood Suffrage," 1086.

114. *Quarterly Review* 116 (1864): 266, 268. Emphasis added. Attributed to Cecil in the *Wellesley Index to Victorian Periodicals*.

Chapter Seven

1. Recent work has begun to address the gap: see Alborn, *Conceiving Companies*; Harris, *Industrializing English Law*; James Taylor, *Creating Capitalism*.

2. Shannon, "Coming of General Limited Liability"; French, "Origin of General Limited Liability"; Bryer, "Mercantile Laws Commission"; Loftus, "Capital and Community."

3. Hickson and Turner, "Genesis of Corporate Governance," 179, 186.

4. Anon., *How to Mismanage a Bank*, 41.

5. Harris, *Industrializing English Law*, 128–9.

6. Ibid., 129–30, 130n41.

7. David M. Walker, *Legal History of Scotland*, 6:725.

8. Quoted in Dubois, *English Business Company*, 97. See also Campbell, *Carron Company*, 24–5.

9. Dubois, *English Business Company*, 97.

10. David M. Walker, *Legal History of Scotland*, 6:734; Freeman, Pearson, and Taylor, " 'Different and Better?,' " 67; Henderson, *Notes on the Law of Scotland*, 4, 8–10.

11. Campbell, "Law and the Joint-Stock Company," 140.

12. 26 Geo. III (1786) c. 106, p. 90. The third company was the Northumberland Fishery Society (1789).

13. Dubois, *English Business Company*, 95–7; 31 Geo. III (1791) c. 55, arts. 1, 3.

14. Harris, *Industrializing English Law*, 129.

15. 48 Geo. III (1808) c. 46, art. 16. Liability for calls is discussed above, chapter 5, pp. 111–4.

16. 5 Geo. IV (1824) c. 49; 7 Geo. IV (1826) c. 48, art. 28.

17. 4 Will. IV (1834) c. 4.

18. Shilts, "Accounting, Engineering or Advertising?"

19. CKS, U2593/B1, Deed for establishing the Kent Insurance Company. See above, chapter 3, pp. 40–1, 52.

20. NMM, GSN/7/1, General Steam Navigation Company, Minutes of the General Meeting, 28 Feb. 1827.

21. Ibid., 31 Aug. 1831.

22. 7 & 8 Vict. (1844) c. 65, art. 36.

23. Malcolm v. West Lothian Railway Company (1835), 13 S. 887.

24. Clowes v. Brettell (1843), 12 LJ Ex 302.

25. Bourne v. Freeth (1829), 9 B & C 632.

26. See chapter 2, p. 28.

27. Two charters did the same: those incorporating the Plymouth Union Bath Company, Patent Rolls, 9 Geo. (1828) IV part 12, no.17; and the Peninsular and Oriental Steam Navigation Company, Patent Rolls, 4 Vict. (1840) part 16, no. 16. See also NMM, P&O/51/17/1, Peninsular and Oriental Steam Navigation Company, Deed of Settlement, 25 Jan. 1841, art. 124.

28. 5 Geo. IV (1824) c. 132, art. 7. The same wording appears in many acts, including 3 Will. IV (1833) c. 32, art. 57 (Exeter Water Company).

29. 6 Geo. IV (1825) c. 144, art. 21 (Paisley Water Company).

30. Davis, *Rise of English Shipping*, 102; Hill, "Kircudbright Shipping Company," 71; Hill, "Galloway Shipping," 106–7; David M. Walker, *Legal History of Scotland*, 5:681–2.

31. Morison, *Decisions of the Court of Session*, 14,667.

32. 4 Geo. IV (1823) c. 41.

33. Davis, *Rise of English Shipping*, 102–4; Harris, *Industrializing English Law*, 186–90. The jurisdiction of the Scottish Court of Admiralty was taken over by the Court of Session when the former was abolished in 1830. David M. Walker, *Legal History of Scotland*, 6:337, 539.

34. Freeman, Pearson, and Taylor, "Technological Change."

35. Boyce, *Information, Mediation and Institutional Development*, 66–9.

36. The following description is based on that of Burt and Kudo, "Cornish Cost Book System,"30–3.

37. 19 & 20 Vict. c.110. There remained some uncertainty, however, as to whether the stannary jurisdiction extended to metalliferous mines outside the southwest.

38. Burke and Richardson, "Cornish Cost Book System"; Burt and Kudo, "Cornish Cost Book System."

39. Burt and Kudo, "Cornish Cost Book System," 34–7; Burke and Richardson, "Cornish Cost Book System," 195.

40. Marke Valley Consolidated Mines, *Description*, 6.

41. Ibid., 20–1. Other mining prospectuses made similar claims. See, for example, Taunton Record Office, Monmouthshire Iron and Coal Company, Prospectus, 11 Nov. 1836. The claim was reiterated in advertisements in the press: for example, *Hull Packet*, 16 Sept. 1836.

42. Henderson, *Notes on the Law of Scotland*, 2.

43. For example, Glasgow University Archive, UGD 84/1/1, Western Bank of Scotland, Contract of Copartnery, art. 31. On the difficulty of recruiting good directors owing to their full liability under partnership law, see the evidence of John Duncan, *SC on Joint-Stock Companies*, BPP (1844) VII, p. 167.

44. Grantham Gas Light Company, *Deed of Settlement*, 46–8.

45. Harris, *Industrializing English Law*, 153–6.

46. For example, NLI, Ir.332.n4, National Bank of Ireland, Deed of Settlement, 6 Jan. 1835, art. 145.

47. NLS, 1976.164(8), Falkirk Gas Work Company, Contract of Copartnery (1829), art. 12. See also GULSC, Mu.17-f.18, Dundee Marine Insurance Company, Contract of Copartnery, 2 Feb. 1836, art. 40.

48. NLS, 1972.193(3), Kirkintilloch Gas Light Company, Contract of Copartnery, 1 Jan. 1838, art. 27.

49. For example, Farmers' and General Fire and Life Insurance and Loan and Annuity Company, *Abstract of Deed of Settlement*, art. 72.

50. The only sectoral exception was bridge companies. The database contains only one unincorporated bridge company.

51. Farmers' and General Fire and Life Insurance and Loan and Annuity Company, *Abstract of Deed of Settlement*, art. 72.

52. See, for example, *Times* (London), 4 Oct. 1842.

53. Walburn v. Ingilby (1833), 1 My & K 61.

54. James Taylor, *Creating Capitalism*, 30–2.

55. 7 & 8 Vict. (1844), c. 110, art. 68.

56. Farmers' and General Fire and Life Insurance and Loan and Annuity Company, *Abstract of Deed of Settlement*, art. 85. This was also the legal advice given, for instance, to the Kent Fire Office in 1802 after the company's application for incorporation had failed. CKS, U2593/B6/1, Kent Fire Insurance Company, DM, 19 Oct. 1802.

57. Quoted in Halket v. Merchant Traders Ship Loan and Insurance Association (1849), 13 QB 960.

58. Harris, *Industrializing English Law*, 143.

59. Robin Pearson, "Shareholder Democracies?," 849; Robin Pearson, *Insuring the Industrial Revolution*.

60. Alchorne v. Saville (1820), 6 Moore. 202(a).

61. Andrews v. Ellison (1821), 6 Moore. 199.

62. Dawson v. Wrench (1849), 3 Ex. 359.

63. Hassell v. Merchant Traders Ship Loan and Insurance Association (1849), 4 Ex. 525.

64. Halket v. Merchant Traders Ship Loan and Insurance Association (1849), 13 QB 960.

65. James, *Practical Application*, 5, 86–7.

66. George Taylor, *A Practical Treatise on the Act for the Registration, Regulation and Incorporation of Joint Stock Companies* (London, 1847), quoted in James, *Practical Application*, 87. Another important case was Hallett v. Dowdall (1852), 18 QB 2, cited in Hunt, *Development of the Business Corporation*, 99–100. See also references to this practice by John Duncan and Henry Bellenden Ker in *SC on Joint-Stock Companies*, BPP (1844) VII, pp. 170–2, 188.

67. Reid v. Allan, and Cross v. Allan (1849), 4 Ex. 326.

68. George, *View of the Existing Law*, 51.

69. 7 Geo. IV (1826) c. 46, art. 13.

70. 4 & 5 Geo. IV (1834) c. 94, art. 3; 7 & 8 Vict. (1844) c. 110, art. 66. For arguments in favor of a three-year extended liability, see evidence of Joseph Parkes, *SC on Joint-Stock Companies*, BPP (1844) VII, p. 232.

71. 19 & 20 Vict. (1856) c. 47, arts. 62–3.

72. NA, BT 3/25, letter from Poulett Thomson to attorney general, 7 June 1834, 154–5.

73. James Taylor, "Company Fraud," 710.

74. *SC on the Limited Liability Acts*, BPP (1867) X, p. 101. See also the evidence of William Drake, pp. 42–3.

75. The following discussion is based on Freeman, Pearson, and Taylor, "'Different and Better?'"; Campbell, "Law and the Joint-Stock Company"; Christie, "Joint Stock Enterprise in Scotland"; F. W. Clark, *Treatise on the Law of Partnership*.

76. Campbell, "Law and the Joint-Stock Company," 145.

77. David M. Walker, *Legal History of Scotland*, 6:717.

78. Ibid., 6:716.

79. Quoted in ibid., 6:717.

80. Adam Smith, *Wealth of Nations*, 2:757–8; McCulloch, *Considerations on Partnerships*.

81. Over half of the English witnesses supported limited liability (eighteen out of thirty-three). James Taylor, *Creating Capitalism*, 151.

82. 21 & 22 Vict. (1858) c. 91. Liability remained unlimited for notes issue until 1879. Carr, Glied, and Mathewson, "Unlimited Liability and Free Banking," 976.

83. On the Anonymous Partners Act, see French, "Origin of General Limited Liability."

84. Munn, *Scottish Provincial Banking Companies*, 106.

85. County of Gloucester Bank, *Deed of Settlement*, art. 13.

86. Munn, *Scottish Provincial Banking Companies*, 29–36, 106.

87. 7 Geo. IV (1826) c. 46, arts. 11–2; 7 & 8 Vict., c. 110, art. 67.

88. See chapter 5, pp. 113–4.

89. In *Dickinson v. Valpy* (1829), for instance, Lord Justice Parke ruled that directors could not bind members of a mining association by accepting a bill of exchange unless authorized to do so, either by the deed of copartnership, by the necessity of such a power to the carrying on of the business, by the usage of similar establishments, or by the express assent of the party sought to be charged. Dickinson v. Valpy (1829), 10 B & C 128. In another case involving a mining company, Parke ruled that managers enjoyed no implied power to borrow, without the explicit sanction of the shareholders. Hawtayne v. Bourne (1841), 10 LJ Ex 224.

90. Anon., *Precipitation and Fall of Mess. Douglas, Heron and Company*.

91. NA, RAIL 250/64, Great Western Railway Company, Minute Book, 31 Aug., 27 Oct. 1837.

92. Hawke and Reed, "Railway Capital," 274.

93. Falkirk Archives, A1800.010/01, Falkirk Gas Work Company, Contract of Copartnery, arts. 4, 12.

94. For example, Aberdeen Central Library, Local Studies Department, P60/8780, Aberdeen Gas Light Company, Contract of Copartnery (1824), art. 10.

95. Quoted in Wilson, *Lighting the Town*, 74.

96. 2 Vict. (1839) c. 3, art. 19.

97. Shareholders were "liable to a share of the losses" and could "be called on for a portion of all sums necessary . . . in proportion to the number of the said shares, which each of the said persons shall respectively hold": Public Record Office of Northern Ireland, D1835/01, Ballymena Gas Light Company, Deed of Copartnership, arts. 2, 12, 17.

98. Ibid., art. 28. See Burt and Kudo, "Cornish Cost Book System," 35–6.

99. Union Lime Company of Aberdeen, *Contract of Copartnery*, art. 6. Five hundred pounds amounted to one-sixth of the total nominal capital of the company.

100. The two companies were the Edinburgh and Leith Shipping Company and the Edinburgh, Glasgow and Leith Shipping Company. NLS, 3.2776(2), London, Leith, Edinburgh and Glasgow Shipping Company, Contract of Copartnery, art. 8.

101. Burt and Kudo, "Cornish Cost Book System," 35–6.

102. But see Hickson and Turner, "Genesis of Corporate Governance," 181.

103. Quoted in Hunt, *Development of the Business Corporation*, 99.

104. Micklethwait and Wooldridge, *The Company*, 147–8.

105. Six of these specified a number of years: British Cast Plate Glass Manufacturers (1772, 21 years); Sierra Leone Company (1791, 31 years); Deptford Creek Bridge (1803, 21 years); Loftsome Bridge (1803, 19 years); Gas Light and Coke Company (1812, 21 years); City of London Gas Light and Coke Company (1817, 46 years).

106. Another, the Victoria Park Company (Manchester, 1837), was a tontine with transferable shares and so was expected to come to an end at some undefined date. It had both general and special rights of dissolution.

107. David M. Walker, *Legal History of Scotland*, 5:697.

108. G. L. Barrow, *Emergence of the Irish Banking System*, 3.

109. Russell, *Reports of Cases*, 1:463–5.

110. Evans v. Stokes (1836), 1 Keen 24; Lyon v. Haynes (1843), 5 Man & G 504; Abraham v. Hannay (1843), 13 Sim 581.

111. Ludlow, *Joint Stock Companies Winding-Up Act*, xxiv.

112. Ibid., xxviii, xxx.

113. Some of these periods, however, were very long: 999 or 1,000 years in five cases and 99 years in three others. Three of the former, all Irish insurance companies, had no provision for dissolution within this time.

114. For example, Clydesdale Banking Company, *Contract of Copartnery*, art. 45.

115. Northern and Central Bank of England, *Deed of Settlement*, arts. 25–6.

116. GULSC, UGD129/2/3/9, National Bank of Scotland, Contract of Copartnery, 1825, art. 31.

117. Agricultural and Commercial Bank of Ireland, *Deed of Partnership*, arts. 5, 158.

118. NAS, GD154/343, Glasgow and Stranraer Steam Packet Company, Draft Contract of Copartnery, 1843, art. 10.

119. Stirlingshire Banking Company, *Prospectus*.

120. Watt, *Theory and Practice of Joint-Stock Banking*, 11. Original emphases. The dissolution clause was also advertised elsewhere as a safety principle shielding shareholders from excessive risks: see Anon., *Remarks on the Objections to Joint Stock Banks*, 13–4.

121. Watt, *Theory and Practice of Joint-Stock Banking*, 11.

122. Ibid.; BSA, CBS/1/1, Central Bank of Scotland, Contract of Copartnership, 1 May 1834, art. 33.

123. *Liverpool Mercury*, 5 Sept. 1834. O'Connell, it should be noted, was a supporter of the rival National Bank of Ireland.

124. Hickson and Turner, "Genesis of Corporate Governance," 181.

125. G. L. Barrow, *Emergence of the Irish Banking System*, 108–20; Hall, *Bank of Ireland*, 158–64.

126. 8 & 9 Vict. (1845) c. 98, art. 21.

127. Checkland, *Scottish Banking*, 124–34; Munn, *Scottish Provincial Banking Companies*, 29–36; James Taylor, "Company Fraud"; Collins, "Banking Crisis of 1878."

128. Burt and Kudo, "Cornish Cost Book System," 34–5.

129. RBS, ASH/8/1, Ashton, Stalybridge, Hyde and Glossop Bank, Minute Book, 31 July 1840.

130. RBS, ASH/7, Ashton, Stalybridge, Hyde and Glossop Bank, Deed of Settlement, 1 July 1836, arts. 105–6.

131. RBS, ASH/8/1, Ashton, Stalybridge, Hyde and Glossop Bank, Minute Book, 28 July, 18 Aug. 1843.

132. *SC on Joint-Stock Companies*, BPP (1844) VII, p. v.

133. See chapter 8 for a more detailed consideration of access to company documents.

134. Quoted in Hunt, *Development of the Business Corporation*, 131.

135. Hunt, *Development of the Business Corporation*, 136–8. Concerns over the destabilizing effects of unlimited liability intensified after the commercial crisis of 1847: James Taylor, *Creating Capitalism*, 161–2.

136. Anon., *How to Mismanage a Bank*, 26–7. Original emphases.

Chapter Eight

1. By attribution in John Poynder, *Literary Extracts from English and Other Works* (1844), vol. 1, cited in *Oxford Dictionary of Quotations*, 547.

2. Bentham, *Rationale of Judicial Evidence*, 1:10.

3. *Times* (London), 23 Sept. 1856.

4. *Times* (London), 21 Sept. 1850.

5. Biagini, "Liberalism and Direct Democracy."

6. Anon., *Remarks on the Objections to Joint Stock Banks*, 19.

7. *Oxford English Dictionary*, s.v. audit, n.

8. Matthews, *History of Auditing*, 12–7, 23–30. Cf. the description of insurance company audits given by four actuaries in *SC on Joint-Stock Companies*, BPP (1844) VII, p. 135. Things had changed by the 1860s when the best auditors, such as Edwin Waterhouse, were checking vouchers and books in great detail *and* giving companies advice on how to improve their bookkeeping systems. Edgar Jones, *True and Fair*, 37–8.

9. Maltby, "UK Joint Stock Companies Legislation"; Stephen P. Walker, "More Sherry and Sandwiches?"; Maltby, " 'A Sort of Guide' "; McCartney and Arnold, "George Hudson's Financial Reporting"; Toms, "Rise of Modern Accounting."

10. Edwards and Webb sampled the accounting and audit provisions of thirty iron and steel companies formed between 1862 and 1900; Edwards, Anderson and Matthews analyzed the audit provisions of 960 companies quoted on the stock exchange in 1886. Edwards and Webb, "Use of Table A"; Edwards, Anderson, and Matthews, "Accountability in a Free-Market Economy."

11. Pratt and Storrar, "UK Shareholders," 206.

12. Edwards, "Accounting Change," 72; Pearson and Richardson, "Business Networking."

13. Reginald Jones, *Local Government Audit Law*, para. 1.5.

14. Welch, "Borough Archives," 67.

15. Glover, *Practical Treatise*, xli.

16. Reginald Jones, *Local Government Audit Law*, para. 1.6.

17. Dubois, *English Business Company*, 302.

18. Ibid., 339. See 6 Geo. II (1733) c. 28.

19. 14 Geo. II (1740) c. 8, p. 191.

20. BSA, ABC/1/1/1, Aberdeen Banking Company, Contract of Copartnery, art. 9; Douglas Heron and Company, "Contract of Copartnery," art. 12.

21. Dubois, *English Business Company*, 339.

22. Caledonian Insurance Company, *Contract of Copartnery*, 8–9.

23. 3 & 4 Will. IV (1833) c. 77, art. 31. This act referred to the parliamentary burghs, which had been enfranchised in 1832; there was a similar clause (art. 32) in 3 & 4 Will. IV (1833) c. 76, which referred to royal burghs.

24. 8 Vict. (1845) c. 17, art. 120.

25. CKS, U2593/B54, United Kent Life Assurance and Annuity Association, Deed of Settlement, 1 Dec. 1824, art. 67.

26. Royal Canal Company, *Charter*, 22.

27. NAS, GD301/58/3, London and Edinburgh Shipping Company, Contract of Copartnery, 1 Dec. 1809, art. 19.

28. Hall v. Connell (1840), 3 Y & C Ex 707. On the other hand, a court in 1841 refused to allow a shareholder to inspect the books of a company for the purpose of framing a defense to avoid paying a call, or as Chief Justice Denman put it, "to fish out a defence from defect in the proceedings." Birmingham, Bristol and Thames Junction Railway Company v. White (1841), 1 QB 282.

29. Brandon Gun Flint Company, *Deed of Settlement*, arts. 27, 88–9.

30. 8 Vict. (1845) c. 17, arts. 9–10.

31. The clause appeared in the constitutional document of 207 corporations of a total of 290 (71.4 percent). All 207 examples of the clause appeared in acts rather than charters.

32. GL, MS 31910/1, County Fire Office, Minutes of County Meetings, 18 Mar. (Yorkshire), 8 Apr. (Warwickshire) 1823.

33. *SC on the Audit of Railway Accounts (House of Lords)*, BPP (1849) X, p. 40.

34. Ibid., p. x.

35. *Railway Times*, 11 Jan. 1840.

36. R. H. Jones, "Accounting in English Local Government," 397.

37. 10 Geo. III (1770) c.114, p. 43.

38. Whitehead, *Railway Management: Letter to George Carr Glyn*, 4.

39. Two eighteenth-century corporations provided rather ambiguously for the provision of summary accounts and for individual shareholder access to the full accounts, viz., the British Society for Extending the Fisheries (1786) and the Northumberland Fishery Society (1789). 26 Geo. III (1786), c. 106, pp. 103, 108; 29 Geo. III (1789) c. 25, arts. 19, 24, 28.

40. By the 1880s, the modal duration of company audits was five weeks. Matthews, *History of Auditing*, 29.

41. Gibbs, *Birth of the Great Western Railway*, 32.

42. NA, RAIL 250/64, Great Western Railway, General Meetings of Proprietors, 27 Feb. 1838.

43. Anon., *Commercial Morality*, 9.

44. NA, RAIL 250/1, Great Western Railway, Board Minutes, 23 Sept. 1836. Emphasis added.

45. LMA, ACC 2558/WM/A/1/7, West Middlesex Waterworks Company Minutes, 24 Jan., 1 May 1827.

46. LTSB, A9b/13, Coventry and Warwickshire Banking Company, Minute Books, 12 Mar. 1839, 8 Mar. 1842, 14 Mar. 1843.

47. McCulloch, *Considerations on Partnerships*, 9.

48. Ibid., 6.

49. *SC on the Companies Acts, 1862 and 1867*, BPP (1877) VIII, pp. 96–7.

50. NA, RAIL 250/64, Great Western Railway Company, General Meetings of Proprietors, 27 Feb. 1840. The board of the County of Gloucester Bank followed suit in 1846: LTSB, A29b/10, County of Gloucester Bank, Minute Book, 6 Feb. 1846.

51. A Member of the Stock Exchange, *Shareholders' Key*, 46.

52. The ubiquity of such a system in England is doubtful, given the views expressed by the anonymous pamphleteer in 1853.

53. *Freeman's Journal and Daily Commercial Advertiser*, 30 Aug. 1844.

54. Dubois, *English Business Company*, 300.

55. 46 Geo. III (1806) c. 136, arts. 12, 14.

56. The Cranstonhill Waterworks (incorporated 1808), the Commercial Bank of Scotland (unincorporated, 1810), and the Insurance Company of Scotland (unincorporated, 1821).

57. Huddersfield Banking Company, *Deed of Settlement*, art. 62.

58. The numbers given in constitutions, however, were often minimums.

59. For unincorporated companies, the figures are £837,657 and £448,211.

60. Evidence of "A. B.," *SC on Joint-Stock Companies*, BPP (1844) VII, p. 104.

61. Robert E. Wright, "Introduction," xvii.

62. LMA, B/EGLC/12, Equitable Gas Light Company, Minute Book, 31 Oct. 1839, 29 Jan. 1840.

63. Some contemporaries thought that directors who paid dividends out of capital, when claiming they were paid out of profits, should be made legally liable to the company. Evidence of John Duncan, *SC on Joint-Stock Companies*, BPP (1844) VII, pp. 183–4.

64. LMA, B/EGLC/12, Equitable Gas Light Company, Minute Book, 29 Jan., 4 Mar. 1840, 16 May 1843.

65. LMA, B/S.Met.G/II/1, South Metropolitan Gas Light and Coke Company, Proprietors' Minutes, 22 Jan. 1835, 27 Jan., 30 June 1836, 23 Jan. 1840.

66. RBS, ASH/8/1, Ashton, Stalybridge, Hyde and Glossop Bank, Minute Book, 28 July 1843. It was even possible for directors to turn the ad hoc audit to their advantage. At the Auchterarder Gas Company in 1843, just before the directors voted to allot themselves additional shares, the board *requested* that the GM appoint a committee to examine the accounts, presumably to preempt criticism of their actions. The committee made a brief and not unfavorable report. Perth and Kinross Council Archives, MS 157/1/1, Auchterarder Gas Company, Minute Book, 20 Jan., 9 June 1843.

67. Stewart, *Audit of Joint-Stock Bank Accounts*, 13–5.

68. LTSB, A32a/2, Burton, Uttoxeter, and Staffordshire Union Banking Company, Deed of Settlement, preamble and arts. 1, 4, 40.

69. Reginald Jones, *Local Government Audit Law*, para. 1.7; Webb and Webb, *English Local Government*, 139–40.

70. 59 Geo. III (1819), c. 12; Webb and Webb, *English Local Government*, 146–7.

71. Snell, *Parish and Belonging*, 341–2.

72. Webb and Webb, *English Poor Law History*, 210–1.

73. Redlich and Hirst, *History of Local Government in England*, 129; Welch, "Borough Archives," 69–70.

74. Reginald Jones, *Local Government Audit Law*, para. 1.2.

75. Jennings, *Principles of Local Government Law*, 175–7; Reginald Jones, *Local Government Audit Law*, paras. 1.23–4.

76. *Times* (London), 6 Nov. 1847.

77. Hardcastle, *Banks and Bankers*, 287.

78. Ibid., 307–8.

79. NA, RAIL 1063/381, Company of Proprietors of the Calder and Hebble Navigation, Incorporating Act of Parliament, 1769, 23.

80. 1 Vict. (1837) c. 83, art. 117. This was the result of a political compromise

between the Liberal-dominated council, who wanted a municipally owned water supply, and the Tory opposition, who supported a private company. The compromise provided the council with the right to nominate half the board of directors and the option of buying the new water company after twelve years. Fraser, "Politics of Leeds Water."

81. 7 & 8 Vict. (1844) c. 77, arts. 92–4.

82. Often, either form was explicitly permitted; in other cases, the actual intention of the constitutional document, if there was one, was unclear.

83. As in the poor-law requirements of 1601, it was standard practice in incorporating acts to include a clause requiring officers—usually the clerk and treasurer—to account for their transactions on relinquishing office, and to give up all company documents in their possession. Unlike poor-law officials, however, officers of joint-stock companies were not chosen annually, and therefore this provision did *not* amount to a regular audit of company affairs.

84. On the "reversionary bonus" in insurance, see Robin Pearson, *Insuring the Industrial Revolution*, 158, 185, 197; Trebilcock, *Phoenix Assurance*, 1:476–80; Alborn, *Regulated Lives*, 176–96.

85. CMA, Clerical, Medical, and General Life Assurance Society, Deed of Settlement, arts. 38, 148–50; Westminster and General Life Assurance Association, *Deed of Settlement*, arts. 23, 39, 42.

86. 8 Vict. (1845) c. 17, arts. 94, 104–11.

87. In life assurance companies, shareholders or policyholders were often chosen as auditors. GL, MS 14312, Provident Institution for Life Insurances and Annuities, Deed of Constitution, art. 41; Rock Life Assurance Company, *Deed of Settlement*, 22–3.

88. James, *Practical Application*, 94–5.

89. Matthews, Anderson, and Edwards, *Priesthood of Industry*, 100.

90. Another example was the "cabal" of auditor-directors running the Kent Fire Office in the 1800s, which was eventually toppled by a shareholders' revolt. Robin Pearson, *Insuring the Industrial Revolution*, 249.

91. An Old Proprietor, *Address to the Shareholders of the Gas-Light and Coke Company*, 2–3.

92. Ibid., 14.

93. Stewart, *Audit of Joint-Stock Bank Accounts*, 6–10.

94. Ibid., 12. Original emphasis.

95. Ibid., 20–1, 28–9, 32.

96. See, for example, Galton, "Railways of Great Britain," 417.

97. Vincent, *Culture of Secrecy*, chapter 2.

98. Spencer, "Railway Morals," 252.

99. Evans, *The City*, 96–7.

100. 4 & 5 Vict. (1841) c. 62, art. 114.

101. Whitehead, *Railway Management: Letter to George Carr Glyn*, 18–9; A

Member of the Stock Exchange, *Shareholders' Key*, 44–5; Hutton, *Suggestions as to the Appointment*; James Taylor, "Company Fraud"; Stephen P. Walker, "More Sherry and Sandwiches?"

102. Edwards, "Accounting Change," 62; Kedslie, *Firm Foundations*.

103. Morgan, *Auditors*; Pixley, *Auditors*.

104. Pratt and Storrar, "UK Shareholders," 209.

105. Rawson, *Diary of a Director*, iii.

106. *Report of the Departmental Committee appointed by the Board of Trade to inquire what Amendments are necessary in the Acts relating to Joint Stock Companies incorporated with Limited Liability under the Companies Acts, 1862 to 1890*, BPP (1895) LXXXVIII, p. 75.

Chapter Nine

1. RBS, DIS/2, Manchester and Liverpool District Banking Company, Deed of Settlement, 30 Apr. 1829, arts. 6, 9; RBS, DIS/3, Manchester and Liverpool District Banking Company, Supplementary Deed of Settlement, 1843.

2. Nine variables were used in constructing the index: for each company, each variable was given a score of 0, 1, or 2, with the higher values attributed to companies with more scope for shareholder participation. The index is calculated as a percentage of the maximum score, which is 18. There are 486 companies, because 28 companies are excluded for which there are missing data either on the number of OGMs per annum, the directors' term of office, or both. The variables are individual access to account books (2 points: access at all times, 1 point: access in a set period, 0 points: no access or not given); GM access to account books (2 points: always presented to OGM, 1 point: could be called by the OGM, 0 points: no OGM access); right of shareholders to dismiss directors (2 points: yes, 0 points: not given); right of shareholders to appoint managers (2 points: yes, 1 point: not given, 0 points: no [i.e., explicitly vested in the board]); right of shareholders to amend constitution (2 points: yes, without approval of board, 1 point: yes, but only with approval of board, 0: not given); number of OGMs per annum (2 points: more than one, 0 points: one or fewer); directors' term of office (2 points: less than 1.5 years, 0 points: 1.5 years or more); smallest shareholders could vote (2 points: yes, 1 point: franchise not given, 0 points: no); cap on number of votes cast by one shareholder (2 points: yes, 1 point: franchise not given, 0 points: no cap).

3. Doyle, "Changing Functions," 301.

4. Ward, *Finance of Canal Building*, chapter 3; Wilson, *Lighting the Town*, 82–9, 113–8.

5. The mean nominal capital of the companies in our sample was £127,685 in the eighteenth century and increased to £562,491 in the period 1825–9 be-

fore falling back to £324,175 in 1840–4. The latter figure was 154 percent greater than the figure for the eighteenth century. This reflected substantial real growth over the period. Price inflation alone would only have raised the mean capital of companies by about 28 percent (calculated using the above figures and the retail price index deflator for 1789–1844 as given at http://www.measuringworth.com, accessed 12 Feb. 2009).

6. *SC on Joint-Stock Companies*, BPP (1844) VII, p. viii.

7. Ibid., pp. vii–viii.

8. McCartney and Arnold, "'Vast Aggregate?,'" 121.

9. *Daily News*, 8 Oct. 1849; *Morning Chronicle*, 9 Oct. 1849; *Leeds Mercury*, 13 Oct. 1849.

10. *Morning Chronicle*, 9 Oct. 1849. Original emphases.

11. *Leeds Mercury*, 13 Oct. 1849.

12. 7 & 8 Vict. (1844) c. 110; 7 & 8 Vict. (1844) c. 113; 8 Vict. (1845) c. 16; 8 Vict. (1845) c. 17.

13. NA, BT1/477/431/50, Francis Whitmarsh to Board of Trade, 7 Feb. 1850.

14. Ibid., George Taylor to Francis Whitmarsh, 1 Feb. 1850.

15. James Taylor, *Creating Capitalism*, chapter 4.

16. Robb, *White-Collar Crime*, 149.

17. A proviso is that the 1844 act did not apply to companies established in Scotland and *only* operating there, but it did apply to companies established in Scotland that had "an office or place of business in any other part of the United Kingdom." 7 & 8 Vict. (1844) c. 110, clause II. For a discussion of the act, see chapter 2, pp. 34–5.

18. See chapter 2, p. 35.

19. Edwards and Webb, "Use of Table A."

20. Edwards, Anderson, and Matthews, "Accountability in a Free-Market Economy."

21. *Railway Record*, 24 July 1852, 476. Emphasis added.

22. *Times* (London), 27 Nov. 1848.

23. Freeman, Pearson, and Taylor, "Technological Change," 585.

24. *Report of the Departmental Committee Appointed by the Board of Trade to Inquire what Amendments are Necessary in the Acts relating to Joint Stock Companies Incorporated with Limited Liability under the Companies Acts, 1862 to 1890*, BPP (1895) LXXXVIII, p. 75.

25. Richard Malins, *SC on the Companies Acts, 1862 and 1867*, BPP (1877) VIII, p. 142.

Select Bibliography

This bibliography contains primary and secondary published works cited and abbreviated in the notes, not all works consulted. Manuscript sources, case law, contemporary newspaper and periodical references, and individual printed official papers—bills, acts, parliamentary reports, accounts, etc.—are cited in full in the notes to the text and are therefore not listed here. For a complete listing of all sources used in the compilation of the database of 514 company constitutions, see Arts and Humanities Data Service (UK), AHDS SN5622, "Constructing the Company: Governance and Procedures in British and Irish Stock Companies, 1720–1844."

Primary Printed Sources

OFFICIAL PAPERS

The Statutes at Large, passed in the Parliaments held in Ireland. 8 vols. Dublin, 1765.

The Statutes at Large, passed in the Parliaments held in Ireland. 21 vols. Dublin, 1786–1804.

The Acts of the Parliaments of Scotland. Edited by Thomas Thomson. 11 vols. Edinburgh, 1814–24.

OTHER DOCUMENT COLLECTIONS

Carr, Cecil T., ed. *Select Charters of Trading Companies, 1530–1707.* London: Selden Society, 1913.

Charters granted to the East-India Company, from 1601; also the Treaties and Grants, Made with, or obtained from, the Princes and Powers in India, From the Year 1756 to 1772. London, 1773.

Glasgow City Council. *Extracts from the Records of the Burgh of Glasgow.* Vol. 6, *1739–59.* Glasgow, 1911.

Morison, W. M., ed. *The Decisions of the Court of Session.* Edinburgh: Bell and Bradfute, 1801–15.

Pearson, Robin, ed. (James Taylor and Mark Freeman, contributing eds.). *The History of the Company: The Development of the Business Corporation, 1700–1914.* 8 vols. London: Pickering and Chatto, 2006–7.

Russell, James. *Reports of Cases Argued and Determined in the High Court of Chancery, During the Time of Lord Chancellor Eldon.* 4 vols. London: J. Butterworth and Son, 1827–30.

Shaw, Patrick, and Alexander Dunlop. *Cases Decided in the Court of Session.* Vols. 6 and 13. Edinburgh, 1827–8, 1834–5.

Wright, Robert E. ed. *History of Corporate Governance.* 6 vols. London: Pickering and Chatto, 2004.

CONTEMPORARY BOOKS, PAMPHLETS, BROADSIDES
(PUBLISHED BEFORE 1900)

Agricultural and Commercial Bank of Ireland. *Deed of Partnership, 10 August 1836.* Belfast: Alexander Markham, 1836.

Anderson, Adam. *An Historical and Chronological Deduction of the Origin of Commerce.* 4 vols. London, 1787–89.

Anon. *Observations upon the Constitution of the Company of the Bank of England, with a Narrative of some of their late Proceedings.* London, 1694.

——. *A Collection of Papers Relating to the East India Trade: Wherein are shewn the Disadvantages to a Nation by confining any Trade to a Corporation with a Joint Stock.* London: J. Walthoe, 1730.

——. "A Caveat against Bubbling, Written in the Year 1732." In Anon., *Essays and Letters on Various Subjects,* 115–23. London: John Brotherton, 1739.

——. *The Precipitation and Fall of Mess. Douglas, Heron and Company.* [1778]. Reprinted in Robin Pearson, ed., *The History of the Company: The Development of the Business Corporation, 1700–1914,* 4:1–250. London: Pickering and Chatto, 2006–7.

——. *A List of Joint Stock Companies, the Proposals for which are now, or have been lately, before the Public.* London: Sherwood Jones, 1825.

——. *Remarks on the Objections to Joint Stock Banks.* London, 1833.

——. *Remarks on the Formation and Working of Banks Called Joint-Stock, With Observations on the Policy and Conduct of the Bank of England Towards These Establishments.* London, 1836.

——. *Oxford Essays, Contributed by Members of the University.* 4 vols. London: John W. Parker and Son, 1855–8.

——. *Commercial Morality: or, Thoughts for the Times.* London, 1856.

——. *How to Mismanage a Bank: A Review of the Western Bank of Scotland*. Edinburgh: Adam and Charles Black, 1859.

Aristotle. *Aristotle's Politics and Athenian Constitution*. Edited by John Warrington. London: J. M. Dent and Sons, 1959.

Bagehot, Walter. *The English Constitution*. [1867]. London: Fontana, 1993.

——. *Collected Works of Walter Bagehot*. 15 vols. Edited by Norman St. John-Stevas. London: The Economist, 1965–86.

Bank of England. *A list of the names of all such proprietors of the Bank of England, who are qualified to vote at the ensuing elections, to be made of governor and deputy-governor, on Tuesday the 5th of April, and of directors on Wednesday the 6th of April, 1803. Together with an abstract of the by-laws concerning elections, for the better direction of members in giving their votes*. London: printed by J. March, 1803.

——. *A list of the names of all such proprietors of the Bank of England, who are qualified to vote at the ensuing election . . . the 7th of April, and . . . the 8th of April, 1812. Together with an abstract of the bye-laws concerning elections*. London: printed by H. Teape 1812.

——. *A list of the names of all such proprietors of the Bank of England, who are qualified to vote at the ensuing election to be made of governor and deputy-governor, on Tuesday the 6th of April, and of directors on Wednesday the 7th of April, 1819*. London: printed by H. Teape, 1819.

——. *A list of the names of all such proprietors of the Bank of England who are qualified to vote at the ensuing election to be made of governor and deputy-governor on . . . the 5th of April and of directors on . . . the 6th April, 1836 : together with an abstract of the bye-laws concerning elections*. London: printed by Teape, 1836.

Bentham, Jeremy. *Rationale of Judicial Evidence*. 5 vols. London, 1827.

Birmingham and Midland Bank. *Deed of Settlement, 15 August 1836*. Birmingham: James Drake, 1836.

Birmingham Banking Company. *Circular*. Birmingham: William Hodgetts, 1829.

Birmingham Flour and Bread Company. *Printed Articles, 22 September 1796*. N.p.

Blackstone, William. *Commentaries on the Laws of England*. 4 vols. [1765–9]. Chicago: University of Chicago Press, 1979.

Blaenavon Iron and Coal Company. *Deed of Settlement, 3 July 1838*. London: J. Unwin, 1840.

Boult, Swinton. *The Law and Practice Relating to the Constitution and Management of Assurance, Banking, and other Joint Stock Companies*. London: J. Ridgway and Sons, 1841.

Bradford Commercial Joint-Stock Banking Company. *Deed of Covenants, 20 February 1833*. Bradford: John Atkinson, 1833.

Brandon Gun Flint Company. *Deed of Settlement, 27 January 1838*. Soham: William Playford, 1838.

Caledonian Insurance Company. *Contract of Copartnery, June 1805*. Edinburgh: Alex. Lawrie, 1805.

Clark, F. W. *A Treatise on the Law of Partnership and Joint-Stock Companies According to the Law of Scotland*. Edinburgh: T. and T. Clark, 1856.

Clifford, Frederick. *A History of Private Bill Legislation*. 2 vols. London: Butterworth, 1885–87.

Clydesdale Banking Company. *Contract of Copartnery, 1838*. Glasgow: James Lumsden and Son, 1838.

Connell, Arthur. *A Treatise on the Election Laws in Scotland*. Edinburgh: William Blackwood, 1827.

Corbet, Thomas. *An Inquiry into the Causes and Modes of the Wealth of Individuals; or the Principles of Trade and Speculation Explained in Two Parts*. London: Smith, Elder, 1841.

County of Devon Banking Company. *Circular*. Exeter: Pollard, n.d.

County of Gloucester Bank. *Deed of Settlement, 26 July 1836*. Gloucester: C. F. Cliffe, Chronicle Office, n.d.

Davenant, Charles. *Reflections upon the Constitution and Management of the Trade to Africa*. London: John Morphew, 1709.

Dickens, Charles. *Martin Chuzzlewit*. [1844]. Oxford: Oxford University Press, 1994.

Dodd, Cyril, and H. W. W. Wilberforce. *A Guide to the Procedure upon Private Bills*. London: Eyre and Spottiswoode, 1898.

Douglas, Heron, and Company. "Contract of Copartnery." [1769]. Reprinted in *The Precipitation and Fall of Mess. Douglas, Heron, and Company, Late Bankers in Air, with the Causes of their Distress and Ruin, Investigated and Considered, by a Committee of Inquiry Appointed by the Proprietors*, appendix 1. Edinburgh, 1778.

Dunlop, Alexander Murray. *The Law of Scotland Regarding the Poor*. Edinburgh: William Blackwood and Sons, 1854.

East India Company. *The Lawes or Standing Orders of the East India Company*. London, 1621.

———. *The Humble Answer of the Governor, Deputy-Governor, and Court of Committees of the East India Company; to a Paper of Propositions for Regulation of the East India Company; received from the Right Honourable the Earl of Nottingham, their Majesties principal Secretary of State*. 28 May 1692. In Lord Somers, *A Third Collection of Scarce and Valuable Tracts, on the most Interesting and Entertaining Subjects: but chiefly such as relate to the History and Constitution of these Kingdoms . . . Particularly . . . of the late Lord Somers. Revised by eminent Hands*, 181–8. London: F. Cogan, 1751.

Eden, Frederick M. *On the Policy and Expediency of Granting Insurance Charters*. London, 1806.

Ellis, Charles Thomas. *Practical Remarks and Precedents of Proceedings in Parliament*. London, 1802.

Emden, Alfred. *The Shareholders' Legal Guide*. London: William Clowes and Sons, 1884. Reprinted in Robin Pearson, ed., *The History of the Company: The Development of the Business Corporation, 1700–1914*, 5:199–375. London: Pickering and Chatto, 2006–7.

English, Henry. *A Complete View of the Joint-Stock Companies formed during the Years 1824 and 1825*. London: Boosey and Sons, 1827.

English and Scottish Law Fire and Life Assurance and Loan Association. *Deed of Settlement, 24 December 1841*. London: J. Wertheimer, 1842.

Evans, David Morier. *The City; or, the Physiology of London Business*. London, 1845.

Farmers' and General Fire and Life Insurance and Loan and Annuity Company. *Abstract of Deed of Settlement*. London: Joseph Rogerson, 1840.

Fenn, Charles. *A Compendium of the English and Foreign Funds, and the Principal Joint Stock Companies, Forming an Epitome of the Various Objects of Investment Negotiable in London, with some Account of the Internal Debts and Revenues of the Foreign States, and Tables for Calculating the Value of the Different Stocks, Etc.* 1st ed. London: Sherwood, Gilbert and Piper, 1837. Extract reprinted in Robin Pearson, ed., *The History of the Company: The Development of the Business Corporation, 1700–1914*, 3:303–80. London: Pickering and Chatto, 2006–7.

Galton, Douglas. "The Railways of Great Britain." *Edinburgh Review* 107 (April 1858): 396–419.

George, John. *A View of the Existing Law, Affecting Unincorporated Joint Stock Companies*. London: S. Sweet, 1825.

Gibbon, Edward. *The History of the Decline and Fall of the Roman Empire*. 2nd ed. Edited by J. B. Bury. 7 vols. [1781]. London: Methuen, 1926.

Gibbs, George Henry. *The Birth of the Great Western Railway: Extracts from the Diary and Correspondence of George Henry Gibbs*. Edited by Jack Simmons. Bath: Adams and Dart, 1971.

Glasgow and Liverpool Royal Steam Packet Company. *Contract of Copartnery*. Glasgow: Robert Weir, 1844.

Glover, William. *A Practical Treatise on the Law of Municipal Corporations*. London: Sweet, 1836.

Grantham Gas Light Company. *Deed of Settlement, 21 October 1833*. Grantham: S. Ridge, 1834.

Hampshire Banking Company. *Deed of Settlement, 2 July 1834*. London: C. F. Cock, 1834.

Hardcastle, Daniel, Jr.. *Banks and Bankers*. London: Whittaker, 1842.

Henderson, Robert. *Notes on the Law of Scotland, in Regard to Joint Stock Companies, with Illustrations from the Law of England*. Edinburgh: Bell and Bradfute, 1846.

Huddersfield Banking Company. *Deed of Settlement, 1 June 1827*. Huddersfield: J. Lancashire, 1827.

Hume, David. *Selected Essays*. [1776]. Oxford: Oxford University Press, 1996.

Hutton, James. *Suggestions as to the Appointment by the Legislature of Public Accountants, to audit the Accounts of all Joint-stock Companies*. London, 1861.

James, James Henry. *A Practical Application of the Joint-Stock Companies' and Friendly Societies' Acts to the Registration and Government of Assurance Societies, with Precedents for a Deed of Settlement, Rules and Forms*. London: Simpkin, Marshall, 1851.

Leeds and West Riding Banking Company. *Deed of Settlement*. BL 8226. dd.13(5). Leeds: T. Wray, 1836.

Ludlow, John Malcolm. *The Joint Stock Companies Winding-Up Act 1848, with an Introduction, Notes and Forms and some Notes of Cases*. London: V. and R. Stevens and G. S. Norton, 1849.

Manchester and Salford Bank. *Deed of Settlement, 15 August 1836*. Manchester: John Harrison, 1836.

Marke Valley Consolidated Mines. *Description and Rules and Regulations*. London: W. Dawson, 1839.

Martyn, Henry. *Considerations upon the East India Trade*. [1701]. Reprinted in Anon., *East Indian Trade, Selected Works, 17th Century*. Farnborough: Gregg, 1968.

May, Thomas Erskine. *The Constitutional History of England Since the Accession of George the Third, 1760–1860*. 11th ed. 3 vols. London: Longmans, Green, 1896.

McCulloch, J. R. *Considerations on Partnerships with Limited Liability*. London: Longman, Browne, Green and Longmans, 1856.

A Member of the Stock Exchange. *Shareholders' Key to the London and North Western Railway Company*. London: Pelham Richardson, 1853.

Metropolitan Marine Bath Company. *Prospectus of the Metropolitan Marine Bath Company*. London, 1824.

Morgan, Henry Lloyd. *Auditors: Remarks on the Qualifications and Duties of Auditors of Accounts of Joint Stock Companies and Other Public Bodies*. London, 1857.

Mundell, Alexander. *The Influence of Interest and Prejudice upon Proceedings in Parliament Stated*. London: John Murray, 1825.

Northern and Central Bank of England. *Deed of Settlement, 13 January 1834*. Manchester: Henry Smith, 1835.

Nottingham, Earl of. *Propositions for Regulating the East India Company, from the Right Honourable the Earl of Nottingham, their Majesties principal Secretary of State.* 11 February 1692. In Lord Somers, *A Third Collection of Scarce and Valuable Tracts, on the most Interesting and Entertaining Subjects: but chiefly such as relate to the History and Constitution of these Kingdoms . . . Particularly . . . of the late Lord Somers. Revised by eminent Hands,* 179–81. London: F. Cogan, 1751.

An Old Merchant. *Remarks on Joint Stock Companies.* London: John Murray, 1825.

An Old Proprietor [James Barlow]. *An Address to the Shareholders of the Gas-Light and Coke Company, on the Financial Accounts of that Corporation.* London: C. and J. Rovington, 1825. Reprinted in Robin Pearson, ed., *The History of the Company: The Development of the Business Corporation, 1700–1914,* 2:119–63. London: Pickering and Chatto, 2006–7.

Pearson, Norman. "Manhood Suffrage on the Principle of Shareholding." *Nineteenth Century* 14 (1883): 1082–5.

Pixley, Francis W. *Auditors: Their Duties and Responsibilities under the Joint-Stock Companies Acts and the Friendly Societies and Industrial and Provident Societies Acts.* London, 1881.

Plymouth and Devonport Banking Company. *Prospectus, 30 September 1831.* Plymouth: Nettleton, 1831.

——. *Prospectus.* N.p., n.d.

Pope, Alexander. *Poetical Works.* Edited by Herbert Davis. Oxford: Oxford University Press, 1978.

Pratt, Isaac. *A Brief Reply to the Several Objections which have been lately handed about in Manuscript by the Opposers of the Worcester Canal.* Worcester, 1786.

Rawson, William. *The Present Operations and Future Prospects of the Mexican Mine Associations Analysed.* London: J. Hatchard and Son, 1825.

——. *Diary of a Director: Notes and Recollections made during the last fourteen Years.* London, 1857.

Richardson, Benjamin Ward, ed. *Thomas Sopwith, with Excerpts from His Diary of Fifty-Seven Years.* London: Longmans, Green, 1891.

Rock Life Assurance Company. *Deed of Settlement, 20 August 1807.* London: John Lambert, 1808.

Royal African Company. *At a generall meeting of all the subscribers to the stock of the Royal Company holden at Drapers' Hall the 19th of December 1671. His Royal Highness present with the Sub-governour and Deputy-governour.* London, 1671.

Royal Bank of Liverpool. *Deed of Settlement, 2 May 1836.* Liverpool: Willmer and Smith, 1836.

Royal Canal Company. *The Charter of the Royal Canal Company, with their Rules.* Dublin: John Chambers, 1789.

Sanders, Francis Williams. *An Essay on the Nature and Laws of Uses and Trusts.* London: E and R. Brooke, 1791.

Scarborough Cliff Bridge Company. *Deed of Settlement, 1828.* York: H. Bellerby, 1828.

Shropshire Banking Company. *Deed of Settlement, 17 May 1836.* Reprinted in Robert E. Wright, ed., *History of Corporate Governance,* 3:1–73. London: Pickering and Chatto, 2004.

Smith, Adam. *An Inquiry into the Nature and Causes of the Wealth of Nations.* [1776]. 3 vols. Indianapolis, 1981.

Smith, John Fairfull. *Proposed Alterations in the System of Joint Stock Banking, with a Defence of the Small Note Currency of Scotland.* Edinburgh: Bell and Bradfute, 1839.

South Sea Company. *A list of the names of all such proprietors of the capital stock of the Governor and company of merchants of Great-Britain, trading to the South-Seas and other parts of America, and for encouraging the fishery. Who are qualified to vote at the ensuing election . . . . on Tuesday the twenty-ninth of January 1805 and . . . on Thursday the thirty-first of the same month: together with part of the seventh by-law concerning elections.* London: printed by H. Teape, 1805.

Spencer, Herbert. "Railway Morals and Railway Policy." *Edinburgh Review* 100 (1854). Reprinted in Herbert Spencer, *Essays: Scientific, Political, and Speculative,* 2:251–311. London: Williams and Norgate, 1878–83.

Stewart, Robert. *The Audit of Joint-Stock Bank Accounts by Shareholders: Is It Practicable or Desirable?* London: Groombridge and Sons, 1853.

Stirlingshire Banking Company. *Prospectus of the Stirlingshire Banking Company, 8 June 1831.* Stirling, 1831.

Taylor, John. *Statements respecting the Profits of Mining in England considered in Relation to the Prospects of Mining in Mexico.* London: Longman, 1825. Reprinted in Robin Pearson, ed., *The History of the Company: The Development of the Business Corporation, 1700–1914,* 3:21–78. London: Pickering and Chatto, 2006–7.

Union Lime Company of Aberdeen. *Contract of Copartnery, 20 July 1827.* Aberdeen: J. Booth, 1827.

Watt, Peter. *The Theory and Practice of Joint-Stock Banking.* New York: Theodore Foster, 1836.

Westminster and General Life Assurance Association. *Deed of Settlement, 30 March 1837.* London: J. Davy and Sons, n.d.

Whitehead, John. *Railway Management: Letter to George Carr Glyn Esq. MP, Chairman of the London and North Western Railway Company.* 2nd ed. London, 1848.

——. *Railway Management: A Second Letter to George Carr Glyn Esq. MP,*

Chairman of the London and North Western Railway Company; in Reply to Capt. Huish's Letter. London: Smith, Elder, 1848.

Williston, Samuel L. "History of the Law of Business Corporations." *Harvard Law Review* 2 (1888): 105–24, 149–66.

Secondary Sources (since 1900)

Acheson, Graeme G., and John Turner. "The Impact of Limited Liability on Ownership and Control: Irish Banking, 1877–1914." *Economic History Review*, 2nd series, 59 (2006): 320–46.

———. "Investor Behaviour in a Nascent Capital Market: Scottish Bank Shareholders in the Nineteenth Century." *Economic History Review*, 2nd series, 64 (2011): 188–213.

Acres, W. Marston. *The Bank of England from Within, 1694–1900.* 2 vols. London: Oxford University Press, 1931.

Alborn, Timothy L. "The Moral of the Failed Bank: Professional Plots in the Victorian Money Market." *Victorian Studies* 38 (1995): 199–226.

———. *Conceiving Companies: Joint-Stock Politics in Victorian England.* London: Routledge, 1998.

———. *Regulated Lives: Life Insurance and British Society, 1800–1914.* Toronto: University of Toronto Press, 2009.

Anderson, Gary M., and Robert D. Tollinson. "The Myth of the Corporation as a Creation of the State." *International Review of Law and Economics* 3 (1983): 107–20.

Arruñada, Benito, and Veneta Andonova. "Common Law and Civil Law as Pro-market Adaptations." Unpublished working paper, 2008. http://d.repec.org/n?u=RePEc:upf:upfgen:1098&r=his.

Ashton, T. S. *Economic Fluctuations in England, 1700–1800.* Oxford: Clarendon, 1959.

Bagwell, Philip S. *The Transport Revolution from 1770.* London: Batsford, 1974.

Barker, Hannah. *The Business of Women: Female Enterprise and Urban Development in Northern England, 1760–1830.* Oxford: Oxford University Press, 2006.

Barrow, G. L. *The Emergence of the Irish Banking System 1820–1845.* Dublin: Gill and Macmillan, 1975.

Barrow, Tony. "Corn, Carriers and Coastal Shipping: The Shipping and Trade of Berwick and the Borders, 1730–1830." *Journal of Transport History*, 3rd series, 21 (2000): 6–27.

Beckett, J. C. *The Making of Modern Ireland, 1603–1923.* London: Faber and Faber, 1966.

Beckett, J. V., and M. E. Turner. "Taxation and Economic Growth in Eighteenth-Century England." *Economic History Review*, 2nd series, 43 (1990): 377–403.

Biagini, Eugenio F. "Liberalism and Direct Democracy: John Stuart Mill and the Model of Ancient Athens." In Eugenio F. Biagini, ed., *Citizenship and Community: Liberals, Radicals and Collective Identities in the British Isles, 1865–1931*, 21–44. Cambridge: Cambridge University Press, 1996.

Bogart, Dan, and Gary Richardson. "Property Rights, Public Goods and Economic Development in England from 1600 to 1815: New Evidence from Acts of Parliament." Unpublished paper presented to the annual meeting of the Economic History Association, Pittsburgh, 2006.

Boot, H. M. "Real Incomes of the British Middle Class, 1760–1850: The Experience of Clerks at the East India Company." *Economic History Review*, 2nd series, 52 (1999): 638–68.

Borsay, Peter. *The English Urban Renaissance: Culture and Society in the Provincial Town, 1660–1770*. Oxford: Oxford University Press, 1989.

Bowen, H. V. "Investment and Empire in the Later 18th Century." *Economic History Review*, 2nd series, 42 (1989): 186–206.

———. "The 'Little Parliament': The General Court of the East India Company, 1750–1784." *Historical Journal* 34 (1991): 857–72.

———. *The Business of Empire: The East India Company and Imperial Britain, 1756–1833*. Cambridge: Cambridge University Press, 2006.

Boyce, Gordon H. *Information, Mediation and Institutional Development: The Rise of Large-Scale Enterprise in British Shipping 1870–1919*. Manchester: Manchester University Press, 1995.

Boyce, Gordon, and Simon Ville. *The Development of Modern Business*. Houndmills: Palgrave, 2002.

Broadbridge, S. A. "The Sources of Railway Share Capital." In M. C. Reed, ed., *Railways in the Victorian Economy: Studies in Finance and Economic Growth*, 184–211. Newton Abbot: David and Charles, 1969.

Bryer, R. A. "The Mercantile Laws Commission of 1854 and the Political Economy of Limited Liability." *Economic History Review*, 2nd series, 50 (1997): 37–56.

Burke, Gillian, and Peter Richardson. "'The Adaptability of the Cornish Cost Book System': A Response." *Business History* 25 (1983): 193–9.

Burt, Roger, and Norikazu Kudo. "The Adaptability of the Cornish Cost Book System." *Business History* 25 (1983): 30–41.

Campbell, R. H. *Carron Company*. Edinburgh: Oliver and Boyd, 1961.

———. "The Law and the Joint-Stock Company in Scotland." In Peter L. Payne, ed., *Studies in Scottish Business History*, 136–51. London: Frank Cass, 1967.

Carlos, Ann M., Karen Maguire, and Larry Neal. "Financial Acumen, Women Speculators and the Royal African Company during the South Sea Bubble." *Accounting, Business and Financial History* 16 (2006): 219–43.

Carlos, Ann M., and Larry Neal. "Women Investors in Early Capital Markets, 1720–1725." *Financial History Review* 11, no. 2 (2004): 197–224.

Carr, Jack, Sherry Glied, and Frank Mathewson. "Unlimited Liability and Free Banking in Scotland: A Note." *Journal of Economic History* 49 (1989): 974–8.

Carswell, John. *The South Sea Bubble.* London: Cresset, 1960.

Casson, Mark, and M. B. Rose. "Institutions and the Evolution of Modern Business: Introduction." *Business History* 39 (1997): 1–8.

Chandler, Alfred D., Jr. *The Visible Hand: The Managerial Revolution in American Business.* Cambridge, MA: Harvard University Press, 1977.

Chauduri, K. N. *The English East India Company: The Study of an Early Joint-Stock Company, 1600–1640.* London: Frank Cass, 1965.

———. "The English East India Company in the Seventeenth and Eighteenth Centuries: A Pre-Modern Multinational Organisation." In Leonard Blassé and Femme Gaastra, eds., *Companies and Trade: Essays in Overseas Trading Companies during the Ancien Regime*, 29–46. Leiden: Leiden University Press, 1981.

Checkland, S. G. *Scottish Banking: A History, 1695–1973.* Glasgow: Collins, 1975.

Cheffins, B. R. "History and the Global Corporate Governance Revolution: The UK Perspective." *Business History* 43 (2001): 87–118.

———. *Corporate Ownership and Control: British Business Transformed.* Oxford: Oxford University Press, 2008.

Christie, J. Roberton. "Joint Stock Enterprise in Scotland before the Companies Acts." *Juridical Review* 21 (1909–10): 128–47.

Clapham, John. *The Bank of England: A History.* 2 vols. Cambridge: Cambridge University Press, 1944.

Clark, J. C. D. *English Society, 1688–1832.* Cambridge: Cambridge University Press, 1985.

Clark, Peter. *British Clubs and Societies, 1580–1800: The Origins of an Associational World.* Oxford: Oxford University Press, 2000.

Clarke, Thomas. "Introduction: Theories of Corporate Governance—Reconceptualising Corporate Governance Theory after the Enron Experience." In Thomas Clarke, ed., *Theories of Corporate Governance: The Philosophical Foundations of Corporate Governance*, 1–30. London: Routledge, 2004.

Cobb, H. S. "Sources for Economic History amongst the Parliamentary Records in the House of Lords Record Office." *Economic History Review*, 2nd series, 19 (1966): 154–74.

Collins, Michael. "The Banking Crisis of 1878." *Economic History Review*, 2nd series, 42 (1989): 504–27.

Cook, Chris, and John Stevenson. *British Historical Facts, 1760–1830.* London: Macmillan 1980.

Cottrell, P. L. *Industrial Finance, 1830–1914*. London: Methuen, 1980.

Crafts, Nicholas. "The Industrial Revolution." In Roderick Floud and D. N. Mc-Closkey, eds., *The Economic History of Britain since 1700*, 2nd ed., vol. 1, *1700–1860*, 44–59. Cambridge: Cambridge University Press, 1994.

Craig, F. W. S. *Chronology of British Parliamentary By-Elections*. Chichester: Parliamentary Research Services, 1987.

Crompton, Gerald. "Rhodes, Thomas (1789–1868)." *Oxford Dictionary of National Biography*. Oxford: Oxford University Press, 2004.

Crook, Malcolm, and Tom Crook. "The Advent of the Secret Ballot in Britain and France, 1789–1914." *History* 92 (2007): 449–71.

Cullen, L. M., ed. *The Formation of the Irish Economy*. Cork: Mercier, 1969.

———. *An Economic History of Ireland since 1660*. London: B. T. Batsford, 1972.

Daunton, M. J. *Progress and Poverty: An Economic and Social History of Britain, 1700–1850*. Oxford: Oxford University Press, 1995.

Davies, K. G. "Joint-Stock Investment in the late Seventeenth Century." *Economic History Review*, 2nd series, 4 (1952): 283–301.

———. *The Royal African Company*. London: Longmans, Green, 1957.

Davis, Ralph. *The Rise of the English Shipping Industry in the Seventeenth and Eighteenth Centuries*. Newton Abbot: David and Charles, 1962.

Deane, Phyllis. *The First Industrial Revolution*. Cambridge: Cambridge University Press, 1965.

Deane, Phyllis, and W. A. Cole. *British Economic Growth, 1688–1959*. 2nd ed. Cambridge: Cambridge University Press, 1962.

Devine, T. M. *The Tobacco Lords: A Study of the Tobacco Merchants of Glasgow and their Trading Activities, c. 1740–90*. 1975. Reprint, Edinburgh: Edinburgh University Press, 1990.

Devine, P. J., et al. *An Introduction to Industrial Economics*. 4th ed. London: Unwin Hyman, 1985.

Dickson, P. G. M. *The Financial Revolution in England: A Study in the Development of Public Credit, 1688–1756*. London: Macmillan, 1967.

Dietz, V. E. "The Politics of Whisky: Scottish Distillers, the Excise, and the Pittite State." *Journal of British Studies* 36 (1997): 35–69.

Doyle, Barry. "The Changing Functions of Urban Government: Councillors, Officials and Pressure Groups." In Martin J. Daunton, ed., *The Cambridge Urban History of Britain*, vol. 3, *1840–1950*, 287–314. Cambridge: Cambridge University Press, 2000.

Dubois, Armand B. *The English Business Company after the Bubble Act, 1720–1800*. New York: Oxford University Press, 1938.

Dunlavy, Colleen. "Corporate Democracy: Stockholder Voting Rights in Nineteenth-Century American and Prussian Railroad Corporations." In Lena Andersson-Skog and Olle Krantz, eds., *Institutions in the Transport and Communications Industries: State and Private Actors in the Making of Institutional Patterns, 1850–1990*, 33–60. Canton, MA: Science History Publications, 1999.

——. "From Citizens to Plutocrats: Nineteenth-Century Shareholder Voting Rights and Theories of the Corporation." In Kenneth Lipartito and David B. Sicilia, eds., *Constructing Corporate America: History, Politics, Culture*, 66–93. Oxford: Oxford University Press, 2004.

Durr, Andy. "William King of Brighton: Co-operation's Prophet?" In Stephen Yeo, ed., *New Views of Cooperation*, 10–26. London: Routledge, 1988.

Edwards, John Richard. "Companies, Corporations and Accounting Change, 1835–1933: A Comparative Study." *Accounting and Business Research* 23 (1992): 59–73.

Edwards, John Richard, and K. M. Webb. "Use of Table A by Companies Registering under the Companies Act, 1862." *Accounting and Business Research* 15 (1985): 177–95.

Edwards, John Richard, Malcolm Anderson, and Derek Matthews. "Accountability in a Free-Market Economy: the British Company Audit, 1886." *Abacus* 33 (1997): 1–25.

Epstein, James. "Some Organisational and Cultural Aspects of the Chartist Movement in Nottingham." In James Epstein and Dorothy Thompson, eds., *The Chartist Experience: Studies in Working Class Radicalism and Culture, 1830–60*, 221–68. Basingstoke: Macmillan, 1982.

Everard, Stirling. *The History of the Gas Light and Coke Company, 1812–1949*. London: Ernest Benn, 1949.

Falkus, M. E. "The British Gas Industry before 1850." *Economic History Review*, 2nd series, 20 (1967): 494–508.

Fama, Eugene F. "Agency Problems and the Theory of the Firm." *Journal of Political Economy* 88 (1980): 288–307.

Fama, Eugene F., and Michael C. Jensen. "Separation of Ownership and Control." *Journal of Law and Economics* 26 (1983): 301–25.

Ferguson, W. "The Reform Act (Scotland) of 1832: Intention and Effect." *Scottish Historical Review* 45 (1966): 105–14.

Fisher, Douglas. *The Industrial Revolution: A Macroeconomic Interpretation*. Basingstoke: Macmillan, 1992.

Foreman-Peck, James, and Robert Millward. *Public and Private Ownership of British Industry 1820–1990*. Oxford: Clarendon, 1994.

Fox, Robin Lane. *The Classical World: An Epic History of Greece and Rome*. London: Penguin, 2005.

Fraser, Derek. "The Politics of Leeds Water." *Publications of the Thoresby Society* 53, miscellany 15 (1971): 50–70.

——. *Urban Politics in Victorian England*. Leicester: Leicester University Press, 1976.

Freeman, Mark. *St. Albans: A History.* Lancaster: Carnegie, 2008.

Freeman, Mark, Robin Pearson, and James Taylor. "'A Doe in the City': Women Shareholders in Eighteenth- and Early Nineteenth-Century Britain." *Accounting, Business and Financial History* 16 (2006): 265–90.

———. "'Different and Better?': Scottish Joint-Stock Companies and the Law, c. 1720–1845." *English Historical Review* 122 (2007): 61–81.

———. "Technological Change and the Governance of Joint-Stock Enterprise in the Early Nineteenth Century: The Case of Coastal Shipping." *Business History* 49 (2007): 573–94.

———. "Between Madam Bubble and Kitty Lorimer: Women Investors in British and Irish Stock Companies." In Anne Laurence, Josephine Maltby, and Janette Rutterford, eds., *Women and Their Money, 1700–1950: Essays on Women and Finance,* 95–114. London: Routledge, 2009.

French, E. A. "The Origin of General Limited Liability in the United Kingdom." *Accounting and Business Research* 21 (1990): 15–34.

Garnett, Jane. "Commercial Ethics: A Victorian Perspective on the Practice of Theory." In C. Cowton and R. Crisp, eds., *Business Ethics: Perspectives on the Practice of Theory,* 117–38. Oxford: Oxford University Press, 1998.

Garrard, John. *Leadership and Power in Victorian Industrial Towns, 1830–80.* Manchester: Manchester University Press, 1983.

Geary, Frank. "The Act of Union, British-Irish Trade, and Pre-famine Deindustrialization." *Economic History Review,* 2nd series, 48 (1995): 68–88.

Gomez, Pierre-Yves, and Harry Korine. "Democracy and the Evolution of Corporate Governance." *Corporate Governance* 13 (2005): 739–52.

Gourvish, T. R. "Railway Enterprise." In Roy Church, ed., *The Dynamics of Victorian Business: Problems and Perspectives to the 1870s,* 126–41. London: Allen and Unwin, 1980.

Gourvish, T. R., and M. C. Reed. "The Financing of Scottish Railways before 1860: A Comment." *Scottish Journal of Political Economy* 18 (1971): 209–220.

Grady, Kevin. *The Georgian Public Buildings of Leeds and the West Riding.* Publications of the Thoresby Society 62, no. 133. Leeds: Thoresby Society, 1987.

Gunn, J. A. W. *Beyond Liberty and Property: The Process of Self-Recognition in Eighteenth-Century Political Thought.* Kingston: McGill–Queen's University Press, 1983.

Hall, F. G. *History of the Bank of Ireland.* Dublin: Hodges Figgis, 1949.

Handlin, O., and M. F. Handlin. "Origins of the American Business Corporation." *Journal of Economic History* 5 (1945): 1–23.

Harling, Philip. *The Waning of "Old Corruption": The Politics of Economical Reform in Britain, 1779–1846.* Oxford: Clarendon, 1996.

Harris, Ron. "Political Economy, Interest Groups, Legal Institutions and the

Repeal of the Bubble Act in 1825." *Economic History Review*, 2nd series, 50 (1997): 675–96.

———. *Industrializing English Law: Entrepreneurship and Business Organization, 1720–1844*. Cambridge: Cambridge University Press, 2000.

Hassan, J. A. "The Growth and Impact of the British Water Industry in the Nineteenth Century." *Economic History Review*, 2nd series, 38 (1985): 531–47.

Hawke, G. R., and M. C. Reed. "Railway Capital in the United Kingdom in the Nineteenth Century." *Economic History Review*, 2nd series, 22 (1969): 269–86.

Herrigel, Gary. "A New Wave in the History of Corporate Governance." *Enterprise and Society* 8 (2007): 475–88.

Hickson, Charles R., and John D. Turner. "Shareholder Liability Regimes in Nineteenth-Century English Banking: the Impact upon the Market for Shares." *European Review of Economic History* 7 (2003): 99–126.

———. "Trading in the Shares of Unlimited Liability Banks in Nineteenth-Century Ireland: The Bagehot Hypothesis." *Journal of Economic History* 63 (2003): 931–58.

———. "The Genesis of Corporate Governance: Nineteenth-Century Irish Joint-Stock Banks." *Business History* 47 (2005): 174–89.

Hill, Carol. "The Kircudbright Shipping Company, 1811–1817." *International Journal of Maritime History* 9 (1997): 69–91.

———. "Galloway Shipping and Regional Development." *Scottish Economic and Social History* 19 (1999): 95–116.

Hilt, Eric. "When Did Ownership Separate from Control? Corporate Governance in the Early Nineteenth Century." *Journal of Economic History* 68 (2008): 645–85.

Hilton, Boyd. *The Age of Atonement: The Influence of Evangelicalism on Social and Economic Thought, 1795–1865*. Oxford: Oxford University Press, 1988.

Holdsworth, W. S. *A History of English Law*. 17 vols. London: Methuen, 1922.

Hoppit, Julian. "Patterns of Parliamentary Legislation, 1600–1800." *Historical Journal* 39 (1996): 109–31.

Hudson, Pat. *The Genesis of Industrial Capital: A Study of the West Riding Wool Textile Industry, c. 1750–1850*. Cambridge: Cambridge University Press, 1986.

Hudson, Sarah J. "Attitudes to Investment Risk amongst West Midland Canal and Railway Company Investors, 1760–1850." Ph.D. thesis, University of Warwick, 2001.

Hunt, B. C. *The Development of the Business Corporation in England, 1800–1867*. Cambridge, MA: Harvard University Press, 1936.

Hurst, James Willard. *The Legitimacy of the Business Corporation in the Law of the United States, 1780–1970*. Charlottesville: University of Virginia Press, 1970.

"Incorporating the Republic: The Corporation in Antebellum Political Culture." Note. *Harvard Law Review* 102 (1989): 1883–903.

Innes, Joanna, and Nicholas Rogers. "Politics and Government 1700–1840." In Peter Clark, ed., *The Cambridge Urban History of Britain*, vol. 2, *1540–1840*, 529–74. Cambridge: Cambridge University Press, 2000.

Ireland, Paddy. "Capitalism without the Capitalist: The Joint Stock Company Share and the Emergence of the Modern Doctrine of Separate Corporate Personality." *Legal History* 17 (1996): 41–73.

Jackson, Gordon. "Government Bounties and the Establishment of the Scottish Whaling Trade, 1750–1800." In John Butt and J. T. Ward, eds., *Scottish Themes: Essays in Honour of Professor S. G. E. Lythe*, 46–66. Edinburgh: Scottish Academic Press, 1976.

Jefferys, J. B. "The Denomination and Character of Shares, 1855–1885." *Economic History Review*, 1st series, 16 (1946): 45–55.

Jenks, Leland Hamilton. *The Migration of British Capital to 1875*. New York: Knopf, 1927.

Jennings, W. Ivor. *Principles of Local Government Law*. London: University of London Press, 1931.

Jensen, Michael C., and William H. Meckling. "Theory of the Firm: Managerial Behavior, Agency Costs, and Ownership Structure." *Journal of Financial Economics* 3 (1976): 305–60.

Johnson, Paul. *Making the Market: Victorian Origins of Corporate Capitalism*. Cambridge: Cambridge University Press, 2010.

Jones, Edgar. *True and Fair: A History of Price Waterhouse*. London: Hamish Hamilton, 1995.

Jones, Reginald. *Local Government Audit Law*. London: HMSO, 1981.

Jones, R. H. "Accounting in English Local Government from the Middle Ages to c.1835." In R. H. Parker and B. S. Yamey, eds., *Accounting History: Some British Contributions*, 377–403. Oxford: Clarendon Press, 1994.

Jones, S., and M. Aiken. "British Companies Legislation and Social and Political Evolution during the Nineteenth Century." *British Accounting Review* 27 (1995): 61–82.

Kedslie, Moyra J. McIntyre. *Firm Foundations: The Development of Professional Accounting in Scotland*. Hull: Hull University Press, 1990.

Keith-Lucas, Bryan. *The English Local Government Franchise: A Short History*. Oxford: Basil Blackwell, 1952.

———. *The Unreformed Local Government System*. London: Croom Helm, 1980.

Kellett, John R. *Railways and Victorian Cities*. London: Routledge and Kegan Paul, 1979.

Kessler, William C. "Incorporation in New England: A Statistical Study, 1800–1875." *Journal of Economic History* 8 (1948): 43–62.

Kim, Kenneth A., and John R. Nofsinger. *Corporate Governance*. Upper Saddle River, NJ: Pearson/Prentice Hall, 2004.

Kirk, Neville. "Post-modernism and the Sublime Myth of the Backward March of Democracy in Nineteenth-Century Britain." *Labour History Review* 59 (1994): 71–8.

Kostal, R. W. *Law and English Railway Capitalism, 1825–1875*. Oxford: Clarendon, 1994.

Kynaston, David. *The City of London*. Vol. 1, *A World of Its Own, 1815–1890*. London: Pimlico, 1994.

La Porta, Rafael, et al. "Law and Finance." *Journal of Political Economy* 106 (1998): 1113–55.

Lambert, Sheila. *Bills and Acts: Legislative Procedure in Eighteenth-Century England*. Cambridge: Cambridge University Press, 1971.

Lamoreaux, Naomi R. *Insider Lending: Banks, Personal Connections and Economic Development in Industrial New England*. Cambridge: Cambridge University Press, 1994.

———. "Partnerships, Corporations, and the Limits on Contractual Freedom in U.S. History: An Essay in Economics, Law and Culture." In Kenneth Lipartito and David B. Sicilia, eds., *Constructing Corporate America: History, Politics, Culture*, 29–65. Oxford: Oxford University Press, 2004.

Lamoreaux, Naomi R., and Jean-Laurent Rosenthal. "Corporate Governance and the Plight of Minority Shareholders in the US before the Great Depression." In Claudia Goldin and Edward L. Glaeser, eds., *Corruption and Reform: Lessons from America's Economic History*, 125–52. Chicago: University of Chicago Press, 2006.

Langton, John, and R. J. Morris, eds. *Atlas of Industrializing Britain, 1780–1914*. London: Methuen, 1986.

Laurence, Anne, Josephine Maltby, and Janette Rutterford, eds. *Women and Their Money, 1700–1950: Essays on Women and Finance*. London: Routledge, 2009.

Lee, Joseph. "Capital in the Irish Economy." In L. M. Cullen, ed., *The Formation of the Irish Economy*, 53–64. Cork: Mercier, 1969.

Levy, A. B. *Private Corporations and Their Control*. 2 vols. London: Routledge and Kegan Paul, 1950.

Loftus, Donna. "Capital and Community: Limited Liability and Attempts to Democratise the Market in Mid-Nineteenth-Century England." *Victorian Studies* 45 (2002): 93–120.

Macaulay, S. "Non-Contractual Relations in Business: A Preliminary Study." *American Sociological Review* 28 (1963): 55–69.

Mackenzie, William Mackay. *The Scottish Burghs: An Expanded Version of the Rhind Lectures in Archaeology for 1945*. Edinburgh: Oliver and Boyd, 1949.

Maclean, Mairi. "Corporate Governance in France and the UK: Long-Term

Perspectives on Contemporary Institutional Arrangements." *Business History* 41 (1999): 88–116.

Maclean, Mairi, Charles Harvey, and Jon Press. *Business Elites and Corporate Governance in France and the UK.* Basingstoke: Palgrave Macmillan, 2006.

Maier, Pauline. "The Revolutionary Origins of the American Corporation." *William and Mary Quarterly*, 3rd series, 50 (1993): 51–84.

Mallin, Christine A. *Corporate Governance.* Oxford: Oxford University Press, 2004.

Maltby, Josephine. "UK Joint Stock Companies Legislation, 1844–1900: Accounting Publicity and 'Mercantile Caution.'" *Accounting History* 3 (1998): 9–32.

———. "'A Sort of Guide, Philosopher and Friend': The Rise of the Professional Auditor in Britain." *Accounting, Business and Financial History* 9 (1999): 29–50.

Mathias, Peter. *The Brewing Industry in England, 1700–1830.* Cambridge: Cambridge University Press, 1959.

———. *The First Industrial Nation: An Economic History of Britain, 1700–1914.* London: Methuen, 1969.

Matthews, Derek. *A History of Auditing: The Changing Audit Process in Britain from the Nineteenth Century to the Present Day.* London and New York: Routledge, 2006.

Matthews, Derek, Malcolm Anderson, and J. R. Edwards. *The Priesthood of Industry: The Rise of the Professional Accountant in British Management.* Oxford: Oxford University Press, 1998.

McCartney, Sean, and A. J. Arnold. "George Hudson's Financial Reporting Practices: Putting the Eastern Counties Railway in Context." *Accounting, Business and Financial History* 10 (2000): 293–316.

———. "'A Vast Aggregate of Avaricious and Flagitious Jobbing?': George Hudson and the Evolution of Early Notions of Directorial Responsibility." *Accounting, Business and Financial History* 11 (2001): 117–43.

McQueen, Rob. *A Social History of Company Law: Great Britain and the Australian Colonies, 1854–1920.* Farnham: Ashgate, 2009.

Michie, Ranald C. *Money, Mania and Markets: Investment, Company Formation and the Stock Exchange in Nineteenth-Century Scotland.* Edinburgh: John Donald, 1981.

———. *The Global Securities Market: A History.* Oxford: Oxford University Press, 2006.

Micklethwait, John, and Adrian Wooldridge. *The Company: A Short History of a Revolutionary Idea.* London: Weidenfeld and Nicolson, 2003.

Mirowski, Philip. "The Rise and (Retreat) of a Market: English Joint Stock Shares in the Eighteenth Century." *Journal of Economic History* 41 (1981): 559–77.

———. *The Birth of the Business Cycle.* New York: Garland, 1985.

Mitchell, Brian R. *Abstract of British Historical Statistics.* Cambridge: Cambridge University Press, 1962.

Mokyr, Joel. "Editor's Introduction: The New Economic History and the Industrial Revolution." In Joel Mokyr, ed., *The British Industrial Revolution: An Economic Perspective*, 1–131. Boulder, CO: Westview, 1993.

Moore, R. J. "John Mill of John Company." In Kenneth Ballhatchet and John Harrison, eds., *East India Company Studies: Papers Presented to Professor Sir Cyril Philips*, 153–82. Asian Studies Monograph Series. Hong Kong: Asian Research Service, 1986.

Morris, R. J. *Class, Sect and Party: The Making of the British Middle Class: Leeds, 1820–1850.* Manchester: Manchester University Press 1990.

———. "A Year in the Public Life of the British Bourgeoisie." In Robert Colls and Richard Rodger, eds., *Cities of Ideas: Civil Society and Urban Governance in Britain, 1800–2000*, 121–43. Aldershot: Ashgate, 2004.

———. "Urban Associations in England and Scotland, 1750–1914: The Formation of the Middle Class or the Formation of a Civil Society?" In Graeme Morton, Boudien de Vries, and Robert J. Morris, eds., *Civil Society, Associations and Urban Places: Class, Nation and Culture in Nineteenth-Century Europe*, 139–58. Aldershot: Ashgate, 2006.

Munn, C. W. "Scottish Provincial Banking Companies: An Assessment." *Business History* 23 (1981): 19–41.

———. *The Scottish Provincial Banking Companies, 1747–1864.* Edinburgh: Donald, 1981.

Murphy, Charlotte. "The Limerick Navigation Company, 1697–1836." *North Munster Antiquarian Journal* 22 (1980): 43–61.

Neal, Larry. *The Rise of Financial Capitalism: International Capital Markets in the Age of Reason.* Cambridge: Cambridge University Press, 1990.

Newton, Lucy. "Change and Continuity: The Development of Joint-Stock Banking in the Early Nineteenth Century." Unpublished typescript, 2008.

Norgate, G. Le G. "Wortley, James Archibald Stuart, first Baron Wharncliffe (1776–1845)." Revised by H. C. G. Matthew. *Oxford Dictionary of National Biography.* Oxford: Oxford University Press, 2004.

North, Douglass C., and Barry R. Weingast. "Constitutions and Commitment: The Evolution of Institutions Governing Public Choice in Seventeenth-Century England." *Journal of Economic History* 49 (1989): 803–32.

Novak, William J. *The People's Welfare: Law and Regulation in Nineteenth-Century America.* Chapel Hill: University of North Carolina Press, 1996.

Ó Gráda, Cormac. *Ireland: A New Economic History, 1780–1939.* Oxford: Clarendon, 1994.

Ober, Josiah. *Mass and Elite in Democratic Athens: Rhetoric, Ideology, and the Power of the People.* Princeton, NJ: Princeton University Press, 1989.

O'Brien, P., T. Griffiths, and P. Hunt. "Political Components of the Industrial Revolution: Parliament and the English Cotton Textile Industry, 1660–1774." *Economic History Review*, 2nd series, 44 (1991): 395–423.

Offer, Avner. "Between the Gift and the Market: The Economy of Regard." *Economic History Review*, 2nd series, 50 (1997): 450–76.

———. *The Challenge of Affluence*. Oxford: Oxford University Press, 2006.

O'Gorman, Frank. *Voters, Patrons and Parties: The Unreformed Electoral System of Hanoverian England 1734–1832*. Oxford: Clarendon, 1989.

Oldham, James. *English Common Law in the Age of Mansfield*. Chapel Hill: University of North Carolina Press, 2004.

The Oxford Dictionary of Quotations. 2nd ed. London: Oxford University Press, 1953.

Patterson, Margaret, and David Reiffen. "The Effect of the Bubble Act on the Market for Joint Stock Shares." *Journal of Economic History* 50 (1990): 163–71.

Pearson, Robin. "Beaumont, John Thomas Barber (1774–1841)." *Oxford Dictionary of National Biography*. Oxford: Oxford University Press, 2004.

———. "Shareholder Democracies? English Stock Companies and the Politics of Corporate Governance during the Industrial Revolution." *English Historical Review* 117 (2002): 840–66.

———. *Insuring the Industrial Revolution: Fire Insurance in Great Britain, 1700–1850*. Aldershot: Ashgate, 2004.

Pearson, Robin, and David Richardson. "Business Networking in the Industrial Revolution." *Economic History Review*, 2nd series, 54 (2001): 657–79.

Pollard, Sidney. *The Genesis of Modern Management*. Harmondsworth: Penguin, 1968.

Pollins, Harold. "The Finances of the Liverpool and Manchester Railway." *Economic History Review*, 2nd series, 5 (1952): 90–7.

———. "The Marketing of Railway Shares in the First Half of the Nineteenth Century." *Economic History Review*, 2nd series, 7 (1954): 230–9.

Porter, Roy. *Enlightenment: Britain and the Creation of the Modern World*. London: Penguin, 2000.

Pratt, Ken C., and A. Colin Storrar. "UK Shareholders' Lost Access to Management Information." *Accounting and Business Research* 27 (1997): 205–18.

Preda, Alex. "The Rise of the Popular Investor: Financial Knowledge and Investing in England and France, 1840–1880." *Sociological Quarterly* 42 (2001): 205–32.

Prest, John. *Liberty and Locality: Parliament, Permissive Legislation, and Ratepayers' Democracies in the Nineteenth Century*. Oxford: Clarendon, 1990.

Raynes, Harold E. *A History of British Insurance*. London: Pitman, 1948.

Redlich, Josef, and Francis W. Hirst. *The History of Local Government in England*. London: Macmillan, 1970.

Reed, M. C. *Investment in Railways in Britain, 1820–1844: A Study in the Development of the Capital Market.* London: Oxford University Press, 1975.

Richards, E. S. "The Finances of the Liverpool and Manchester Railway Again." *Economic History Review*, 2nd series, 25 (1972): 284–92.

Robb, George. *White-Collar Crime in Modern England: Financial Fraud and Business Morality, 1845–1929.* Cambridge: Cambridge University Press, 1992.

Robbins, Michael. *The Railway Age.* London: Routledge and Kegan Paul, 1962.

Roe, Mark J. *Political Determinants of Corporate Governance: Political Contexts, Corporate Impact.* Oxford: Oxford University Press, 2003.

Rose, M. E. "The Administration of the Poor Law in the West Riding of Yorkshire (1820–1855)." D.Phil. thesis, Oxford University, 1965.

Rutterford, Janette. "From Dividend Yield to Discounted Cash Flow: A History of UK and US Equity Valuation Techniques." *Accounting, Business and Financial History* 14 (2004): 115–49.

Rutterford, Janette, et al. "Who Comprised the Nation of Shareholders? Gender and Investment in Great Britain, c. 1870–1935." *Economic History Review*, 2nd series, 64 (2011): 157–87.

Rydz, D. L. *The Parliamentary Agents: A History.* London: Royal Historical Society, 1979.

Salmon, Philip. *Electoral Reform at Work: Local Politics and National Parties, 1832–1841.* Woodbridge: Boydell and Brewer, 2002.

Salter, Malcolm S. *Innovation Corrupted: The Origins and Legacy of Enron's Collapse.* Cambridge, MA: Harvard University Press, 2008.

Scott, William Robert. *The Constitution and Finance of English, Scottish and Irish Joint-Stock Companies to 1720.* 3 vols. Cambridge: Cambridge University Press, 1912.

Searle, G. R. *Morality and the Market in Victorian Britain.* Oxford: Clarendon, 1998.

Shannon, H. A. "The Coming of General Limited Liability." *Economic History*, 2 (1931): 267–91.

——. "The First Five Thousand Limited Companies and Their Duration." *Economic History* 3 (1932): 396–424.

——. "The Limited Companies of 1866 and 1883." In E. M. Carus-Wilson, ed., *Essays in Economic History*, 1:380–405. London: Arnold, 1954.

Shilts, Wade E. "Accounting, Engineering or Advertising? Limited Liability, the Company Prospectus and the Language of Uncertainty in Victorian Britain." *Essays in Economic and Business History* 22 (2004): 47–62.

Shleifer, Andrei, and Robert W. Vishny. "Survey of Corporate Governance." *Journal of Finance* 52 (1997): 737–83.

Simpson, A. W. B. *Victorian Law and the Industrial Spirit.* London: Selden Society, 1995.

Smith, Dennis. *Conflict and Compromise: Class Formation in English Society, 1830–1914.* London: Routledge and Kegan Paul, 1982.

Snell, K. D. M. *Parish and Belonging: Community, Identity and Welfare in England and Wales 1700–1950.* Cambridge: Cambridge University Press, 2006.

Snow, Vernon F. "The Reluctant Surrender of an Absurd Privilege: Proctorial Representation in the House of Lords, 1810–1868." *Parliamentary Affairs* 29 (1976): 60–78.

Spadafora, David. *The Idea of Progress in Eighteenth-Century Britain.* New Haven, CT: Yale University Press, 1990.

Ste. Croix, G. E. M. de. *The Class Struggle in the Ancient Greek World.* London: Duckworth, 1981.

Stedman Jones, Gareth. "The Language of Chartism." In James Epstein and Dorothy Thompson, eds., *The Chartist Experience: Studies in Working Class Radicalism and Culture, 1830–60,* 3–58. Basingstoke: Macmillan, 1982.

Sutherland, Lucy S. *The East India Company in Eighteenth-Century Politics.* Oxford: Clarendon, 1952.

Sweet, Rosemary. *The English Town, 1680–1840: Government, Society and Culture.* Harlow: Pearson Education, 1999.

Sykes, Joseph. *The Amalgamation Movement in English Banking, 1825–1924.* London: King, 1926.

Taylor, James. "Commercial Fraud and Public Men in Victorian Britain." *Historical Research* 78 (2005): 230–52.

———. *Creating Capitalism: Joint-Stock Enterprise in British Politics and Culture, 1800–1870.* Woodbridge: Boydell, 2006.

———. "Company Fraud in Victorian Britain: the Royal British Bank Scandal of 1856." *English Historical Review* 121 (2007): 700–24.

Thomas, D. L. "Morgan, William (1750–1833)." Revised by Robin Pearson. *Oxford Dictionary of National Biography.* Oxford: Oxford University Press, 2004.

Thomas, P. D. G. *The House of Commons in the Eighteenth Century.* Oxford: Clarendon, 1971.

Thomas, W. A. *The Stock Exchanges of Ireland.* Liverpool: Cairns, 1986.

Thompson, Dorothy. *The Chartists: Popular Politics in the Industrial Revolution.* Aldershot: Wildwood House, 1984.

Toms, J. S. "The Rise of Modern Accounting and the Fall of the Public Company: The Lancashire Cotton Mills, 1870–1914." *Accounting, Organizations and Society* 27 (2002): 61–84.

Trebilcock, Clive. *Phoenix Assurance and the Development of British Insurance.* 2 vols. Cambridge: Cambridge University Press, 1985, 1998.

Trotsky, Leon. *The History of the Russian Revolution.* 3 vols. New York: Anchor Foundation, 1980.

Vamplew, Wray. "Sources of Scottish Railway Share Capital before 1860." *Scottish Journal of Political Economy* 17 (1970): 425–40.

Vernon, James. *Politics and the People: A Study in English Political Culture.* Cambridge: Cambridge University Press, 1993.

Vincent, David. *The Culture of Secrecy: Britain, 1832–1998.* Oxford: Oxford University Press, 1998.

Walker, David M. *A Legal History of Scotland.* 7 vols. Edinburgh: Green Lexis-Nexis UK, 1988–2003.

Walker, Stephen P. "More Sherry and Sandwiches? Incrementalism and the Regulation of Late Victorian Bank Auditing." *Accounting History* 3 (1998): 33–53.

Wall, Maureen. "Catholics in Economic Life." In L. M. Cullen, ed., *The Formation of the Irish Economy*, 37–52. Cork: Mercier, 1969.

Wallis, John Joseph. "Constitutions, Corporations, and Corruption: American States and Constitutional Change, 1842 to 1852." *Journal of Economic History* 65 (2005): 211–56.

Wallis, John Joseph, Barry R. Weingast, and Douglass C. North. "The Corporate Origins of Individual Rights." Unpublished paper presented to the annual meeting of the Economic History Association, Pittsburgh, 2006.

Ward, J. R. *The Finance of Canal Building in Eighteenth-Century England.* Oxford: Oxford University Press, 1974.

Webb, Sidney, and Beatrice Webb. *English Local Government: Statutory Authorities for Special Purposes.* London: Longmans Green, 1922.

——. *The Development of English Local Government, 1689–1835.* London: Oxford University Press, 1963.

——. *English Poor Law History, Part II: The Last Hundred Years.* London: Cass, 1963.

Welch, Edwin. "Borough Archives in England and Wales." *Archivum* 13 (1963): 61–72.

Willan, T. S. *The Early History of the Don Navigation.* Manchester: Manchester University Press, 1965.

Williams, O. Cyprian. *The Historical Development of Private Bill Procedure and Standing Orders in the House of Commons.* 2 vols. London: H. M. Stationery Office, 1948–49.

Wilson, John F. *Lighting the Town: A Study of Management in the North West Gas Industry, 1805–1880.* London: Paul Chapman, 1991.

——. *British Business History, 1720–1994.* Manchester: Manchester University Press, 1995.

Wilson, John F., and Andrew Thomson. *The Making of Modern Management: British Management in Historical Perspective.* Oxford: Oxford University Press, 2006.

Wright, D. G. *Popular Radicalism: The Working-Class Experience, 1780–1880.* London: Longman, 1988.

Wright, Robert E. "Introduction." In Robert E. Wright et al., eds., *History of Corporate Governance: The Importance of Stakeholder Activism*, 1:xi–xxi. London: Pickering and Chatto, 2004.

Yeo, Eileen. "Some Practices and Problems of Chartist Democracy." In James Epstein and Dorothy Thompson, eds., *The Chartist Experience: Studies in Working Class Radicalism and Culture, 1830–60*, 345–80. Basingstoke: Macmillan, 1982.

Index

Aberdare Canal, 83, 106

Aberdeen, Leith, and Clyde Shipping Company, 154–55

Aberdeen Banking Company, 117

accountants, 207, 214, 227, 229, 233, 235, 236, 238–39, 250

accounts, 1, 10, 15, 35, 55, 180, 211–39, 257n32; advance circulation of, 225–26; in cost-book mines, 187–88, 207; individual access to, 123, 207, 208–9, 216, 219, 220, 221, 222, 227–28, 237, 239, 241, 246, 247, 294n39; inspection by committees, 226–31, 295n66; inspection by groups of shareholders, 216, 219; inspection confined to specified periods, 215–16, 222, 248; parish, 231–32; presented to GM, 35, 206, 221–26, 241, 246, 261n54; public access to, 238; publication of, 34, 206, 232, 233; summary, 34, 213, 215, 222–25, 238, 239, 241, 246, 249, 294n39. *See also* auditors; audits

acts of incorporation, 2, 15, 35, 40, 58, 181, 242, 264n35, 268n101, 293n31; cost of, 51–52; drafting of, 63; procedure for obtaining, 8, 11, 31, 41, 45–53, 75–76; right to amend provisions of, 138–41; rights and responsibilities conferred by, 14, 27, 46, 113, 127–28, 130, 132, 139, 161, 164, 184, 185, 220, 252; in the United States, 3, 31

Adamson, Alexander, 135

admiralty law, 53, 186. *See also* Registration Acts of 1786 and 1823

agency theory, 4–5, 7, 96

Agricultural and Commercial Bank of Ireland, 202, 203, 204, 206, 273n82

Albion Flour Mill, 182

Alborn, Timothy L., 13, 67–68, 111, 145–46, 150–51

Alchorne v. Saville (1820), 193

Alexander, Robert, 135–36

Alison, Archibald, 61

Alliance British and Foreign Life and Fire Assurance Company, 114

Alliance Marine Company, 273n82

American and Colonial Steam Navigation Company, 73, 102

Anderson, Adam, 77

Andrews v. Ellison (1821), 193

Anne, Queen, 46

annuities, 21, 24, 199

Anonymous Partners Act of 1782, 28, 185, 186, 197, 258n46

arbitration. *See* shareholders: arbitration between

Arigna Iron and Coal Company, 156–57, 160, 170

Aristotle, 143

Arms Bank (Glasgow), 25

Arran Fishing Company, 195

Ashby v. Blackwell and Million Bank Co. (1765), 266n68

Ashby-de-la-Zouch Canal Company, 48, 73, 81, 90–91, 112–13

Ashton, Stalybridge, Hyde and Glossop Bank, 115, 207–8, 229–30

assemblies of shareholders. *See* general meetings (GMs)